A Distant Front in the Cold War

COLD WAR
INTERNATIONAL HISTORY
PROJECT SERIES

James G. Hershberg
Series Editor

WOODROW WILSON CENTER PRESS
STANFORD UNIVERSITY PRESS

A Distant Front in the Cold War

The USSR in West Africa
and the Congo, 1956–1964

Sergey Mazov

Woodrow Wilson Center Press
Washington, D.C.

Stanford University Press
Stanford, California

EDITORIAL OFFICES

Woodrow Wilson Center Press
Woodrow Wilson International Center for Scholars
One Woodrow Wilson Plaza
1300 Pennsylvania Avenue, N.W.
Washington, D.C. 20004-3027
Telephone: 202-691-4029
www.wilsoncenter.org/press

ORDER FROM

Stanford University Press
Chicago Distribution Center
11030 South Langley Avenue
Chicago, Il 60628
Telephone: 1-800-621-2736; 773-568-1550
www.sup.org

Library of Congress Cataloging-in-Publication Data

Mazov, S. V. (Sergei Vasilévich)
    A distant front in the Cold War : the USSR in West Africa and the Congo, 1956–1964 /
Sergey Mazov.
        p. cm. — (Cold War International History Project series)
    "Portions of this book were originally published as Politika SSSR v Zapadnoi Afrike,
1956–1964 : neizvestnye stranitsy istorii kholodnoi voiny (Moscow : Nauka, 2008);
translated by the author"—T.p. verso.
    Includes bibliographical references and index.
    ISBN 978-0-8047-6059-1 (hardcover : alk. paper)
    1. Africa, West—Foreign relations—Soviet Union.   2. Soviet Union—Foreign
relations—Africa, West.   3. Congo (Democratic Republic)—Foreign relations—Soviet
Union.   4. Soviet Union—Foreign relations—Congo (Democratic Republic)
5. Khrushchev, Nikita Sergeevich, 1894–1971—Political and social views.   6. Africa,
West—Foreign relations—20th century.   7. Congo (Democratic Republic)—Foreign
relations—20th century.   8. Soviet Union—Foreign relations—1953–1975.   I. Mazov,
S. V. (Sergei Vasilévich). Politika SSSR v Zapadnoi Afrike, 1956–1964.   II. Title.
    DT476.5.M39   2010
    327.4706609'045—dc22   2010017490

Portions of this book were originally published as *Politika SSSR v Zapadnoi Afrike, 1956– 1964: Neizvestnye stranitsy istorii kholodnoi voiny* (Moscow: Nauka, 2008). Translated by the author.

Woodrow Wilson International Center for Scholars

The Woodrow Wilson International Center for Scholars is the national, living U.S. memorial honoring President Woodrow Wilson. In providing an essential link between the worlds of ideas and public policy, the Center addresses current and emerging challenges confronting the United States and the world. The Center promotes policy-relevant research and dialogue to increase understanding and enhance the capabilities and knowledge of leaders, citizens, and institutions worldwide. Created by an Act of Congress in 1968, the Center is a nonpartisan institution headquartered in Washington, D.C., and supported by both public and private funds.

Conclusions or opinions expressed in Center publications and programs are those of the authors and speakers and do not necessarily reflect the views of the Center's staff, fellows, trustees, or advisory groups, or any individuals or organizations that provide financial support to the Center.

The Center is the publisher of *The Wilson Quarterly* and home of Woodrow Wilson Center Press and *dialogue* television and radio. For more information about the Center's activities and publications, including the monthly newsletter *Centerpoint*, please visit us on the web at www.wilsoncenter.org.

The Cold War International History Project

The Cold War International History Project was established by the Woodrow Wilson International Center for Scholars in 1991. The project supports the full and prompt release of historical materials by governments on all sides of the Cold War and seeks to disseminate new information and perspectives on Cold War history emerging from previously inaccessible sources on the "the other side"—the former Communist world—through publications, fellowships, and scholarly meetings and conferences. The project publishes the *Cold War International History Project Bulletin* and a working paper series, and maintains a website, http://www.cwihp.org.

At the Woodrow Wilson Center, the project is part of the History and Public Policy Program, directed by Christian F. Ostermann. The project is overseen by an advisory committee that is chaired by William Taubman (Amherst College), and includes Michael Beschloss; James H. Billington (Librarian of Congress); Warren I. Cohen (University of Maryland at Baltimore); John Lewis Gaddis (Yale University); James G. Hershberg (George Washington University); Samuel F. Wells Jr. (Woodrow Wilson Center); and Sharon Wolchik (George Washington University).

The Cold War International History Project has been supported by the Leon Levy Foundation (New York), the Henry Luce Foundation (New York), the Korea Foundation (Seoul), the John D. and Catherine T. MacArthur Foundation (Chicago), the Ratiu Family Foundation (London), and the Smith Richardson Foundation (Westport, CT).

Contents

Series Preface
James G. Hershberg

Half a century later, with Africa mired in a seemingly unending series of woes—from poverty to AIDS to civil wars, coups, and corruption to environmental catastrophes and more—it seems hard to remember that as the 1960s began, the continent seemed on the dawn of a promising new era. The world watched, fascinated, as colonial empires receded and nationalist movements evicted them in sometimes orderly and euphoric, but often turbulent, chaotic, or bloody struggles to achieve independence ("liberation"). In the space of a few years, dozens of new countries emerged where European overlords had dominated for decades or centuries. "Nobody knew what would happen when 300 million people stood up and demanded the right to be heard," recalled one observer. "People wanted to know what was happening on the continent: where was it headed, what were its intentions?"[1]

The murky nexus between decolonization and Cold War rivalry magnified global interest and local intrigue. In Africa, as in the rest of the third world, Washington and Moscow eagerly vied for the affections of new states and their often charismatic leaders—and alongside the zero-sum East-West competition, an internecine East-East contest for influence broke out as the Sino-Soviet schism split the Communist world and Mao Zedong and Nikita Khrushchev each claimed to lead a model society.[2] The Cold War struggle for Africa peaked in the late 1950s and early 1960s dur-

---

1. Ryszard Kapuściński, *The Soccer War* (New York: Alfred A. Knopf, Inc., 1991; Vintage, 1992), pp. 20–21.

2. See Odd Arne Westad, *The Global Cold War: Third World Interventions and the Making of Our Time* (Cambridge, UK: Cambridge University Press, 2005).

ing the era of Nikita Khrushchev. Far more than Stalin, who paid little attention to the continent (or the rest of the third world, for that matter), Khrushchev fervently tried to project Soviet influence and to gain the favor of key figures he saw as opposing "imperialism" and undercutting American interests, from Patrice Lumumba in the Congo to Kwame Nkrumah in Ghana.

Sergey Mazov's *A Distant Front in the Cold War* offers a fresh perspective on those tumultuous times. Scholars have long been able to tap declassified U.S. records to probe and recount American attempts to preserve and extend its sway in the new Africa during the heyday of decolonization—Dwight D. Eisenhower's comparatively modest efforts (influenced by John Foster Dulles' distaste for neutralism) and John F. Kennedy's avid courting of key African nationalist leaders.[3] However, traditional Communist secrecy (not to mention linguistic and other practical barriers) frustrated attempts to understand and assess Moscow's activities in Africa.

Meticulously exploiting recently opened Soviet archives, Mazov offers an unparalleled view inside the making and implementation of the Kremlin's policy in the region. In this provocative and trail-blazing study, he carefully scrutinizes its role in the crisis surrounding the Congo's independence from Belgium—the African affair that most dramatically seized the international spotlight—and in courting moderate Liberia and three "radical" and assertively "non-capitalist" newly independent West African states: Ghana, Guinea, and Mali. At a time when the nonaligned movement reached the apex of its prestige, Khrushchev's wooing of these countries and their leaders seemed to confront Washington with an even worse peril—that Soviet Communism might capture the hearts, minds, and resources of the decolonizing world, in Africa and beyond, through a sinister array of blandishments and tools ranging from economic and military aid to ideological appeal and propaganda to covert operations. As Mazov shows, however, Khrushchev's charm offensive in West Africa, though menacing at the time to U.S. policymakers, was hardly a smooth or, ultimately, successful operation, hamstrung by many of the same limitations that undercut Soviet policy elsewhere in the world.

Though West Africa was a relative backwater in the Cold War, lacking the intensity or danger of escalation of such hotspots as Berlin, Cuba, or the Taiwan Straits, it exemplified an important aspect of the global strug-

---

3. See, e.g., Richard D. Mahoney, *JFK: Ordeal in Africa* (Oxford University Press, 1983), and Philip Muehlenback, *Betting on the Africans: John F. Kennedy's Courting of African Nationalism* (Oxford University Press, forthcoming).

gle at a crucial moment when the international system underwent a period of volatile change and superpowers viewed battles for influence in seemingly obscure or "distant" fronts (from West Africa to Southeast Asia) as potentially pivotal. It is hardly the last world on this complex tale. In addition to lamentably missing Soviet pieces of the puzzle, Chinese sources are only beginning to emerge[4], and Africa's own archives and perspectives, for example, still only rarely grace narratives of the duel between Washington and Moscow for that continent. Yet, by lifting the veil on the Soviet side of this story, Mazov enriches our understanding of the Cold War and its legacy in a still-troubled area of the world.

---

4. China's foreign ministry archives have now opened substantial records through 1965, opening the possibility for far more serious study of Beijing's efforts to gain influence in Africa.

Acknowledgments

I owe thanks to my colleagues and friends, whose encouragement, support, advice, and inspiration made this book possible. I had the privilege to be a scholar associated with the Cold War International History Project at the Woodrow Wilson International Center for Scholars from February to May 2003, and I am extremely grateful to the project's director, Christian Ostermann, for making my months of fellowship so meaningful. I am deeply thankful to James Hershberg, the editor of the Cold War history series of the Woodrow Wilson Center Press, for reading my manuscript critically and making extensive and useful comments. I am greatly indebted to the reviewers, Svetlana Savranskaya and Ilya Gaiduk, and also to an anonymous Africanist reviewer, for valuable critical comments and proposals. I express my heartfelt thanks to Lise Namikas, who provided me with her dissertation on the Congo crisis and enlightened me on many nuances of U.S. Congolese policy. I am especially grateful to Joseph Brinley, director of the Woodrow Wilson Center Press, whose suggestions helped me respond to the reviewers' observations, and who professionally guided the manuscript through the publication process. I enjoyed the support of Yamile Kahn, managing editor of the Press, who clarified many important issues for me. A book written in English by an author for whom English is not native requires much editorial assistance, which I received from Alfred Imhoff, the copy editor, whose numerous corrections made my manuscript much more readable in English. I greatly appreciate the kind assistance of the staff of the Archive of Foreign Policy of the Russian Federation (Archiv vneshnei politiki Rossyiskoi Federatsii), the Russian State Archive of Contemporary History (Rossyiskyi gosudarstvennyi archiv noveisheyi istorii), the U.S. National Archives, and the Manuscript Division of the Library of Congress. And I particularly thank my colleagues at the Institute of World History of the Russian Academy of Sciences, especially Apollon Davidson, the chief of the Center for African Studies.

My greatest gratitude is to my wife, Marina Tarasova, for encouraging, supporting, and sustaining me. She patiently shared all the difficulties and setbacks I suffered during the long course of this project and helped me to overcome them.

Sergey Mazov

affect Soviet policy? Did they contribute much to frustrating Soviet plans? To clarify these issues, I rely extensively on U.S. archival sources. The American archives offer generous access to many documents covering both the domestic and international aspects of the Cold War in West Africa. The most useful records that I obtained were those of the Department of State collected in the U.S. National Archives and the Papers of Averell Harriman collected in the Manuscript Division of the Library of Congress. They contain assessments of Soviet policy in West Africa as well as analyses of American responses to Soviet initiatives. The documents produced by U.S. federal, intelligence, and military agencies are full of useful, reliable information on Soviet policy in Africa, and the objectivity and professionalism of many of these reports, particularly those from the Central Intelligence Agency, are impressive.

I had no opportunity to work in non-Russian archives on the Congo crisis. Besides officially published documents,[7] a bit of help was found in a collection of materials, including archival documents, that was prepared for an international conference on the Congo crisis held in Washington in 2004.[8]

Access to Russian and American archives has allowed me to set Soviet behavior in West Africa and the Congo in a broad international context. I have sought to avoid the tendency to reach back to the 1960s and write about the Cold War in Africa only from the perspective of the superpowers, while marginalizing Africa and African experiences. Instead, to bring in a real international perspective, I have examined the Soviet-U.S.-African triangle of relations that evolved with respect to West Africa and the Congo.

Studying the African position in this triangle is fraught with challenges, which Kevin Dunn defined in a book that explores the imaginings and reimaginings of the Congo, tracing changes in "discursive landscapes." Since the nineteenth century, Dunn concludes, Westerners have regarded the Congo as a mysterious and dangerous "heart of the darkness," occupied by irrational and childlike people who are hopelessly backward and savage. As he explains, during the period leading up to and directly following 1960, when the Congo achieved independence, external actors continued to conceptualize "events in the Congo by employing colonial images and . . . old racial stereotypes and by privileging Western definition of State, sovereignty, and security."[9] In the 1960s, he asserts, "for many Western observers, the Congo symbolized the inherent inability of Africans to rule themselves."[10] One of the repercussions of this image was the United States' decision to intervene in the country to prevent a Soviet takeover. Dunn warns against two dangers: "overemphasizing external hegemonic actors without addressing African agency or resistance," and focusing "exclusively on the production of African 'imagined communities' without sufficient attention to international contexts."[11]

In writing this book, I tried to steer between these two problems. I did not rely uncritically on external—whether Western or Soviet—assessments of African leaders presenting their views. Conversely, assessing the veracity of external opinions through African perspectives was very difficult. I did not have an opportunity to work in African archives and was limited to published materials. For obvious reasons, they are inferior to U.S. and Soviet archival documents in reconstructing "what actually happened." For example, the correspondence between Kwame Nkrumah and Nikita Khrushchev collected in the AVP RF contains much more information on Nkrumah's perception of the Soviet line in the Congo crisis than Nkrumah's own long book *Challenge of the Congo*,[12] in which he did not mention Khrushchev at all. African sources and derivative writings regarding Nkrumah, about whom I have myself written elsewhere,[13] are contradictory—some portraying him as the black star of Africa, the father of African nationalism and champion of African unity,[14] but others as a dictator, tyrant, and Leninist tsar.[15] As I worked in the various archives, however, I found a new Nkrumah, a practical and pragmatic politician.

This book covers the period from 1956 to 1964. In 1956, the Soviet Union began to be very active in the developing world, and the Twentieth Congress of the CPSU was held, which worked out the Soviet "new deal" toward Afro-Asian countries. In January 1956, the USSR and Liberia established diplomatic relations, an act that inaugurated practical Soviet policy in West Africa. In October 1964, Khrushchev was ousted, and—for a while—Soviet policy toward Sub-Saharan Africa was modified to become more pragmatic and less ideological.

The need to retrace the evolution of Soviet policy toward West Africa and the Congo in the light of Cold War events has influenced how this book has been structured. Chapter 1 examines the period 1956–59. It briefly analyzes the changes in Soviet policy toward the developing world, Africa in particular, after Stalin's death. I argue that Khrushchev was not guided by a global strategy to take over Africa; there was no established Soviet African blueprint per se, only some drafts of it, based on flawed knowledge of the continent and its inhabitants. The chapter examines Soviet-Liberian diplomatic contacts in detail. In January 1956, a Soviet government delegation arrived in Monrovia to participate in William Tubman's presidential inauguration. The Soviet diplomatic debut in Tropical ential tribal leaders," and "the disinclination of the rural masses to accept the revolutionary doctrine of Communism."[1]

There were also external factors restricting the Communist expansion in Tropical Africa. For the time being, the USSR and its allies did not want to penetrate this area. The Soviet leadership considered it relatively unimportant in terms of geopolitics.

In June 1945, Maxim Litvinov, the chairman of the USSR's Commission on the Preparation of Peace Treaties and Postwar Settlement and the deputy commissar for foreign affairs, submitted two top-secret memorandums to the commissar for foreign affairs, Vyacheslav Molotov, titled "On the Issue of Acquiring Trusteeship Territories" and "Additional Considerations on the Issue of Trusteeship Territories." These memos defined and substantiated the "ratings"—if we can use this modern term—of the territories under mandate rule. The value of each territory for the USSR was established in accordance with the traditional Russian geopolitical aims in the southern direction, which entailed control over the Black Sea Straits—including penetrating the Mediterranean and establishing strongholds there—and a breakthrough to the Pacific Ocean.

The Dodecanese Islands, situated close to the Black Sea Straits, had the highest rating. The acquisition of these islands, or "at least some of them," was, according to Litvinov, of the "greatest importance." A trusteeship for Palestine was deemed "extremely desirable." The former Italian colonies were also rated highly. Libya was characterized as a "proper object" for acquisition; there, "we could establish a firm foothold in the Mediterranean basin." Eritrea and Italian Somalia could be of interest as "intermediate bases between the Black Sea and the Far East, as well as an instrument of influence on the neighboring Arab countries and Abyssinia." Somalia's ports were viewed as "naval (and air force) bases threatening four important sea routes, having much significance for England."[2]

The lowest rating was given to the African territories lost by Germany after World War I: Cameroon, Tanganyika, Togo, Rwanda-Urundi, and Southwest Africa. "I do not think that . . . mandate territories in a part of the world so distant from our naval bases could be of interest to us," Litvinov wrote. Judging from Molotov's comments on this memo, this was the only point to which he objected. The commissar underlined the paragraph and made a pencil note on the margin: "Politic[ally they] can!"[3]

In Stalin's foreign policy regarding geopolitically valuable territories, security imperatives clearly outweighed ideological considerations. The architects of Soviet foreign policy were interested in the geostrategic position of Libya, Somalia, and Eritrea rather than in the prospects for any revolutionary developments there. Soviet diplomacy showed remarkable persistence and flexibility (the official position changed four times) in trying to achieve a Soviet presence in the Mediterranean—the traditional priority for Russian geopolitical aspirations.[4]

The Stalinist outlook featured a rigid, dualistic view of the world, and the African countries had been considered a standby of the West. According to the two-camp theory, countries that were not firmly embedded in the Eastern Bloc's socialist camp were simply relegated to the West's imperialist one. The independence movements and their leaders in the colonies were regarded as mere pawns of the Western colonial powers, which were manipulating them into accepting a fake independence.

The substance of the Soviet stance was formulated by Joseph Stalin in his instructions to Molotov concerning the creation of the Trusteeship Council, the issue that the UN General Assembly discussed in November and December 1946: "Those days when the USSR could consider itself an insignificant state regarding all kinds of mandate territories have passed. . . . Only this position enables us to play an active role in the issue of mandates and, in case of necessity, to make concessions to our partners in exchange for their concessions." One thing was most important for Stalin: the affirmation of the Soviet Union's great power status, making it impossible to settle any international issues without its participation. But he regarded the colonies' political leaders with disfavor because of their conformism: "We should not be more leftist than the leaders of these territories. These leaders, as you well know, in their majority are corrupt and care not so much for the independence of their territories as for the preservation of their privileges with regard to the population of these territories. The time is not yet ripe for us to clash over the fate of these territories and to quarrel over their future with the rest of the world, including their corrupt leaders themselves."[5]

For Stalin, it was possible to comprehend the world in terms of both class struggle and the USSR's international position. In the areas where the Soviet Union could not claim direct influence as a state, its leadership would use an ideologically driven policy and the dogmatic Communist approach to domestic elites. Whenever they did not fit into the Soviet scheme of implementing its national interests, the "national bourgeoisie" would immediately be termed "corrupt," "imperialist lackeys," "compromises," or "puppet figures"—in the spirit of orthodox Communist theory and its world revolutionary strategy.

Soviet authors were guided by the postulate that each national bourgeoisie was prone to compromise with its "colonial masters" and thus was incapable of completing the task of national liberation. Thus, writing in 1953 about the Gold Coast (now Ghana), which was then still a British colony—however, with an African government led by Kwame Nkrumah's Convention People's Party—Ivan Potekhin, the leading Soviet expert on Africa from the end of World War II until his death in 1964,[6] declared: "The government of the People's Party is basically a screen concealing the actual rule of English imperialism. . . . The People's Party, representing the interests of the big national bourgeoisie of the Gold Coast, deceived the confidence of the people, and the leaders of the party made a sharp turn to the right, to the side of collaboration with English imperialism."[7]

Stalin's death in March 1953 and the sweeping tide of decolonization in the African colonies paved the way for changes in the Soviet orientation toward the international situation in general and the developing world in particular. In 1954, Nikita Khrushchev emerged as the dominant political figure in the collective leadership that had succeeded Stalin. And as Khrushchev developed a much more expansive view of the Soviet security environment than Stalin's, he discarded the Stalinist concepts regarding the African scene.

The Khrushchevian approach contained a strikingly different evaluation of political independence. It replaced the two-camp theory with a more sophisticated worldview by recognizing neutralism as a separate and positive force and considering most African countries as being anti-imperialist rather than the preserves of imperialism.

Two major international events in 1955 contributed to the shift in Soviet policy toward Africa and the rest of the developing world. In April, the summit of the leaders of nonaligned Asian and African countries in Bandung, Indonesia, manifested the appearance of a new group of actors in the international arena. And in July, at a Geneva summit, Khrushchev and U.S. President Dwight Eisenhower agreed for the first time that no nation could really win a thermonuclear war. This meant that Soviet political advances in the developing world could be made without heightening the risk of a highly destructive war with the United States.

Khrushchev started his breakthrough to the East with an arms deal with Gamal Abdel Nasser of Egypt, and in September 1955 Czechoslovakian weapons began to pour into Egypt, sending shock waves across the Western world.[8] Khrushchev's much-publicized tour of India, Burma, and Afghanistan followed in November and December of the same year. Agreements for trade and technical assistance were concluded with the host governments. The success of Khrushchev's mission gave credence to the euphoria of rising optimism about Soviet prospects in the developing world. Many in the highest Soviet circles believed that the East had been opened for a peaceful, victorious advance by the USSR. The old revolutionary guard hoped that the accelerating Soviet efforts to win the sympathies of the newly emerging countries would hasten the collapse of the capitalist system.

The academician Ivan Maiskyi expressed such expectations in a personal letter to Khrushchev and Premier Nikolai Bulganin dated December 30, 1955. The venerable scholar and experienced diplomat believed that the next stage of "the battle for the world supremacy of socialism would involve the liberation of colonial and semicolonial nations from imperialist exploitation. . . . At this time, conditions for this struggle in Asia, Africa, and Latin America look more favorable than in Europe and the United States. Way back in the 1930s, when I was the Soviet ambassador in London, it occurred to me that great masses of the British proletariat would follow a truly socialist way only after England had lost its empire or at least the bulk of it. Now this moment is not far off."[9]

Khrushchev was not so optimistic, but he considered Africa and other territories undergoing decolonization to be a new front in the Cold War— one that was more promising for the socialist camp than the countries of the West, where the prospects for revolution looked bleak. His knowledge about the developing world was vague, but he had a hunch that nonalignment implied "disalignment" from the West. So there was now a historical chance to penetrate the soft underbelly of imperialism and to channel the anti-Western sentiments of the "bourgeois nationalist" leaders into support for Soviet foreign policy.

Soviet social scientists promptly updated the theory to validate the new policy. The national liberation movement was proclaimed an integral part of the "world revolutionary process," and its leaders were now deemed plausible allies in the anti-imperialist struggle, provided they were willing to adopt "progressive" policies. Potekhin, too, was quick to abandon the old stereotypes and approaches. As he saw it, most African political parties led by the national bourgeoisie were no longer being accused of pursuing policies of accommodation. "Not all bourgeois parties were attached to the progressive camp, but the very fact of creation of mass political organizations in all colonies during a short period of time signifies the beginning of a new historical stage in the life of African people," he asserted in 1956.[10] Now he saw the situation in the Gold Coast in a different light. The Convention People's Party's winning of parliamentary elections became a "great victory of the Africans." The steps taken by Nkrumah's government strengthened "the positions of the leftist forces," "weakened the positions of English imperialism," and undermined the influence of "the feudal elite, which represents the social mainstay of imperialism."[11] Thus Nkrumah and other African leaders, previously labeled "the colonizers' minions," were transformed into progressive and promising partners of the USSR.

To recruit reliable partners, a comprehensive African strategy would be needed. Would the Soviets be able to develop and implement such a strategy?

Did Khrushchev Have a Special African Strategy?

How Westerners answered the question of whether Khrushchev had a special African strategy depended on the state of relations between the Cold War adversaries. In the late 1950s and early 1960s, when the Cold War was in full swing, Khrushchevian policy toward Africa was identified with a "Communist takeover" of the continent. The USSR's actions in West Africa and the Congo were considered part of a holistic African strategy, a subtle and detailed Kremlin's master plan to dominate Africa.

In this vein, the U.S. scholar (and later policymaker) Zbigniew Brzezinski, in a collection of essays issued in 1963, described Soviet plans in Africa in terms of a military offensive. During the first stage, "with anticolonialism serving as the bridge establishing empathetic access, economic and political penetration is meant to create an initial beachhead." The essence of this stage was the training of a procommunist fifth column among the domestic educated elites, to establish a community of "politically sympathetic rulers, growing more hostile to the West and perhaps also experiencing pressure from various sub-elites (students, young intellectuals, impatient planners, etc.)." After entrenching themselves on the beachhead, the Soviets planned to develop it and launch an offensive. These indoctrinated elites "will then move step by step toward emulating Soviet experience, adopting its organizational forms, then justifying this doctrinally by Marxist argumentation." In the final stage, the ultimate goal was to be achieved—the "transformation of a 'national democracy' into a proletarian dictatorship."[12]

With the advent of détente, however, it became commonplace to deny the existence of a Soviet strategy to take over Africa. "Moscow's policies show no evidence of following any master plan but appear rather as pragmatic responses to developments on the continent since the onset of independence in the late 1950s," the authoritative British Africanist Colin Legum emphasized in a volume published in 1987.[13] Many other scholars also asserted that, in fact, there existed no special Soviet strategy concerning Africa, and the Communist threat there was exaggerated.[14]

One exceptionally well-informed Soviet expert, Karen Brutents, does not confirm the existence of an all-inclusive, long-term Soviet strategy regarding Africa. Moreover, Brutents, who spent three decades working for the International Department of the Central Committee of the Communist Party of the Soviet Union (CC CPSU), maintains that he "never dealt with a document making an attempt to expound our African strategy. No document of this kind has existed."[15]

Archival materials suggest that there was no document specifying an established Soviet African doctrine per se. But in several documents, certain long-term objectives of the USSR for the continent were formulated, and the ways to achieve them were delineated. These documents include two top-secret decrees of the CC CPSU,[16] along with materials from the Conference of Soviet Orientalists held behind closed doors in Moscow from October 28 to November 1, 1958.[17] Apart from scientists, the conference was attended by high-ranking party and government officials, representatives of the union republics, and journalists. The next subsection explores the dimensions of the objectives and plans to achieve them that emerge from these documents.

The Soviet Plan to Penetrate Africa

Propaganda for the Communist ideology and dissemination of the experience of the USSR's socialist construction were chosen as the main instruments for spreading Soviet influence in Africa. The first-priority role was assigned to radio as the mass medium most available to Africans. Special attention was paid to broadcasts in African languages. The State Committee for Radio and Television was "to organize broadcasting to African countries in Swahili, Amharic, and Hausa" and "explore the possibilities to create bureaus for Soviet radio in Black African countries." It was planned to invite African broadcasters to implement radio programs in these languages.[18]

Provisions were made to distribute Soviet printed matter to Africa. It was considered worthwhile to arrange "publishing sociopolitical and imaginative literature in Swahili, Amharic, and Hausa," including "series of illustrated booklets highlighting the economic, scientific, and cultural achievements of the peoples of the Soviet Union, especially of Central Asia and Transcaucasia," and to establish a network of the Telegraph

Agency of the Soviet Union (Telegrafnoye Agentstvo Sovetskogo Soyuza, TASS) and central newspapers' bureaus in African countries. The CC CPSU committed the Ministry of Culture and the All-Union Corporation Mezhdunarodnaya Kniga (International Book) "to arrange the distribution of Soviet films and literature in African countries."[19] The fall 1958 Conference of Soviet Orientalists recommended "examining the issue of providing aid for domestic [African] publishing firms . . . in printing Soviet publications." The Ministry of Foreign Trade was recommended to send printing machinery to African countries and "to sell (in installments) modern typographic equipment to friendly entrepreneurs." These firms "might publish not only our booklets, but also journals and bulletins." There was a need to "engage more widely the services of progressive scientists, journalists, and writers in composing brochures and articles exposing the imperialistic essence of U.S. policy toward the Middle East, Southeast Asia, and Africa, and articles, reportage, and the like on the peaceful foreign policy of the USSR, its disinterested aid to the countries of these regions, and their cultural relations with the USSR."[20]

It was necessary to back this Soviet stirring up in Africa with a similar effort to shape a positive image of "the Black Continent" in Soviet public opinion. "Measures aimed at acquainting the Soviet general public with the history, life, culture, and art of the Africans" included "organizing exhibitions, holding conferences of Soviet Arabists and Africanists, and publishing translations of the national imaginative and other literature of these peoples."[21] The CC CPSU instructed the Ministry of Culture and the Writers' Union to include in the plans of publishing houses the issuing of creative literature written by African and African American writers and prescribed measures "to improve the covering of the situation in Black African countries, the progress of the national liberation movement of African people, and the exposure of the colonialist policy of Western Powers."[22]

To penetrate Africa, it was necessary not only to rely on "progressive" and "friendly" Africans but also to train them. The CC CPSU recognized that it was it advisable "to increase the admission of secondary, undergraduate, and graduate students from Black African countries for study in Soviet higher and secondary special educational institutions" and "to raise the number of annual scholarships and grants assigned by the Soviet Union to African countries to 300."[23]

It was impossible to elaborate an African policy without an overall development of Soviet African studies. The CC CPSU instructed the Ministry of Higher and Secondary Education "to jointly determine with the

USSR Ministry of Foreign Affairs [Ministerstvo inostrannykh del, MID] and the USSR Academy of Sciences' Presidium the personnel requirements for specialists in African affairs and to organize their training in the educational and scientific institutions of African countries; trainees are also to be sent to the Soviet embassies in Africa." Steps should be taken "to increase the number of Africanists studying at Leningrad University," "to bring in appropriate specialists in African languages from abroad for work at this University," and "to establish ties between the corresponding Soviet educational institutions and the universities and colleges of Black African countries."[24]

The key point of many speeches at the Conference of Soviet Orientalists was the necessity to send Soviet scientists to Eastern countries to work for long periods of time. For instance, the influential journalist Georgii Zhukov, chairman of the State Committee for Cultural Relations with Foreign Countries (Gosudastvennyi komitet po kul'turnym svyazyam s zarubeznymi stranami), which was under the USSR Council of Ministers, declared:

> The snag is that our Orientalists are working mostly in their home country and come to speculative conclusions by basing their knowledge only on the literature that we receive from foreign countries. This is the crucial difference between our Orientalism and bourgeois Orientalism; bourgeois Orientalists have been residing in the countries they study for many decades. . . . Historically, we have the situation when Orientalists have been considered for 20 to 30 years to be the people who, I should say, are divorced to some extent from daily life and are preoccupied with exploring abstract matters. Life has left us behind, and we happen to be unprepared for creating the theory of dealing with Asian and African countries, the theory to be effectual for our diplomacy, policy, and economic and propagandistic activity in these countries. We should begin a "great migration" of our Orientalists to the Oriental countries; they must live there not for one or two months, but for years and maybe decades. Then we will be able to discourse learnedly on how Asian and African countries are developing and which way they will choose. We need our Soviet missionaries, our Soviet Doctor Schweitzers, sent by the Slavs of the West, our compatriots who have been living in these countries for a long time.[25]

For the USSR to penetrate into Africa required that the work of the MID be adjusted to modern realities. Therefore, the CC CPSU committed the MID "to intensify its work with African countries, to strengthen the embassies by staffing them with persons with good knowledge of the native languages and these countries."[26] Also stressed at the Conference of Soviet Orientalists was the necessity to engage specialists in the affairs of Oriental countries in diplomatic work. Zhukov stated: "It would be right to have people who have chosen Orientalism for their academic careers among our embassies' personnel, among the diplomats. Otherwise, in the Soviet embassies in Asian and African countries, there will remain people who used to work at the embassies in Paris or Stockholm, then they were sent to Thailand, and then to Latin America. Meanwhile, professional Orientalists are sitting in Moscow and studying literature on the situation in Asian and African countries."[27]

An important aspect of "opening up" Africa to Soviet influence was assigned to three public organizations—the Central Council of Trade Unions (Vsesoyuznyi Tsentral'nyi Sovet Proffessional'nykh Soyuzov), the Soviet Afro-Asian Solidarity Committee (Sovetskyi Komitet Solidarnosti stran Azii i Afriki), and the USSR Committee of Youth Organizations (Komitet molodeznykh organizatsyi). The CC CPSU entrusted these organizations with the task "of striving to expand the ties with the corresponding organizations of Black African countries, of searching out various ways to maintain and strengthen the contacts with the national liberation and workers' movements of these countries, and to give these movements full-fledged assistance."[28]

Overcoming Obstacles
It was much easier to elaborate the concept of Soviet penetration into Africa than to implement it. Those developing this concept had poor knowledge of Africa, were full of fanciful expectations, and were guided by theoretical perceptions based on Marxist postulates that were "abstract matters" in the context of African realities.

Brzezinski reasonably believed that the USSR would need to overcome formidable obstacles to achieve its goals in Africa: "The Communist states were not only economically weaker than the West; they were politically and ideologically inexperienced in African ways, linguistically and culturally alien, and often even unable to grasp the importance of tribal loyalties (instead of class conflicts) in Africa."[29] But Brzezinski saw the main safeguard against Africa's falling under Communist domination in the Africans themselves. "The fundamental sense of values held in the African states," he predicted, would "keep them, at least for the near future, partially immune to the proselytizing zeal of the Communists."[30]

Soviet radio broadcasts to Africa began in April 1958. Initially, they were confined to 15 minutes daily in English and French. At the end of 1959, the broadcasts were stepped up to 31.5 hours a week. Occasional broadcasts in Swahili became regular in February 1960. By the end of 1961, Radio Moscow's weekly programs for Africa were of these durations: in English, 21 hours; in French, 21 hours; in Swahili, 14 hours; in Amharic, 7 hours; in Portuguese, 7 hours, and in Italian, 3.5 hours.[31] The first broadcast in Hausa was made on November 4, 1961.[32]

The propagandistic effectiveness of Radio Moscow's broadcasts to Africa was low. The CC CPSU Presidium admitted this in a special resolution adopted in July 1961. Among other things, it stated: "Materials are being written in a complicated language that African listeners can hardly understand, without due regard to the conditions and peculiarities of individual countries, and the political and cultural level of the population. Specialists in African problems are not drawn into broadcasting." To improve this situation, the Presidium resolved that abstract reasoning about the advantages of socialism should be avoided and that the authors of programs should "carefully take into consideration the situation in different African regions, the economic, the political and cultural development of individual African countries, and the fact of their population having little information on world events and often distorted knowledge as regards the Soviet Union, socialism, and communism." In broadcasting, it was necessary to involve "the Soviet [citizens] who have visited Africa, and representatives of African peoples during their stay in the USSR."[33]

The volume of political radio programs increased significantly, whereas previously they were merely entertaining and designed to build up a listening audience. For instance, strong anti-Western and anticolonial rhetoric was characteristic of the program regularly presented by Ivan Potekhin on behalf of the Soviet-African Friendship Association that he chaired. And the Soviet Union and socialism were depicted in the floweriest terms on the program *As Africans See the USSR*, which consisted of talks about the USSR given by African students studying at Soviet universities and by Africans visiting Russia.

Still, many programs could hardly draw the attention of most African listeners. Viktor Laptukhin, who worked in the African editorial office of Radio Moscow and was engaged in broadcasting in Hausa from its inception, recalls that he and his colleagues faced serious problems deriving mainly from "the differences in cultural traditions and mentality" between the audience and the authors of the programs. But "the leaders of the State Committee for Radio and Television thought that the problems could be resolved by flooding our listeners with information on our achievements in culture and the arts. Folk songs and melodies from classical operas and ballets, mixed with ideological commentary, took up the bulk of the broadcasting time. Attempts to change anything in this routine were resolutely prevented."[34]

The Soviet Union also began to disperse its printed products in Africa. From January to August 1961 alone, it sent 54,000 books and 13,500 copies of periodicals. The books were mainly the classics of Marxism-Leninism and propaganda. The largest Soviet libraries organized the exchange of "books and other materials with libraries and museums in African countries."[35]

African subjects were also reflected in Soviet publishing programs. The Publishing House Inostrannaya Literatura (Foreign Literature) was a vivid example of this process. The CC CPSU adopted a special resolution on its work, one of whose main reprimands was that it did not issue enough books by African authors: "The Publishing House acquaints the readers with the life of the people of colonial and nonindependent countries by producing literature that comes out not in these countries but mainly in the United States, England, France, and misrepresents the situation in underdeveloped countries."[36] In accordance with the directive of the CC CPSU, the Publishing House revised its work plan for 1961–62, which its director forwarded to the CC CPSU Department of Propaganda and Agitation in the Union Republics. The list of books to be published evoked criticism, partly because only a few were by African authors: "There are still no books on Africa. Of 171 titles, only 2 books concern Africa."[37]

However, it was difficult for the Publishing House Inostrannaya Literatura to carry out its task, because it faced a lack of interpreters and encountered selling problems. Another difficulty was in choosing those African languages into which the books designed for Africa should be translated in the first instance.[38] Despite these obstacles, the Publishing House increased its production of books by African writers and the translations of Russian literature into African languages. Conversely, the African theme was heavily represented in the work plan of another publisher, the Publishing House Vostochnaya Literatura (Oriental Literature), which was established in 1957.

The Soviet press began to pay much more attention to African problems and events. In 1957, a bureau of the important Soviet newspaper *Pravda* was established in Ghana; and in 1958, a bureau of the TASS was established in Guinea.

Along with the USSR's radio and print initiatives, to engage Africa, it also conducted student exchanges, formed new government agencies, established Peoples' Friendship University, and created the Institute for African Studies. The number of students from black Africa enrolled in various Soviet higher educational establishments was growing quickly. In December 1959, 114 young people from Sub-Saharan Africa (including 42 Sudanese) were studying in the USSR;[39] by January 1961, there were 527.[40] At Khrushchev's personal initiative, Peoples' Friendship University (Universitet Druzhby Narodov, also known as Patrice Lumumba University), was established in Moscow in February 1960. The reality of life in the USSR sometimes caused disillusionment among these young Africans, with unexpected and unpleasant consequences for Soviet authorities, such as racial conflict, "anti-Soviet sentiments," the formation of unauthorized organizations by African students, and general problems with selecting reliable student cadres from African countries (see chapter 4 for more on these problems, and on Peoples' Friendship University).

The Soviet leadership allocated significant resources to the study and understanding of Africa. Leningrad University began to train more specialists in African affairs. A chair of African studies was established at Moscow University. And in 1959, the Institute for African Studies was set up within the USSR Academy of Sciences.

The story of the creation of the Institute for African Studies resembles a detective novel, for it involved a struggle among three rival groups in high Soviet circles advocating different approaches to the problems of African studies.[41] The supporters of the first approach, a group of Africanists led by Ivan Potekhin, wanted to establish a specialized institute where it would be necessary to organize integrated studies of the African continent, including its history, culture, and languages. W. E. B. Du Bois, the patriarch of Pan-Africanism and a fighter for the civil rights of African Americans, actively helped this first group. When in Moscow in January 1959, he was received by Khrushchev and handed him a letter expounding the main principles of Potekhin's approach.

The chief advocate of the second approach, the academician Babadjan Gafurov, did not disagree with Potekhin and DuBois in principle as regards the subjects of African studies, but he believed that, from an organizational point of view, African studies should be carried out at the Institute of Oriental Studies of the USSR Academy of Sciences. The third approach was fundamentally different. Its proponents, patronized by the CC CPSU secretary, Nuritdin Mukhitdinov, proposed reducing African studies mainly to exploring "pressing problems"—that is, those connected to the current political situation.

Initially, Mukhitdinov's party won the day. On May 18, 1959, the CC CPSU adopted a resolution stipulating that "the urgent economic and political problems of African countries" should be studied not at a specialized institute but at the Institute of the World Economy and International Relations of the USSR Academy of Sciences.[42] Nevertheless, on June 29, the same commission—most probably at Khrushchev's orders—passed a resolution on the establishment of the Institute for African Studies within the Academy of Sciences and declared the previous resolution to be null and void.[43] On July 2, the CC CPSU Presidium made the decision to create the Institute for African Studies within the framework of the Academy of Sciences. The institute's sphere of competence covered various issues of African history, culture, economy, and national relations.[44] Potekhin was appointed its first director.

The formation of the Institute for African Studies was difficult. There was a lack of professional personnel. It was necessary to combine fundamental and integral study of Africa with efforts to solve many practical problems. "A very specific knowledge of each African country, of the different sides of its life, of the things that had never been dealt with before was much more needed than general information on Africa," recalls Apollon Davidson, one of the institute's first staff members.[45] As a result of the intrigues of the adherents of the third approach led by Mukhitdinov, the institute's activity was subjected to criticism by the CPSU, and in June 1962, it was transferred from the academy's History Department to its Economics Department, and its research subjects were correspondingly redirected.

The Institute for African Studies did not have much influence in the making of Soviet African policy. In that respect, it was not an exception among the other academic institutions. Karen Brutents admitted that, in general, its impact on the "production" of the CC CPSU International Department was relatively weak:

> First of all, there was no considerable gap between our professional knowledge and what scientists could give us—not to mention some specific issues, of course. Besides, they knew whither and for what purpose they were writing, and the mechanism of self-censorship began to work; they were writing

while having it in mind that their materials should correspond to the official line. Some were writing for form's sake, only in order to be left alone and to proceed with their own matters. There were, of course, some interesting materials. But they were also ignored completely if they differed from the previously adopted background assumptions. The top brass, or at least some of them, believed that they, by definition, possessed the ultimate truth. Their belief that by virtue of their position they knew everything was further strengthened by their access to the sources of information not available either to the staff or to the scientists. They needed science to substantiate previously approved concepts rather than for anything else.[46]

The "Africanization" of the MID had been gaining momentum since the late 1950s. In July 1958, the African Department was established within its structure. Heretofore, Africa had been dealt with by the European departments responsible for the countries that had African colonies. In 1961, the African Department was divided in two—one for North Africa, and one for Sub-Saharan Africa. In 1959 and 1960, Soviet embassies were established in the former Belgian Congo, Ghana, Guinea, Mali, Somalia, and Togo.

Naturally, the creation of these new departments and the corresponding increase in the number of personnel could not automatically solve the numerous complicated problems faced by the Soviet Foreign Service. A memorandum from the deputy foreign minister, Vasilyi Kuznetsov, to the CC CPSU provides some insight into these problems. Kuznetsov wrote this memo in connection with the comments made by the first deputy chairman of the USSR Council of Ministers, Anastas Mikoyan, on the MID's proposals concerning the seemingly large number of employees—twenty-eight—at the Soviet Embassy in the Central African Republic. In the memo, distributed to the members of the CC CPSU Presidium on January 9, 1961, Mikoyan asked: "Why don't we have a staff of twelve to fifteen persons in these small states?"[47]

Kuznetsov countered that reducing the numbers of personnel in the embassies in Africa would make the only source of reliable information on Africa run dry: "The staff of the Ministry of Foreign Affairs in African countries is extremely limited in numbers. Its further reduction will deprive the Embassies of the opportunity to carry out necessary work and to submit to the center even a minimum of information. Meanwhile, we have a very poor knowledge of Africa, and it is impossible to draw it from literature."[48]

Having analyzed the embassies in seven African countries (Ghana, Guinea, Mali, Morocco, Somalia, Togo, and Tunisia), Kuznetsov argued that they were understaffed. There were twenty-seven "secret service agents" among the total embassy personnel of seventy. It was necessary to give permanent posts to junior diplomatic personnel in order to be able to train them as professional Africanists, for "now there is a lack of them in the MID." Due to severe climate conditions, embassy personnel were entitled to long leaves. The embassies in Africa also had to do the work assigned to the Union of Soviet Societies of Friendship and Cultural Relations with Foreign Countries, because it had no representatives of its own in Africa. The existing embassies were also charged with the duty to study the African countries where there were as yet no Soviet legations. As a result, diplomatic personnel were overloaded with work. The embassies were short of operating personnel, and so they had to enlist the services of "the diplomatic personnel having security clearance (ministers and first secretaries)" to have the premises watched at nighttime. "Stewards, drivers, clerical personnel, and sometimes even diplomatic personnel" had to participate in protecting the embassies' buildings. And it was forbidden to fill the vacancies of technical personnel with natives, "for reasons of security and of preserving state secrets."[49]

Kuznetsov also presented the corresponding data on the numbers of embassies' and other agencies' personnel of the leading Western powers in African countries. The Western powers, he asserted, "attach great importance to Africa and have flooded it with their diplomats, secret service agents, servicemen, and other people. . . . In these circumstances, it is very difficult to understand why the Soviet Union should further reduce the already-minimum volume of work aimed at developing the USSR's relations with African countries and at strengthening our positions in Africa, the work that our embassies are able to cope with only with great difficulty."[50] However, the CC CPSU ignored Kuznetsov's arguments and decided that the personnel of the Soviet Embassy in the Central African Republic should number sixteen, and not twenty-eight as the MID had requested.[51]

Even when taking into account the officials' habit to amplify, in the eyes of those in higher echelons, their difficulties with personnel, it is obvious that the life of Soviet diplomats working in Africa in the late 1950s and early 1960s was not easy. As the Soviet Union was establishing itself in Africa, the proficiency of the MID's personnel grew. But there was an obstacle—that is, the secret principle of foreign policy with regard to developing countries—"which was guided by the vestigial maxims of employing personnel in various spheres—diplomacy, intelligence, political work, economics, and the like. Predominantly professionally weak people were sent to these countries, especially to the farthermost and the poorest countries."[52] And there were many such countries in Africa.

The State Committee for Cultural Relations with Foreign Countries, established in 1957 "to direct foreign policy propaganda and coordinate the activity of the organizations maintaining cultural relations with foreign countries,"[53] and the State Committee for Foreign Economic Relations, which were both under the USSR Council of Ministers, were paying more and more attention to Africa. The Union of Soviet Societies for Friendship and Cultural Relations with Foreign Countries and the Soviet Afro-Asian Solidarity Committee also became important driving belts for achieving Soviet aims in Africa. They pretended to resemble "nonpolitical" and "nongovernmental" organizations, but actually they were established by the CC CPSU's decrees, were under the rigid control of the party and governmental structures, and were funded from the government budget. Speaking at the Conference of Soviet Orientalists in 1958, Georgii Zhukov specified the role of "the formally nongovernmental organizations" in Soviet propaganda to Africa—they "should smooth the official overtones in our propaganda."[54]

In 1957, the CC CPSU issued a decree to reorganize the All-Union Society of Cultural Relations with Foreign Countries (Vsesoyuznoe obshestvo kulturnoi svyazi s zagranitsei) into the Union of Soviet Societies for Friendship and Cultural Relations with Foreign Countries (Soyuz sovetskikh obshestv druzby, SSOD), which obtained the status of a public organization. The SSOD was established in February 1958; initially, it had a Department of Near Eastern and Middle Eastern Countries and Africa staffed with nine persons. One of the SSOD's tasks was "the acquaintance of Soviet people with the history, culture, and languages of foreign peoples."[55] On April 15, 1959, the CC CPSU accepted the offer of the SSOD to organize a Soviet-African Friendship Association. Ivan Potekhin was appointed its chairman.[56] In its infancy, the SSOD was mainly preoccupied with establishing Soviet cultural centers in Africa, and the Friendship Association organized celebrations of memorial dates in African history and held meetings with African politicians and public figures.

The Soviet Afro-Asian Solidarity Committee was established in 1958. It was a member of the Afro-Asian Peoples' Solidarity Organization (AAPSO), with headquarters in Cairo. The Soviet Afro-Asian Solidarity Committee (again, Sovetskyi Komitet Solidarnosti stran Azii i Afriki,

SKSAA) received African politicians and public figures in the USSR, organized mass actions of solidarity with African peoples and international conferences, awarded scholarships to the African students studying in the USSR, answered letters from the African listeners to Radio Moscow's overseas broadcasts, and the like. The CC CPSU instructed the SKSAA "to take measures to establish and extend relations with the national solidarity committees and with the progressive organizations of Asian and African countries by using primarily the AAPSO and its Permanent Secretariat in Cairo to achieve this purpose."[57]

The SKSAA also performed more specific political and propagandistic tasks in the AAPSO Permanent Secretariat. In his memo to the CC CPSU, its representative at the secretariat, G. Abdurashidov, noted: "The Permanent Secretariat in its daily practical work faces numerous difficulties caused mainly by the fact that it is situated in the [United Arab Republic]."[58] He convincingly proved that the Egyptian authorities were seeking to gain control over the African national liberation movement and to transform the AAPSO into "an instrument of the United Arab Republic's political, economic, and cultural penetration into African countries."[59] Abdurashidov believed that in such circumstances, Soviet representatives "should concentrate their activity on extending and strengthening their relations and contacts with African national organizations outside the Permanent Secretariat, so as to study events in Africa carefully and particularly." He proposed not only studying events but also doing the following:

(1) To reorganize the activity dealing with the holding of meetings and talks with representatives of African national organizations so that as much information as possible could be obtained on their activity, political programs, and methods of struggle; the base they rely on; and on the actual potential they have. (2) To organize the preparation of detailed letters of information and memo files on the most prominent leaders of the African national liberation movement. (3) To study periodicals published by various African organizations in order to clinch the matter of providing them with material aid, and also of using these periodicals and organs for the dissemination of Marxist-Leninist literature in Africa, as well as books and booklets casting light on the situation in socialist countries and exposing the aggressive intentions of the imperialist powers. (4) To work more actively with the African students being sent

to the Soviet Union to study, in order to organize the students' selection and to enroll them in educational institutions in a more expeditious manner.[60]

Abdurashidov asked the CC CPSU to allocate the funds necessary for increasing the size of the staff of the sksaa agency in the Permanent Secretariat, as well as for paying the rent "of rooms for the agency that may become a center, of sorts, of political work among Africans in Cairo." Also, one more car, "preferably a Volga," was needed, because the Egyptians, in order to impede contacts between the Permanent Secretariat members and African public figures in Cairo, had sold the cars belonging to the Permanent Secretariat.[61] The CC CPSU decided to meet the sksaa request, though not in full.[62]

The United States Retaliates

As explained above, archival documents make it clear that at least some drafts for a Soviet strategy in Africa did exist. This strategy's main goal was to penetrate Africa and strengthen the Soviet influence there. But there was no formulated Soviet strategy for spreading Communism in Africa and taking it over. The Soviet Union did not aim to expel the West from Africa but sought to have Western interests reduced.

As became evident in retrospect, in the late 1950s and early 1960s, many in Western leadership roles apprehended that "the Communist ghost" might have indeed materialized in Africa. The common American vision of Soviet aspirations in Sub-Saharan Africa was presented in a secret memorandum prepared by the U.S. Department of State in March 1960. This memo's authors believed that the USSR and its allies would eagerly seize the opportunity to establish a foothold on the continent provided by the breakup of the colonial empires. The Eastern Bloc's objective was not only "to weaken the West by stimulating hostility between the new Africa and its former masters." It also sought "to align the new states of Africa on its side in the long-term struggle against the West, which it terms 'peaceful coexistence.'" There could be no genuine nonalignment of these countries, for "in the Soviet vision of a polarized world, neutrality for developing states is regarded merely as a way station on a journey out of the Western and into the Communist field of attraction." The peaceful declarations of the Soviet Union were concealing its true goals: "(a) to stimulate the 'national liberation' movement so that Western economic as well as political interests are reduced or swept away; [and] (b) to prevent the U.S. from replacing the metropolitan powers [i.e., the colonial powers] as a stabilizing Western influence."[63]

Soviet activity in Africa was characterized as a total challenge to the West "in every sphere of life—political, diplomatic, economic, social and military." The failure of the West to take "adequate" ("as total in concept") countermeasures was pregnant with strategic losses in the Cold War confrontation: "Penetration of Africa would permit the Bloc to encircle NATO to the South, to have access to new markets and raw materials, and to establish a potential for bases in the area. In the longer run, the growth of Soviet influence in Africa at the expense of the West will increase the over-all power position of the Bloc in world affairs, have a damaging effect on the world-wide Western position, and would encourage a dangerous mood of overconfidence in Moscow." Even if the Communists' efforts "to subvert African states" failed, NATO would face serious problems in Africa all the same, for these states were "jealous of their newfound independence" and could succeed "in so stimulating extremist, racist, and divisive forces on the African continent that orderly progress and cooperation with the West become increasingly difficult."[64]

The stakes in the rivalry for Africa, which was "both a prize and a battlefield in the worldwide political and strategic contest," were high.[65] The strategic value of Sub-Saharan Africa stemmed principally from its geographic location and its strategic raw materials. A policy document adopted by the U.S. National Security Council in August 1957 remarked that alternate air and sea routes to the Far East passed through the area: "In the event of war or loss of Western access to the Mediterranean," the control of these routes "could be of considerable importance." If the Eastern Bloc won "the prize," it could "pose a serious threat to communications in the Atlantic, the Indian Ocean, and the Red Sea, as well as to our important North African strategic facilities, the Mediterranean littoral, and the flank of NATO." Losing control of the area could result in "both economic dislocation for Western Europe and Communist access to strategic materials."[66]

The balance of forces on the African "battlefield" was changing in favor of the East. The seeds of anticolonial and anti-imperialist propaganda had fallen on fertile soil, and the Eastern Bloc had gotten the better of the colonial powers, along with the United States. The authors of "Communist Penetration in Africa," a document prepared by the Department of State, stated: "Unhindered by ties with the colonial powers, the Soviet Union and its allies are able openly and constantly to champion nationalist causes of the world stage, especially in the UN and through the Afro-Asian Peoples' Solidarity Conference in Cairo. . . . In the minds of Africans yearning for independence, the Soviet Union is increasingly winning recognition as the leading anti-colonialist power or, at least, as a most useful goad to Western countermeasures involving political and economic support for Africa."[67]

U.S. policy vis-à-vis Africa was being torn by a basic dilemma. As one scholar noted in 1958, it was animated "by a natural sympathy on the one hand for the legitimate nationalist aspirations of self-determination, equality and social progress, and on the other hand, the recognition that advances in this direction often threaten vital strategic bases and economic interests of the United States and the Western World."[68] It was impossible to adopt any courses of action that would "directly undermine the Metropolitan powers," for two reasons. First and foremost, it implied ignoring "the constructive work they are doing." Second, it could arouse the resentment of the NATO allies, which could "weaken our general position." At the same time, the United States could not afford "to ignore the aspirations of the Africans, since our silence would be construed as opposition."[69]

With the Cold War in full swing, this dilemma in American practical policy was predominantly solved in favor of the former colonial powers. "It was a dual policy with a 'theory' of anticolonialism and practice of support for colonial elites," Arne Westad noted.[70]

At a meeting of American, British, and French politicians, diplomats, experts, and military officers in Washington in April 1959, Robert Murphy, the U.S. deputy undersecretary of state for political affairs, assured his European allies that

> for its part, the United States is concentrating primarily on the extension of economic, technical, and in some areas small amounts of military assistance to the newly independent countries and in the dependent areas is endeavoring to cooperate with the metropolitan powers in their development programs. With regard to self-determination, we support an orderly evolution toward this objective, while making clear that self-government imposes important responsibilities which the peoples concerned must be ready and able to discharge. In brief, we neither wish nor intend to supplant European interests in Africa, nor do we approve the violent rush toward independence now being pushed by the extreme nationalists.[71]

Murphy exhorted France and Great Britain not to "bottle up African nationalism" and to make every effort "to channel it into constructive directions."[72]

In the United States, as also in the other metropolitan regions, many politicians were anxious to clamp down on the jinni of African nationalism that was now on the loose. In Eisenhower's administration, it was the people who treated the anticolonial movement suspiciously as a powerful and potentially anti-Western force who were setting the pace in policy-making. The staff of the State Department's Bureau of African Affairs believed that, despite the scope of the rise of "African consciousness"—local, regional, or continental—this consciousness would be "emotional, irresponsible, exaggerated and xenophobic."[73] Secretary of State John Foster Dulles regarded African nationalism not as a natural and justified reaction to colonialism but as the result of the intrigues of world communism. Many U.S. officials shared his contempt for nonalignment policy, which he considered to be an amoral stance in a Manichean Cold War struggle between the free world and atheistic communism and denounced as "immoral" and "obsolete."[74]

The participants in the 1959 tripartite talks on Africa in Washington agreed that it was necessary "to avoid African nationalism turning into a massive anti-European movement which the Communists could exploit."[75] It was a difficult task, because the socialist methods of modernization were attractive for Africans, who were "restive about their underprivileged status." "The dramatic example of rapid industrial development in the USSR and elsewhere," the Department of State noted, "has convinced them that quick material progress is possible even for areas that are initially far behind the West. The administrative and economic models of the USSR and Communist China are seen as useful guides by some of the more radical elements."[76]

The Africans' "vulnerability" to Communist ideology and their "receptivity" to the Soviet political and economic overtures also sprang from the traditional scheme of life: "Most Africans are still primarily villagers who live largely from subsistence agriculture and receive their social services from a traditional system that emphasizes sharing rather than individual acquisition." Because they are used to egalitarian principles of distribution, people in African societies showed "a greater degree of sympathy and understanding for authoritarian socialism than for democratic processes."[77]

It was the necessity to counteract the "Communist threat" that significantly stimulated the United States to become active in Africa and get down to elaborating its own African strategy. Thus, in February and March 1957, Vice President Richard Nixon went on a three-week tour of Ghana, Morocco, Ethiopia, Sudan, Libya, Tunisia, Liberia, and Uganda. Upon his return to Washington, he reported to the president that Africa was "the most rapidly changing area in the world today" and could become "the decisive factor in the conflict between the forces of freedom and international Communism."[78] Nixon recommended that, to effectively counteract Soviet expansionism, the policy of "containment of Communism" being followed in Europe should be transplanted to Africa. To achieve this goal, he believed that it was necessary for the Department of State to "take immediate steps to strengthen its representation in Africa, both quantitatively and qualitatively."[79]

In August 1958, the Bureau of African Affairs was established within the Department of State, and the Office of Assistant Secretary of State for African Affairs was set up. In its press release, the Department of State noted that this move "constitutes recognition of the African Continent" and "is vital to the efficient conduct of our relations with that Continent."[80] There was another important reason for establishing the bureau. In July 1958, Joseph Satterthwaite, the assistant secretary of state for African affairs and the future head of the bureau, had stressed, in a speech to Congress, "the need for positive and aggressive programs . . . to counter the activities in Africa of nations whose ideologies are unfriendly to the United States."[81] The Bureau of African Affairs became the think tank charged with the task of analyzing the African policy of the USSR and its allies and elaborating the methods of thwarting the Communist ambitions for domination in Africa in order to keep it "oriented toward the free Western World."[82]

The U.S. administration had to begin solving this problem in West Africa, which had become the first part of Sub-Saharan Africa to encounter Khrushchev's breakthrough to the developing world. To provide a context for these developments, it is necessary to examine those Soviet-Liberian diplomatic contacts that highlight the beginning of the Cold War in Sub-Saharan Africa and illustrate the materialization of the Khrushchevian approach to the developing world as applied to West Africa.

The Liberian Debut of Soviet Diplomacy

It has become common practice to trace the beginning of the Cold War in Sub-Saharan Africa from October 1958, when Guinea became independent, or from July 1960, when the Congo crisis erupted. However, archival documents suggest that these current opinions ignore the Liberian debut of Soviet diplomacy.

On July 30, 1955, Soviet foreign minister Vyacheslav Molotov received a message from the acting Liberian secretary of state, George Padmore (the namesake of a prominent exponent of Pan-Africanism, to be mentioned below). He was inviting a Soviet delegation to visit Monrovia to participate in the celebrations marking the inauguration of President William Tubman.[83]

Only a couple of years earlier, this visit would have been unthinkable. The Soviet leadership considered Liberian independence to be "fictitious," and not without reason. Liberia was established in 1847 by the Americo-Liberians—emancipated slaves whose ancestors had been shipped from Africa to America. People who were brought to Liberia by the "love of freedom" became the ruling caste and treated the natives even worse than European colonizers were doing. While waging incessant wars with the indigenous population and constantly in financial difficulties, the Americo-Liberians had only one guarantee to ensure their survival and the preservation of their master status: the massive and comprehensive aid coming from the United States—their "second," but "true," fatherland. Liberia always supported U.S. foreign policy without reservation.

President Tubman, the protégé of the conservative wing of the Americo-Liberian ruling elite and a convinced enemy of "atheistic Communism," who came into office in 1944, was ready to support the United States, viewing this as a form of compensation for U.S. assistance to his country. While the United States and the USSR were allies in World War II, he sanctioned Soviet-Liberian negotiations on the establishment of diplomatic relations, but soon after the Cold War erupted, he ordered the negotiations to be suspended. He decided that it was imperative to join America's crusade against Soviet Communism and declared Liberia's willingness "to support the free world against Communism even when certain selfish actions or sacrifices are required."[84] The negotiations were broken off in April 1946, never to be resumed. Yet this did not prevent Tubman from inviting Soviet representatives to his first and second inauguration ceremonies, though his missives were left without an answer.[85] Then, in July 1955, after being elected to a third term, Tubman sent Molotov an invitation to his third inauguration ceremony.[86]

In the mid-1950s, Liberia's foreign and domestic policies remained mainly unchanged. Thus the USSR's Information Committee, under the MID, emphasized that "the Liberian Government headed by Tubman, who is actually the country's dictator, advocates the maximum encouragement of American investments in the Liberian economy. . . . Both the foreign and internal policies of the Liberian Government are controlled by the U.S. ruling circles, which causes resentment on the part of opposition elements in the country."[87] But this assessment did not take into considerations the problems Tubman faced as the anticolonial struggle in the neighboring West African countries was gaining momentum. A Liberian student of Tubman's policy formulated his new dilemma as follows: "How to appear credible to the nationalist leaders of West Africa and to maintain his inflexible pro-Western stance in international affairs?"[88] So Tubman decided to make a gesture to the Communist Bloc in order to obtain the needed credibility.

Tubman's unequivocal commitment to U.S. foreign policy did not stop the Soviet Union from seeking contacts with Liberia, then the only independent country in Tropical Africa. On August 20, 1955, Molotov signed a positive reply to Padmore's missive and ordered that it should be passed to the Liberian side through the USSR's ambassador in Paris.[89]

Establishing Diplomatic Relations

The first official Soviet delegation to Tropical Africa visited Liberia from December 31, 1955, to January 12, 1956. It was headed by A. P. Volkov, chairman of the Union of the USSR Supreme Council, and included V. I. Bazyhkin, deputy head of the MID's Department of American Countries, and A. G. Myshkov, a secretary-interpreter. According to the guidelines received by the delegation, its main goal was that of "making personal contacts with Liberian statesmen and resuming the negotiations on the establishment of diplomatic relations between the USSR and Liberia, which were conducted by the Soviet and Liberian embassies in 1945–1946 in Washington."[90]

The reception of the Soviet guests in Monrovia was not free from certain breaches of diplomatic protocol. When introducing the head of the Soviet delegation to President Tubman, the chef de protocol mistook Volkov for Egypt's representative. According to the delegation's report, another incident was even funnier:

> The foreign delegations leaving the President's residence were to get into cars in the same order as they had been introduced to the President. But when the moment came for the Soviet delegation to depart, it turned out that the car set aside for it was out of order and could not be sent up to the front door. After some confusion, a car with an English flag arrived and, in the presence of the numerous people watching the departure of the delegations, the Negro chauffeur removed the little English flag and replaced it with a Soviet one. Those present reacted to all these manipulations with liveliness.[91]

The delegation used its contacts with Liberian officials to clarify the prospects for the establishment of USSR-Liberia diplomatic relations. For the first time, this issue was raised on January 2 in a short talk with President Tubman during a military parade. Members of the delegation asked for an audience with the president to discuss the possibility of resuming the negotiations. Tubman agreed.[92]

Tubman regularly reported to the U.S. ambassador in Monrovia, Richard Jones, on the particulars of Soviet-Liberian contacts. On that very day, January 2, Tubman informed the ambassador that the Soviet representatives had intimated that they had instructions to hold confidential talks with him on several subjects, "one being the exchange of diplomatic representation between our two countries."[93]

On January 5, Jones told Tubman that the U.S. government "would be gravely concerned if the Government of Liberia accepted a [Soviet] diplomatic mission in Monrovia," and made it clear that if this indeed happened, Liberia would experience problems with foreign investments. Tubman himself did not consider it expedient to establish full-fledged relations with the USSR. He said that "he was fully aware of the dangers inherent in accepting a Soviet mission" and offered to rebuff the Soviets on the matter of exchanging diplomatic missions by dragging it out "for a long, long time."[94]

The next day, at a meeting with the Soviet delegation, Tubman reverted to delaying tactics. He said that although he did not object to establishing diplomatic relations, the national budget for 1956 had already been approved, and it would be difficult to raise the $150,000 to $200,000 a year needed to maintain a Liberian diplomatic mission in the USSR. The president promised to urge Congress to allocate this sum for the next financial year. The parties agreed to formalize the arrangement to establish diplomatic relations through an exchange of letters and by issuing a joint communiqué. The Liberian acting secretary of state, Momolu Dukuly, and Bazyhkin were charged with preparing the drafts. At the end of the talks, Tubman remarked that "the credentials the delegation submitted did not provide for full powers to conduct negotiations and to sign documents concerning the establishment of diplomatic relations between Liberia and the USSR."[95]

Half an hour later, Tubman met with Ambassador Jones and told him about the results of the meeting with the Soviets. There was only one important difference between the information Tubman related to Jones and the report submitted by Bazyhkin and Volkov to the MID. The Soviets did not mention having discussed any future Soviet-Liberian economic cooperation or any possible Soviet aid. At the same time, in his telegram to the Department of State based on Tubman's story, Jones informed Washington that "Volkov expressed Soviet interest in the economic and cultural development of Liberia and stated that the USSR was prepared to offer economic assistance to Liberia."[96]

Apparently, no economic issues were discussed. Had they been touched upon, Volkov and Bazyhkin would have certainly mentioned this. Tubman needed the bluff about hypothetical Soviet aid to receive additional financial injections from the United States. Tubman, in a special letter, assured President Eisenhower: "Our patent regard for the agreement entered into between our two governments for economic assistance in our development programs cannot be bartered nor sold by any new traducing ideology and the visit of the Soviet delegation to Liberia seeking to effect arrangements for an exchange of diplomatic representatives and economic assistance will have no effect on the Liberian Government's attitude and policy."[97]

Meanwhile, Bazyhkin and Volkov had to send a telegram to Moscow asking for "an urgent delivery to the Liberian Embassy in London of the appropriate document empowering the delegation to conduct negotiations and to sign agreement on establishing diplomatic relations." The next day, a telegram signed by Molotov was received, stating that the Soviet Embassy in London had actually sent a note to the Liberian Embassy confirming the full powers of Volkov, the head of the delegation, and that "the President of Liberia was notified of this by telegraph.[98]

On January 7, Dukuly received Bazyhkin and Myshkov, the secretary-interpreter. Killi Tamber, head of the International Organizations Bureau of the Liberian Department of State, was present at the meeting. According to the Soviet delegation's information, Tamber had studied in the USSR and knew Russian. He was not introduced to Bazyhkin and Myshkov and avoided socializing with them. The drafts proposed by the parties proceeded from different premises. The Soviet side wanted the exchange of embassies to follow the establishment of diplomatic relations. The Liberian draft noted that "nowadays the exchange of embassies is impracticable, for the government has neither the legislative body's authorization nor sufficient budgetary allocations."[99]

This was a flimsy argument. Tubman had brought the Legislature under his personal control and packed it, according to an opposition Liberian politician, with "his servants, cronies and favorites, many of them illiterate."[100] Nevertheless, the agreed-on text of the joint communiqué was much closer to the Liberian draft. The time of the establishment of diplomatic missions was not set: "The parties have agreed that the exchange of embassies between the USSR and the Republic of Liberia will take place after the Liberian Government has received the authorization of the Legislature of Liberia and sufficient budgetary allocations."[101] This enabled Tubman to handle the problem of exchanging diplomatic missions at his own will—or as he told the U.S. ambassador, to drag it out "for a long, long time."

On the evening of January 7, the Soviet delegation held a reception in honor of the president of Liberia. Addressing the president, Volkov expressed the hope that the contacts made with Liberian officials "would develop and strengthen" and "would make for establishing friendly and mutually beneficial relations between the two countries." When speaking in his turn, Tubman did not mention the prospects for Soviet-Liberian relations but emphasized that he shared " the principles of noninterference in internal affairs and of respect for national sovereignty in interstate relations." Despite the reticence of his speech, Tubman was by no means indifferent to the gifts he received from the delegation. As Bazyhkin and Volkov reported, "At the end of the reception, in a separate room, we handed the gifts to the President, the Vice President, the Secretary of State, and the Chairman of the House of Representatives. Everybody was greatly pleased with the gifts. When the Presidents' aides-de-camp were. carrying the gifts to the cars, Tubman loudly warned them that his gifts should be put in a separate place. The next day, Tubman's wife appeared at an official reception wearing a Soviet brooch."[102]

On January 11, Tubman received the Soviet representatives. He approved the text of the joint communiqué. He had reasons to be satisfied with the results of the negotiations. Liberia had established relations with all the great powers and had not assumed any obligations to the USSR. The president did not repeat the flimsy argument about the necessity of the Legislature's sanction and explained the delay as being for financial reasons, saying that at the moment there was no money to maintain a Liberian embassy in Moscow, but he promised that the necessary funds would be allocated "at the earliest opportunity."[103]

Tubman seemed to care more about the propagandistic effect of the communiqué than about its practical implementation. He asked the Soviet representatives to let him "inform the pressmen unofficially that the agreement concerning the establishment of diplomatic relations between the USSR and Liberia had been reached" before the settled date of publishing the document (January 20, 1956). They had no objections, and this information was published in a local newspaper the next day, January 12. Tubman readily agreed to be photographed, on the veranda in the company of the Soviet delegation, by Soviet, American, and Liberian cameramen. They parted in a friendly way. Tubman said he would like to take a shot of vodka to mark the establishment of diplomatic relations and noted that the three shots of vodka he had drunk at the Soviet reception "had a good effect on him."[104]

On this very day, January 12, at the Liberian Department of State, Volkov and Dukuly signed the Russian and English texts of the joint communiqué on the establishment of diplomatic relations and "exchanged the letters." The Russian text was handwritten. Apparently there was no typewriter with Russian characters in Monrovia. On January 20, 1956, the communiqué and the letters were published in the main Soviet newspapers.

Vain Overtures to Tubman

Even with these diplomatic developments between the USSR and Liberia, the U.S. administration was still sure that Tubman would not let the Russians penetrate West Africa. On January 27, Eisenhower wrote him: "I am confident that, thanks to your understanding of international affairs and the motivations of certain governments, your intention to protect the Liberian people and nation from the insidious aims of Communism will enable you to remain firm in your resolve to resist the pressures to these ends now being brought to bear upon your Government."[105] In the instructions for the U.S. ambassador in Liberia attached to the letter, the U.S. secretary of state, John Foster Dulles, noted that the "President has expressly avoided mention of an exchange of diplomatic representatives between Liberia and the USSR because the possible release at any time of a public letter with this phrase could result in a Soviet propaganda advantage." Dulles instructed the ambassador not to divulge the contents of the president's message because of its "personal and confidential nature."[106]

Tubman did his best to freeze relations with the USSR at the existing level—nearly zero. The Soviet side, for its part, tried vainly to obtain some practical results from the documents signed in Monrovia. On February 22, 1956, the MID's Department of the Middle East recommended to the Soviet ambassador in London, Yakov Malik, that he should meet with the Liberian ambassador to "discuss the specific issues of economic and cultural relations" and find out Tubman's attitude toward "his possible invitation to visit the USSR."[107]

On March 27, Malik met with Liberia's chargé d'affaires in London,

John Marshall. The Liberian diplomat indicated that the president was likely to accept the invitation. But Tubman was not forthcoming. He declined the invitation on the pretext that "the Liberian Legislature does not permit him to undertake such a journey in 1957 as he already went abroad in the previous year, 1956 (to West European countries)."[108]

There was no progress on the issue of the exchange of embassies. On April 20, 1956, the USSR's ambassador to the United States, Georgii Zarubin, in a conversation with the Liberian ambassador, George Padmore, conjectured that "for the convenience of both countries, they will exchange diplomatic missions in the foreseeable future." Padmore reacted skeptically, calling into question the capability of Liberia to maintain an embassy in Moscow, given that the world prices of rubber, the Liberian staple export, had plummeted. At the end of the conversation, he hinted that this was the official explanation, but the real obstacle was the "pro-American figures" in the Liberian leadership who "would impede the exchange of diplomatic missions."[109]

In the autumn of 1956, an idea was born in the middle echelon of the MID that a diplomatic demarche with regard to Liberia should be undertaken. On September 26, the Department of the Middle East prepared a memorandum to the CC CPSU in which, among other things, it was stated that "so far the Liberian Government has not announced either its readiness to exchange embassies or the date when this will happen, and therefore is indefinitely delaying the resolution of this issue." The department proposed sending a note to the Liberian Department of State. The draft it submitted reminded the Liberian side of Tubman's statement that he "does not anticipate any difficulties with receiving the sanction of the Liberian Legislature to establish diplomatic relations between our countries." In this connection, it was supposed that "during the elapsed time, the Liberian Government has received both the sanction and the funds to maintain its embassy in Moscow." The Department of State was asked to announce "when it would be most suitable to conduct concrete negotiations between our representatives concerning the date of the exchange of embassies and the corresponding measures connected therewith."[110] But the note was not approved by the MID's upper echelon and was not dispatched.

The Liberian tactic was transparent: to confine the matter to vague generalities and to mark time in order to avoid complications in relations with the United States. This situation did not suit the Kremlin, which spurred the MID into putting forth new initiatives.

In January 1959, Deputy Foreign Minister Vladimir Semenov informed the USSR's ambassador to the United States, Mikhail Men'shikov, that

"the question of developing relations with Liberia is under consideration."
The ambassador was asked to advance his opinion on "our possible measures to stimulate Soviet-Liberian relations."[111] The answer from Washington did not give a reason for optimism. The chargé d'affaires, Mikhail
Smirnovskii, reported that his talks with Liberian diplomats showed that
the Liberian government was not yet ready to exchange diplomatic representatives with the USSR.[112]

In the summer of 1959, the Liberian government, via its embassy in
London, invited delegations from the USSR, Ukraine, and Byelorussia to
come to Monrovia in January 1960 to participate in the inaugural celebrations for Tubman, who had been reelected to a fourth term in May 1959.
The MID recommended that the CC CPSU should send all the three delegations, "considering our interest in developing relations with Liberia,"
and should appoint "a prominent Soviet statesman" to head the USSR
delegation. However, the CC CPSU Presidium decided to send only one
delegation, from the USSR, headed by Nuritdin Mukhitdinov, chairman of
the Commission for Foreign Affairs of the Soviet of Nationalities of the
USSR Supreme Soviet.[113]

Mukhitdinov's memoirs offer no details of his meeting with Tubman:
"We exchanged opinions, came to mutual understanding and decided that
the embassies headed by Ambassadors should be established in both capi-
tals, along with trade missions."[114] Archival materials indicate that another
important subject was also touched upon. Tubman said that "he would like
to invite Khrushchev to visit Liberia as the President's guest" and "if
Khrushchev accepts his proposal, he will send an official written invitation." The president made it clear that he was ready to make a visit to the
USSR, but "so far certain circumstances have prevented him from making
use of the Soviet side's invitation."[115]

Two memorable events happened during Mukhitdinov's stay in Liberia.
It turned out that all the guests at the inauguration ceremony in Monrovia
had to be clad "according to international protocol: ladies in evening
dresses, gentlemen in tuxedos, striped pants, white shirts and bow ties.
Such attire for gentlemen was not tailored in the USSR, and the CC CPSU
Economic Board found a tailor from the Bolshoi Theatre." In three days,
the required suit was ready for Mukhitdinov. The other members of the
Soviet delegation also had to tackle the sartorial problem. One of them
rented a suit at a theater. When he was trying it on in Monrovia, the seams
snapped. The next day, the man had to be present at the inauguration ceremony, and now he was holding his pants, "or, more exactly, the two
halves of them torn apart and distantly resembling in shape Africa and

America." The chef de protocol of the Liberian Ministry of Foreign Affairs was called up, he consulted Tubman, and the president permitted the Soviet representatives to wear "any clothes convenient for them." They attended the ceremony in their suits.[116]

The second episode was not so funny. During a trip to the Atlantic seaboard, Mukhitdinov decided to have a swim, and his companions went sightseeing. His swim nearly ended in tragedy: "I took off my clothes, entered the water. I walked about 30 meters, but the water was waist-deep—not an inspiring adventure at all. Suddenly I find myself deep under the water—a steep slope! I do not know how deep the water is. The surf is strong, and the waves alternately draw me into the ocean and toss me against the rocks as a matchbox; I cannot touch bottom. I am already scratched and bloodied by being tumbled into the rocks, and still cannot overcome the waves." Luckily, everything was taking place very close to the president's country seat. Somebody noticed that the head of the Soviet delegation was in trouble and called for help. The unfortunate swimmer was rescued from the water with the help of a long pole.[117]

The Soviet delegation received exceptional treatment. Mukhitdinov was the only foreign guest who was asked to deliver a short speech during the inauguration ceremony, Tubman's wife invited him for a dance at the state reception, and he was decorated with a Liberian order.[118] Nevertheless, the visit brought no practical results.

On January 18, 1960, at the MID's proposal, the CC CPSU Presidium made a decision "to send W. Tubman a letter of invitation to make an official visit to the USSR at any time convenient for him." The Soviet ambassador to Guinea was assigned to hand Tubman the invitation. The ambassador was authorized to inform the president that if Khrushchev received an official invitation, "he would be glad to visit Liberia during his trip to other African countries."[119]

The counselor of the USSR's Embassy in Guinea, Ivan Marchuk, was charged with the mission to deliver Khrushchev's missive to Tubman. He received Marchuk on February 23. On reading the missive, the president "thanked him for the invitation to visit the USSR and said that he accepted it with pleasure." He also instructed Secretary of State Rudolph Grimes to prepare an invitation for Khrushchev right away, and he told Marchuk that Grimes would pass it to him the next day. The next morning, Grimes handed Marchuk a sealed envelope containing an official invitation for Khrushchev to visit Liberia at any time that was convenient for him.[120]

According to Marchuk, Tubman "was visibly pleased by receiving N. S. Khrushchev's missive and reaching the agreement on the exchange of visits." The president invited the Soviet diplomat to the reception on the occasion of his wife's birthday, where he introduced Marchuk to a number of Cabinet members and told them that the latter "has brought to him a message from Khrushchev." Some of the foreign diplomats present at the reception asked Marchuk about the purpose of his visit. Marchuk answered that he had arrived "on an official mission." The diplomats interpreted this as meaning that they had reached an agreement on exchanging diplomatic missions. The Ethiopian and British ambassadors even offered help in finding a building for the Soviet Embassy in Monrovia.[121]

On March 4, 1960, the information on Khrushchev's upcoming visit to Liberia and on Tubman's to the USSR was published in the Soviet press. Among other things, it was said that the dates of the visits "will be agreed upon through diplomatic channels."[122]

The visits did not take place. In August 1960, Grimes informed Georgii Zhukov, chairman of the State Committee for Cultural Relations with Foreign Countries, that Tubman "intends to visit the USSR in 1961," though previously the president had mentioned the second half of 1960.[123]

There was no progress in Soviet-Liberian relations. As of November 1960, the MID stated that "nowadays there exists no systematic trade with Liberia. There are also no regular contacts in the sphere of culture."[124] Nevertheless, the Liberian president did not fail to receive political dividends from his contacts with the Communist nations. On December 20, 1960, the Soviet Union endorsed Liberia's selection as the first black African country to have a seat on the UN Security Council.[125]

Tubman faithfully kept his promise to the Americans—to drag out the matter of exchanging diplomatic missions with the USSR "for a long, long time." No relations were established between the two countries during Tubman's administration. He died in 1971, and only in 1972 did Moscow and Monrovia exchange diplomatic missions.

In his dealings with the Soviet Union, Tubman from the very beginning was aiming at taking maximum advantage of the confrontation between the superpowers. All African leaders were trying with varying success to implement this strategy. Tubman, one of the most experienced African politicians, was a shrewd gambler and reaped the rewards. Guided by the considerations of his regime's survival in the situation of the Cold War and the collapse of colonial empires in Africa, he decided to make overtures to the USSR. In so doing, he managed to avoid sacrificing his fundamental principles (pro-Americanism, anticommunism) and, moreover, did not enter into any commitments and skillfully abstained from any practical steps to establish full-fledged relations with the Soviet Union.

Having considered the developments in Liberia, we next turn to the USSR's efforts to build bridges to Ghana. Initially, the prospects for close Soviet-Ghanaian relations did not look promising.

Establishing Relations with Ghana

Officials in Washington had no doubts as to the reliability of Liberian president William Tubman—an American proxy—but they were concerned with the prospects for Communist penetration into West Africa, where the British colony of the Gold Coast was set to become independent Ghana in March 1957. The very possibility of intercourse between the Soviet and the Gold Coast delegations at President Tubman's January 1956 inauguration in Monrovia seriously alarmed the West. At the direction of the Department of State, the U.S. Embassy in Monrovia made a thorough investigation to clear up "what contacts, if any, occurred between the members of the Gold Coast delegations and the Russians." The conclusion of Donald Lamm, the American consul general in Accra, was not frightening in this respect: "There was no official meeting of the Gold Coast delegations with the Russians, and "one or more members of the delegation did have a private chat with them."[126]

The Gold Coast Becomes Independent Ghana

On February 20, 1956, the U.S. undersecretary of state, Herbert Hoover Jr., informed the U.S. Consulate in Accra that the probability of the Soviet Union being invited to the ceremonies celebrating the independence of the Gold Coast, not to mention the possible establishment of diplomatic relations between the two countries, had been causing uproar at the Department of State. He expressed anxiety that Ghana might have been turned into the beachhead for Communist penetration into the hinterland of West Africa: "In the light of Soviet policy since the end of World War II, it can be safely assumed that Russia's primary objective in establishing diplomatic and consular offices in Africa is to undermine the fledgling political institutions of countries just emerged from colonial status to independence. The principal Soviet tool used to bring about the Communist penetration of these countries and surrounding areas would be the offers of economic aid and technical assistance, with significant political strings attached. Another, most effective tool would be the organization and direction of cadres of Africans, already trained in Communist schools abroad, to proselytize and win over to Communism the tribal peoples of the West African hinterland."[127] This is one of the earliest documents where "containment thinking" was formally applied to Africa independently from the considerations of European defense.

In December 1956, Lamm assumed that "owing to the financial situation, and the shortage of personnel, the Gold Coast" would not be able to send its representatives to the USSR and Communist China "for a considerable time after independence, even if they were inclined to do so." But this did not mean, the consul believed, that the native government would "react adversely to a proposal from these countries" to establish relations in view of "(1) enhanced prestige to the Gold Coast (2) possibilities of increased trade (e.g., cocoa with Russia), and (3) the implied threat to both the United Kingdom and the United States that arrangements could be made with the Russians if sufficient aid is not forthcoming from the West."[128]

The British position was outlined by Francis Cumming-Bruce, adviser to the governor of the Gold Coast on external affairs. He told Lamm that it would, "of course, be the policy of the British Government subsequent to independence to discourage the Gold Coast" from establishing relations with Communist countries, but the British had "very few weapons in their arsenal to use as arguments."[129] British officials seemed to reconcile themselves to the appearance of the Eastern Bloc's representatives in West Africa.

The United States tried to prevent or delay this. Lamm asked for the Department of State's permission to discuss the matter "with any senior Africans." He believed that it would be "quite useless" to appeal to "high moral principles, the dangers of Communism, etc." He proposed to base the approach to them "on a very gentle hint that the presence of Russian or Communist Chinese representatives in the Gold Coast might possibly have a slightly adverse effect on American investment."[130]

On January 4, 1957, the prime minister of the Gold Coast, Kwame Nkrumah, sent to the chairman of the USSR Council of Ministers, Nikolai Bulganin, a letter informing him that "the House of Commons of the United Kingdom had passed the law granting independence to the Gold Coast within the British Commonwealth." The law was to come into force on March 6, 1957, and the new state named Ghana would emerge. Nkrumah invited Soviet representatives to attend the Independence Day celebrations. He emphasized that this preliminary notification was at his own initiative, because time was drawing on. On January 23, Bulganin answered that, on receiving an official invitation, the Soviet government "would be glad" to send its delegation to Accra.[131]

The very same day, Nkrumah informally invited U.S. secretary of state John Foster Dulles to attend the celebrations in Accra, but Dulles declined, being of the opinion that Vice President Richard Nixon should lead the U.S. delegation. The Department of State's arguments were expounded in a memorandum to Nixon: "The Communist Bloc, as you know, has been displaying an increasing interest in the continent of Africa. In addition to various efforts at penetration and subversion in northern Africa, the Soviet Union and its allies have seized every opportunity to further their interests South of the Sahara. At the inauguration ceremonies for President Tubman of Liberia last year, for example, the Soviets sent a powerful delegation, sought to establish diplomatic relations, and made vague offers of economic assistance. We may expect a similar, or even greater, effort during the Gold Coast ceremonies." Under these circumstances, the Department of State considered the vice president's leadership "as extremely significant in demonstrating the American interest in Africa."[132] Nixon agreed to head the U.S. delegation.

Nixon was not the only one to try to influence Nkrumah. Dulles instructed the U.S. Embassy in Monrovia to give careful consideration to the suggestion "that the Liberian delegation to the Ghana ceremonies might take the opportunity to recommend to Ghana that they avoid establishment of relations with the USSR." The secretary of state was not sure that the Liberians would be able to cope with this problem: "The Liberian officials involved may not effectively present such a delicate issue. Ghana officials are not likely to accept such suggestions from their not-too-respected West African neighbors."[133]

On February 27, the U.S. Embassy in Monrovia informed Dulles that it had discussed with Liberia's secretary of state, Momolu Dukuly, the issue of joint action to prevent the USSR and Ghana from establishing relations. The embassy was of the opinion that "[the government of Liberia's] experience with Soviet efforts establish relations here, if properly told, may suggest to Ghana a method for handling the situation if it arises."[134] Dukuly informed the Liberian president about the discussion.

Faithful Tubman made no delay in complying with the American request. On February 28, Dukuly brought to the U.S. Embassy two of Tubman's letters to be sent to Nkrumah. One of them contained an emotional appeal that was quoted "almost verbatim" in the telegram that the embassy had sent to Dulles: "I [Tubman] earnestly pray you, Nkrumah, take all measures to prevent introduction in West Africa any harmful ideology, i.e., Communism."[135]

On March 6, 1957, the Gold Coast became the independent nation of

Ghana—the first of scores of Sub-Saharan African colonies to obtain political independence. Ghana emerged as a symbol of black pride and potential, while its charismatic leader, Kwame Nkrumah, was viewed as a champion of African liberation. He had been born in 1909 in the Gold Coast, had trained as a teacher, and in 1935 had gone to the United States for advanced studies. He entered Lincoln University in Pennsylvania and, after graduating in 1939, obtained master's degrees from Lincoln and from the University of Pennsylvania. He studied the literature of socialism, notably Karl Marx and Vladimir Lenin, and of black nationalism, especially Marcus Garvey. Nkrumah left the United States in 1945 and went to England, where he played an important role in organizing the Fifth Pan-African Congress in Manchester.

In December 1947, Nkrumah returned to the Gold Coast to serve as the general secretary of the United Gold Coast Convention, which was composed of Western-educated elites (mostly lawyers), entrepreneurs, and chiefs—a native "political class" that had a stake in the colonial system. They sought gradual reforms that would benefit their class, rather than the destruction of this system by radical methods. Having become frustrated with the conservative vision of the convention's leaders, in 1949 Nkrumah created the Convention People's Party, a mass-based nationalist party that called for "Self-Government *Now*." Nkrumah's tactic included strikes, boycotts, and demonstrations to exert continuous pressure on the colonial authorities to implement fundamental political reforms. After his "positive action" campaign caused disturbances in 1950, he was jailed, but when the Convention People's Party won the 1951 elections, he was freed to form a government and led the Gold Coast to independence.

The status of the Soviet delegation that went to Accra to participate in the independence celebrations was not high; it was headed by I. A. Benediktov, minister of state farms. This reflected the Kremlin's cautious attitude toward Nkrumah. Ghana had achieved its independence by peaceful means, and he was not viewed as a "true revolutionary" or a promising ally. The limitations of Ghanaian political independence were apparent, and Ivan Potekhin called it "illusive."[136] The former metropolitan country, Britain, left in Ghana its governor, many public officers, teachers, and the like. Nkrumah's power as prime minister was circumscribed. Colonial laws, institutions, and economic structures remained.

The Soviet press described the festivities in Accra with a certain reticence, avoiding any prognoses about Soviet-Ghanaian relations. The *Pravda* correspondent, Nikolai Pastukhov, admitted that achieving Ghanaian independence was an important component of the national liberation movement of "the awakened Asian and African nations," but he noted that "the economy of the new state is still in the hands of foreign, mainly English and American, monopolies."[137] The journal *Novoye vremya* published Nkrumah's biographical information without mentioning his political commitments. There was only one quotation from his statements: "Ghana's aspiration is to live in concord with all nations of the world."[138]

Nkrumah received Benediktov twice and "had long and friendly talks with him, in the course of which they agreed, in principle, to establish diplomatic relations between the Soviet Union and Ghana."[139] (In my research, I was unable to find out the details of these negotiations because the Soviet delegation's report remains classified.) In his public lecture, delivered at the Polytechnic Museum in Moscow, Benediktov avoided any political issues and devoted his narration to Ghanaian history, "the hardworking people of Ghana and its customs, as well as the luxuriant and boon nature of the country."[140]

Ghana's minister of finance, Komla Gbdemah, shared with an American diplomat some details of the Soviet delegation's stay in the country. The Russians "pressed them [the Ghanaian side] hard for the establishment of diplomatic relations, pointing out that the United States had an embassy here." The Ghanaians could find only one explanation, and a rather old one, for their position. The Russians were told that "the countries which had already established consulates had priority. Establishing relations with these countries would absorb all of Ghana's capacity to support diplomatic establishments overseas for some time to come."[141] Tubman's message seemed to have reached Nkrumah.

Much more is known about the U.S. delegation's stay in Ghana. The record of the talks between Nixon and Nkrumah has been published.[142] The highest-priority subject of the talk was economic problems. Nkrumah complained about the lack of funds to finance the building of a dam and power complex on the Volta River. He emphasized that the Volta River Project "would go far towards realizing Ghana's goal of economic independence." This was an invitation to participate in a project in which Canadian and British aluminum companies had already shown interest. The vice president assured the prime minister "that the United States would continue to watch the situation carefully." Nixon diplomatically hinted that developing diplomatic relations with Communist countries was undesirable. He asked whether he would be correct in describing Ghana's foreign policy as "nationalist" or "neutralist." He preferred "nationalist," for this term "more accurately described the fact that such nations are determined to secure and defend their independence." The vice president added that "the United States has shown by words and actions its devotion to the principle of independence. We believe that the best assurance we can have of our own independence is the independence of others. Unfortunately, other countries are not so motivated." It was clear what countries he had in mind as "other." Nkrumah replied that Ghanaian policy would be "one of non-involvement and non-alignment in the East/West struggle," but "Ghana could never be neutral." At this point, the secretary for external affairs, A. Adu, intervened "to say that although no final decision had yet been taken, Ghana might find it necessary to establish some kind of representation with the Soviet Bloc." Nkrumah confirmed this. The Ghanaians were beginning to play the Soviet card. They made it clear that the price of their "correct" foreign policy vis-à-vis the United States was financing the Volta River Project.

America and the USSR Compete

Ghana became the priority focus of U.S. policy in West Africa. Nixon recommended "follow[ing] most closely the evolution of this state [Ghana], realizing that its success or failure is going to have profound effect upon the future of this part of Africa." He also suggested that the possibility of assisting, "to a limited extent," in the implementation of the Volta River Project should be considered.[143]

In 1957, Ghana established relations, exchanged embassies, and concluded economic cooperation agreements with the United States, Great Britain, and France.[144] It also slowly negotiated these types of connections with the USSR and other socialist countries.

When talking with Western diplomats, Nkrumah emphasized that he understood the Russians and did not trust them. This resulted in a less-alarmist Western attitude toward the possible appearance of a Soviet diplomatic mission in Accra. U.S. ambassador William Flake sent a telegram to the Department of State: "Each time I have discussed USSR with Prime Minister I have noticed a growing caution on his part towards USSR overtures. I feel we should not try for impact in this direction but should merely hold to our present course of tactful persuasion that USSR is dangerous companion. Even if Prime Minister should eventually permit small USSR mission here I believe he is now sufficiently suspicious to make him control it severely."[145] In another telegram, the ambassador wrote about the specific tactic in the event of Ghana's exchanging embassies with the Soviet Union: "We should try to delay exchange [of embassies between the

USSR and Ghana] as long as possible and at the same time give [the government of Ghana] series of inoculations to make it resistant to activities of USSR mission when it eventually arrives."[146]

Nkrumah always linked the issue of Soviet-Ghanaian relations to that of American aid in financing the Volta River Project. According to Flake, "He is not interested in 'half of Volta.' It must be all or nothing."[147] On April 4, Minister of Finance Gbdemah declared that if Western countries did not grant loans for the project, "we would have to look for them in another place."[148] It was to be in the East; in October 1957, in London, representatives of the USSR and Ghana had arranged for a visit of a Soviet delegation to Accra to negotiate the exchange of diplomatic missions and the conclusion of a trade agreement.

Nkrumah tried to gain an advantage from the visit even before it started. On November 6, he held a meeting with diplomats from the United States, the United Kingdom, India, Canada, and France. The prime minister said he had agreed to the establishment of the Soviet mission in Accra very reluctantly. The agreement in principle had been reached in March, the USSR was "pressuring," and he could see "no valid basis to continue holding off." In a private talk with Flake, Nkrumah said that "he would not care what consequences might follow a rebuff to the USSR if he could get economic development started." It was the ambassador's impression that "we might persuade the Prime Minister to use a new formula to postpone indefinitely USSR exchange . . . by showing there is no need to have the USSR in reserve for reasonable economic projects."[149]

On November 15, Nkrumah sent a letter to Eisenhower asking him "to consider the possibility of participating in this great scheme, bearing in mind its vital importance to our political future." Eisenhower, in a brief message to Nkrumah dated November 21, promised to give the matter "prompt and careful consideration."[150] At that time, the Soviet delegation had already arrived in Accra.

On November 19, the first secretary of the USSR's Embassy in London, Dmitrii Safonov, and the counselor of the USSR's trade mission, Valentin Smirnov, arrived in the Ghanaian capital. Safonov recollected that they were given the red carpet treatment. Ghanaian newspapers published information on the visit on their front pages "under splash headlines in large print." Aside from meetings with Nkrumah and other leaders, the program included "everyday dinners and lunches, cocktail parties," and trips around the country. "Apparently the Ghanaians," Safonov wrote ironically, "were going to prolong our visit for ten days at least to have as much fun as they could, to eat and drink at the feasts arranged in our honor. And we, with

Valentin Iovich, hoped to perform our task within two or three days. We could scarcely convince the hosts to at least slightly reduce the duration of our visit; we have spent seven or, maybe, even eight days there."[151] The pompous reception of the Soviet delegation obviously had a political explanation. It was necessary to demonstrate to the West that the words about looking for financial aid in "another place" had not been a bluff.

Safonov indicated that Nkrumah was enthusiastic about the proposal to exchange embassies. The delegation "easily came to an agreement with Nkrumah on the date of opening our embassy, the size of its personnel, the terms for the Embassy being provided with adequate premises, and other issues." According to Safonov, "approximately two months later," a small group of diplomats headed by Ambassador Mikhail Sytenko arrived in Accra via London.[152]

The Soviet Embassy was opened in Accra in August 1959. Safonov dated his visit to the same year.[153] But this is a mistake. U.S. archival documents reveal that Safonov and Smirnov visited Ghana from November 19 to 27, 1957.[154] Safonov mentions his meeting with Potekhin in Ghana, when the scholar was on a study tour there, and this leaves no doubt that the visit took place in 1957. One and a half years had elapsed between reaching the agreement on exchanging diplomatic missions and the establishment of the Soviet Embassy in Ghana.

There was a pause in Soviet-Ghanaian relations. N. A. Makarov, the attaché of the USSR's Embassy in London, believed that they "were developing very slowly" due to the attitude on the Ghanaian side. It "apparently protracts the exchange of diplomatic missions between the two countries," and also thus "delays or avoids" intended journeys to the USSR by the prime minister, Nkrumah, and the minister of agriculture. Makarov explained the nonconstructive position of the Ghanaian government "first and foremost by Ghana's heavy dependence on England, and secondly by Nkrumah's fear 'to spoil' his relations with England and the USA and thereby to reduce the chances for receiving their economic aid as a result of establishing normal diplomatic, trade, and other relations with the Soviet Union." The diplomat did not consider the situation irreversible and predicted that "if Ghana fails to receive considerable economic aid from England and the United States in the nearest future, it might change its position toward relations between our countries and even apply to the Soviet Union for assistance."[155]

The American forecasts regarding the prospects for Soviet-Ghanaian relations were similar. Ambassador Flake felt "that during these past 15 months since independence the Prime Minister has moved noticeably from the left towards the center in his views, and that he has become increasingly aware of the dangers inherent in any close association with the USSR. He has been warned by certain other independent states in Africa about the danger of trying to do business with the Soviets, and such Soviet emissaries that have come to Ghana during the past year have been watched closely by the police. Communist literature arriving in Ghana by post is intercepted and destroyed. The Prime Minister has adopted an effective 'go-slow' in exchanging diplomatic missions with the USSR."[156] The ambassador had the impression that the United States' considerable financial investments in Ghana could prevent its rapprochement with the Soviet Union: "He [Nkrumah] will stay in power for a long time, and he will continue a policy of close and friendly relations with the United States so long as he is convinced that the United States wishes to help him raise the standard of living in Ghana."[157]

An important indication of the United States' favorable attitude toward Nkrumah's policy was its unwillingness to support the internal opposition in Ghana, the United Party. On November 27, American diplomats met for an evening of conversation with the United Party's leaders. Kofi Busia and Joseph Danquah, the old and implacable enemies of Nkrumah, were among them. The second secretary of the U.S. Embassy, Archie Lang, concluded that the opposition leaders "had no coherent ideas on policy to present to the public." But they believed they had something that could impress the Americans. Joe Appiah launched "a long tirade against what he alleged to be Communist control of the [Convention People's Party]." According to Appiah, Nkrumah was "actually carrying out orders from the Communist Party to turn Ghana into the first Communist state in Africa," and thus to become "the starting point for an eventual Union of Socialist Soviet Republics of Africa." Lang admitted that the embassy "was not aware of any substantiation" of Appiah's charges about a Communist plot and pointed out that "he is widely reputed to be a loudmouthed, highly partisan and given to exaggeration."[158]

Judging by Russian archival materials, the plan for a Communist coup in Ghana did exist, but Nkrumah had nothing to do with it. During the independence celebration in Accra in March 1957, two Ghanaians, Mai Alale and Odoi Annan, met behind closed doors with a member of the Soviet delegation. They presented themselves as the leaders of the Jan Tamraro ("Red Star" in Hausa) Party, or the Communist Party of West Africa. Alale and Odoi handed the Soviet delegate a letter in which they asked the CC CPSU to receive a Jan Tamraro delegation in Moscow. In the letter, Nkrumah's regime was called "a clique of traitor-opportunists who have betrayed the interests of the common people of the Gold Coast."[159]

In the autumn of 1957, Alale and Odoi arrived in Moscow and presented to the CC CPSU International Department the program of their party. It was a whimsical mixture of Trotskyism, Stalinism, and Pan-Africanism, aimed at "the liberation of all West African countries from the yoke of colonialism" and their subsequent unification into one state as a result of armed struggle. The party leaders were ready "to enter upon the formation of clandestine administrative, economic and military structures of the future West African Republic and the creation of the Armed Forces." They applied to the CC CPSU for a loan of £5 million to launch this program.[160] The CC CPSU International Department, concluding that Jan Tamraro had "made serious mistakes of a leftist sectarian character," refused to give the loan and suggested that legal methods of political struggle and tactics in keeping with a "broad united national democratic front" should be applied.[161] The Soviet leadership considered interstate relations with the established and legitimate, even if not genuinely "progressive," governments of the newly independent countries to be of a higher priority than the contacts with the radical left opposition.

The main concern of the United States in Ghana was not a nonexistent "Communist plot" but instead the interest Nkrumah paid to the Soviet experience of accelerated industrialization. According to Potekhin, who was received by Nkrumah in Accra on September 1957,

> When we turned to the issues of economic development of the country, Nkrumah asked me what I thought of the report on the country's path to industrialization written by his economic expert (Professor Lewis of Manchester University). I replied that the report was very inadequate. Then he asked what my opinion was about the ways to industrialize Ghana. I replied that there were only two ways: (1) the division of labor and the cooperation of African countries; (2) the establishment of economic ties with socialist countries. He replied that he liked these ideas very much and would base his report at the forthcoming conference of African nations on them. Right then he took his notebook, asked me to repeat my formulation, and wrote it down. Then he asked me to put my ideas on paper in more detail. A few days later, I sent to him my observations, written out on five pages.[162]

When Nkrumah visited the United States from June 23 to 26, 1958, President Eisenhower made it clear that the U.S. government was not going to foot the bill for Ghana's accelerated industrialization. He advised that private capital should serve as a base for the implementation of the Volta River Project and emphasized that "the construction of a strong, viable economy is a long process."[163] Nkrumah, in return, made a rather blunt public statement: "Africa has no choice. We have to modernize. Either we shall do so with your interest and support—or we shall be compelled to turn elsewhere. This is not a warning or threat, but a straight statement of political reality."[164]

The U.S. position was not changed, even when it became clear that the exchange of embassies between Ghana and the USSR was inevitable. During his meeting with American officials, Secretary for External Affairs Adu said that his government had been "bulldozed into relations with the USSR at the time of independence"; and that Ghana had since then used every device to drag its feet, but the exchange of diplomatic missions would eventually have to be made with the USSR. Joseph Palmer, second deputy assistant to the U.S. secretary of state, replied: "We are deeply concerned at the possibilities for subversion both in Ghana and other areas in Africa which will result from the establishment of a Soviet Mission. However, the decision is one which Ghana must make and whatever that decision, it would not, of course, affect in the slightest the friendly ties between the United States and Ghana."[165]

The U.S. Embassy in Accra wrote about the expectations of future favors to which Nkrumah's visit to the United States had given rise among the Ghanaians: "For them the central questions are how and when will the United States make a substantial financial contribution to Ghana's development? How and when will the U.S. support the liberation of Africa and the fight against racial discrimination on this continent?"[166]

However, the United States and other Western countries were reluctant to grant Ghana considerable credits, primarily because of Nkrumah's African policy, whose two basic principles were anticolonialism and Pan-Africanism. Nkrumah was convinced that "an African organic unity . . . could alone make political independence worthwhile, or even make it reality."[167] Addressing a rejoicing throng on the night of independence, he declared: "We have done with the battle and we again re-dedicate ourselves in the struggle to emancipate other countries in Africa, for our independence is meaningless unless it is linked up with the total liberation of the African continent."[168]

In April 1958, Nkrumah succeeded in calling the first conference of independent African states in Accra. The declaration adopted at the conference partly read: "We pledge ourselves to apply all our endeavors to avoid being committed to any action which might entangle our countries to the detriment of our interests and freedom, to recognize the right of the African peoples to independence and self-determination, and to take appropriate steps to hasten the realization of this right." In an address of welcome to the conference, Nkrumah said that the continent's independent countries had the responsibility "to hasten the total liberation of Africa, the last stronghold of colonialism."[169]

In keeping with these sentiments, Ghana became a magnet for all those fighting for the liberation of African colonies. There they received moral support, material aid, and military training in special camps personally supervised by Nkrumah.[170] In 1957, he invited to Ghana the notable exponent of Pan-Africanism, George Padmore,[171] who was duly appointed his adviser on pan-African affairs. Padmore was elected the first secretary-general of the permanent secretariat set up by the first All-African People's Conference held in Accra in December 1958, which brought together more than three hundred political and trade union leaders representing twenty-eight African countries and colonies. The conference vehemently condemned "colonialism and imperialism in whatever shape or form these evils are perpetuated" and declared "its full support to all fighters for freedom in Africa, to all those who resort to peaceful means of nonviolence and civil disobedience, as well as to all those who are compelled to retaliate against violence to attain national independence and freedom of the people." The delegates considered unity and solidarity to be key strategies in the fight against colonialism and neocolonialism and called for the establishment of Africa-wide organizations, including trade and youth unions.[172]

The West was watchful of Nkrumah's pan-African initiatives. Some Western observers and African leaders saw his personal ambitions and Ghanaian hegemonism behind his appeals for African unity.

It was high time for Nkrumah to establish full-fledged relations with the Soviet Union. On April 10, 1959, the first Soviet ambassador to Ghana, a career diplomat, Mikhail Sytenko, received an agreement. The embassy was opened in Accra in August, with its personnel being limited to eighteen.[173]

On June 10, an agreement on establishing trade relations between the USSR and Ghana was signed in Accra. It provided for the negotiation of a long-term trade agreement.[174] The negotiations revealed that the Ghanaians were eager to obtain special privileges but the Russians were not ready to grant them. The Soviet government committed the Ministry of Foreign Trade (Ministerstvo vneshnei torgovli) "to conduct negotiations and conclude an agreement, for the period of three to five years, on annually purchasing in Ghana 20,000 to 30,000 tons of cocoa beans. To reach an agreement with the Ghanaians on the partial payment for the cocoa beans to be effected in Soviet goods, in percentage of the value no less than, in 1960, 10 percent; in 1961, 20 percent; in 1963, 40 percent; and in 1964, 50 percent, and to pay in hard currency for the remaining part."[175] But the Ghanaians did not agree with these terms, which were willingly accepted by other developing countries. The negotiations were suspended "in consequence of the refusal of the Ghanaian side to purchase Soviet goods as a partial payment for the USSR's import of cocoa beans."[176]

At the end of 1959, the volume of Soviet-Ghanaian trade was still very small; by November 1, Ghana had bought Soviet goods worth 575,200 rubles, and the Soviet Union had bought Ghanaian goods worth 6.5 million rubles. And even with such a meager volume of trade, there were obvious circumstances "hindering the development of Soviet-Ghanaian trade and successful business struggles with foreign firms." One of the main obstacles was the lack of entrepreneurial market skills within the Soviet establishment. Other foreign commercial firms operating in Ghana practiced credit selling and the system of three- to five-month installment payments; they supplied their customers with any required quantities of goods, had well-equipped exhibition halls to demonstrate their machinery in action, and provided catalogues and user manuals in English. Soviet trade organizations gave credits on very unfavorable terms, offered too large or too small quantities of goods without due regard to the demand in the Ghanaian market, and did not care to advertise their machinery or to provide instructions, even in Russian.[177]

Soviet propaganda in Ghana was not free from blunders, either. By the end of the 1950s, the only form of ideological work was lectures. The embassy's staff was saddled with the task of "disseminating the truth about the Soviet Union" among Africans. Diplomats were reluctant to fulfill such exacting obligations, viewing them as an additional load. They were amateurs at propaganda, easily thrown off balance by such basic and frequently asked questions from the Africans as "What advantages does the socialist system have over the capitalist one?" Besides, their English was usually not fluent enough to attract or to convince a local audience.[178]

There existed objective circumstances, which, though not exactly favorable for the task of "disseminating the truth about the Soviet Union," were clearly capable of reducing the efficiency of anti-Soviet propaganda in Ghana. As Peter Rutter, counselor of the U.S. Embassy, observed, "It is likely not more than half of the population are in any way affected by such media as press, radio, periodicals, books. The predominant mode of communication is by word of mouth." The diplomat lamented: "It seems fairly certain that opinion here takes virtually no interest in the East/West struggle or is aware of the Communist menace. In fact, attempts to persuade Ghanaians to side with the free world against the Communists can easily be counterproductive, because to many Ghanaians the danger of Communism is a fable invented by imperialists to prolong European control of Africa."[179]

Soviet relations with Ghana fared much better than those with Liberia. But the USSR leadership had no grounds to expect that Ghana would move into the Soviet orbit of influence. With this in mind, we next turn to Soviet-Guinean relations. The price that Guinea had paid for achieving its independence was a total rupturing of all its ties with France, its former parent state. Could Guinea survive? The "Guinean experiment" attracted the attention of the whole world and evoked the superpowers' responses.

The Beginning of the "Guinean Experiment" and the Superpowers' Responses

The role of Guinea as a Cold War battlefield remains debatable. The historian Fred Marte claims that the Cold War affected that country "indirectly," because the postindependence situation was determined by a conflict of personalities—by the encounter between two "strong politicians," the "authoritarian" French president Charles de Gaulle and the Guinean "radical charismatic leader" Sékou Touré.[180] Another historian, Lanciné Kaba, developing the theme of a "personal vendetta," maintains that it is possible to suggest that the Cold War existed only between Guinea and France.[181] But such an appraisal ignores the international dimension of the French/Guinean "quarrel," in which the main global antagonists have been involved.

Opening Salvos

The Soviet leaders searched among newly independent countries for those capable of modernizing in accordance with the Soviet recipe and turned into reliable allies, attractive showcases, and beachheads for spreading Communist influence. The "exhumed" conception of socialist orientation, or noncapitalist development, became the theoretical base necessitating the existence of at least one "revolutionary democratic" regime in each region of the developing world.[182]

One of the elaborators of this theory, Georgii Mirskii, admitted that it was created by direct political order from above and was designed for real policy:

> In practice, of course, the theory of noncapitalist development was rooted not in science but in Khrushchev's foreign policy. In fact, everything began in 1955 when Khrushchev decided to provide Nasser with Soviet weapons legalizing it as a trade deal between Egypt and Czechoslovakia. Diplomats of the old school were against rapprochement with Nasser's regime. The then–Soviet ambassador in Egypt, [Daniil] Solod, was horrified with the possibility of entering into an alliance with "these *makhnovtsi*" [these were the followers of the Ukrainian anarchist Nestor Makhno, 1889–1934]. But Khrushchev, with his inherent courage and unorthodoxy, neglected any considerations of abiding by classical theory. Apparently knowing nothing about the East, he grasped the advantages for his practical policy in lending a helping hand to Asian and African nationalists with anti-imperialist views. The Cold War was going on, the revolutionary process in Western countries was frozen, and the opposing sides were facing each other from their European trenches on both sides of the "iron curtain." On the contrary, the world of the newly independent countries emancipated from colonial rule might still be converted into a theater of mobile warfare, where there were chances of using the anticolonial inertia to penetrate into "the soft underbelly of imperialism" by enlisting support of the millions of people awakened to the new life. At that time it seemed to be a very promising line of policy. Moreover, it granted Khrushchev an opportunity to show himself as a flexible and dynamic politician in comparison with his main political rival Molotov, an orthodox and dogmatist. . . . Therefore, our task was to place theoretical "base" of Marxism-Leninism under Khrushchev's course.[183]

At the end of 1958, there emerged a state in Tropical Africa which, as the Kremlin believed, could well opt for the "socialist choice." On October 2, French Guinea became the independent Republic of Guinea. The next day, its leader, Sékou Touré, sent a telegram to "the President of the

USSR" informing him of the desire "of the sovereign and independent Guinean state" to establish diplomatic relations with the USSR.[184]

Officials in Moscow were sure that they had every reason to believe that the expected rapprochement between the USSR and Guinea would be rapid and smooth. Guinea had achieved its independence in a rigid confrontation with the metropolitan country—Guinea had been the only French colony whose electorate rejected de Gaulle's new Constitution and membership in the French Community, in a referendum on September 28, 1958. In Soviet eyes, Touré had the reputation of a revolutionary. At the age of fifteen, he was expelled from his lycée for having participated in a strike. He studied the fundamentals of Marxism-Leninism in one of the circles organized in French West Africa by the French Communists, and he was active in Guinea's first Marxist-Leninist study group, established in Conakry in 1944. He was the founding father of Guinean trade unions and collaborated with the French General Confederation of Labor, which was controlled by the left. He was a member of the World Federation of Trade Unions' General Council. In 1951, his trade union and political activity had taken him to Berlin and Prague, as well as Warsaw. He founded the Parti Démocratique de Guinée and transformed it into a well-organized mass party.[185]

It has been widely believed for a long time that Touré was "a longstanding and unwavering Leftist." Recent studies based on extensive archival research have challenged this view. Elizabeth Schmidt has argued that Touré was a pragmatic politician who altered his stance. By the mid-1950s, he "had abandoned his once radical politics and was seeking accommodation with the interterritorial Rassemblement Démocratique Africain and the colonial administration." Only under pressure from the grass roots did he decide to vote for immediate independence and to break with the Rassemblement Démocratique Africain over this issue. Schmidt concluded that "Guinea's radical position on the 1958 constitution was not a foregone conclusion, but the result of a long internal struggle that was won by the Left only in the final hour."[186]

But the Kremlin was ignorant of these nuances. The information on Guinea prepared by the MID noted that, "according to our French friends [Communists], the political views of Sékou Touré are close to Marxism."[187] The Soviets reacted to Touré's telegram promptly. On October 3, the deputy minister of foreign affairs, Vasilyi Kuznetsov, stated the position of his department in a memorandum to the CC CPSU: "The MID of the USSR considers the question of recognition of Guinean Republic by the Soviet Union and of exchanging with it diplomatic representatives to be predetermined in principle."[188] The mark written on the document informs that the CC CPSU Presidium adopted a proper resolution on October 4. The very same day, the chairman of the USSR Supreme Council Presidium, Klim Voroshilov, telegraphed Touré that "the Soviet Government solemnly declares its recognition of the Guinean Republic as an independent and sovereign state and expresses its readiness to establish diplomatic relations and to exchange diplomatic representatives with it."[189]

Western countries were in no hurry to recognize Guinea. Officially, Paris insisted on the conclusion of a French-Guinean agreement defining the status of Guinea. France had strong motivations for taking this stand. It was also expounded specifically in a confidential memorandum of the U.S. government: "(1) There is a tendency to 'punish' Guinea for having decided to break with France; (2) the whole future of the French Community could be jeopardized if the leaders of the other African territories, who voted in favor of the Constitution, got the impression that Guinea benefited by its negative vote; (3) one of the leading French African figures, [Ivorian] Minister of State [Félix] Houphouët-Boigny, is personally jealous of Sékou Touré and is strongly urging that the French Government do nothing to enhance the latter's position."[190]

The United States was faced with a complicated dilemma. France was a strategic ally, and it was desirable to receive its consent for recognizing Guinea. It was not clear how soon the former metropolitan country would back down. On October 4, the French ambassador in Washington, Hervé Alphand, assured Robert Murphy, deputy undersecretary of state for political affairs, that negotiations with Guinea "would not take long."[191] But there were no contacts between France and Guinea.

The delay in recognizing Guinea did not meet U.S. national interests. It was damaging to the image of the United States as an advocate of the cause of national self-determination and an opponent of colonialism. The American consul in Dakar, Donald Dumont, stated with regret that "helping France to do her homework on a colonial issue" would mean losing "some degree of propaganda prestige in anti-colonial circles."[192] But for the United States, it was more than a loss of prestige. The USSR might have obtained freedom of action in Guinea, as well as a bridgehead in West Africa. The staff of the U.S. Embassy in Moscow believed that "the Soviet Union has been presented with a classical opportunity for penetration into an important area of Africa through prompt offers of economic assistance to Guinea."[193]

The U.S. administration decided not to hurry with the recognition of Guinea, and Secretary of State John Foster Dulles explained the motives in a telegram to the embassies in Paris and London and to the consulate in Dakar: "We fully appreciate many factors causing France hesitate in recognizing Guinea. Moreover we have no desire to press France to reward Guinea for negative vote by giving it as favorable treatment as other French African territories, nor to rush or otherwise embarrass necessary French-Guinea negotiations by the early establishment of diplomatic relations or condoning similar efforts by Soviets or other undesirables. Finally we do not wish in any way to favor premature independence of dependent areas."[194]

Touré, in his turn, sent a telegram to President Eisenhower stating that "Guinea wishes the establishment of relations in the diplomatic field" with the United States.[195] He did this on October 2, 1958, the day before he dispatched a similar cable to the Kremlin. Only six days later, Dumont informed Touré, by an "ordinary cable," that a reply to Touré's October 2 message would be sent "when all aspects of the judicial position of Guinea are clarified."[196]

On October 9, a special emissary from Touré, Joseph Diallo, arrived in Dakar and met with Dumont. Diallo delivered a letter from the Guinean leader to Eisenhower that confirmed the intention to establish diplomatic relations with the United States. Diallo said that Touré attached great political and economic importance to Guinea's recognition by the U.K. and U.S. governments and assured that "it is to Guinea's interest to remain with the Western Bloc." Diallo informed Dumont that, "while not denying his Marxist training," Touré "deeply resented such nonsensical rumors that he was Communist and prepared to sell out his country to the USSR."[197]

Touré's assurance of his loyalty did not change the American position. Dumont, in compliance with Dulles' instructions, notified Touré that "the United States Government is giving due consideration to the question of the recognition of your country as an independent state." Dumont did not indicate when this matter would be considered and what should be expected from these deliberations.[198]

Then an amazing thing happened. On October 19, Touré sent Dumont a message expressing his gratitude for "United States recognition of Guinea" and promising to send a goodwill emissary to the United States. The message was broadcast over Radio Conakry and published in the Guinean press.[199]

This evoked bewilderment in Washington. Dumont received instructions from the Department of State to urgently leave for Conakry and to tell the Guinean leadership that the question of recognition was still under consideration.[200] On October 22, Dumont had a three-and-a-half-hour conversation with Touré and the minister of internal affairs, Fodéba Kéi'ta. Touré explained the misunderstanding as due to an "incorrect translation." The consul compared the text of his telegram of October 18 with the French translation submitted by the Guinean side and concluded: "Even admitting their inaccurate rendition of 'is giving due consideration' by the phrase 'accordela consideration votlue' [sic], the French translation could not properly be considered as constituting recognition." He told Touré that the Department of State was likely to come out with an official refutation if "world press began investigation." On hearing this, Touré made a long face, but his gloomy mood did not last long. The conversation was interrupted by a telephone call from the vice consul in Dakar, which led Dumont "to infer recognition by U.S. Government might forthcoming soon." He shared his impressions with Touré.[201]

The U.S. position changed on October 21, when French foreign minister Maurice Couve de Murville met with Dulles in Rome and told him that "the French Government no longer objected to immediate recognition of Guinea by friendly powers."[202] On receiving this information, the State Department sent Dumont a telegram countermanding the previous instructions, but when it reached Dakar, he was already on his way to Conakry.[203]

Dumont had the impression that the boycott of Guinea as an independent state by the Western powers was the most serious problem for Touré: "The non-recognition of his Government by the western powers was 'eating' him. . . . He was worried that somehow things might not succeed unless he could achieve soon the international blessing of his regime which Western (particularly U.S.) recognition would mean to him."[204]

On October 31, Dulles informed Eisenhower that the French government "unwillingly" agreed with recognition of Guinea by friendly powers.[205] The next day, November 1, 1958, the U.S. president informed Touré of the United States' "formal recognition" of Guinea.[206]

In the particulars of his visit to Guinea, Dumont conveyed "some further notions of the character and mentality of the Prime Minister of the new independent state of Guinea." Touré had proved himself to be "an enigmatic character, to say the least," unlike the image of him created by the mass media. His recently adopted tactics were to wear a "native boubou robe and Mohammed V–like woolen cap." Nevertheless, he received Dumont in "European clothes, just a little too broad in the shoulders and slightly too slim at the waist, and a bit too Yalish (high water mark) for the trouser length." He was "well proportioned, not too tall," with a "handsome" figure, and "in physiognomy," he had "something of the Indochinese about him—his eyes particularly."

Touré personally met the consul at the airport and was "most cordial in receiving" him. Touré was "soft and gentle, courteous, almost to the point of timidity." Dumont could not escape the conclusion that "the new responsibilities of State were weighing heavily on him." He "displayed a certain distraughtness at times." He smoked heavily, consuming most of Dumont's Camels.

Speaking on Guinean-Western relations, Touré stressed that "despite the gossip, his own ties had always been with the West. He frankly confessed that his training had been in Marxist ideas, but he energetically emphasized that being this and being a Communist were two different things."[207] Dumont summed up his impressions on Touré as follows:

1. He is a tough-minded leader, not easy to turn from a given stand or policy he has decided on.
2. He is a hard bargainer, a wily negotiator.
3. He is susceptible to the direct, frank approach, and prefers bluntness in personal face-to-face contacts.
4. At this particular juncture he may show less than his usual levelheadedness in responding to what he may interpret as attacks on his regime. . . .
5. The Prime Minister, something of a genius in politics, seems to have rather naïve economic and financial ideas.[208]

Dumont suspected that an authoritarian regime of personal power was developing in Guinea and that it would be difficult to deal with: "Our future relations with the Republic of Guinea are not going to be easy. We shall be dealing with a West African government organized along strong authoritarian lines. Its comportment will be less democratic and less 'reasonable' at times [than that] of Mr. Nkrumah's. Relations with Mr. Touré's advisers and ministers will reveal an ostensible inferiority complex and a supersensitivity to criticism of undemocratic methods. We must be prepared to see internal strong-arm political methods employed at the slightest opposition manifested toward Mr. Touré's regime."[209]

Dumont's predictions turned out to be generally true. His description of Touré's views and political style was far more authentic and comprehensive than the information provided by the French Communists on which the Soviet leadership had to rely.

It was very difficult to establish official contacts between the USSR and independent Guinea. At the end of October 1958, the MID decided to send the *Pravda* correspondent in Paris, Georgii Ratiani, to Conakry. But the trip did not take place, because the French authorities refused him the right of passage through the territory of French West Africa.[210]

Before the referendum on the new French Constitution, General de Gaulle had warned that any overseas territory that voted against it would receive independence but "bear the consequences."[211] After saying "no" to the Constitution, the Guineans instantly understood that de Gaulle had been absolutely serious in his warnings. As soon as the results of the voting became known, the French government issued a communiqué stating that "Guinea could no longer enjoy the assistance of the Administration of the French State or obtain supplier's credits."[212] French administrators, technicians, military personnel, doctors, and teachers were recalled from Guinea. "Before leaving they destroyed documents, ripped out telephones, smashed light bulbs and stripped the police of uniforms and weapons. Touré's Guinea had been condemned to death."[213] Touré's birth certificate was also destroyed.[214] Many enterprises and all military facilities were dismantled, and the archives were taken away. What could not be taken away was burned. What could not be burned was sunk in the ocean. All transfers of funds from France were canceled, and all French-Guinean commercial transactions were suspended.

The USSR's Testing Ground—and America's Wait-and-See Policy
The whole world was watching the Guinean experiment. Could one of the poorest of the former colonies survive with all ties to its former metropolitan country severed? The Soviet Union could not keep aloof. Its leadership saw Guinea as the testing ground for its African policy.

Touré began to look for help "from any possible quarters." Not surprisingly, the starting point of his quest was France. In October and November 1958, Guinea repeatedly proposed to Paris that diplomatic relations should be established, and expressed its readiness to join the French Community and to remain in the franc zone (i.e., the zone of the Communauté Financière Africaine franc, the monetary unit of French colonies in West Africa and Equatorial Africa). The French government either did not respond or bluntly rejected those proposals.[215]

The United States became the second recipient of Touré's pleas. During his visit to Liberia on November 22, 1958, Touré, who was elected president by the Parliament, asked President William Tubman "to intercede with the United States to obtain certain arms and ammunition" for Guinea's police force.[216] For Tubman, this request was most welcome. The second secretary of the U.S. Embassy in Monrovia, Robert Allen, had reported to the Department of State that because the Liberian president was "unable to offer Touré any material help or even technical assistance, Tubman's main play is apparently to pose as the influential mediator who can obtain United States recognition and possibly aid."[217] Tubman hoped to block a rapprochement between Ghana and Guinea and thus to obstruct Nkrumah's efforts to create a Union of Independent African States, considered by Tubman a "dangerous chimera."

Touré was an outspoken critic of the balkanization of francophone Africa, and, like Nkrumah, he championed pan-African political and economic unity. From the Liberian capital, Touré made his way to Accra, where on November 23 he and Nkrumah signed a treaty establishing a Ghana-Guinea Federal Union to form the nucleus of an eventual "Union of West African States." In a joint statement, Nkrumah and Touré promised to coordinate their economic, defense, and foreign policies and would begin to discuss a unified constitution. Ghana granted Guinea a credit in the amount of £10 million "to afford Guinea such . . . aid as may be necessary to strengthen the new state." The two leaders appealed to other African nations for support and said that Ghana and Guinea "would welcome adherence to this Union of other West African states."[218]

On November 24, the Liberian ambassador to Washington conveyed Touré's request for arms and ammunition to Joseph Satterthwaite, assistant secretary of state for African affairs. Satterthwaite indicated that "thorough consideration would have to be made of the matter."[219]

On December 17, the Guinean foreign minister, in a conversation with Tubman, made it clear that "Guinea desires to purchase arms and ammunition from the United States." The president replied that his ambassador to the United States "had already approached the United States Government and that he had been advised by him that the U.S. Department of State had suggested since President Touré's special representative was expected in Washington, directly from Guinea, the matter should await his arrival."[220]

Touré publicly expressed his "disappointment" with this state of affairs when the first American ambassador to Guinea, John Morrow, presented his credentials.[221] The Guinean president could not wait. He felt compelled to accept aid from socialist countries.

In November 1958, on the initiative of Soviet foreign minister Andrei Gromyko, the CC CPSU decided to send the counselor of the Soviet Embassy in the United Arab Republic, Peter Gerasimov, to Guinea "to discuss the prospects for Soviet-Guinean relations with representatives of the Government of Guinea and to explore the Guineans' attitude to the possibility of establishing a Soviet embassy in Conakry."[222]

Gerasimov was in Guinea from December 1 to 13, 1958. His talks with Touré and the senior ministers confirmed Dumont's opinion that Touré was "a wily negotiator." The disastrous financial situation and unwillingness of Western powers to provide economic aid seemed to leave him no space for maneuvering as regards the line of policy toward his only potential savior. However, Gerasimov was told that for the time being it would be premature to establish diplomatic relations between Guinea and the USSR. Sékou Touré's half-brother, Ismaël Touré, the minister of public works, informed Gerasimov that "the President is of opinion that initially Guinea should exchange diplomatic representatives at least with one capitalist country. If Guinea begins with exchanging diplomatic representatives with socialist countries, France might accuse it of joining the socialist camp and try to strangle the Guinean Republic in cooperation with Great Britain and the USA. . . . The President feels certain of friendly support of socialist countries and is of the opinion that Guinea for the present is called upon to maneuver and to balance, to pursue a policy of positive neutralism, to exploit contradictions between capitalist countries."[223]

From the Guinean ministers, Gerasimov heard action-oriented proposals for establishing military and economic cooperation between the USSR and Guinea. The minister of internal affairs, Fodéba Kéi'ta, stated that "the creation of the National Army requires armaments, namely rifles, carbines, submachine guns, machine guns and ammunition." The minister of cooperation, Abdurrahman Diallo, "suggested that the Soviet Union should buy in the Guinean Republic bananas, coffee, and other goods." Because Gerasimov was not authorized to make decisions on such issues, it was decided that "a Soviet delegation should urgently arrive in Conakry to conclude an agreement on trade and cultural relations between the two countries."[224]

Touré himself did not ask for aid. He said that despite its current difficulties, Guinea was a worthy partner of the USSR, for its vocation was to carry out some "special mission" in Africa" and "to show other African nations the correct course they should follow to reach national independence and unification of the African people."[225] Touré's concept of the "correct course" was intentionally vague, and he refrained from associating it with any specific socialist reforms.

The president rightly calculated that he would receive Soviet aid without pledges concerning his internal and foreign policy. The Kremlin, in its turn, saw in Guinea, clean from "colonial filth" and Western rivals, the first potential Soviet stronghold in Sub-Saharan Africa. And there was another factor favorable to Guinea. Touré's anticipations were justified, as the Russians viewed the "special mission" of Guinea in the light of socialist orientation. Gerasimov's report described the promising prospects for building a socialist society in Guinea: "According to members of the Government and party figures, their aim is to build a socialist cooperative society. Many trading cooperatives have already been created in the country. They are beginning to organize production cooperatives. The typical feature of the political and social situation in Guinea—in contrast, for example, with Ghana—is the absence of a national bourgeoisie. The country has objective conditions for the transition from the presently prevalent communal social order to a socialist society if the Government and the Party pursue a correct policy and outer support is provided by the socialist camp."[226]

In Gerasimov's opinion, it was necessary, "not wasting time," to develop relations with Guinea without emphasizing the question of exchanging embassies.[227] The CC CPSU's draft resolution, "On the Development of Relations between the USSR and the Guinean Republic," prepared by the MID on December 26, 1958, envisaged that all the requests put forth by the Guinean leadership should be complied with before the establishment of diplomatic relations. It was planned to charge "the corresponding Ministries and Departments" with preparing, within a week, and introducing to the CC CPSU their proposals for "urgently purchasing a certain quantity of bananas and other Guinean goods to be paid for partly in kind and partly in free currency," for "supplying the Guinean Government with a certain quantity of small arms for the national armed forces on preferential terms or as a gift," and for "admitting 50 to 60 Guinean students to the educational establishments of the USSR and granting them stipends."[228]

The CC CPSU's attitude was more cautious and balanced. On December 30, 1958, its Secretariat sanctioned the dispatch to Conakry of a Soviet delegation to negotiate the terms of the trade agreement. It was decided to take up all the other issues, including the supply of arms, "after the establishment in Guinea of the Soviet embassy."[229]

On January 30, 1959, the delegation arrived in Conakry. During the twenty-day visit, it was received by President Touré and had meetings with the ministers in charge of economic matters. The Guineans said they would welcome Soviet assistance in such areas as minerals prospecting, the mechanization of agriculture, and the organization of cooperatives. They showed interest in "the experience of building up" the Soviet Army, the achievements of the USSR in "eliminating illiteracy and developing the methods for creating written languages," and "the issue of admitting Guinean students to Soviet higher educational establishments."[230]

The economic situation in Guinea was becoming desperate, and this time the Guinean leaders did their best to convince the potential sponsors that Guinea's internal policy would be adjusted in accordance with their wishes. Members of the delegation heard that the Parti Démocratique de Guinée intended to make use of the Soviet experience in reforming the economy and in party building, and was ready "to restrict the activity of foreign companies."[231]

Touré not only showed himself to be a friend and admirer of the Soviet Union; he also tried to discredit his West African rivals for Soviet aid. The head of the delegation, L. Ezhov, wrote in his report:

> Sékou Touré believes that Ghana and Guinea are very different states. Ghanaian independence is nominal: as in the past, the English have complete domination in the country, the feudal top and the Government are bribed and corrupted by the English, corruption is flourishing, and a comprador bourgeoisie is being cultivated. Guinea had to enter into union with Ghana, but, according to Touré, this union is purely symbolic. The Guineans are always ready to demonstrate to the outside world the reputed strength of the Guinea-Ghana Union in order to propagandize the idea of the future united state of the free peoples of Black Africa.[232]

Touré, like many other politicians, conducted a secret diplomacy that differed from his public one.

On February 13, Ezhov and the minister of agriculture and cooperation, Abdurrahman Diallo, signed an agreement on commodity circulation and payments between the USSR and Guinea that entered into force on the date of signing.[233] The economic blockade of Guinea had been broken.

Guinea became the first country in Tropical Africa where a Soviet embassy was opened. And Gerasimov became the first ambassador. When he arrived in Conakry on April 16, 1959, the reception was pompous—the guard of honor, the brass band that failed to play the USSR's national anthem properly, the escort of motorcyclists, the cheering crowds in the streets, the repeated broadcasting of the speech Gerasimov delivered at the airport. And on April 20, the Soviet ambassador presented his credentials to President Touré.[234]

Touré also solved the problem of arming his army and police. On March

20 and 27, two shipments of arms arrived in Conakry from Czechoslovakia. According to U.S. intelligence, they included "machine guns, several thousand rifles, and possibly armored vehicles and antitank and antiaircraft artillery." Simultaneously, a Czechoslovakian technical mission of eighteen persons arrived. The State Department characterized this as "the Bloc's most serious attempt to date to penetrate and influence political development in Black Africa."[235]

Guinea received not only rifles but also heavy armaments, including a number of rather obsolete armored vehicles. When displayed in a military parade in Conakry, they created a commotion. Robert Rinden, chargé d'affaires of the U.S. Embassy in Guinea, reported to the State Department:

> It was after a dramatic pause in the stream of paraders that the crowd suddenly came to life with the loudest cheering yet heard in Conakry by Embassy reporters. The enthusiasm rippled down the avenue, accompanying a formation of some 25 natty motorcyclists speeding along the avenue on their Czech machines. These were followed by half a dozen military sidecar motorcycles, machine-gun mounted. Then came trucks towing four anti-aircraft guns, and others towing six or eight light field artillery pieces (105s and anti-tank). The pièce de résistance was the smooth rumbling of three light tanks (75 mm armament), which were especially widely applauded by the viewers. The motley assortment of three or four ambulances, repair cars, and supply trucks which followed came as an anti-climax. All the equipment—though not of recent manufacture—was well painted and appeared in good working condition. The tanks are reported to be a 1953 revision of a 1946 Skoda model.[236]

The leadership of the major Western powers appraised the Soviet arms deliveries to Guinea as a serious challenge. During the tripartite talks on Africa held in Washington on April 16 to 21, representatives of the United States, Great Britain, and France expressed concern that Guinea "might turn into a Communist cancerous growth."[237]

Then, on April 24, Robert Murphy, the U.S. deputy undersecretary of state for political affairs, required the Guinean ambassador, Telli Diallo, to explain "the circumstances which caused such a large quantity of arms to arrive in Guinea at the same time as Communist Bloc specialists and a Soviet diplomatic mission." The ambassador replied that his country "made general requests for assistance from all nations in a position to offer it, and Czechoslovakia had come forward with arms." He stressed that acceptance of the arms "did not symbolize Guinea's capitulation to any political terms which the Communist Bloc countries might have in mind."[238]

Secretary of State Christian Herter sent a memorandum to President Eisenhower containing a proposal to officially invite Sékou Touré to the United States. This visit would be "the most effective in counteracting the rapidly developing Communist influence in Guinea." At the beginning of May, an official invitation to visit the United States in October 1959 was handed to the president of Guinea.[239]

On April 27, Joseph Satterthwaite proposed to Douglas Dillon, under-secretary of state for economic affairs, to revise the principle of leaving "to France the leading political and economic role in Guinea since independence." Satterthwaite pointed to the growing influence of the Soviet Bloc in Guinea and the apparent unwillingness of its government to rely on France alone for aid: "I believe it is now essential to determine that it is in the interest of the United States to provide assistance to the Republic of Guinea." Satterthwaite suggested granting "surplus rice" as a friendly gesture. Dillon agreed.[240]

While implementing this initiative, the United States ran into unforeseen difficulties. Touré confirmed his reputation as a wily negotiator who was very sensitive to the slightest infringements of his country's sovereignty. According to the set procedure, the American side provided food aid on certain standard terms. Most of the rice was to be delivered to the Fouta Djalon region, where food was in short supply, and it was required that American personnel would be in charge of its distribution.

On May 12, Robert Rinden had to hear strong objections from Sékou Touré. The president said that Guinea would never accept aid on such terms. The United States should stop telling the Guinean government to what regions the food aid was to be destined, and the government itself would ensure its fair distribution. He asked "if the US, in extending aid to France, had prescribed the exact areas of France to be assisted or whether it left such determination to the discretion of the French Government?" Finally, on May 15, after lengthy discussions with Telli Diallo, it was agreed that the Guinean government would "inform representatives of American Government of the results" of the aid program.[241] In June, the U.S. government decided to offer Guinea 5,000 tons of rice and 3,000 tons of flour.[242]

The first Guinean official delegation visited the USSR from August 14 to 25, 1959. The delegation was headed by Saifulaye Diallo, who was chairman of the National Assembly (Parliament) and political secretary of the Parti Démocratique de Guinée. The members of the delegation included Ismaël Touré and the general secretary of the government, Jean Faragué Tounkara. They conducted negotiations with their Soviet partners, whose delegation was headed by the first deputy chairman of the USSR Council of Ministers, Anastas Mikoyan; were received by Khrushchev, who was on vacation in the Crimea; and visited Baku, Kiev, and Leningrad. The Soviet-Guinean agreement on economic and technical cooperation was signed in Moscow on August 24. The USSR granted Guinea, on easy terms, a credit of 140 million gold rubles.[243]

During their tour of the USSR, the members of the Guinean delegation constantly showed that they were full of admiration for the Soviet reality. According to the Soviet officials who accompanied the Guineans, their charges were deeply impressed by Azerbaijan's achievements. Thus, Ismaël Touré was heard to say: "This is how I imagine Guinea when it becomes truly independent." The guests were fascinated with a lot of things in Ukraine, where they saw "abundance and prosperity everywhere." There were many compliments to Khrushchev. Diallo told M. D. Yakovlev, deputy foreign minister of the Russian Soviet Federal Socialist Republic, that "Khrushchev is great in his simplicity. Now I understand why the imperialists are so afraid of frank and direct talks with him; they prefer to keep their distance and argue with him through the medium of the press. Reactionaries are helpless against his logic and arguments." After such encomiums, the Guineans often expressed their resolute desire "to build a socialist society in Guinea." Usually, this was the prelude to requests for "immediate free assistance" to be granted besides the credit so that the delegation "could return home with concrete results."[244]

The Guineans succeeded in their requests for aid. On the eve of the delegation's departure, the USSR Council of Ministers decided "to render Guinea free aid as a gift of the Soviet government to the extent of 7.5 million rubles in export prices." It was planned to spend this money on constructing a radio station in Conakry, on supplying twenty-four trucks and the various types of machinery needed to establish a large state-owned rice-growing farm, and on covering the expenses for the work of the Soviet specialists to be engaged in these projects.[245] In November and December, the first groups of specialists left for Guinea.

After the August visit, Soviet-Guinean relations developed successfully. Despite being well hidden from the public eye, the beginning of military cooperation was an important expression of rapprochement between the two countries. Declassified archival documents shed light only on isolated details of Soviet military aid to Guinea. In mid-October 1959, the two sides reached an agreement on training Guinean military personnel in the USSR. On October 18, the Soviet chargé d'affaires in Guinea, Ivan Marchuk, and the state secretary for national defense, N'Famara Kéi'ta, discussed the problems dealing with the sea carriage of 150 Guinean military men to the Soviet Union, where they were to be trained. It was decided to transport them under the guise of tourists on board the ship *Sedov*, sailing from Conakry to Kaliningrad. The Soviet side prepared this operation thoroughly. Marchuk informed Kéi'ta that "a heated crew's space will be made available for the Guinean military men, and measures will be taken to prevent them from catching cold. Warm civilian clothing will be delivered to Kaliningrad." The two officials agreed that "it will be better if the military men say goodbye to their relatives and friends not in the port but somewhere else," in order not to attract any attention.[246]

The character of military training to be received by the Guineans had not yet been determined. Marchuk could only tell Kéi'ta that "the Soviet military authorities are ready to train two commanding officers of small patrol ships.[247] Other declassified documents indicate that there were fifty-five flight cadets from Guinea in the USSR in September 1960.[248] On January 25, 1960, the CC CPSU Presidium approved the directive of the Council of Ministers, establishing that "the training and upkeep of Guinean military personnel should be gratis," paid for from the budget of the USSR Ministry of Defense.[249]

By the autumn of 1959, the USSR and its allies had firmly entrenched themselves in Guinea, which had concluded bilateral trade agreements with five socialist countries, "theoretically, account[ing] for one-third of the country's foreign trade." About 150 technicians from the Soviet Bloc "replaced French officials, so that the key officers in many vital ministries [were] from Eastern Europe."[250]

The United States, after lingering long with the recognition of Guinea, did not hurry to substantially assist this country or to invest in its economy. But this did not mean that the U.S. administration had abandoned its plans to challenge the Communist influence in Guinea.

Assistant Secretary of State Satterthwaite, in his memorandum to Undersecretary of State Dillon, called Guinea the country that "has assumed a critical importance among all the French-speaking areas of West and Equatorial Africa." Satterthwaite put forth two arguments in order to substantiate this thesis. First and foremost, "because Guinea accepted General de Gaulle's challenge and voted for independence, its experiment is being closely watched by all its French-speaking neighbors." If it succeeds, it will "almost certainly act as a magnet to the surrounding area." Second, if the Soviet Union achieves a dominant position in Guinea, "it will undoubtedly use Guinea as a bridgehead for expanding its influence throughout West Africa."[251]

In the existing situation, the optimal tactic for the United States was a waiting game. Its substance was formulated in the same memorandum: "Our principal objective in Guinea is to maintain the presence of the United States and the West in the country and to establish a position for future United States action to stem the flood of expanding Soviet influence when this flood recedes."[252] This forecast that the flood would recede was based on two premises. The first was that Touré was believed to be a politician who could not become a Soviet puppet. "Also, we believe that while Touré cannot be considered wholly satisfactory from the West's point of view, he nevertheless represents a stable element strongly committed to neutrality and, as such, is worthy of our support," Satterthwaite wrote.[253]

There was also another prediction that the Soviet efforts to gain the upper hand in Guinea would be frustrated due to Soviet miscalculations. John Morrow, the first U.S. ambassador to Guinea, who arrived in Conakry in July 1959, recollected: "To those who persisted in asking me if I did not feel that I was being sent into a rather hopeless situation, particularly since the Communist Bloc countries had a nine-month advantage, I replied with an unhesitating No. The Communist Bloc countries had had nine months in which to make mistakes. My only hope was that the Guineans were becoming increasingly conscious that the Communists were not twelve feet high."[254]

Touré was eager to disprove by word and deed the assertions of the Western media that Guinea had become "the Kremlin's satellite" and a "bastion of Communism in Africa." His first state visit outside the African continent was to the United States, from October 25 to November 9, 1959. The beginning of his conversation with Eisenhower was encouraging. The American president noted that "Guinea had acquired its independence by peaceful means" and deplored "any actions which make Guinean problems more difficult." This meant a recognition of the Guinean regime's legitimacy and that French views no longer much mattered. Touré tried to convince his interlocutor that Guinea had established ties with socialist countries perforce, after having been driven into a corner. France had done everything to "ruin the economy of Guinea." The situation had been so desperate that the Guineans "would have accepted help from the devil himself at that juncture." Right off, the missions from the Eastern Bloc countries arrived and offered acceptable barter arrangements. The Guinean leadership took this as the only chance to prevent economic collapse. Guinea did not apply to the Eastern European countries for aid, but it received, on a grant basis, "some 2,500 rifles, three tanks, six tractors, a number of field kitchens and several thousand steel plows." The one country the Guineans did approach for help was the United States. It refused to deliver small arms for the Guinean security forces, but "the French were at this time introducing automatic weapons into the country surreptitiously and getting them into the hands of their former soldiers. A thousand such arms have been seized." Eisenhower dismissed the matter with a joke; he "smilingly remarked that this at least meant they [the Guinean authorities] were receiving arms for their security forces in this way."[255]

At the meeting with Secretary of State Christian Herter, Touré hinted that massive U.S. investments were welcome in Guinea and guaranteed security for invested capital. "Such developed countries as the United States should do more than just concentrate on a single school building in Conakry or a dam elsewhere," he said. But Herter showed interest only in Guinea's economic situation.[256]

American knowledge of the Guinean leaders was substantially enlarged by the observations and comments of Arva Floyd, who had accompanied Touré and his party on their trip around the United States in the capacity of interpreter. In her opinion, Touré was an outstanding leader and enjoyed indisputable authority within his entourage. He "tried to avoid wherever possible the appearance of monopolizing the honors," but he "was nevertheless first among equals." In the United States, Touré "lived up to his reputation for vigor and strength of personality and for preferring frankness and directness of approach." He again showed himself as a wily negotiator, and he "seemed to have an open mind on matters of secondary concern to him but to hold passionate convictions on questions which he considered of central importance." He "relished the free give and take of press conferences and the like," was "quick-witted and handled himself well," and "all his speeches except that at the United Nations were made without notes or prepared texts."

Among the members of Touré's team, Floyd distinguished the president of the National Assembly, Saifoulaye Diallo, and the minister of internal affairs, Fodéba Kéi'ta, as the "most competent and influential." Initially, they "undoubtedly tended to think of American foreign policy in terms of militaristic bluster and malevolent capitalist schemes for exploiting weaker countries." But the reality they saw in the United States and their intercourse with American politicians made them drop this stereotype. All the members of the Guinean delegation were "very ignorant of the United

States." Touré, for example, once asked where Oxford University was located in America.[257]

The "discovery" of America by the Guinean leaders was far more important than the rather modest results of the official visit (the conclusion of an agreement on cultural cooperation). Those in Guinea's top circles who favored socialist orientation now began to reconsider their preferences. According to U.S. ambassador Morrow, Kéi'ta, on returning from the United States, confessed that "he had been prejudiced by propaganda which was now being proven false." The minister felt that "the scales had been removed from his eyes," praised the leadership of Eisenhower and "the humanity and statesmanship" of Herter, and admitted his "admiration for the technical skill and progress of America." Initially, Kéi'ta discussed this with his subordinates and then with Louis Lansana Béavogui, the minister of the national economy, and with Diallo. They agreed with him on many points. Kéi'ta, who had never attended anything sponsored by the U.S. or other Western embassies, began to visit the U.S. Embassy not only to participate in official events but also to have private talks with Ambassador Morrow.[258]

Ten days after his departure from the United States, Touré arrived in Moscow on November 19, 1959, and stayed until November 27. It was the first time that the head of one of the states of Sub-Saharan Africa had gone on a visit to the USSR. The Guinean delegation visited Leningrad, Tbilisi, and Gagry, where it was received by Khrushchev, and it conducted negotiations with other Soviet leaders. The joint Soviet-Guinean communiqué reflected the absolute coincidence of opinions on the problems discussed— disarmament, the elimination of colonialism, the Congo crisis, Soviet-Guinean relations. The two sides also signed an agreement on cultural cooperation.[259]

Touré did not publicly ask for Soviet aid and always emphasized that the foreign and domestic policies of his country were independent. He affirmed that "the world is not divided into the East and the West" and "we don't submit to the laws of any doctrine and philosophy."[260] The full records of the Soviet-Guinean talks have not yet been declassified, but the published materials give grounds to suppose that in his confidential conversations with the Soviet leaders, the Guinean president told them something more pleasant. Khrushchev remembered Touré as an educated person who understood the substance of both the class struggle and the struggle for national independence.[261] It transpired from the public speeches of the other Soviet leaders that they were delighted with the fact that at last a worthy strategic ally had been found in Sub-Saharan Africa.

The first deputy chairman of the USSR Council of Ministers, Frol Kozlov, when addressing a meeting devoted to Soviet-Guinean friendship, called Touré "one of the most prominent leaders of contemporary Africa" and noted a certain similarity between the historical destinies of the two countries:

> A little more than a year has passed since Guinea took the road of independence. One year is a very short period of time, but the Guinean people has already managed to achieve much all the same. Certain persons in the West predicted the collapse of the "Guinean experiment" and shouted about the inevitable failure of the incipient economic conversion. We, the Soviet people, know very well that such "prophecies" coming from foreign ill-wishers. We heard them constantly when converting our motherland into a mighty and advanced power. The prophets of doom are likely to be equally hasty with regard to the Guinean Republic.[262]

Kozlov made it clear that the USSR would provide material aid to sustain the Guinean experiment at any price, and would make Soviet-Guinean relations a model for those with other African countries as well.[263]

2. Achievements and Failures in the "Year of Africa," 1960

The year 1960 became known in history as the "Year of Africa," when the continent's political map was rapidly transformed with seventeen new independent states. And this collapse of the colonial system in Africa gave credence to the rising optimism of Soviet policymakers about the future of the continent. In Soviet eyes, the successful struggle of emergent African states for independence, accomplished however peacefully, automatically placed them among those revolutionary forces strengthening the anticolonial and anti-imperialist front.

On this basis, the Soviet Union could accept as allies most of the new African governments. Comparing the slogans used at the First All-African People's Conference (in Accra, December 1958) with those used at the second conference (in Tunis, January 1960), *Izvestiya*'s African correspondent, Vladimir Kudryavtsev, noted emphatic progress. At the first conference, the "nationality and contents" of the slogans "reflected the callowness of African liberation movement, and above all the lack of unity in views on Africa's present and future." But at the second conference, participants united behind the single slogan "Independence and Unity." On seeing this slogan, Kudryavtsev realized the extent to which the struggle of African people "had grown and matured politically."[1]

Such assessments reflected the hopes of the Soviet elite that sweeping decolonization would turn Africa, a sphere of Western influence, into the West's Achilles' heel by opening it to Soviet penetration. According to this logic, Africa was expected to infuse new life into the decaying world revolutionary process. Thus, the journal *Sovremennyi Vostok*, in the first issue of 1960, declared: "Africa has become the forefront of the national liberation struggle of the oppressed people."[2]

As it became obvious that colonialism was finished in Africa, the U.S. government showed more understanding and sensitivity toward the aspirations of independent African countries. The United States' approach to its contacts with the Communist world changed to a more balanced, pragmatic, and realistic policy. A document prepared in January 1960 by the State Department's Bureau of African Affairs read: "It would be counterproductive . . . for the United States to try through undue pressure to discourage contacts between Africa and the Sino-Soviet Bloc. The African governments, especially the new ones, are jealous of their sovereignty and are intent in most cases on maintaining a truly neutralist position. . . . They intend to develop diplomatic and economic relations with both sides, regardless of United States views, to expand their contacts with both."[3] Another document from the bureau stressed the necessity of drawing a clear distinction "between ordinary diplomatic, commercial, and cultural contacts, which cannot be prevented by the West, and Bloc efforts, [such as] propaganda and subversion, which must be countered promptly and effectively."[4]

Because it was impossible to distinguish between "ordinary" and "subversive," and the more so propaganda activity, the real U.S. policy was based on the fundamental constant that the Soviet presence in Africa was subversive and detrimental to Western interests. Thus, on April 9, 1960, the National Security Council issued the policy objective for the United States in West Africa of "maintenance of the Free World orientation of the area and denial of the area to Communist domination."[5] This formulation would be upheld by the successive administrations of Dwight Eisenhower, John Kennedy, and Lyndon Johnson.

In the middle of 1960, the Congo crisis erupted. This crisis became an ordeal for Khrushchev with respect to his African policy, forcing him to reexamine optimistic assessments of Soviet perspectives on the continent and to take a more realistic look at African realities.

The Eruption of the Congo Crisis: The First Open Challenge

The Congo was destined to become the first "hot spot" of the Cold War in Sub-Saharan Africa, ushering in an era of U.S. and Soviet military involvement in the region. With its vast territory strategically located in the "heart of Africa" and richly endowed with mineral resources, the Congo was accurately considered to be the key to the African continent. And therefore the Western powers were not going to wait and see what would happen in the Congo, as they had done with respect to Guinea.

The role of the USSR in the Congo crisis is the least explored and most debatable issue. The most widespread approach is clearly expressed in three major studies by American scholars.[6] They describe Soviet Congolese policy as a typical example of Khrushchev's adventurism, his emotional reaction to events based on ideology, in contrast to the pragmatic American approach. However, these books, as well as the bulk of writings on the Congo crisis, were written when Russian archival materials were unavailable. Published sources are full of harsh Soviet statements condemning an "imperialist plot" against the Congolese people and promising them moral support and comprehensive aid. But Khrushchev's actions were far less decisive. This afforded some authors ground for revising the role of the Soviet Union in the crisis, suggesting that it was rather limited and determined by self-interest. Thus, the Belgian sociologist and writer Ludo de Witte assumes that the "Kremlin had neither the political will nor the means to threaten the West's supremacy in the Congo" and was indifferent to the needs of rising Congolese nationalism, treating the nationalists as "throwaway items."[7] The American historian Lise Namikas, the first and for the moment the only Western researcher who has worked in the Russian archives on the Congo crisis, has taken a less guarded and more balanced view. She argues that Soviet behavior in the Congo was another demonstration of a complicated and flexible correlation between security and ideology imperatives in Soviet foreign policy.[8]

The Congo as a Likely Trouble Spot

On January 30, 1960, after a few weeks of painstaking negotiations between the Belgian government and Congolese politicians within the framework of the Round Table Conference in Brussels, parliamentary elections were set for May and independence for June 30. The Belgians hoped to vest power in "reliable" Congolese who would cooperate constructively with their former mother country.

U.S. officials were not optimistic about the Congo's prospects. They believed that Belgium would fail to hold its ground in the Congo after independence and that turbulence would ensue. They feared that the key to Africa might become ownerless, or even worse fall into Communist hands. The National Security Council foresaw "a variety of problems arising as the Congo approaches the June 30 independence date amid frantic efforts by Brussels to help Congolese get ready for independent government and resolve economic difficulties. . . . Confusion in Congo may facilitate Communist penetration."[9]

The risk for the Congo of the sudden transition to independence was certainly great. As independence approached, recriminations grew between Belgians and the Congolese. Ian Scott, first Britain's consul and then its ambassador in the Congo, had the impression that many Belgians saw "the Congolese as a sort of sub-human species"[10] and believed that they were not capable of running an independent state. Independence was a new concept for most Belgians, and they lacked the pragmatic approach to new relationships: "We were good with them [the Congolese]; but we used to go ahead of them in a queue and now we can't face calling them 'Monsieur' and waiting behind them."[11] The Africans reciprocated by charging colonial oppression and humiliation. Racial incidents became routine events in both the cities and the countryside, and there was a heightening of tensions among both Europeans and Africans.[12]

As a result of these tensions, there was an increasing exodus of Belgian families. And without such Belgian specialists, economic and administrative collapse was inevitable. There were no Africans in the top levels of government and administration. The Belgians concentrated on training medical assistants, nurses, clerks, primary school teachers, mechanics, and the like. Higher education was minimal among the Congolese. There were no native cadres of doctors, engineers, lawyers, or business executives. By 1960, out of 14 million people, there were only fifteen university graduates in the Congo.[13]

The Congo's territorial integrity was very fragile. The Congo River united the territory geographically, but there were many disintegrative factors: vast distances; difficult communication; a scattered population, often divided by impenetrable jungle; and hundreds of separate ethnic groups that had been forcibly united within artificial colonial boundaries. For many Congolese, ethnicity was the behavioral and mental determinant of their identity.

The Congo's political situation mirrored its ethnic diversity. More than forty parties competed for parliamentary seats. However, this external variety of political colors was deceptive. The parties called themselves socialist, progressive, popular, democratic, national, African, and the like, but most of them were essentially based on a tribe's or region's efforts to protect its local interests and thus favored a federal system that would give their domains considerable autonomy.

The Mouvement National Congolais (MNC), which advocated a unitary state and was the only party with national rather than local ambitions and a nationwide organization, was successful in the parliamentary election of May 1960. The MNC won 41 out of 137 seats in the Chamber of

Representatives and 19 out of 74 seats in the Senate. The fragmentation of the new Parliament meant that even though the MNC's leader, Patrice Lumumba, headed the largest grouping, he would have to create a broad coalition to obtain a majority. He succeeded in setting up the government through agreements with regional parties, but it could hardly function effectively, given that twelve parties shared twenty-two ministerial chairs.[14] Moreover, these ministers, who were appointed by him, often had opposite views on crucial problems pertaining to the Congo's state structure and its domestic and foreign policies.

The politicians who took the two key political offices personified the contradictions in the Congolese elite. The most important post, prime minister, was assumed by Lumumba, a thirty-five-year-old commoner with a primary school education who was a member of the small Tetela tribe living in the middle reach of the Lualaba River. He tried many jobs and rose to become a postal clerk in Stanleyville. Tall, thin, and agile, he was a luminous speaker and charismatic leader but was also temperamental and impulsive. His political platform was a mixture of leftist nationalism, militant anticolonialism, positive neutralism, and Pan-Africanism. He denounced tribalism and advocated a highly centralized government.

The leader of the Alliance des Bakongo, Joseph Kasavubu, who became president, the other key political office, was a sharp contrast to Lumumba. He was forty-three years old and from a noble family, and he had a strong tribal base among the Bakongo who lived in Leopoldville and the surrounding area. He had studied for the Roman Catholic priesthood but instead became a teacher and civil servant. As a defender of the traditions of the Bakongo, he aimed for their self-rule, envisioning a loose confederation of ministates in the Congo Basin. He reacted allergically to Communist and Pan-Africanist slogans, but unlike Lumumba he was a canny, inscrutable politician who could conceal his genuine views and intentions. Though he was thus more skillful than Lumumba behind the scenes, Kasavubu was only an average orator and was heavyset, phlegmatic, and inferior to the prime minister as a public politician.

Making Dispositions for Independence

The chief Cold War adversaries were preparing for the coming encounter in the Congo. The United States began in good time to thoroughly strengthen its positions in this strategically and economically important area to prevent the USSR from attempting "Communist penetration" after the end of colonial rule. The United States had a vested interest in defending the Congo. The U.S. atom bombs dropped in 1945 on Hiroshima and Nagasaki had a "filling" of Congolese origin—from the uranium mines in Shinkolobwe. And though, in the 1950s, the United States declined to purchase uranium in the Congo, due to discoveries of uranium in Canada and South Africa, the Congo remained an important source of strategic materials for the Western world. In 1959, 9 percent of the world's copper, 49 percent of its cobalt, 69 percent of its industrial diamonds, and 6.5 percent of its tin came from the Congo.[15] The United States received three-quarters of its imported cobalt and half its tantalum from the Congo. Both minerals were widely used in the nuclear and aerospace industries.[16]

On February 18, 1960, high-ranking officials of the Department of State, including Undersecretary Douglas Dillon, discussed "steps the United States might take in the light of the Congo's coming independence" with the U.S. ambassador to Belgium, William Burden, who urged his country to "avoid a repetition of the Guinean experience, when the Soviet Bloc moved into a vacuum after the French had left." He recommended increasing the staff of the U.S. Consulate General in Leopoldville and providing economic assistance to the Congo, arguing that because it was the third-most-populous African country with "a potentially explosive situation," it required "unusual attention."[17]

The ambassador's call was heard. After a delegation of American businessmen headed by David Rockefeller, the president of Chase Manhattan Bank, visited the Congo, it was granted a loan of $325 million.[18] The staff of the Leopoldville Consulate was increased so that it could begin to function as an embassy at the time of independence. Clare Timberlake, an experienced career diplomat, came from Bonn to become the American ambassador. He "saw the world in stark Cold War terms"[19] and was characterized by Lawrence Devlin, the Central Intelligence Agency (CIA) station chief in the Congo from 1960 to 1967, who worked under diplomatic cover, as "a natural leader, prepared to make rapid, tough-minded decisions, the right man in the right spot at the right time."[20] The consulate general accelerated its propagandistic efforts, and began to publish two weeklies and a bulletin reviewing the American press. U.S. consulates, offices of trade firms, cultural centers, and bureaus of periodicals were established in provincial centers and big towns, and missionaries were active in the countryside.

Some prominent Congolese politicians also visited the United States at official invitation. Two of them deserve special mention. Moise Tshombe, a businessman and administrator with an American missionary education, had his tribal base among the Balunda in southern Katanga, the rich min-

81

ing province, and enjoyed financial support from the powerful Union Minière du Haut Katanga, the giant holding company that controlled the province's economy. Tshombe formed the Confédération des Associations Tribales du Katanga (Conakat), which was dominated by Belgian mining interests. He talked about a federal government, but his plan would have given the provinces almost complete autonomy. Albert Kalonji, the leader of the Baluba tribe living in the southern part of Kasai Province, controlled another Congolese source of mineral wealth. He began his political career with the MNC, but after a split with Lumumba, he founded his own party—the MNC-Kalonji.

The U.S. administration foresaw that the United Nations would play an important, if not the key, role if a crisis in the Congo erupted and took measures to prevent the UN from giving the green light to Communist penetration there. The UN secretary-general, Dag Hammarskjöld, a Swedish aristocrat, believed that the UN should become a stabilizing factor in Africa's decolonization and guide the process toward continued Western domination and further Westernization. He shared the opinion that Belgium would fail to keep its control over the situation in the Congo after independence and that the UN would have to intervene.

In January 1960, on returning from a swing visit to twenty-four African territories, Hammarskjöld held a meeting with the high-ranking UN officials whom he trusted completely. All were Americans—Ralph Bunche, undersecretary-general for special political affairs; Andrew Cordier, executive assistant to the secretary-general; and Heinz Wieschhoff, Hammarskjöld's adviser on African affairs and a professional anthropologist. They worked out specific measures to establish the UN's presence in the Congo.[21] And Hammarskjöld appointed Bunche, the first African American Nobel laureate, as the special representative of the secretary-general in the Congo.

On the eve of Congolese independence, there were no Soviet personnel, vested interests, or institutions in the Congo. But Soviet leaders had already identified the Congolese politicians who deserved their support. Lumumba has been stereotyped as "pro-Soviet," "Red," or a Communist disguised in nationalist clothes. However, the archival materials suggest that his relations with the Soviet Union were far more complicated. He was not the first Congolese politician who applied to the USSR for assistance. In early January 1959, the police dispersed participants in a meeting organized in Leopoldville by the Alliance des Bakongo (or the Abako, for short), demanding independence for the Congo. Mass anti-Belgian riots followed. Dozens of Congolese were killed in clashes with the police and troops. On January 10, "members of the Abako and sympathizers" dispatched a letter to the Belgian government demanding that it "grant the Belgian Congo independence immediately." On January 20, a copy of this letter, with the Abako's seal, was received by the Soviet Foreign Ministry (Ministerstvo inostrannykh del, MID). It contained a notification, which partly read: "Transmit the copy to His Excellency Khrushchev—we hope to receive your military aid before January 19, 1959."[22] In the report to the MID, the Soviet Embassy in Brussels identified Kasavubu's Abako as "the most influential political organization" and "the avowed leader of the national liberation movement in the Congo," while the MNC led by Lumumba was labeled "more moderate."[23] The MID's African Department spent four weeks making thorough inquiries about the Abako and other Congolese political organizations and movements and eventually recommended "not to react to the Abako's letter and leave it without an answer."[24] The recommendation was accepted.

Riots in Leopoldville and the growing movement for independence stimulated Soviet interest in the Belgian colony as a likely trouble spot. The Belgians strictly limited Communist Bloc relations (except Czechoslovakia) with the Congolese right up until independence. The Soviet Union, therefore, had to establish contacts and conduct dialogue with the Congolese unofficially. In April 1959, Lumumba participated in a session of the Steering Committee of the Conference of All-African Peoples held in Conakry, the capital of Guinea. One of the leading officials of the Parti Démocratique de Guinée introduced him to Peter Gerasimov, the USSR's ambassador to Guinea, and they arranged to meet at the Soviet Embassy. Lumumba told Gerasimov that his party, the MNC, demanded that the Congo be granted independence by January 1960 and at this time was preparing "to form the future national government." He also promised that "as soon as we come to power, we will immediately exchange diplomatic representations with the USSR." Lumumba expressed a desire to visit the Soviet Union and alluded to the desirability of giving financial aid to his party for the conduct of internal propaganda, including "against anti-Soviet slander." Gerasimov limited his response to boilerplate rhetoric: "The Soviet people watch the fight for national liberation in Africa with great sympathy, and they are true friends of the African people."[25]

From Conakry, Lumumba headed to Brussels, where he and the secretary of the Central Committee of the Communist Party of Belgium (CPB), Albert de Conninck, had an "unofficial meeting that lasted about five hours." On April 27, De Conninck, in a conversation with the first secretary of the Soviet Embassy in Belgium, B. A. Savinov, characterized Lumumba and his party in very complimentary terms. "De Conninck said," Savinov reported to Moscow, "that the MNC is currently the strongest political organization in the Congo and leads the national liberation movement, Lumumba holds a progressive position and is greatly under the influence of the President of the Guinean Republic, Sékou Touré. Before coming to Belgium, he was in Conakry and met several times with Sékou Touré. Reasoning about the future of the Congo, he always refers to the experience of the Guinean Republic and to Sékou Touré's hints."[26] In the spring of 1959, it was the highest praise for an African politician in the eyes of Soviet authorities to be identified with the Guinean president, who was at that time the USSR's only ally in Sub-Saharan Africa.

On April 30, the Central Committee of the Communist Party of the Soviet Union (CC CPSU) decided to comply with the request of Lumumba, "a public figure of the Congo, to invite him to the USSR for two weeks for acquaintance with the life of Soviet working people and trade unions' activity."[27] The MID ordered the ambassador in Conakry to inform Lumumba that his applications for Soviet aid "would be discussed after his arrival in Moscow."[28]

Lumumba had not yet visited Moscow, and the Kremlin had not decided whether to provide him with assistance. In October 1959, when in Accra, Lumumba handed the Soviet ambassador a letter "with an official request for help in organizing propaganda and preparing cadres." The Soviet side was again noncommittal, and did not respond.[29]

Lumumba's next meeting with a Soviet representative took place in Brussels, on February 19, 1960, when he spoke with Savinov in the apartment of a Belgian Communist lawyer, Jan Terfe. Lumumba did not mince words in requesting Soviet assistance. He "emphasized that now, as the fight for complete independence and the establishment of democratic regime was entering its decisive stage, the matter of material aid acquired a very acute and urgent character, because the election results will very much depend on the organization and propaganda work." Lumumba asked Savinov "to clarify the answer to his request for aid and whether or not he could count on any aid from the Soviet Union." Savinov promised to convey his request to Moscow. In his report to the MID, Savinov admitted that Lumumba, as the leader of the MNC, "the largest political movement in the Congo," enjoys "enormous popularity" and predicted that he may become "one of the main contenders for the post of premier or president." But, he cautioned, Lumumba's "ideological and political views are still not fully developed."[30] This ambivalence about Lumumba shows "in its full irony U.S. fears that he was a Communist disguised in nationalist clothes and could be unduly influenced by the Communists."[31] The Kremlin seemed to be waiting for the result of the elections to choose its favorite.

It is widely believed that the MNC received subsidies from Moscow.[32] However, the available archival materials do not confirm that the USSR funded the electoral campaigns of the MNC or other Congolese political parties. All reports on alleged Communist financing were investigated by U.S. government agencies. In March 1960, Victor Nendaka, vice president of the MNC, resigned and made public statements to the effect that he had documentary proof of Lumumba's acceptance of Communist support. On March 25, he was invited to the U.S. Embassy in Brussels to speak with the second secretary, Robert McKinnon, and the attaché, Lawrence Devlin, who, as noted above, was actually a CIA officer. Nendaka failed "to produce documents or to provide specific information concerning Lumumba's dealings with the Soviets and the CPB," but "the Embassy officers continued to ply him with questions on the subject." His replies were "extremely vague and often contradictory." Nendaka had produced nothing important that would compromise Lumumba in American eyes. He could not provide his interlocutors with documents proving that "the CPB, through an intermediary, is arranging to have a Belgian firm with an office in the Congo give Lumumba 5,000,000 francs for use in the electoral campaign." The only compromising information that seemed plausible was Nendaka's story about Soviet brochures dealing with "the Seven-Year Plan, the life of an average worker or peasant in the USSR, agricultural cooperatives in the Soviet Union, etc.," that he allegedly saw at MNC headquarters. To tarnish Lumumba's reputation, Nendaka had to speculate that "he [Nendaka] specifically referred to Lumumba as a 'trained' orator, and then said that the Soviet Bloc trains Africans to propagate the ideals of revolution. Thus, by implication, he suggested that Lumumba is under the influence of the Soviets."[33]

Soviet financial gifts, if there were any, were not substantial and could hardly have exerted real influence on the elections' outcome. The Congolese politicians Philippe Kanza and Thomas Kanza, in a conversation with officials of the Soviet Embassy in Brussels, expressed regret that the USSR was "insufficiently active in aiding the national liberation movement in the Congo" and "badly conducts its propaganda" there. The Congolese "made reference to the activism of the United States, the Federal Republic of Germany [West Germany], Israel and other capitalist countries. They noted that the United States organizes trips by its officials to the Congo, invites Congolese leaders to the United States, gives financial aid to the newly created Political Institute of the Congo, and grants stipends to Congolese students."[34]

The Soviet Union was, in fact, very cautious in offering aid to Congolese political organizations and leaders. On December 28, 1959, the USSR's chargé d'affaires in Guinea, Ivan Marchuk, received Pierre Mulele and Raphael Kinki, two leading officials of the Parti Solidarité Africain (PSA), and the Abako's general secretary, Antoine Kingotolo. Without making any advances concerning future Congolese-Soviet relations, they asked for "financial aid from the USSR to organize party activity in the Çongo" and for "material aid if the Congolese were forced, in view of the obstinacy of Belgium, to take up an armed struggle." According to Marchuk, "Additionally, they wanted from us a number of advisers to help with the most effective organization of the fight for national liberation in the Congo, and in particular they asked about the possibility of using Moscow radio to transmit appropriate instructions to those fighting for the independence of the Congo." Marchuk replied that "the Soviet government doesn't give such aid to anyone or in any circumstances" and "doesn't interfere in problems of internal organization of colonial peoples' struggle." The Congolese asked to be excused if some of their requests "seemed indiscreet." However, "now understanding the position of the Soviet Union, they would like to come to Moscow if the possibility presents itself in order to establish contacts with Soviet organizations and in particular the Afro-Asian Solidarity Committee."[35]

The CC CPSU International Department decided to invite Antoine Gizenga—the leader of the PSA, not an Abako representative—to the USSR, reflecting growing Soviet suspiciousness about moderate organizations such as the Abako that leaned toward an alliance with the West.[36] As for Gizenga, it was a good choice. The PSA joined the MNC's electoral bloc, which won a plurality of seats in the Parliament. Lumumba appointed Gizenga deputy prime minister and Mulele minister of education.

Only when Lumumba finally emerged as the Congo's leader, and the Belgians made it clear that they would not accept him, did Khrushchev publicly announce his support for the Congolese prime minister. On June 29, Khrushchev sent Lumumba a greeting informing him that the Soviet government "affirms its recognition of the Congo as a free and sovereign state and offer to establish diplomatic relations and to exchange diplomatic missions."[37] The official Soviet delegation—consisting of twelve members headed by Mirzo Rakhmatov, vice chairman of the Presidium of the Supreme Soviet of the USSR and chairman of the Presidium of the

Supreme Soviet of Tadjikistan—left for Leopoldville to participate in the independence celebrations.

Independence—and Anarchy

The Congo descended into chaos and anarchy a few days after independence was declared on June 30, 1960. The trouble started on Independence Day, which opened with a special ceremony at the Parliament Building in Leopoldville. King Baudoin of Belgium delivered a patronizing speech, praising the "genius" and "tenacious courage" of King Léopold II and the subsequent development of the country by "Belgian pioneers." Kasavubu's conciliatory speech was full of gratitude. But in his highly emotional speech, Lumumba made no attempt to conciliate the Belgians. "Our wounds are still too fresh and painful for us to be able to forget them at will," he proclaimed. He spoke of the need "to bring an end the humiliating slavery imposed on us by force" and invoked the struggle for independence, which had involved "tears, fire and blood." He promised to "show the world what the black man can do when he is allowed to work in freedom" and to "make the Congo the focal point of all Africa."[38]

Lumumba's speech was warmly applauded by the Congolese, but it was at once taken by the Belgians as an assault and affront to the king and the whole of Belgium. King Baudoin almost left the ceremony. Lumumba subsequently made some conciliatory public remarks, but his performance was taken in high U.S. circles as evidence of "personal instability," "erraticism," and "inexperience—qualities which might make the Congo more vulnerable to instability and Soviet penetration."[39]

The situation in the Congo was highly explosive, and its army was a perfect "detonator." Though the Congo had become independent, nothing had changed in its army, except the name—the colonial Force Publique had become the Armée Nationale Congolaise (ANC, Congolese National Army). The soldiers had a feeling that independence had passed them by. They were still under the command of white officers, for no Congolese held a rank higher than sergeant. Unlike all government employees, they did not receive a pay raise. On July 4, 1960, the ANC's commander in chief, General Emil Janssens, in a clumsy attempt to instill discipline, wrote "After Independence = Before Independence" on a blackboard for all the soldiers to read.[40]

The ANC soldiers mutinied immediately, throwing the country into chaos. They demanded a raise in salaries, immediate Africanization of the officer cadres, and the recall of Janssen. Joined by fringe urban population groups, soldiers roamed the streets pillaging, arresting, insulting, and attacking white civilians. Murders, rapes, and physical violence were rare, and whites more often were suffering from moral terror and mockeries in public, for the Congolese wanted to demonstrate that they were now the bosses. A representative incident involved Devlin, the newly appointed CIA station chief in Leopoldville. When the crisis erupted, he halted his vacation in Paris and rushed to reach his new post. He was picked up by a band of soldiers in the center of Leopoldville and taken to a military base, where he refused to kiss one soldier's feet, and they played Russian roulette with him. A soldier put his revolver to Devlin's head. Five times the Congolese pulled the trigger, and the pistol's hammer clicked, hitting an empty chamber that should have contained at least one cartridge out of six. Fortunately, however, the revolver was not loaded. It was a joke—"Congolese roulette."[41] Devlin found the U.S. Embassy surrounded with rebel soldiers, and full of white refugees. A stage-three alert had been declared, and personnel were burning documents.[42]

The Soviet delegation in Stanleyville also came to harm. On July 7, it met Prime Minister Lumumba and President Kasavubu. An accord was concluded for the establishment of diplomatic relations and for the exchange of ambassadors between the USSR and the Congo.[43] Mirzo Rakhmatov, the head of the delegation, explained the riots as the actions of "provocateurs supported by the bribed leaders of pro-Belgian parties." He wrote in his memoirs that the Congolese soldiers who were searching Belgian paratroopers and checking the documents of residents of the Stanley Palace Hotel, where the Soviets were staying, were treating them in a "very friendly" way. On the night of July 8, Rakhmatov ventured out into the city for a stroll with friends. Suddenly they were stopped by an ANC military patrol. "The soldiers," Rakhmatov remembers, "mistook us for representatives of some foreign stock company and for this reason they treated us at first with suspicion. I explained that we had arrived in the Congo from the USSR for the feast. Then one of the soldiers said: 'Khrushchev! Sputnik!' Everybody began to smile, hearing us attentively. I asked what did they contest against. They replied that they wanted freedom and would fight for it to the bitter end." The Russians were released immediately.[44]

According to another witness—the first Congolese representative in the UN, Thomas Kanza—the Soviet delegation had to survive several hair-raising episodes. Kanza recalled that some Congolese soldiers believed rumors that Lumumba had brought in Russian paratroopers to disarm them. They invaded the delegation's rooms in the Stanley Palace Hotel and manhandled the Russians. No one was badly hurt. When informed of this, Lumumba asked his foreign minister, Justin Bomboko, "to take charge of the security, and make it possible for the Soviets to leave unhindered." Bomboko begged Kanza, his only subordinate with a university education, to collect the Russians from the hotel and drive them under military escort to Ndjili Airport. Rahkmatov, remaining calm, "made a most energetic protest in the name of his government at the unfriendly way that his delegation had been treated." Kanza "simply rejected his protest, and made it clear to him, through the Russian interpreter, that the Congolese government was doing its best to ensure the safety of its guests."[45]

Another incident happened at the airport. Kanza described it as follows: "The special Soviet plane was surrounded by Congolese soldiers, who were anxious to go aboard in order to inspect all the luggage. Belgian propaganda had borne fruit: the Congolese soldiers honestly believed that Lumumba had brought in Russian troops. There was a rumor that the Soviet plane at the airport was the last to have arrived: others have arrived earlier, and left again after depositing Russian soldiers. This plane must therefore be inspected. The Soviet delegates let me negotiate with the Congolese soldiers, and agreed to get into their plane, leaving their luggage behind for the moment." Kanza and Bomboko, who arrived in the airport soon after, managed to convince the soldiers that there were no Russian troops concealed in the plane. Kanza and Bomboko were invited aboard and offered a glass of vodka. Bomboko's toast "pleased everyone."[46]

On July 8, Janssens was dismissed, and the government decided to Africanize the ANC's command. Victor Lundula, Lumumba's uncle, a retired staff sergeant in the Force Publique, was appointed the ANC's commander in chief and was awarded the rank of general. An ANC staff sergeant, Joseph Mobutu, who was a member of the MNC and Lumumba's private secretary, was promoted to colonel and appointed the ANC's chief of staff. The garrisons returned to normal, and the murders and looting stopped.

The mutiny set off an exodus by the Congo's panic-stricken white community. The Western media was full of often-exaggerated stories of atrocities committed by the mutineers. The American, British, and French consuls in Elisabethville, the capital of Katanga Province, made a joint plea for Belgian military intervention.[47] On July 10, Belgium sent troops into the Congo to protect its citizens and economic interests.

The Soviet reaction was severe. "The people of the Congo want to establish genuine order, to kick away the colonizers. Congolese soldiers did not want to obey Belgian officers. And they do what is right exactly, for Belgian officers are also colonizers," Khrushchev stated on July 12. He elaborated his proposition that the Belgian invasion was part of a broader NATO plan of aggression: "These measures against the Republic of the Congo affirm once more the aggressive reality of the military blocs of the imperialists, and their efforts to maintain the methods of the colonizers. The military blocs of the imperialists have been established to pursue a predatory policy. It is not only Belgium that has sent troops to the Congo. It is NATO that has sent these troops to crush the people of the Congo by force of arms."[48] A propaganda war over the Congo had begun.

While the troops were consumed with protecting and evacuating Europeans, the situation remained calm. Lumumba even gave his permission for Belgian troops to stay in Kasai Province for two months.[49]

Katanga's Secession and the Internationalization of the Crisis
The situation changed abruptly on July 11, 1960, when two events occurred that made an internationalization of the crisis inevitable. Belgian troops landed at the docks of the port city of Matadi after all the Europeans who wanted to be evacuated had left. The nearest Congolese garrison to Matadi, in Thysville, resisted the invasion, and twelve Congolese were killed and thirteen Belgians were wounded in armed clashes.[50] Congolese radio operators, using the ANC's own circuit, alerted units of the army around the country and demanded help. Activated by revenge, the soldiers unleashed another round of anti-European pogroms.

The very same day, Katanga, the richest Congolese province, holding more than half of the country's known mineral resources, seceded from the independent Congo, with support from Brussels, taking with it the country's major sources of revenue. The head of the provincial government, Moise Tshombe, read the declaration of Katanga's independence. He called the central Congolese government procommunist and "extremist" and explained that independence was a move to avoid "the danger we are in of being forced to an even longer subjection to the communizing will of the central government." He called the province's independence "total" but asked Belgium to continue "technical, financial and military aid; and also to help us in reestablishing public order and security."[51]

The Soviet Union reacted sharply to Katanga's secession. In the Soviet government's statement, Tshombe was characterized as "protégé of foreign monopolies." It warned "that any attempt to tear away provinces from the Congo Republic is unlawful and felonious act dictated by the selfish ends of the tiny circle of financial and industrial magnates of the colonial powers."[52]

Tshombe responded wittily to this Soviet condemnation. On July 14, he dispatched a telegram to Moscow addressed to "Mister Minister of Foreign Affairs" that partly read: "Taking into account that the Charter of the United Nations solemnly proclaims the right of nations for self-determination, . . . the people of Katanga through their elected representatives address the Free World countries with request to recognize Katanga's independence."[53] The telegram was left without an answer.

News of Katanga's secession reached Lumumba and Kasavubu in Lu-luabourg, the capital of Equateur Province. They immediately flew to Elisabethville, but when their plane was over the airport, Godefroid Munongo, Katanga's influential minister of the interior, who had gone especially to the control tower, refused landing permission. He said that Tshombe would be happy to receive Kasavubu, but, in the present circumstances, not Lumumba. To back Munongo's words, a scratch force of European mercenaries had rolled steel gasoline drums across the runway.[54] The central government had no choice but to call in an outside force to restore law and order in the country and its territorial integrity.

On July 12, in the absence of Lumumba and Kasavubu, the Congolese Council of Ministers decided to ask for U.S. intervention. The request, signed by Foreign Minister Bomboko and Vice Premier Gizenga, stressed the urgent need to have "a foreign neutral army" on the spot "in order to assure peace and order in collaboration with the Congolese Army."[55] U.S. ambassador Clare Timberlake was present at the meeting and immediately transmitted the request to Washington.

Having analyzed the ambassador's cables to Washington, the journalist and scholar Madeleine Kalb concluded that "Timberlake believed that anarchy in the Congo would have repercussions far beyond the immediate crisis: it would play directly into the hands of the Russians by providing an opportunity for radical forces to take over and undermine Western interests in this rich and strategic part of Africa. At the same time he realized that the only action capable of preventing anarchy—intervention by Belgian troops—would also play into Soviet hands: it would antagonize the new Congolese government and give the Russians an excellent opportunity to stress their anti-imperialist solidarity with the new African states." So "the best way out of the impasse was to place the intervention under the UN umbrella." The great powers would not participate directly. Timberlake metaphorically formulated this principle in his cable to Secretary of State Christian Herter and Undersecretary Douglas Dillon, dated July 10: "This should keep bears out of the Congo caviar."[56]

After the Congolese Cabinet meeting on July 12, Bomboko called on Timberlake and was told that while the ambassador had not yet heard from Washington, he personally "did not believe U.S. troops would be sent to the Congo unless they arrived under the auspices of the United Nations." Timberlake pointed out "that Khrushchev had already made a statement accusing us of trying to reimpose colonialism on the Congo."[57] Hours later, President Eisenhower's press secretary stated: "The United States believes that any assistance to the Government of the Congo should be through the United Nations and not by any unilateral action by any country, the United States included."[58] The U.S. administration quickly pressed Dag Hammarskjöld to take a leading role. With the UN umbrella, Eisenhower could eliminate an opportunity for the Soviet Union to expand its influence while limiting the United States' involvement in Africa.

Meanwhile, Kasavubu and Lumumba returned to Stanleyville. On July 13, they cabled the United Nations, making it clear that the military aid requested for the Congo from the UN "is not for the purpose of reestablishing the internal situation of the Congo, but of protecting national territory against aggression of metropolitan Belgian troops."[59] This formulation gave no grounds for interference in the Congo's internal affairs.

Khrushchev really did make the statement condemning the United States to which Timberlake referred. Speaking at a press conference in the Kremlin on July 12, the Soviet leader called the Congo government's decision to apply to the UN Security Council for help "adequate," but he dropped a hint of doubt that the council would react properly: "It is obvious that a fair claim of the Congolese people will hardly receive sympathy from the Security Council. One ought to expose this authority to let all the people know that the United States of America has turned it into an instrument for suppressing lovers of liberty and holding peoples in colonial slavery."[60] The official Soviet position on the UN's involvement in the Congo was stated on July 13: "The USSR Government considers that the grave situation created in the Congo threatens the peace and security of the people. The United Nations Organization must take urgent measures to bring the aggression to an end, and to reestablish completely the sovereign rights of the independent Republic of the Congo."[61]

Both the United States and the Soviet Union had ulterior motives for supporting the UN operation. Eisenhower was more interested in shielding the Congo from "Communist penetration." Khrushchev, conversely, tried to exploit the opportunity to expand the USSR's influence as the leading opponent of colonialism and imperialism. He upheld the UN operation mainly for two reasons. First and foremost, the UN forces replaced the troops of Belgium, a NATO member. Second, he believed that the Congo crisis provided him with a good chance to tip the balance of forces within the UN that were unfavorable for the USSR and its allies.

The "Congo Club" in the United Nations

In the United Nations, the General Assembly was dominated by the Western and Latin American countries, which needed only twelve votes from African and Asian countries to achieve a two-thirds majority. And the Western powers also enjoyed a predominant position in both the Security Council and the Secretariat. In the Security Council, they held four of the five permanent seats and on average three of the six elected seats. In August 1960, of 102 senior posts in the Secretariat, 23 were held by Americans, 16 by the British, 10 by the French, 8 by Russians, and 5 by Indians.[62]

Conor Cruise O'Brien, the UN secretary-general's representative who directed UN operations in Katanga in the fall of 1961, described an offstage decisionmaking mechanism with respect to the Congo in high UN circles. The only reliable sources of information on what was actually going on in the Congo were cables dispatched by the UN staff in Leopoldville to Secretary-General Hammarskjöld. These telegrams, "taken together, made a picture quite sharply different from the rounded contours of the one created for us by the official reports, circulated to delegates in the General Assembly and the Congo Advisory Committee." Only people who read the telegrams, O'Brien argued, "had the full materials necessary for an adequately informed discussion, and adequately motivated decisions, on the UN operation in the Congo." The secretary-general did not make the telegrams available either to the Security Council or the General Assembly. The only powerful body that he kept fully informed of all important Congolese dispatches was "the highly informal, and perhaps rather eccentrically composed, 'Congo Club' within the [UN] Secretariat itself," which was the real "Cabinet" for the Congo operation and which "played its cards remarkably close to its chest." This club's members included citizens of Britain (Alexander MacFarquhar), India (C. V. Narasimhan and General Indar Jit Rikhye, the chef de cabinet to the secretary-general), Ireland (O'Brien), Nigeria (Francis Nwokedi), and the United States (Ralph Bunche, Andrew Cordier, and Heinz Wieschhoff). The reality of the inner circle was that there was an American monopoly in the decisionmaking process. Hammarskjöld heavily relied on "a small group of advisers who happened to be Americans"—Bunche, Cordier ("a senior member of the group"), and Wieschhoff ("a gray eminence"). The other members took little part in the club's proceedings.[63]

Socialist countries were not represented in the Congo Club, and "care was taken to see that no member of the Secretariat who was a citizen of a Communist State saw the Congo telegrams." Georgyi Arkad'ev, an official temporarily reassigned from the service of the Soviet Union who was then UN undersecretary for political and Security Council affairs, did not have access to the Congo files in the custody of his subordinate, director and deputy to the undersecretary for political and Security Council affairs, Heinz Wieschhoff—who in practice, though not in theory, worked directly for Hammarskjöld, ignoring his superior officer, Arkad'ev.[64] O'Brien's argument was that this state of affairs could be justified by the fact that the Americans surrounding the secretary-general "were governed by the high Hammarskjöldian conception of loyalty to the international organization alone," in contrast to "a loyal servant of Soviet Russia and Communism," Arkad'ev,[65] but this was obviously not convincing to Khrushchev.

"The Russians," Kalb notes, "felt that, in general, they themselves were not sufficiently well represented at the decisionmaking levels of the UN Secretariat, and in the specific case of the Congo, UN officials—American, European, or Afro-Asian—were working to further Western interests and to frustrate Soviet interests."[66] What, then, was Khrushchev thinking in letting himself in for this risky UN game?

The Security Council Approves the UN Operation in the Congo
An urgent meeting of the UN Security Council was held on the evening of July 13, 1960. Mongi Slim of Tunisia, unofficially representing the Afro-Asian Bloc of countries in the United Nations, introduced a draft resolution. Its first paragraph called upon Belgium "to withdraw its troops from the territory of the Republic of the Congo." The second paragraph authorized the secretary-general "to take the necessary steps, in consultation with the Government of the Republic of Congo, to provide the government with such military assistance as may be necessary until, through the efforts of Congolese government with the technical assistance of the United Nations, the national security forces may be able, in the opinion of the government, to meet fully their tasks."[67] The Soviet UN representative, Arkadyi Sobolev, submitted three suggested amendments, "(1) to in-

sert a point condemning Belgian armed aggression against the Congo, (2) to point to the necessity of immediate withdrawal of Belgian troops from the Congo, and (3) to add to paragraph 2 of the draft after the words 'military assistance' the words 'provided by African State Members of the United Nations.'"[68]

The "Africanization" of the UN forces was seen by Khrushchev as a chance to turn them into an instrument for protecting Lumumba's government and securing Soviet interests. The idea of carrying out the UN operation in the Congo with only African troops was popular among African and Asian states. On July 13, Ghanaian president Kwame Nkrumah stated: "The present difficulties in the Congo should be solved primarily through the efforts of the independent African states within the framework of the United Nations machinery. Intervention by Powers from outside the African continent, in the view of the Government of Ghana, is likely to increase rather than lessen tension."[69] Tunisia and Ceylon, elected members of the Security Council, voted against condemnation of Belgian aggression but supported the third Soviet amendment. All the Soviet amendments were defeated, and the resolution submitted by Slim was adopted by eight votes to none, with three abstentions (the United States and the USSR voted for it).

The resolution gave the Western powers serious advantages. Belgium had not been accused of aggression. The paragraph on the UN force's mission in the Congo, though deliberately vague, made it clear that its primary task was not to expel Belgian troops but to restore order in the country, the problem with which Lumumba's government had failed to cope. The secretary-general received a free hand concerning the national structure of the UN forces and its command.

On July 14, Lumumba and Kasavubu sent Khrushchev a public telegram reading as follows: "Given the threats to the neutrality of the Republic of the Congo from Belgium and various Western nations conspiring with her against our independence, we ask you to watch the Congo situation closely. We might be led to ask help from the Soviet Union if the Western camp does not stop its aggression against our sovereignty."[70] The Congolese leaders did not want the USSR to interfere directly. Kanza assumed rightly that the telegram "represented a means of pressure and propaganda rather than any wish to have Soviet or American troops replacing the Belgians in the Congo."[71]

In his reply on July 15, Khrushchev publicly pledged Soviet aid "that might be needed for the victory of your rightful cause." He supported the UN actions in the Congo, but left the door open for further unilateral measures if the UN force did not accomplish what he regarded as its proper objectives: "In the atmosphere of peoples' growing indignation to imperialist aggression in the Congo, the UN Security Council did useful things having made the decision urging withdrawal of Belgian troops from the Congo. If the aggression continued, despite this decision, the Soviet would insist on taking more resolute measures both by the UN and by peace-loving nations sympathizing with the Congo's cause."[72] The United States labeled Khrushchev's remarks "intemperate, misleading and irresponsible."[73]

Khrushchev meant hypothetical measures, refrained from making any commitment, and Hammarskjöld set about "telephoning all over the world for troops, aircraft, staging areas, and supplies, composing instructions and directives, setting up a command and staff organization, and choosing a name for the new operations—ONUC (Organisation des Nations Unies au Congo)."[74] On July 15, just 48 hours after the Security Council's decision, 3,500 UN troops from Ghana, Tunisia, Morocco, and Ethiopia arrived in the Congo. In a week, 11,500 UN troops had been deployed in all five provinces except Katanga.[75]

UN Forces in the Congo
The United Nations operation in the Congo was planned to provide the United States with a considerable role, though only neutral countries sent contingents of troops. These UN troops were flown to the Congo by U.S. military planes. Upcountry, the troops were transported by planes and armored personnel carriers with American crews. The U.S. Army maintained communication between the ONUC units and provided communication with the outer world. And though Americans predominated among the civilian personnel whom the UN sent to the Congo to fill the key posts in the institutions of the former colonial administration, the U.S. government formally maintained aloofness, participating only in operation "Safari"—ferrying food assistance from American military bases in Europe to the Congo.

The Soviet Union, which was displeased with excessive American involvement in the UN operation, reacted by sending, at the request of Hammarskjöld, 10,000 tons of food supplies by planes and special ship, as a gift to the Congo.[76] To provide ONUC with truck transportation, it shipped "100 trucks GAZ-63 with canvas cover, car-making units, and an auto service workshop," as well as a group of instructors to "help with vehicle operations."[77]

96

The USSR did not miss the chance to provide planes for ferrying the UN troops. Ghana was totally dependent on the great powers to get its troops to the Congo. Nkrumah approached the British for aid, and they promised to help, but only after receiving the Security Council's sanction. Soviet ambassador Mikhail Sytenko offered Ghana the use of two Ilyushin-18s (IL-18s), which were accepted without reference to the UN Secretariat. This incurred Hammarskjöld's displeasure.[78] On July 21, three Soviet planes loaded with food supplies landed in the Congolese capital. Right off the bat, they were used to ferry troops and munitions to the Congo. Shortly, another two IL-18s began to maintain an Accra-Leopoldville airlift.[79]

In a note dated July 23, the Soviet government informed the UN secretary-general that Soviet planes would ferry not only Ghanaian troops to the Congo but also "motor transport, communications equipment, food supplies, and other types of cargo sent by the Ghanaian Government to the Congolese Government to assist the latter." In reply, Hammarskjöld reminded the USSR that according to the ground rules set by the Security Council, the transport aircraft of its permanent members could not carry cargo inside the Congo.[80]

The extent of the Soviet airlift to the Congo remains debatable. A declassified, undated top-secret memo prepared by the MID Department of African countries clarifies the number of Soviet planes sent to African countries "in connection with aid to the Republic of Congo":

1. *Five* IL-18s have been given to the government of Ghana and flown to Accra (P. 294/20 of 30.7,[81] P. 294/63 of 3.8.60);

2. *One* IL-14 was sent on August 11 as a gift to the Prime Minister of the Republic of Congo, Patrice Lumumba (P. 293/55 of 27.8.60);

3. *Ten* IL-14s designated to the government of the Congo for a period of up to one year flew from Moscow with foodstuffs on August 28; *five* AN-12s, also for the government of the Congo, are to fly with military consignments [*spetsimushestvo*] from Moscow to Conakry on September 1 (P. 297/12 of 20.8.60);

4. *Ten* AN-2s and five MI-14 helicopters will be delivered to the government of the Congo for one year by sea transport (USSR Council of Ministers Instruction 2471 of 15.8.60);

5. *Two* IL-14s for the government of Guinea (a decision of the highest authority [the Instantsiya, the CPSU leadership] of 25.8.60).

Total: for the Congo—26 planes and 6 helicopters; for Ghana—5 planes; for Guinea—2 planes.[82]

With these planes, the USSR was far behind the United States, which used ninety aircraft and "a number of helicopters" to maintain the UN operation in the Congo.[83]

A *Pravda* correspondent who accompanied one of the IL flights to Rabat, Accra, and Leopoldville described the difficulties involved in the Soviet airlift. They had to fly "not along the coast, on a well-established route dotted by airports" but to take an uncharted route "over deserts of the Sahara Desert, the Atlas Mountains and the Atlantic Ocean where there are not any terrain features." They faced many unforeseen problems before they reached their destination. While landing at the Leopoldville airport, where Americans "had captured the radio station," the plane's radio fell silent "at the most critical point," when a Soviet pilot needed landing instructions. He happily managed to avoid a crash landing.[84]

Lumumba Is "a Castro or Worse"

Lumumba, with some justice, regarded the Belgian military presence as the prime cause of the grave situation in the Congo. Ralph Bunche assured the Congolese government that Belgian troops, "in accordance with the decisions taken by the Security Council, were to leave the Congo upon the arrival of United Nations forces." But now the UN forces had arrived; yet the Belgian troops were still there. On July 17, 1960, Lumumba and Kasavubu signed an ultimatum addressed to the UN, saying that "if by July 19, . . . the United Nations is unable to discharge the mission which we have entrusted to it, regretfully we may be obliged to call upon the Soviet Union to intervene."[85]

The ultimatum did have the immediate effect of putting pressure on Belgium to withdraw its forces. The United States, working with Hammarskjöld, helped to produce an agreement with Belgium that its troops would leave Leopoldville by July 23. In this limited sense, Lumumba's tactics succeeded, but his move backfired in several important ways.

In Leopoldville, the Senate refused to approve Lumumba's ultimatum and rejected any possible intervention by the Soviet Union.[86] A meeting of the UN African Bloc on July 18 unanimously opposed the Congo's threat to call in Russian troops.[87]

This ultimatum enraged the West, particularly the United States. On July 18, the Belgian government recalled its ambassador from Moscow.

On July 19, the U.S. Embassy in Brussels dispatched a telegram to the Department of State sharply criticizing Lumumba and suggesting for the first time the need to oust him: "Whatever circumstances may have led to present situation, Lumumba has now maneuvered himself into position of opposition to West, resistance to United Nations and increasing dependence on Soviet Union and on Congolese supporters (Kashamura [the minister of information, Anicet Kashamura], Gizenga) who are pursuing Soviet ends. Only prudent, therefore, to plan on the basis that Lumumba government threatens our vital interests in Congo and Africa generally. A principal objective of our political and diplomatic action must therefore be to destroy the Lumumba government as now constituted, but at same time, we must find or develop another horse to back which would be accepted in rest of Africa and defensible against Soviet political attack."[88]

Speaking at the National Security Council meeting held on July 21, the CIA director, Allen Dulles, gave Lumumba a damning characteristic. "In Lumumba," he said, "we were faced with a person who was a Castro or worse." Dulles described Lumumba's background as "harrowing," recalling all his "sins":

> In 1956 Lumumba had been convicted of embezzling 100,000 francs and had received a two-year jail term. There were strong Leftist and Communist trends in his background. He had attended a Communist youth meeting in 1959. Lumumba has clearly been promised assistance by the Communist Party of Belgium. We do not know how much assistance they are giving, but it is clear that the Belgian Communist Party is being used as a channel. It is safe to go on the assumption that Lumumba has been bought by the Communists; this also, however, fits with his own orientation.[89]

Considering various scenarios of possible Soviet actions in the Congo, American analysts believed that Soviet military intervention was unlikely. A July 22 memorandum of the Joint Chiefs of Staff noted that bringing troops to the Congo "poses great practical difficulties for the Soviets" if they tried "airlifting forces into the area or sealifting them."[90] To forestall a Soviet decision to intervene in the Congo, the United States "did station an attack carrier near the mouth of the Congo River."[91] The USSR could not sustain a military challenge to the Western powers. Its naval capacity was rather limited, and it lacked aircraft carriers and the airlift capability to ferry and supply forces thousands of miles from home.

The U.S. intelligence services did not find Communist influence inside the Congo dangerous enough to frustrate ONUC's mission. The director of the U.S. State Department's Bureau of Intelligence and Research, which was tasked with analyzing information on the situation, reported to the secretary of state on July 25: "The Communists do not have an efficient and well-established apparatus in the Congo that would permit them to manipulate existing forces, judging from available intelligence. They were effectively excluded from the Congo throughout virtually the whole period of Belgian colonial administration and thus were not able to recruit and build up local Communist Party organizations."[92]

The leverage of the Soviet Union on the Congo was rather limited. Its only stake was Lumumba. And the prospect of Soviet peaceful penetration worried the USSR's Cold War adversaries not less than plausible Communist military intervention. In Washington in late July, Lawrence Devlin outlined to CIA chief Allen Dulles his belief that

> if the Soviets achieved their objective of influencing and eventually controlling Lumumba, they would use the Congo as a base to infiltrate and extend their influence over the nine countries or colonies rounding the Congo—Congo-Brazzaville, the Central African Republic, Sudan, Uganda, Rwanda, Burundi, Tanganyika, Rhodesia, and Angola. Had the Soviets gained a position of control or influence in the nine countries and colonies, they would have had an extraordinary power base in Africa. In addition to gaining control or influence over the minerals, raw materials, and oil produced in Africa, it would have greatly increased their influence in the third world, as well as extending their influence within the UN.[93]

Devlin's impression was that Dulles "had probably already reached the same conclusion."[94]

On July 21, another UN Security Council meeting was held at the request of the USSR's new representative to the United Nations, Vasilyi Kuznetsov, to discuss the Belgian presence in the Congo. He accused the Western powers of attempting to dismember the Congo and reserve for themselves the economic riches of Katanga, with the assistance of "a certain lackey Tshombe," whose secessionist activity "evokes exultation among industrial and financial tycoons." Kuznetsov submitted a strongly worded resolution insisting upon the withdrawal of Belgian troops from the Congo within a period of three days and demanding respect for the territorial integrity of the Congo. "If aggression continues," he warned, "then of course more active measures were to be taken, both by the United Nations and by peace-loving states which are in sympathy with the Congo's cause."[95]

The U.S. representative to the United Nations, Henry Cabot Lodge Jr., interpreted this statement as a threat of Soviet military intervention, and promised, "We will do whatever may be necessary to prevent the intrusion of any military forces not requested by the United Nations." It was "regrettable," he said, that the Soviet Union was "seeking to bring the Cold War to the heart of Africa."[96]

Kuznetsov's draft UN Security Council resolution did not win support, but he did win a general agreement that the continued Belgian presence in the Congo made it necessary to clarify the original resolution. Tunisia and Ceylon introduced a new resolution that was softer than the Soviet draft but more critical of the Belgians than the first resolution, calling on the Belgian government to withdraw its troops "speedily" and authorizing the secretary-general to "take all necessary action to this effect." It requested all states "to refrain from any action which might undermine the territorial integrity and the political independence of the Republic of the Congo."[97] This new resolution was adopted on July 22.

Lumumba's Wasted Visit to the United States

Lumumba welcomed the UN Security Council resolution and stated that "Russian aid is no longer necessary."[98] He made this statement on July 22, 1960, en route to New York. He wanted to reconcile with the United Nations and the West, to receive U.S. economic assistance, and to convince Hammarskjöld and Eisenhower to enter Katanga to restore the control of the federal Congolese government. He was foiled on all points.

When Lumumba arrived in New York, he implored Hammarskjöld to recognize the necessity for UN troops to suppress Tshombe's military regime. But the secretary-general did not budge from his position and told Lumumba that he would not order UN troops to enter Katanga under the current conditions. The Congolese representative to the UN, Thomas Kanza, who participated in the negotiations, explained their breakdown as due to Lumumba's inflexibility:

> We [the Congolese officials who accompanied Lumumba] felt most uneasy, for we were witnessing a real conflict of personalities, and one which could have serious results on the whole future between the central Congolese government and the UN.

The two principals were equally determined to get their point of view across, and each persistently underestimated the other. All the rest of us made attempts to reason with Lumumba in Lingala; counseling tact and diplomacy in the answers and suggestions that he made to the UN authorities we were confronting and of whose goodwill we had such need. But Lumumba remained extremely demanding and impatient, while Hammarskjöld simply noted down his suggestions and continued to promise continued assistance to the Congo and its government.[99]

Thereafter, relations between the prime minister and the secretary-general continued to deteriorate. Lumumba believed that Hammarskjöld was working mainly for Western interests and that he could not be trusted. Hammarskjöld judged Lumumba as a political self-destroyer without good sense. He told Kanza at parting: "Let him play with fire if he wants to—but he'll certainly get burnt."[100] Afterward, the secretary-general visited the Congo many times, but he never met Lumumba, restricting contacts with him to correspondence.

From New York, Lumumba went to Washington, where he could not see President Eisenhower, who was vacationing in Newport, Rhode Island, but spent a frustrating half hour with Secretary of State Christian Herter. Herter rebuffed each of three requests from the prime minister—to persuade the Belgians to withdraw their troops from the Congo; to provide Lumumba's government with money, technicians, and an official loan; and to supply Lumumba and Kasavubu with a "small aircraft." Herter told Lumumba that all U.S. aid would have to be channeled through the United Nations.[101] Fifteen years later, Undersecretary Douglas Dillon, who had been present at the meeting, testified that the "willingness of the United States government to work with Lumumba vanished" after this meeting.[102]

Lumumba was also disappointed and was convinced that neither the West nor the United Nations was ready to take the kind of action he believed necessary to stop Katanga's secession. Now he was ready to accept aid from outside the UN.

The United Nations Attempts to Settle the Katanga Problem—
and Lumumba Retaliates
The Russians did not hesitate to exploit Lumumba's mood. While in America, he met with two Soviet diplomats, Deputy Foreign Minister

Kuznetsov, on July 24 and 30, 1960, and the ambassador to Canada, Suren Arutyunyan, on July 29. According to the CIA's intelligence, at Lumumba's meeting with Kuznetsov, "Soviet arms aid to the Congo was discussed."[103] I did not have an opportunity to take a look at archival documents confirming or refuting this assertion, but published materials give ground for supposing that Soviet representatives agreed to supply vehicles to Lumumba's government, bypassing the UN. On July 31, the Soviet government stated that the 100 trucks it would send to the Congo "in the nearest future" were intended not for ONUC but for transporting by road cargo "needed by the Congolese people and the government to conduct a fair fight against imperialist aggression."[104]

This was unacceptable to those in the U.S. administration, who believed that "exclusive reliance on the UN for the rehabilitation of the Congo provided the best means of keeping out Soviet assistance and its inevitable subversive accompaniments."[105] On August 1, the Department of State issued a declaration that partly read: "The Soviet leaders must be aware that this kind of public statement can only add to the problems of those who are seriously trying to restore peace and order in the Congo."[106] On August 6, the department sent a circular telegram asking to have it explained to friendly governments that the United States' decision to give aid through the UN was "motivated by the belief that bilateral assistance from the United States, which would be followed by bilateral assistance from the Soviet Union and other Communist countries, would have transformed the Congo rehabilitation into a Cold War competition which would not be to the advantage of the Congo, of Africa, and of the entire Free World."[107]

Yet it was impossible to avoid a Cold War competition while the Katanga problem, Lumumba's vulnerable spot, remained unresolved. Since its secession on July 11, Katanga had been operating as an independent state, and quickly acquiring the attributes of one. The Provincial Parliament became the National Parliament. The Constitution elaborated by the Belgians came into effect, endowing President Tshombe and his appointed government with full executive power. The flag and anthem of independent Katanga appeared, and Katangan coins were minted. Victor Lundula, the man whom Lumumba had appointed the ANC's commander, was first arrested and then expelled from the province. Army units in Katanga were purged from the military disloyal to Tshombe and reinforced with white mercenaries.

With both the United States and the Soviet Union now interested in the outcome of the crisis in the Congo, Hammarskjöld tried to do his best to avoid a showdown. With U.S. help, he persuaded the Belgian government to make a public commitment to withdraw its troops from the province, and in late July he arrived in Leopoldville. The then-assistant to the secretary-general's special representative in the Congo, Brian Urquhart, vividly described "the madhouse" that the secretary-general found in the Congolese capital: "When he [Hammarskjöld] landed in Brazzaville, his welcome was taken over by the Abbé Fulbert Youlou of the French Congo who, white Dior soutane streaming in the wind, insisted on bringing him across the river to Leopoldville in his own speedboat. At a reception in Hammarskjöld's honor, Vice Prime Minister Antoine Gizenga made a long and insulting speech while members of the Soviet Embassy circulated among the guests distributing anti-UN propaganda. At Hammarskjöld's meeting with the Congolese Cabinet, which arrived hours late, a curtain was suddenly raised, revealing the entire Leopoldville press corps."[108]

On August 2, Belgium agreed to allow UN troops into Katanga. The very same day, Hammarskjöld announced that UN forces would enter Katanga on August 6. Bunche was dispatched to Elisabethville on August 4 to prepare the way, but on his arrival, he was told by Tshombe that the entry of the UN forces would mean war. To illustrate his determination, Tshombe had prepared redoubtable "visuals." Bunche saw with his own eyes how "bulldozers, Jeeps, oil drums and other items were being placed on the runway" to prevent the impending landing of UN troops.[109] Bunche had to return to Leopoldville, his mission a failure. Taking into account the relative strengths in personnel and equipment between Katanga and ONUC, Tshombe's talk of war was in fact nothing but a bluff. But Bunche recommended that the entry of UN troops into Katanga be delayed. Hammarskjöld agreed and left for New York to convene the Security Council for further discussions.

Hammarskjöld's decision was followed by a hail of protest from the Congolese Cabinet and Moscow. Gizenga—in the absence of Lumumba, who was still traveling abroad—made a speech on the radio.

The Soviets also reacted sharply. In a statement on August 6, the Soviet government for the first time strongly criticized the command of UN troops in the Congo. It charged that "instead of helping the legitimate government," UN forces "were very often employed outside their competence," illegally disarming the ANC struggling against the Belgian aggressors and "even coming into armed collision" with it. The statement made the suggestion to "replace this command and appoint a new one, which will be faithful in the performance of duties imposed on them by the Security Council" and "remove all Belgian troops from the Congo."[110]

The leaders of three African countries—Ghana, Guinea, and the Congo—supported this statement. Ghanaian president Kwame Nkrumah was more active than any other African politician in supporting the Lumumba government. On August 6, he "informed the Soviet chargé d'affaires in Accra that the government of Ghana intends to act decisively regarding the issue of the Congo, even to the point of forming a joint command with the Congolese government to carry out combat operations against the Belgians in the Congo." The president asked directly "if combat operations begin, whether he could count on such aid from the USSR as would not draw the USSR into an open conflict with the great powers."[111]

On August 8, Nkrumah and Lumumba, paying an official visit to Ghana, signed two documents. In the first, a joint communiqué, they expressed their intention to establish "a Combat High Command of military forces to bring about a speedy withdrawal" of Belgian troops from the Congo, if the UN failed. The second document was a secret agreement on a union between the two countries, with a federal government responsible for foreign affairs, defense, the issuing of a common currency, economic planning, and development.[112]

On August 11, Khrushchev informed the Ghanaian president that "the Soviet government regards the decision of the government of Ghana directed at defending the independence of the Republic of the Congo and extending the necessary aid to the legitimate Congolese government in order to remove the Belgian troops from the Congo as quickly as possible with complete understanding." The Soviet leader expressed "readiness, if the need arises, to give the government of Ghana possible assistance, in particular, by delivering weapons to the government of Ghana."[113]

Soviet weapons were delivered to Ghana in the autumn of 1960. In February 1961, Nkrumah "extended many thanks for providing Soviet weapons" to the chairman of the Supreme Soviet, Leonid Brezhnev, when he made a state visit to Ghana.[114]

In a letter to Hammarskjöld dated August 7, Lumumba suggested sending to the Congo a group of observers from Asian and African states "to ensure on the spot and without delay, the strict application of the decisions concerning the withdrawal of Belgian troops from the whole of Congolese national territory and more particularly from Katanga and to ensure the political independence of the Republic of the Congo."[115]

The position of the Afro-Asian Bloc countries in the United Nations with respect to the Congolese crisis did not align with the Western strategy and extended the playing area for the USSR substantially. At the UN Security Council meeting on August 8 and 9, Kuznetsov called Lumumba's proposal a noteworthy initiative that "might facilitate the Secretary-

General's task of implementing the Security Council's decisions." The Soviet representative noted that the refusal to bring UN troops into Katanga was a concession to Belgian aggressors and to "a dummy figure" of Tshombe, "who is maintained by the foreign occupiers and not recognized by the Republic of the Congo."[116] Kuznetsov submitted a draft resolution that called for "the speedy withdrawal of Belgian troops from the territory of the Congo and the maintenance of the territorial integrity and political independence of the Congo" and imposed on the secretary-general the obligation "to take decisive measures, without hesitating to use any means to that end, to remove the Belgian troops from the territory of the Congo and to put an end to acts directed against the territorial integrity of the Republic of the Congo."[117]

Because the draft lacked necessary support, the Soviet Union did not insist on a vote. Kuznetsov voted for the Tunisia-Ceylon resolution, which was adopted with two abstentions. The resolution was ambivalent. It called on Belgium to "withdraw immediately its troops from the Province of Katanga under speedy modalities determined by the Secretary-General" and declared that the entry of UN forces into Katanga "is necessary for the full implementation of this resolution." Conversely, the fourth paragraph of the resolution reaffirmed the principle of nonintervention in the internal affairs of the Congo: "The United Nations Force in the Congo will not be a party to or in any way intervene in or be used to influence the outcome of any internal conflict, constitutional or otherwise."[118] It guaranteed the immunity of Tshombe's regime from the UN, for Katanga's secession could have been interpreted as an "internal conflict."

Tshombe had taken advantage of the situation right off the bat. On August 9, in what resembled an ultimatum, he issued ten conditions under which he would permit the UN's entry into Katanga. The UN would incur a commitment, in particular, not to allow its planes and vehicles to be used to bring officials of the central Congolese government into Katanga.

On August 12, the secretary-general arrived in Elisabethville with two companies of Swedish troops from the UN force. He handed Tshombe a prepared document in which he set out an interpretation of the fourth paragraph of the August 9 resolution on the UN's action in Katanga that was favorable to Tshombe's regime. In cooperation with the commander of the Belgian troops in Katanga, Hammarskjöld arranged the timetable for their withdrawal. It began in a week, and the UN troops were deployed in the provincial towns.[119]

Hammarskjöld considered this a diplomatic victory, his personal triumph. But Lumumba was furious—the secretary-general had concluded an agreement with the leader of the separatists while ignoring the head of the central government. So a bitter dispute began between Hammarskjöld and Lumumba on the terms of the UN mandate. Hammarskjöld took the position that Katanga's breaking away was an internal political matter and should be resolved by Lumumba and Tshombe working together. Lumumba maintained that the UN should expel the Belgian military from Katanga and take action to end Tshombe's secession. After an exchange of angry letters, Lumumba decided to break off relations with Hammarskjöld and wrote him a final letter declaring that the "government and people of the Congo have lost their confidence in the secretary-general of the United Nations" and asking for a group of Asian and African representatives "to ensure the immediate and entire application of the Security Council resolutions of July 14 and 22 and August 9."[120]

Hammarskjöld's refusal to help Lumumba end the Katanga secession intensified Lumumba's suspicions of the UN and the Western powers and spurred the Congo's rapprochement with the Soviet Union. To bolster Lumumba's position, the Soviet government appointed its first ambassador to the Congo, Mikhail Yakovlev, who had been the foreign minister of the Russian Soviet Federal Socialist Republic, the USSR's largest constituent republic. On August 6, he arrived in Leopoldville and submitted his credentials to President Kasavubu and also handed Lumumba a personal message from Khrushchev. The Soviet leader compared the situation in the Congo with the first years "of the existence of our state, which was invaded by foreign imperialist powers right after people took power in their hands." He expressed confidence that "the Congolese people will win their just struggle for expulsion of foreign interventionists from their country, retaining the territorial integrity and political unity of the Republic of Congo, for their freedom and independent development." Khrushchev reaffirmed the readiness of the Soviet Union to fulfill its commitments to provide the Congo with economic aid.[121]

On August 10, the Soviet merchant ship *Leninogorsk* called at the Congolese port of Matadi, carrying 9,000 tons of wheat, 1,000 tons of sugar, and 300,000 cans of milk. The sugar and milk came in handy, for the Congo had been suffering an acute shortage of foodstuffs, but the wheat was not unloaded due to the unavailability of milling facilities. According to Ambassador Yakovlev, the Congolese government "applied with request to deliver the wheat to the port of Dakar to have it milled or sold." On August 17, the CC CPSU Presidium sanctioned shipping the wheat to Dakar "at the expense of the surplus fund of the USSR Council of Ministers." But on August 27, on the way to Dakar, the *Leninogorsk* dropped anchor, because the Ministry of Foreign Trade had prohibited its captain from calling at Dakar. The internal situation had changed there. The Federation of Mali had disintegrated (see below in this chapter), and the Soviet authorities did not want "the wheat to come into the hands of the French puppet, [Mali Federation president Leopold] Senghor, and it is unknown whether the Congolese government receives something for it or not as contract for the sale has not been signed." For more than two weeks, negotiations on the ill-fated cargo were conducted with Morocco, Tunisia, and Guinea. Eventually, the Moroccans agreed to take it.[122] Lawrence Devlin was right to conclude that such unintentional parodies occasionally undermined "the Soviets' image of unwavering support for Africa's downtrodden people."[123]

According to Devlin's estimation, based on the information supplied by agents, "several hundred" Soviet personnel arrived in the Congo in July and August 1960. The CIA "assumed that many, if not most, of the Soviets were intelligence officers, but this was impossible to confirm."[124] And it was an exaggeration.

In his memoirs, General Vadim Kirpichenko, one of the Soviet Intelligence Service's top officials, named three intelligence officers: "With the risk to their lives, Leonid Gavrilovich Podgornov, Georgiy Arsen'evich Fedyashin, and Oleg Ivanovich Nazhestkin used to obtain information and establish the necessary contacts in the Congo, which was enveloped in the flames of war."[125] These three were the ones who staffed the station of the KGB (Komityet Gosudarstvennoy Bezopasnosti, Committee for State Security of the USSR) in the Congo. Podgornov was the station's chief. He and Nazhestkin worked under diplomatic cover, and Fedyashin was a correspondent for the Telegraph Agency of the Soviet Union (Telegrafnoye Agentstvo Sovetskogo Soyuza, TASS). The KGB station was entrusted with the following tasks: "The USSR government needs information about the plans and designs of the Western powers in the Congo. We also need intelligence on the Congolese political parties and leaders, their attitudes, and their foreign-policy orientation."[126]

The KGB men were in the first group of personnel to leave Moscow for the Soviet Embassy in Leopoldville. The arrangements must have been made in a great hurry. Nazhestkin remembers: "Our plane was already preparing for flight, but several people from the embassy staff had not yet received their diplomatic passports. Finally, a panting courier from the MID's consular section handed over to us the documents in mint state, and our Odyssey started."[127]

Nazhestkin's memoir reveals what flawed knowledge functionaries in

Moscow had about the situation at the Soviet Embassy in Leopoldville. For the first several weeks there, the embassy's staff had to work in a hotel, where the KGB could not use its radio station. As Nazhestkin recalled:

> Immediately a long and expensive telegraphic correspondence with the MID began. Moscow instructed us that buying a house for the Embassy would be more profitable than renting one, that we should carefully examine the real estate market, conduct sustained negotiations to seek lower prices, etc. Everything was bureaucratically true, but it did not fit the case, as our Embassy staff had arrived in a crisis-ridden country, which was on the brink of civil war and under foreign intervention. After reading yet another "wise" dispatch from the MID, Ambassador Yakovlev, in warm blood, spit several by-no-means-diplomatic phrases out and resolutely sat down to write a telegram addressed personally to N. S. Khrushchev, the First Secretary of the CC CPSU. The response from Moscow came the next morning. We would be allowed to settle the housing problem at our discretion.

Finally, an Italian agreed to rent his two-story villa in the city center to the embassy.[128]

The fourth paragraph of the August 9 Security Council resolution had inspired not only Tshombe. On August 9, Albert Kalonji, the Baluba leader of South Kasai, declared his region an independent state that would have close ties with Katanga. An agriculturalist by education, Kalonji had begun his political career in Lumumba's Mouvement National Congolais. Soviet diplomats in Belgium observed that "he is awfully ambitious, a good orator, has authority with Baluba."[129] It is not surprising that Lumumba and Kalonji soon parted ways. In the summer of 1959, he accused Lumumba of "dictatorial manners" and, as mentioned above, established his own party, the MNC-Kalonji.

This second secession was a heavy blow to the central Congolese government. Kasai Province abutted Katanga from the northwest and was a protective buffer for Tshombe's regime. There were very considerable deposits of industrial diamonds in South Kasai, and the loss of territory deprived the Congo of an important source of export revenues and further threatened its political and economic viability.

The Kasai situation was very difficult for Lumumba. To survive politically and even physically, he had to crush separatism and to get the country under control. His reliance on the Soviet Union would now need to deepen for him to have any chance of succeeding. He decided to attack Katanga and Kasai using the ANC, but he needed additional military assistance. On August 15, he wrote Khrushchev and asked him to immediately send transport planes, trucks, "sundry armaments of high quality," "up-to-date military transmission equipment," and "food rations for troops in the field"—all needed "to assure the territorial integrity of the Republic of Congo, which is being seriously threatened."[130]

In responding to this request, Khrushchev was faced with a complicated dilemma—"how to balance the risk of confronting the United States with the risk of losing the respect of the Third World radicals, who had become a cornerstone of his policy."[131] Being fully aware of the impossibility of sustaining any sort of military challenge to the entrenched Western powers thousands of miles from home, Khrushchev preferred limited military aid in the form of planes, trucks, and advisers. The risk seemed to him well calculated and justified. He only equalized chances for the opposing Congolese forces and believed that Soviet moves would not cause direct military intervention by the West.

Soviet military assistance was minimal and could not have been decisive in an attack against Katanga. But it did help get the offensive off the ground. The arrival of hundreds of Soviet trucks in Matadi and of ten Ilyushin transport planes in Stanleyville made Lumumba's troops genuinely mobile.

Trucks that had initially been promised by the Soviet Union to ONUC were diverted by barge up the Kasai River to Port Franqui, and overland to Luluaburg, the point of departure for Lumumba's offensive in South Kasai and Katanga. It began on August 24 and made a good start. The central government's troops, transported by Soviet trucks, and "under the command of three military advisers from Czechoslovakia,"[132] had captured Bakwanga, the capital of South Kasai. Kalonji had fled to Elisabethville. On August 30, ten IL-14s with Congolese wing marks arrived in Stanleyville. Each plane had a crew of eight, including backup personnel, technicians, and interpreters.[133] On September 5, Soviet planes began to ferry reinforcements to Bakwanga. By that time, it was clear that Lumumba's troops would not gain an easy victory. Having been deprived of logistical support, they had to confiscate vehicles and foodstuffs. Benalulua soldiers used the situation to take revenge against the local Baluba population for the pogroms against their tribesmen in the spring of 1959. Hundreds of the Baluba were massacred, the army had been involved in interethnic warfare, and its fighting efficiency had been destroyed and its morale shattered.

The West could not help interpreting Soviet bilateral assistance to Lumumba as a prelude to a Communist triumph. "In those days," Devlin remembers, "when everything was measured in Cold War terms, we were convinced that we were observing the beginning of a major Soviet effort to gain control of a key country in central Africa for use as a springboard to control much of the continent."[134]

Kasavubu Ousts Lumumba; Lumumba Ousts Kasavubu

Khrushchev's and Lumumba's actions did not catch the U.S. administration napping. The Department of State and the Joint Chiefs of Staff worked out three contingency plans for the Congo. The first plan dealt "with things that should be done in the event Lumumba remained in power but asked the UN to withdraw." The second plan was "of an operational nature" and concerned "covert activities to bring about the overthrow of Lumumba and install a pro-Western government." The third plan had been worked out not only on the chance of "the possible arrival of Soviet military forces in the Congo but also dealt with the possibilities of denying access to the Congo to military supply flights not authorized by the United Nations."[135]

On August 25, 1960, a meeting of the National Security Council's Special Group decided to get rid of Lumumba. On August 26, the CIA chief, Allen Dulles, cabled the station in Leopoldville: "In high quarters here it is the clear-cut conclusion that if (Lumumba) continues to hold high office, the inevitable result will at best be chaos and at worst pave the way to Communist takeover of the Congo with disastrous consequences for the prestige of the UN and for the interests of the free world generally. Consequently we conclude that his removal must be an urgent and prime objective and that under existing conditions this should be a high priority of our covert action."[136] The CIA station thus began to put into effect the plan to remove Lumumba from power.[137]

In executing the third plan at the urging of the Defense Department, the State Department agreed to dispatch a naval task force to the west coast of Africa that included two destroyers and two amphibious vessels with landing craft, helicopters, and about five hundred Marines. The official aim of this force was "to make a series of 'show-the-flag,' courtesy, people-to-people friendship visits to ports along the entire coast." But its chief mission was "to serve notice to the Soviets, at least implicitly, that the United States prepared to act militarily to keep them out of the Congo."[138]

Pushed by the Belgians and assured by U.S. ambassador Clare Timberlake and Hammarskjöld's newly appointed representative in the Congo, Andrew Cordier, of indirect U.S. and UN support, President Kasavubu was on the edge of ousting Lumumba. The CIA station in Leopoldville drafted and passed to the president via an intermediary "a how-to" paper outlining "step-by-step the actions he should take before dismissing Lumumba and what he should do in the aftermath."[139]

On the evening of September 5, Kasavubu declared on a Leopoldville radio station that Lumumba and six of his ministers had been dismissed and that Joseph Ileo, the president of the Senate, had been named to form a new government. Kasavubu accused Lumumba of plunging "the nation into fratricidal warfare." The president called on the UN to assume responsibility for "peace and order" in the Congo.[140] Having concluded his radio statement, Kasavubu returned to the presidential palace and went to bed. Thus he had ignored American advice and failed "to control the radio station, a key place in such a volatile situation and one we had emphasized in our paper."[141]

In the evening, Lumumba went to the same radio station and spoke three times to the population. He proclaimed that Kasavubu "is no longer the head of state," called his actions "a public betrayal of our nation," and begged "the United Nations and the free world not to interfere in the internal affairs of the Congolese state."[142]

Lumumba seemed to have bested his rival. Kasavubu was fearful of riots and stayed at his residence and so was unseen by the people, while Lumumba acted vigorously. During the night of September 5, the Council of Ministers published a communiqué declaring that the chief of state was deprived of his functions for having violated the fundamental law, nullifying the latter's revocation of the government. On September 7, after an effective address by the prime minister, the Chamber of Representatives voted 60 to 19 to approve a motion declaring the reciprocal ousters of Lumumba and Kasavubu "null and void." The following day, the Senate voted 41 to 2 to repeal Kasavubu's attempt to dismiss Lumumba. The Senate vote came after Lumumba had appealed to it for support against UN and Belgian efforts to impose "slavery" on the Congo.[143]

In this total chaos, only UN forces acted coherently and purposefully, according to a plan preapproved by Hammarskjöld. On September 6, they closed the Leopoldville radio station to get Lumumba off the air and seized control of all major airports to prevent Lumumba from bringing forces loyal to him from Orientale and Kasai provinces to tilt the balance in the capital in his favor.

To stop the ferrying of troops to Kasai by Soviet planes, Brian Urquhart was sent to Stanleyville, Lumumba's political and tribal base, in the northeastern part of the country. On arriving there on September 5, he found out that the UN soldiers stationed there were Ethiopians who were convinced that the order to prevent any more troops taking off "was the wrong thing to do." "The main source of tension," he remembers, "was the ANC, but additional complication was the Soviet personnel, 'doctors,' and other *soidisant* experts, who were attached to the Soviet transport aircraft. A strong propaganda effort was under way to promote Soviet prestige and undercut United Nations activities, and this in turn made the remaining Europeans uneasy. They were especially fearful that Lumumba might turn up in Stanleyville in person." Urquhart spent most of the next day "urging our Ethiopian commander to block the runway and thereby prevent further movements of troops to Kasai in the Soviet IL-14s. To avoid a fight with the Congolese Army over this, we arranged a distribution of beer to 3,000 Congolese soldiers at the airport and put oil barrels across the runway during the night while they were sleeping it off."[144]

The Congolese crisis now entered its most dangerous phase. On September 7, President Eisenhower stated at a Washington news conference that "the United States deplores the unilateral action of the Soviet Union in supplying aircraft and other equipment for military purposes to the Congo, . . . aggravating an already serious situation which finds Africans killing other Africans." Thus, he continued, the UN program of collective aid for the Congo was "threatened by the Soviet action, which seems to be motivated entirely by the Soviet Union's political designs in Africa."[145]

The next day, Governor Averell Harriman of New York (1956–58), who was on a fact-finding tour of eight African nations for the U.S. Democratic presidential candidate, John Kennedy, arrived in Leopoldville. On September 9, he joined forces with Ambassador Timberlake "to try to galvanize Kasavubu into action." The president "was certain that he had made the right decision when he dismissed Lumumba, who was 'surrounded by Communist advisers' and had an 'evil influence' on the country; but he had no idea what he should do next." After a talk with Lumumba, Harriman concluded that he "was not a Communist but that he was out of his depth if he believed he could use the Russians for his purposes without being used by them in turn."[146]

Before his departure from the Congo, Harriman had a private meeting with Ambassador Yakovlev. As Nazhestkin, who was an interpreter at this meeting, recalled, "The American diplomat [Harriman] tried to convince Yakovlev that it was necessary to maintain relations with the immature Congolese government and to lend it assistance only through the United Nations. 'Why do you act in circumvention of the UN?' Harriman asked. 'Because UN assistance as the case stands and under your command is the noose on the Congolese nation's neck!' Yakovlev replied. Such was the rhetoric of the Cold War in those days, and it was far from diplomatic etiquette."[147]

Harriman did not leave a favor unanswered. According to Madeleine Kalb, "he warned the Soviet diplomat that if his country kept interfering in the Congo's affairs, it might not only fail to help Lumumba, but it might antagonize the Congolese so much that they would expel the Soviet Embassy."[148] As he was leaving the embassy, Harriman told the reporters waiting for him that "the exhausts of Soviet aircraft have poisoned the political atmosphere in the Congo."[149] This phrase spread around the world and dispelled the faint hope for a Soviet-American trade-off in the Congo.

The Soviet Union also rebuffed Hammarskjöld's reprimands. On September 5, the UN secretary-general sent a note to the USSR's mission at the UN, calling into question the legality of Soviet supplies to the Congo and the status of Soviet individuals and equipment there. In return, the Soviet government issued a statement on September 9 strongly criticizing Hammarskjöld personally for what the UN was doing in the Congo. The UN secretary-general, the statement read, "has turned out to be the part of the organization's machinery which openly works to the advantage of the colonizers, thus compromising the UN." The USSR demanded that the UN withdraw its troops from the Congolese airports; return national radio stations to the "full and unlimited control of the Congolese government"; dismiss the ONUC command, which "misemployed troops, sent to the Congo in accord with the Security Council's decision"; and allow "the legitimate government" an opportunity "to exercise authority and sovereign rights over the whole Congo without any UN representatives' interference or making difficulties."

These demands by the USSR were radical, but no effective mechanism had been worked out to implement them. The September 9 statement proposed to act through the Security Council where there were no chances to pilot the resolutions needed. If "the Security Council for some reason or another refuse to perform its obligation," the Soviet government exhorted friendly states "to provide the legitimate Congolese government with comprehensive aid in a pinch."[150] This was a call primarily to the United Arab Republic, Ghana, and Guinea, which had threatened to withdraw their troops from the Congo unless the UN gave up its control of the Leopoldville radio station and the Congolese airports.

The Soviet leadership seemed to have made a decision not to provide Lumumba with military aid under any circumstances. The phrase about "the possibility of military assistance to the legitimate government of the Congo" was deleted from the draft of the statement prepared by the Soviet Foreign Ministry.[151]

The Soviets who happened to be living in Leopoldville in those days felt threatened. Valeriy Subbotin, a research fellow of the Institute for African Studies of the USSR's Academy of Sciences, described this mood of anxiety:

> Lumumba's position is precarious, President Kasavubu keeps silence, but the ministers with whom we meet, including an energetic Gizenga, say that things will be straightened out. The city's newspapers, which seem to be directed by the Belgians, blame ultranationalists and Moscow's henchmen for the economic mess and unemployment. There is a habitual caricature in the newspaper: a python with the inscription "USSR" stifles a wretched African. . . . We sit in a bar, with the radio playing, tuned by a Belgian barkeeper to Radio-Brazzaville, which explains that Russia is responsible for all the troubles, and that there are Russian agents, undercover and overt, all round. Opposite us at the table, two Belgians nod their heads knowingly.[152]

It became obvious that Kasavubu did not enjoy popularity and support to counterbalance Lumumba. On September 12, Kasavubu ordered Lumumba's arrest, and he was arrested, but he was shortly thereafter released at the request of the soldiers guarding him. On September 13, a joint session of the Parliament voted 88 to 25 to grant Lumumba "special powers" to oppose Kasavubu's efforts to overthrow his regime.[153]

Mobutu's Coup

This was a deadlock, but it did not last long, for the third force had stepped out of the shade to change the situation radically. "U.S. officials," Madeleine Kalb notes, realized that Kasavubu's dramatic dismissal of Lumumba was only the first step toward the elimination of Soviet influence in the Congo and that Lumumba could not be counted out just yet."[154] It was decided to replace the cautious and ambitious Kasavubu with a strongman. The ANC's chief of staff, Colonel Joseph Mobutu, was chosen for this role because the CIA believed he had the requisite leadership qualities.

Lawrence Devlin recalled that on the night of September 13, 1960, he was invited to the Presidential Palace, where he had a confidential meeting with Mobutu. The colonel had touched the most sensitive issue for a CIA officer by saying that "the Soviets are pouring into the country" and that the Congolese "didn't fight for independence to have another country to recolonize" them. Mobutu showed Devlin the books and pamphlets he said "the Soviets were handing out to the troops." Most of them were in English, and this "defeated the Soviet objective to influence the thinking of the Congolese soldiers, since they hardly spoke broken French, let alone English." Lumumba, Mobutu continued, refused to prevent "Soviet efforts to penetrate the army." He declared: "Here is the situation: The army is prepared to overthrow Lumumba, but only on the condition that the United States will recognize the government that would replace Lumumba's." Devlin hesitated, for he did not have the authority to guarantee the United States' support for a coup d'état, nor its recognition of a new Congolese government; as he recalled, "although I did not believe that [Lumumba] was either a Communist or a Soviet agent, I was convinced that he was being manipulated by the Soviets and that he would, sooner rather than later, fall under their control." Devlin assured Mobutu that the United States would recognize "a temporary government composed of civilian technocrats." He also promised Mobutu $5,000 to provide for Mobutu's "senior officers," and that he "would be available and arrange to meet him in his office early that morning."[155]

On September 14, Mobutu declared on the National Radio that he was assuming power and "neutralizing the head of state, and the two rival governments now in office, as well as both houses of the Parliament until December 31, 1960."[156] Mobutu acted decisively. His troops dispersed an attempted Senate meeting on September 15 and occupied the Parliament the following day. Lumumba was arrested, and only the involvement of Ghanaian troops from ONUC saved him from lynching by soldiers from the Kasai Baluba, who had been decimated by the central government's forces. He retreated to the shelter of his home, guarded by the UN troops, and was put under house arrest.[157]

Mobutu managed to slow down the offensive of the central government's troops in Kasai and Katanga. On September 18, he ordered that it be stopped. Agitators were sent to the soldiers, who were promised that their wages would be paid if they retreated. Hammarskjöld had released

$1 million to pay the troops, and money for Mobutu was also forthcoming from Brussels.[158] Having become exhausted from battles and poor supplies, the soldiers agreed. At the end of September, they were paid and ferried by UN planes to their garrisons. On October 17, the UN put the finishing touch on the operation with an agreement with Tshombe whereby neutral zones would be established in northern Katanga, within which only the UN Blue Berets could operate.

At his first press conference after the coup, Mobutu announced the severance of diplomatic relations between the Congo and the USSR and ordered all Soviet Bloc diplomats, technicians, and other personnel to leave the Congo within 48 hours. The Soviet ambassador, Yakovlev, made several attempts to call on Kasavubu, but he was brusquely rebuffed. On the evening of September 15, Yakovlev visited Hammarskjöld's newly appointed representative, Rajeshwar Dayal, an Indian. Dayal writes in his memoirs that he "expressed shock at the discourteous treatment of the envoy of a great country and asked the Ambassador if I should try to intercede on his behalf, at least to allow him a little more time to make his preparations. But the Ambassador had made up his mind, and I subsequently learned that all day long smoke had been billowing from the Embassy chimney as documents were being destroyed."

Yakovlev asked for the UN's assistance in allowing two Soviet planes to land at Ndjili Airport to fly Soviet and Czechoslovakian citizens home. Dayal "readily agreed." The ambassador's request for a plane to evacuate Soviet personnel from Stanleyville was also granted. Dayal, in return, "asked about the medicines and other stores and pressed that they be left behind as a humanitarian act since the United Nations was in very short supply." Yakovlev had no objection, and "the crates came in very handy subsequently as many were found to contain considerable quantities of vodka, which proved to be a blessing to our hard-pressed Ethiopian troops in Stanleyville."[159]

On September 17, the Soviet and Czechoslovakian embassies were closed down, and all Soviet Bloc personnel left the Congo. The night before, Nazhestkin recollects, in the embassy, surrounded by the Mobutu's troops, "all night long we were burning documents. Yakovlev was calm and active; he did not show any signs of perplexity. The personnel shared the ambassador's mood; everybody was preparing for the evacuation in an orderly way. Finally, the Soviet flag was hauled down and we got into our cars. The gate was thrown open, and the soldiers made a lane for the motorcade, which started for the airport."[160]

The country to which the Soviets had been sent to help overcome its

117

colonial legacy and maintain national sovereignty had turned out to be inhospitable and alien. They had often found themselves in situations beyond their understanding and encountered unexpected hazards. Yakovlev seemed to have expressed the general mood of his countrymen in the Congo when he privately asked Dayal if he knew "what was going on in the country." Dayal turned the question back on the ambassador and "said he was extremely puzzled."[161]

Equally puzzled was Yakovlev himself when Congolese soldiers with fixed bayonets dashed inside the Stanley Palace Hotel and seized him as a "Communist spy." He shared good company with two other "spies" that had just been caught—Ralph Bunche and the Israeli ambassador to the Congo. Devlin, who watched the soldiers emerging from the hotel with their prisoners, described the scene ironically:

> Bunche and the Israeli knew that discretion was the better part of valor and promptly obeyed the order to get into the back of the army truck. The Soviet ambassador, who had yet to appreciate the value of that stratagem, remonstrated loudly in English. He proclaimed that he was the ambassador of the USSR sent to help the poor, downtrodden, oppressed Congolese masses. Unfortunately, he did not speak French or any African language, and the Congolese soldiers did not understand English. He refused to climb into the truck. Without further ado, the soldiers stepped forward, grabbed him, and tossed him into the vehicle as casually as if he had been a sack of Soviet wheat.[162]

Soviet doctors and specialists sent on a mission of mercy to the Congo's Orientale Province as part of bilateral aid were puzzled. Some of them were beaten by the Congolese because they were dressed in shorts, Belgian colonial style, "thus making themselves indistinguishable from the detested Flemish."[163]

On September 20, Soviet planes, delivered to the Lumumba government, landed in Cairo on their way back to Moscow. The Soviet trucks were left in the Congo and fell into the hands of Mobutu's army and police. They were sometimes used in a way that Soviet officials could not imagine even in their nightmares—for repressions against Lumumba's supporters. When in Moscow, participating in the World Trade Unions Congress in January 1962, Edward Mutombo, general secretary of the Congolese Working People's Union, told his Russian interlocutor that "Congolese revolutionaries were being driven away to be shot" in Soviet trucks. Mutombo himself was arrested and hauled to a police station in a Soviet truck.[164]

Khrushchev learned about Mobutu's coup while crossing the Atlantic Ocean onboard the *Baltika*, making his way to New York to participate in the Fifteenth Session of the UN General Assembly. According to his speechwriter, Oleg Grinevskyi, he closely followed events in the Congo and labored intensively over policy with his assistants while sailing across the Atlantic. He was disappointed on hearing the stream of bad news from Leopoldville. "American imperialists," he said, "are, of course, at the head of the plot against Congolese people and their chief Lumumba. Taking the advantage of 'Ham's' [a derogatory shortening of Hammarskjöld; in Russian, *ham* means boor] weakness, the Americans managed to make the UN command work for their purpose. And now the Secretary-General retreats and watches with tender emotion the final act of the Congolese tragedy developing. The Congo is slipping through our fingers, but we must not condone it." With his hands tied inside the Congo, Khrushchev's only opportunity to influence the situation was to mount an offensive in the international arena. He chose Hammarskjöld as his main target. "I spit upon the UN," Khrushchev cried in anger. "It is not our organization. And the poor fish Ham is sticking his nose in important affairs that are none of his business. He has seized authority that doesn't belong to him. He must pay for that. We'll really make it hot for him."[165]

The recent events at the United Nations had not favored putting Khrushchev's intentions into effect. The Security Council discussed the Congolese issue from September 9 to 17. On September 15, two conflicting resolutions were introduced. The U.S. resolution expressed confidence in the secretary-general, urged contributions to a UN fund for the Congo to be controlled by Hammarskjöld, and asked states to "refrain from any action which might tend to impede the restoration of law and order," a clause that would have broadened considerably the possible scope of Hammarskjöld's action against the Soviet Union.[166] The Soviet resolution proposed that Hammarskjöld and the UN command "put an end to all forms of interference in the internal affairs of the . . . Congo" and withdraw its guards from airports and radio stations. It demanded dismissal of the UN command for "gross violation" of council orders and appealed for donations of economic aid directly to the Congolese government.[167] Neither draft resolution received the necessary support.

Ceylon and Tunisia, which had sponsored the three earlier Security Council resolutions, came up with a third draft resolution. But this time it was not the result of compromise and was close to the U.S. proposal. In particular, it called "upon all states to refrain from the direct or indirect provision of arms or other materials of war and military personnel and other assistance for military purposes in the Congo during the temporary period of military assistance through the United Nations, except upon the request of the United Nations through the Secretary-General."[168] It was a vote of confidence in Hammarskjöld and of disagreement with the concept of supplying bilateral aid to the Lumumba government.

The newly appointed Soviet representative to the UN, Valerian Zorin, tried to play on African fears that the UN, if given an exclusive role, might end up taking the Congo under trusteeship, which was associated in Africans' minds with colonial times. "The representatives of Ceylon and later the representative of Tunisia themselves," he declared, "stated that we have no right to deprive the government of military assistance. They also said that that such assistance should, according to the proposal, be provided exclusively through United Nations channels, but this is precisely a violation of a basic principle of the United Nations, the principle of sovereign rights of all states. This would mean the imposition of a United Nations trusteeship on the Republic of the Congo."[169] Zorin was not a success. Soviet amendments to the draft were rejected, and on September 16 the USSR vetoed it.

This was the first Soviet veto of a resolution concerning the Congo that was backed by the Afro-Asian Bloc in the United Nations. The U.S. representative, James Wadsworth, proposed an emergency session of the General Assembly. Over Zorin's protest that it was illegal to call a special session without Soviet approval, the council voted 8 to 2 (the 2 being the USSR and Poland), with France abstaining, to summon a new forum on September 17 to 20.[170] On September 19, the Ghanaian representative, Alex Quaison-Sackey, speaking for sixteen Asian and African nations, introduced a draft resolution that followed the lines of the vetoed Tunisian-Ceylonese draft, including the provisions opposed by Zorin; it requested that the secretary-general "continue to take vigorous action" to carry out the Security Council's resolutions on the Congo, appealed "for urgent voluntary contributions to a United Nations Fund for the Congo," and called upon all states to refrain from sending arms or military personnel into the Congo except through the United Nations.[171] The following day, the Afro-Asian resolution was adopted 70 to 0, with 11 abstentions, the Soviet Bloc among them. At the behest of the United States, the key section calling for cessation of all outside military aid to the Congo was put to a separate vote. The USSR voted in favor.[172]

Khrushchev Drops a Bombshell at the UN General Assembly

The Soviet attack on Hammarskjöld at the United Nations had backfired, convincing the Afro-Asian Bloc of states to rally support for the secretary-general. When, on September 19, 1960, Khrushchev's ship docked in New York, he discovered that he had been outmaneuvered not only in the Congo but also at the General Assembly. "One of his chief reasons for coming to New York," Madeleine Kalb notes, "was to court the new African heads of state and to start building a socialist-neutralist alliance which would form a numerical majority in the Assembly. Now it seemed that the combination of a Soviet veto in the Security Council and a Soviet abstention in the General Assembly—on two major Afro-Asian initiatives dealing with the Congo crisis—had isolated him from the very people he was trying to reach."[173] Though this did not bowl Khrushchev over, his prestige was at stake. The Fifteenth General Assembly session was a grandiloquent meeting. Khrushchev had proposed that the leaders of the world's nations come to New York, and more than half had agreed. He was eager to establish himself as the chief defender of Afro-Asian interests in the struggle against colonialism.

In his first speech to the General Assembly on September 23, Khrushchev, with characteristic bravado, refused to admit that the Soviet Union had suffered a defeat in the Congo, calling such assertions "absurd." He claimed that "we have suffered no set-back in the Congo, nor was any set-back possible, since there neither were nor could not have been any of our troops in the Congo, nor any interference by us in that country's domestic affairs." The countries which "style themselves the 'free world,'" he said, "are celebrating too soon, "because theirs is a Pyrrhic victory." He then fiercely attacked Hammarskjöld for his position on the Congolese crisis:

> When the colonialists realized that the Government of the Republic of the Congo, which had been legally elected and had received a vote of confidence from Parliament, had firmly embarked on an independent policy and was resolved to be guided solely by the interests of the Congolese people, they immediately resorted to every possible means of overthrowing that Government. They set out to secure the establishment of a puppet government, a government which, though ostensibly "independent," would in fact carry out the wishes of the colonialists. . . . It is deplorable that they have been doing their dirty work in the Congo through the Secretary-General of the United

121

Nations and his staff. That is a disgraceful state of affairs. . . . The Assembly should administer a rebuff to the colonialists and their followers; it should call Mr. Hammarskjöld to order and ensure that he does not misuse the position of Secretary-General.[174]

Khrushchev now not only "made it hot" for "Ham" but also launched a full-scale assault on the office of the secretary-general per se. The Soviet government, he continued, "has come to a definite conclusion" that "the post of Secretary-General, who alone directs the staff and alone interprets and executes the decisions of the Security Council and the sessions of the General Assembly, should be abolished." So the Soviet leader proposed replacing the office of the secretary-general with "a collective executive organ of the United Nations consisting of three persons"—a troika "invested with the highest trust of the United Nations" and representing "members of the military blocs of the Western powers, socialist states and neutralist countries."[175] This bombshell proposal stunned most of the delegates with its vehemence and far-reaching nature. But it was well crafted to appeal to the delegates from the Afro-Asian Bloc of states, whose support presumably could be gained if they were offered a greater say in top UN Security Council affairs.

Hammarskjöld did his best to persuasively explain his conception of the office of the secretary-general to the leaders of the neutral nations gathered in New York. On September 26, not referring directly to Khrushchev's troika proposal, he said:

The General Assembly is facing a question not of any specific actions but of principles guiding United Nations activities. In those respects it is a question not of a man but of an institution. . . . Use whatever words you like—independence, impartiality, objectivity—they all describe essential aspects of what, without exception, may be the attitude of the Secretary-General. Such an attitude . . . may at any stage become an obstacle for those who work for certain political aims which would be better served or more easily achieved if the Secretary-General compromised with this attitude. But if he did, how gravely he would then betray the trust of all those for whom the strict maintenance of such an attitude is their best protection in the world for power and influence.[176]

Hammarskjöld received a thunderous ovation from the assembly.

Khrushchev replied on October 3 with another attack on the secretary-general, this time biting and personal:

The responsibility for interpreting and executing all the decisions of the General Assembly and the Security Council at present falls upon one man. But there is an old saying that there are not, and never were, any saints on earth. . . . Mr. Hammarskjöld has always been prejudiced in his attitude toward the socialist countries; he has always upheld the interests of the United States and other monopoly-capitalist countries. The events in the Congo (Leopoldville), where he played a simply deplorable role, were the last drop which filled the cup of our patience to overflowing. . . . In order to prevent any misinterpretation, I should like to repeat we do not place confidence in Mr. Hammarskjöld. If he himself cannot muster the courage to resign in, let us say, a chivalrous way, we shall draw the inevitable conclusion from the situation. There is no room for a man who has violated the elementary principles of justice in such an important post as that of Secretary-General.[177]

Hammarskjöld did not offer excuses, but he ably played on sensitive strings for neutral states:

By resigning, I would, therefore, at the present difficult and dangerous juncture, throw the Organization to the winds. I have no right to do so because I have a responsibility to all those member states for which the organization is of decisive importance, a responsibility which over-rides all other considerations. It is not the Soviet Union or indeed any other big Powers which need the United Nations for their protection. It is all the others. In this sense, the Organization and I deeply believe in the wisdom with which they will be able to use and guide it. I shall remain in my post during the term of office as a servant of Organization in the interest of all those other nations as long as they wish me to do so.[178]

This compelling statement again brought the assembly, except for the delegates from the Soviet Bloc, to their feet in a standing ovation that lasted for several minutes.

Khrushchev left for Moscow on October 13, not waiting for a decision on the Congo. It was obvious that his plan to gain a majority in the UN by enlisting the Afro-Asian Bloc's backing for his policy toward the Congo had been frustrated. It had been based on the miscalculation "that Hammarskjöld's policy toward the Lumumba government was so outrageous that the Africans would feel obliged to support Moscow's strong personal attacks on the Secretary-General."[179] A considerable number of Afro-Asian states were displeased with certain aspects of Hammarskjöld's Congo policy, but they all still considered the UN the strongest bulwark against any attack on their sovereignty that might have prevented the Cold War from penetrating Africa. And Khrushchev's troika proposal, advertised by Soviet propagandists as the way to "reform" the United Nations, would inevitably destroy the UN's usefulness. So the emerging states did not support the troika proposal—the "three-headed god," as Jawaharlal Nehru, the Indian prime minister, called it—considering it to be nothing more than diplomatic maneuvering and propaganda.

The Neutralization of Lumumba

Events in the Congo also did not move to the Soviet Union's advantage. Lumumba had been sidelined and isolated in the prime minister's residence, surrounded by UN troops, which protected him against arrest by Mobutu's forces. The UN guards were in turn surrounded by a ring of ANC soldiers trying to prevent Lumumba from leaving the house. The U.S. administration still considered Lumumba very dangerous and remained concerned that he might find a way to return to power. As the CIA director, Allen Dulles, cabled to Lawrence Devlin on September 24, 1960, "We wish to give every possible support in eliminating Lumumba from every possibility of resuming governmental position or if he fails in Leo[poldville], setting himself up in Stanleyville or elsewhere."[180]

Mobutu had been hanging onto power and had progressively consolidated it. He appointed an interim body, the College of High Commissioners, to administer the government.[181] It was headed by Justin Bomboko and consisted mainly of young Congolese students and graduates. However, the real authority was the so-called Binza Group, named for the hilly district in the suburbs of Leopoldville where most of its members lived. Devlin, who supervised the group's activities, recalls that it had its own troika—the core (Mobutu, Bomboko, and Victor Nendaka, the head of the Sûreté, the semiautonomous state security agency), with "other influential individuals also involved," later including the prime minister, Cyrille Adoula. The Binza Group "operated in many ways, sometimes as a pressure group and sometimes individually," and "no major political decisions were taken without its approval." It was far more influential than President Kasavubu, being the unofficial "power behind the presidency."[182] A secret CIA document called the Congolese central government "the Mobutu military dictatorship working through the Council of Commissioners."[183]

On September 29, Kasavubu formally turned over all "executive and administrative authority" to the College of High Commissioners.[184] But it was an unconstitutional body, and the Mobutu government's lack of legality remained an acute problem. Devlin recalled that Hammarskjöld's representative, Rajeshwar Dayal, "refused to accept commissioners as the legal government of the Congo and he refused to take many, if any, of the Congolese players seriously. Despite his extremely limited experience in the Congo—less than one month—Dayal argued that the political impasse could not be solved without Lumumba. Our view was the direct opposite: the crisis could not be resolved *with* Lumumba actively involved because he was the main obstacle to a solution."[185] Without Lumumba being neutralized, it was impossible to establish a legal government that could obtain parliamentary approval. Timberlake lamented: "Lumumba is the central problem. There is always the danger that no matter how firm the opposition lines up, Lumumba's oratory plus threats can turn it [a parliamentary session] into a victory for himself."[186]

The CIA launched an assassination plot against Lumumba as the most workable solution. Its operatives developed several schemes of clandestine operations.[187] In his memoirs, Devlin recounted previously publicly unknown details about "a specific, highly sensitive operation" that he was directed to plan and implement. At the end of September 1960, "Joe from Paris," a senior CIA officer and "a highly respected chemist," had delivered to Leopoldville "deadly poisons to assassinate Lumumba." "Joe" handed them to Devlin, who was to do the job, and informed him that the operation was authorized by President Eisenhower. "Joe" also made it clear that the details were up to Devlin, who could choose other methods of assassination, "providing it was not traceable to the U.S. government."

Devlin was shocked. He believed that "it was morally wrong for me or anyone under my orders to kill Lumumba, an act that I could not justify by any argument or rationalization." He was convinced that "the Congolese would solve the Lumumba problem themselves" by less drastic methods. But he kept it to himself, knowing that the refusal "would mean my immediate recall and replacement by a more compliant officer, in effect, the end of my career." It was hard to locate a non-American agent with the access to Lumumba's kitchen and living quarters. The primary obstacle was the protection provided for the legitimate prime minister by the United Nations. Devlin's plan was "to stall, to delay as long as possible in the hope that Lumumba would either fade away politically as a potential danger, or that the Congolese would succeed in taking him prisoner."[188] Devlin's calculation turned out to be correct.

Lumumba seemed to be at a loss. At first, he threatened to use force against the UN troops in the Congo, then repeatedly appealed to the UN with requests to recognize his government as the only legitimate one in the Congo. All his appeals were ignored. Now he was going to leave for Stanleyville, his political and tribal base; then he clamored for a plane to fly to New York to address the UN General Assembly. His mind was distracted by grief. His daughter had died from tuberculosis in Switzerland. The coffin containing her body arrived in Leopoldville, and custom required burying the girl at the place where she was born. Lumumba asked for a UN plane so he could take the coffin to Stanleyville for burial, but his request was denied.[189] The last straw for him was the General Assembly voting on November 22 to seat the Kasavubu delegation in the UN rather than the envoys sent to UN headquarters by Lumumba. The Soviet Bloc and a number of countries belonging to the Afro-Asian Bloc opposed this decision, which implied the UN's recognition of the Mobutu-Kasavubu regime.[190] The vote had definitely cut off all chance of Lumumba's returning to power by legal means; retaking the capital from Stanleyville, his stronghold, had become the only realistic option.

On the night of November 27, during a tremendous thunderstorm, Lumumba evaded cordons of Congolese and UN troops guarding his Leopoldville home and drove away with a few friends in the direction of Stanleyville, 800 miles to the east. He did not act like a fugitive, making stops along the way to rally his supporters. No wonder he was captured by Mobutu's forces, which had been provided with planes and helicopters by the U.S. Embassy, and the ONUC command was sent to search for him. He was arrested, beaten, and transported to the prison at Camp Hardy in Thysville. Without UN protection, his life was in danger.

On December 5, the Soviet government issued a statement demanding Lumumba's release, calling for an immediate meeting of the Security Council, and accusing Hammarskjöld "of playing the role of the colonizers' lackey."[191] The Security Council was called into session on December 7. The Soviet representative to the UN, Valerian Zorin, put forward a draft requesting the release of "the prime minister of the Republic of Congo, Patrice Lumumba," his restoration to power, and the disarming of "the terrorist bands of Mobutu."[192] A Western draft reaffirmed the UN's support

$1 was exchanged for 450 Guinean francs on the black market, although the official exchange rate was $1 to 246 Guinean francs.[209]

This situation was exacerbated by the reform of domestic trade. The Bureau of Home Trade, created by the government's decree, tried to control all trade operations, including goods receipts in the port, warehousing, the execution of documentation, and the distribution of goods to state-owned and private retail outlets. This system created favorable conditions for profiteering and a famine of goods. The French historian Jean Suret-Canale, who answered the call of Touré "to save the Guinean revolution" and arrived in Guinea in 1959, found its state-owned shops quite ineffective: "Too often these shops were empty or furnished poorly. There were a lot of nontraded commodities while fast-moving goods disappeared and were smuggled to neighboring countries and sold there at excessive prices. Many state-owned shops derived revenue that could hardly cover paying small salary to a shop assistant. Incompetence of personnel (many shop assistants could not make elementary calculations) and widespread corruption brought state trading to the edge of financial catastrophe."[210]

In the spring of 1960, Guinea faced a food crisis. Rice, the staple food of most of the country's population, was unobtainable, and edible oil, wheat flour, and meat were in severely short supply. There were long waiting lines, and people fought for the few supplies available. In some places, the police had to be summoned to prevent violence.[211]

In March 1960, the Guinean director of foreign commerce, Framoï Bérété, inquired about obtaining flour in the United States. But by April, when the U.S. government gave its suggestions, the Guinean side had lost interest, having found at least another partial solution to its food crisis. For, also in April, a ship containing 2,500 tons of rice had arrived from Odessa and a shipload of potatoes had arrived from "an eastern European port." In May, the Guinean government announced that the People's Republic of China had made a gift of 10,000 tons of rice "as a token of the friendship between the people of China and the people of Guinea."[212]

During his second visit to the USSR (September 6–8, 1960), the Guinean president tried to convince the Soviet leaders that Guinea still held the "vanguard role" in Africa and therefore deserved additional assistance. Speaking in the Kremlin on September 7, he stressed that "ridiculous agreements" had been imposed on "approximately fifteen" African countries, allowing the former colonial powers to exercise complete control over all important spheres, including foreign policy. In these circumstances, Touré continued, it was very important for the socialist bloc to grant aid to a country that "truly fights for its economic, political and cultural liberation." If this aid was delayed, he warned, neocolonialists "would settle in Africa again, but this bout under new masks."[213]

Although the officials in the Kremlin did not share Touré's opinion that almost all newly independent states were "puppet regimes," they did consider Guinea the Soviet African favorite, and therefore they felt it should be given aid regardless of economic expediency. So the Soviet-Guinean protocol signed September 8 became the real lifeboat for the Guinean economy. The Soviet government added 86 million rubles to its credit of 160 million rubles provided earlier.[214] Overall, credits from socialist countries, mainly the USSR, were the main financial source for Guinea's three-year development plan; internal savings provided only 15 to 20 percent of the money needed.[215] A Soviet-Guinean trade agreement, signed September 7, allowed a disparity in mutual trade in Guinea's favor.[216] By July 1960, the Soviet Union had sold to Guinea commodities valued at 22 million rubles and bought Guinean commodities worth 10.5 million.[217]

The Guinean economy depended completely on aid from socialist countries, but Touré secretly sought new donors. When the Liberian president, William Tubman, paid a state visit to Guinea in May 1960, Touré told him that "Guinea had not been overly pleased with the aid it had received from the Soviet Bloc," and "he had become distressed at the devious way in which the bloc appeared to conduct its affairs." Therefore, "he did not know how long Guinea would be able to accept" this aid.[218] Touré was sure that Tubman would inform the Americans of this conversation. It was a part of Touré's big game around the building of the Konkouré Dam and power station. He wanted the Americans, not the Russians, to finance and implement this key project.

Touré's Game around the Konkouré Dam
Guinea had the richest and the most extensive bauxite deposits in the world, along with the world's largest and most modern plant for producing aluminum at Fria. The Konkouré Dam was planned to provide energy for mining new deposits and producing aluminum. At a discussion of the situation in Guinea held at the Department of State in Washington on April 23, 1960, Stanley Osborne, the president of Olin Mathieson Chemical Corporation, declared: "If this plum should fall into Russian hands, they could deliver aluminum to the rest of the world at a profit for ten cents a pound cheaper than the West could possibly afford."[219] The U.S. ambassador in Conakry, John Morrow, wrote to the Department of State about

the Konkouré Dam: "If the Soviets take over the project, they will greatly facilitate consolidating and completing their penetration and control."[220]

In a letter dated July 19, Touré asked President Eisenhower to allocate money for the construction of the Konkouré Dam: "We appealed to friendly powers that sincerely desire to help us achieve rapid progress on the African Continent and a better future for mankind."[221] This was a hint that Guinea had approached the USSR with an analogous appeal. In his letter of reply, Eisenhower assured Touré that "the United States Government is prepared to undertake immediately a study to bring up to date the survey of the dam as an essential first step in approaching this project."[222] Guinea handed over to the United States the original survey for the Konkouré Dam project done by the French, but Eisenhower wanted to "update" it—a time-consuming process that did not involve commitments to construct the dam.

On October 6, Touré informed the U.S. assistant secretary of state, Joseph Satterthwaite, that the USSR had offered Guinea a long-term loan to finance the construction of the Konkouré Dam and was prepared to send all the technicians and equipment necessary to begin work on January 1, 1961. Guinea was ready to accept the Soviet offer, but Touré wanted the United States to construct the dam. "If the United States should make an offer now equivalent to that of the Soviets', however, there would be no question that Guinea would accept the U.S. offer instead," he said. Satterthwaite indicated that "the Guineans might find they had committed themselves too heavily to the Soviets and were no longer in a position to choose who would or would not participate in projects in Guinea."[223] The American side did not make any new proposals about the dam. Refusing to succumb to Touré's blackmail with the "Russian threat," they believed that building the dam would serve their interests, if "the political atmosphere in Guinea were to change rather substantially."[224]

The USSR Ignores Danger Signals
Changes in Guinea that were favorable for the United States began to unfold in the spring of 1960. In April, Guinea's three-year development plan was revised to "smooth the revolutionary sharpness of political formulations" and "delete all socialist statements."[225]

New trends also began to appear in foreign policy. The Soviet newspaper *Izvestiya* published information that on March 9, 1960, the Guinean ambassador to the USSR, Seydou Conté, paid a visit to the East German leader, Walter Ulbrecht.[226] On March 15, the U.S. Embassy in Moscow reported to the Department of State that Conté told the Canadian ambassador that he "had presented his credentials to the East German regime and that he was also the Ambassador to the [German Democratic Republic, East Germany]."[227] West Germany recalled its ambassador from Conakry, threatening to break off diplomatic relations if official relations were established between Guinea and East Germany. Before leaving for Bonn, the West German ambassador, Herbert Schröder, was assured by Morrow that the latter "would call unofficially on the Guinean Government to urge that every possible step be made to clear up this misunderstanding." One conversation between Morrow and acting president Abdurrahman Diallo, who was the minister of state (Touré was away from Conakry), was enough. In the short run, the Guinean ambassador to France informed the West German government that the East German Trade Mission in Conakry would not be raised to the status of an embassy.[228]

The Western media created the image of Guinea as a country where the Soviet Bloc ideologically dominated, conducting intensive brainwashing. The West German journalist Fritz Schatten saw significant evidence "of large-scale [Communist] political and propagandist infiltration":

> Officials of the Soviet Bloc countries delivered lectures in the State schools on DIAMAT [the Communist acronym for "dialectical materialism"], and on the principles and practice of current Soviet policy in Africa. Instructors of the Communist-dominated World Federation of Trade Unions [WFTU] were active in the so-called trade-union university of Conakry and at the trade-union school in Dalaba. . . . The bookshops and the book depots run by the Youth League and the [Parti Démocratique de Guinée] were becoming centres for the distribution of vast quantities of Communist literature. The works of Mao Tse-tung, Khrushchev's speeches, the works of Lenin, and the "classics of socialist realism" were all to be had at low prices, and often free. In the same way the *World Communist Review*, *Humanité*, and various periodicals and publications of the WFTU were easily obtainable. The formulae and slogans of Communist agitation were becoming more and more strongly impressed on public opinion in Guinea.[229]

Archival documents reveal a somewhat different picture, however. The first secretary of the Soviet Embassy, V. I. Ivanisov, who toured remote places of Guinea in November 1959, found out that the majority of Guin-

Soviet Embassy arrived in Accra. This brought the number of personnel beyond their legal limit (eighteen persons)—as the Ghanaian Foreign Ministry reminded the Soviet ambassador. But the Soviets did not reduce the size of their staff, which suggests that Nkrumah supported them.[241]

On April 30, in the midst of U.S.-Ghanaian negotiations on the Volta River Project, the first Ghanaian official delegation, comprising members of Parliament and Cabinet officials, arrived in the USSR. It was led by Kojo Botsio, chairman of the Parliament and minister of the economy. The main purpose of his mission was concealed. Shortly before the delegation left Accra for Moscow, Nkrumah hinted at the subject, talking with Mirzo Rakhmatov, the head of the Soviet delegation participating in the celebration of Togolese independence. Nkrumah said that the delegation that was to arrive in Moscow was "more economic than parliamentary" and that Botsio was carrying Nkrumah's personal letter to Khrushchev. Botsio asked the Soviet ambassador in Ghana if he and Ambassador Elliot could find an opportunity to have a confidential talk with Khrushchev.[242]

The veil of secrecy was so dense that Nkrumah did not trust his plans to paper. In his letter to Khrushchev, Nkrumah confirmed Botsio's "full powers to discuss some substantial matters" and stressed that he "enjoys his confidence."[243]

On May 5, during negotiations at the Ministry of Overseas Trade, Botsio submitted to Minister Nikolai Patolitchev the list of joint projects, with the construction of a hydroelectric power plant among them. Botsio said that "the Government of Ghana is interested in receiving Soviet economic and technical assistance" in building these projects and raised the question of Ghana receiving 100 million pounds credit. Botsio again insisted that the USSR should pay for Ghanaian cocoa "mainly in free currency."[244] As a matter of fact, he repeated the position that had hampered the signing of the Soviet-Ghanaian trade agreement in 1959.

The Soviet side "expressed benevolence on the establishment of economic and technical cooperation between the Soviet Union and Ghana" and suggested sending expert Soviet personnel to Ghana "for working out proposals and recommendations." Botsio was told that "the Soviet Government would be ready to give consideration to the question of credit as soon as Soviet organizations studied specific Ghanaian applications for assistance needed to implement certain projects." Purchases of Ghanaian cocoa were geared to concluding trade agreements "along the lines of agreements concluded by the Soviet Union with African countries, Guinea, Ethiopia, Sudan, Tunisia, and Morocco in particular."[245] These agreements stipulated payment for Soviet goods not only with traditional export goods but also with hard currency.

On May 6, Khrushchev received the Ghanaian delegation in the Kremlin. His protocol-observing meeting with all the delegates lasted about ten minutes. Then he had a more lengthy confidential talk with Botsio and Elliot, but its record remains classified.[246]

The Ghanaians publicly praised the Soviet reality, the USSR's policy, and Khrushchev personally. On May 5, they were guests at a session of the USSR Supreme Soviet, hung upon Khrushchev's every word while he was making his speech, and often applauded him. They enthusiastically welcomed the news of the abolition of taxes and the reduction of working hours in the USSR. The Ghanaians welcomed the news that an American high-altitude U-2 plane had been shot down over the Soviet Union and exclaimed: "That is it!" Members of the delegation told the Soviets who accompanied them that they admired Khrushchev's "great activity in strengthening peace the world over."[247]

In private talks, Botsio described Ghana's dismal prospects if it did not receive Soviet aid. On May 16, he asked to bring to the Soviet government's notice the following:

> There was much talk about socialism in Ghana, but there were no practical results. Staying in the Soviet Union convinced them that they had not had a clear idea about socialism yet. Thanks to their visit, they saw what advantages socialism had over the other systems. Now Ghana has a lot of enemies in connection with its fight for independence and presidential republic. On returning to Ghana, they will get down to implementing what they have seen in the USSR and the imperialists will press them, for the Ghanaian economy is totally dependent on the West. So we want the Soviet Government to believe that we have a settled intention to build socialism in Ghana and to grant economic and political aid without hesitation.[248]

This looked like a rather awkward attempt to bargain, to make a deal promoting the "socialist orientation in Ghana in exchange for Soviet aid." But no agreements were reached.

On August 3, 1960, the Ghanaian government's second delegation arrived in Moscow. It was led by Emmanuel Ayeh-Kumi, "roving ambassador and perhaps the richest Ghanaian of the time," and included Tawia Adamafio and John Tettegah, head of the Ghana Trade Union Council.[249]

The next day, a Soviet-Ghanaian agreement for economic and technical cooperation was signed in the Kremlin. The Soviet government assumed the obligation to give Ghana technical support in "geological exploration, in the construction of building materials producing plants, hydroelectric stations of medium capacity, edible fish industry plants, in establishing model state farms, in the construction industry and in other branches of economy." The agreement made provisions for sending Soviet experts to Ghana to explore the economic feasibility of specific objects to be constructed with Soviet assistance. And the dispute over the terms of the Soviet loan to Ghana had been solved in Ghana's favor. The substantial sum of 160 million golden rubles (i.e., rubles that were convertible as hard currency) was loaned at an interest rate of 2.5 percent a year, to be paid by Ghanaian export commodities "and/or pounds or any other hard currency." So, unlike the other developing countries, Ghana received the privilege to pay its debt mainly with export goods.[250]

Nkrumah trusted Adamafio to deliver his personal secret letter to Khrushchev. Knowing that "our mission would be a failure if by some act of carelessness the contents of the letter got into the hands of the West," Adamafio decided to carry it on his own person—which was prudent, because after the delegation's plane made an intermediate stop in London, his bag was misplaced and "arrived in Moscow three days later, no doubt, thoroughly screened!"[251]

Adamafio handed Nkrumah's letter to Khrushchev in the Crimea, where the Soviet leader was on vacation. Only two members of the delegation, Adamafio and Tettegah, along with Ambassador Elliot, arrived there to negotiate with Khrushchev. According to the Soviet press, they had a "cordial, long talk on the live issues in Soviet-Ghanaian relations and also on the recent situation in Africa. Both sides fully shared points of view on all the problems discussed."[252]

Much later, Adamafio and Tettegah revealed some of the details of these negotiations. "We had many useful discussions with Niki [sic]," Adamafio recounts, "and he offered to build the Akosombo Dam [on the Volta River] for us. He wrote back to Kwame, and Nkrumah was quite happy. From then on, our relations with the Eastern countries developed quite rapidly and resulted in the great tour of the whole of Eastern Europe in 1961."[253] Tettegah, in an interview with Thompson, confirmed that Khrushchev "promised them that if the West delayed the Volta River Project, he would build it for them, just as he was building Nasser's dam."[254]

Both sides decided to give to the world the text of the August 4 agreement by mutual arrangement. Nevertheless, a report about it reached the Western press prematurely. This was to Ghana's advantage. Khrushchev's

141

promise to build the dam and grant a considerable Soviet credit called to mind the fact that the ineptitude of American and British policy over the Aswan Dam in Egypt had played into Soviet hands. Nkrumah received strong arguments in negotiations over the Volta River Project with his Western partners. The calculated leak must have been orchestrated by the Ghanaians. The head of the Ghanaian chancery in Moscow, F. E. Boaten, was blamed for this, but the punishment was light. He was recalled to Accra and "nearly dismissed from the service."[255] News of the signing of the agreement appeared in the Soviet press on August 29, but without noting a firm date.[256] The Ghanaian Ministry of Information confirmed the news on August 31.

The Congo Crisis Pushes Ghana toward the East

The advent of the Congo crisis produced a fundamental change in Ghana's position in relation to the West—pushing it toward the East. Ghana and the USSR took similar positions on how the Congo crisis should be resolved and cooperated closely in supporting the Lumumba government (see the earlier part of this chapter).

Nkrumah's hopes that the Cold War could be kept out of the country by dispatching the Ghanaian contingent to the Congo as part of the UN's peacekeeping force were dashed. The Ghanaian troops in the Congo under the UN command were led by the British general H. T. Alexander, who had been appointed by Nkrumah as the chief of staff of Ghana's Armed Forces. He maintained that "there was in fact no occasion when they failed to obey United Nations' orders as opposed to the conflicting orders which may have been issued either by the resident Ghanaian ambassador or direct from Accra."[257] At a crucial moment of the coup against Lumumba on September 6, 1960, by Alexander's order, the Ghanaian troops prevented Lumumba's forces from taking over the radio station in Leopoldville.

The U.S. Embassy in Accra considered Nkrumah's policy in the Congo not a "drift toward the Soviets" but a reflection of Ghana's determination "to pursue more actively its policy of positive neutralism." In a telegram dated August 25, 1960, Ambassador William Flake recommended not trying "at every turn to thwart [Ghanaian] contact with Soviet Bloc" and "show Ghana by our deeds that we are truer friends than USSR."[258]

The Eisenhower administration followed this advice. On September 1, the Department of State dispatched to the Accra Embassy a telegram informing it that the United States was ready to provide Ghana with $30 million to implement the Volta project. The terms of the loan were usual: "a $20 million loan from the Development Loan Fund at 3.5 percent with a 30-year term and a $10 million loan from the Export-Import Bank at 5.75 percent with a 25-year term." When Flake let Nkrumah know about the loan, the president "was pleased" with the news. He had succeeded in borrowing money for his favorite project at last. Nkrumah said he had come to the U.S. government because it "is his first friend."[259]

An important problem of the rates for electric power that Ghana was to deliver to Valco remained unresolved. During the Fifteenth Session of the UN General Assembly, on September 22, Eisenhower and Nkrumah met in New York. Nkrumah thanked his interlocutor for "all the assistance he had given Ghana toward the realization of the Volta project" and said that the question of rates could be solved "with an additional loan of 10 million pounds." The reply was noncommittal. The Americans wanted to clarify Nkrumah's views on the Congo crisis before pouring additional money into the Volta project. Nkrumah said nothing that contradicted the official American position. He stressed that the problems of the Congo must be worked out through the UN and said he thought much of the UN secretary-general, Dag Hammarskjöld.[260]

Addressing the UN General Assembly the next day, Nkrumah touched on other aspects of the situation in the Congo. He criticized the command of the UN troops and supported Lumumba as the head of the legitimate government. He spoke of the failure of the UN to distinguish between legal and illegal authorities, which had led to the most "ludicrous results, embarrassing both the Ghanaian forces who were called upon to carry them out and the United Nations itself, which was exhibited in a ridiculous light. For instance, the very troops which Ghana sent to help the legitimate Lumumba Government at the request of Lumumba were employed by the United Nations in preventing Lumumba, the legitimate Prime Minister of the legal Government of the Congo Republic, from performing the most obvious functions of his office—for instance, using his own radio station."[261]

Nkrumah's speech at the UN was far from echoing the Soviet line. He did not approve of Khrushchev's plan to substitute a troika for the secretary-general (see above), saying that "it would be entirely wrong to blame either the Security Council or any senior officials of the United Nations for what has taken place." Nkrumah expressed his personal appreciation "on the way the Secretary-General has handled the most difficult task." The Ghanaian president again argued strongly in favor of the African states' role in solving the Congo problem:

I am sure that the independent African States will agree with me that the problem in the Congo is an acute African problem which can be solved by Africans only. I have on more than one occasion suggested that the United Nations should delegate its functions in the Congo to the Independent African States, especially those African States whose contribution in men and material make the United Nations effort in the Congo possible. The forces of these African States should be under a unified African Command with responsibility to the Security Council, under which the United Nations troops entered the Congo Republic.[262]

Nkrumah received an ovation from the delegates of the African countries and the Eastern Bloc, and Khrushchev "heatedly shook his hand."[263] But high U.S. circles appraised Nkrumah's speech otherwise. On September 24, the assistant secretary of state for African affairs, Joseph Satterthwaite, in a telephone conversation with the Ghanaian representative to the United Nations, Alexander Quasion-Sackey, expressed surprise at the contents of Nkrumah's speech. "I pointed out," the American diplomat reported to the Department of State,

that except for Nkrumah's personal praise of Secretary Hammarskjöld, it was difficult to find a word in the speech showing any understanding of the position of the West in the East/West conflict. Moreover, in Nkrumah's discussion of the Congo, no mention was made of the unilateral intervention of the Soviet Union outside United Nations channels involving the arrival of several hundred Soviet technicians. Certainly, therefore, the content of the Nkrumah and Khrushchev speeches and the display attached to the reception by the Eastern Bloc delegates of the Nkrumah speech gave us every reason to believe there had been collusion between the two.[264]

Nkrumah's performance at the UN session made a "most unfortunate impression" on the secretary of state, Christian Herter, who concluded that "by actions as well as words Nkrumah seemed determined to abet the Soviet cause."[265]

Khrushchev and Nkrumah met twice in New York, on September 25 and 29. The records of their talks remain classified. Reports in the Soviet press were short and of a general character. The available documents indirectly suggest that the contacts between the two leaders were fruitful and prepared the ground for further rapprochement. At the CC CPSU Presidium meeting on October 15, 1960, Khrushchev noted that "Nkrumah made a good impression. He said that there was no other way for Africa than the way of socialism."[266]

In the light of Ghana's apparent drift toward the East, the West grew alarmed at Nkrumah's willingness "to use subversion and Communist aid in pursuit of his [Pan-African] ambitions."[267] Herter cabled the U.S. Embassy in Accra on October 13, 1960:

> We do not wish to take action to encourage Nkrumah's role in Africa unless and until he shows greater signs of stability and that his actions are not furthering Soviet objectives in such matters as Congo and UN machinery. This does not mean, however, that our relations with Nkrumah or [the government of Ghana] should be any less cordial than before, and we hope frequent personal contact will make Nkrumah realize where his interests lie and make him aware he cannot indefinitely take one line in private with us as he did with the President and a completely opposite line in public as he did at [the General Assembly meeting].[268]

Two days after Nkrumah's return from New York, on October 7, 1960, Ambassador Flake directly explained to him what Ghana's position should be in the Cold War confrontation. He drew the president's attention to the inadmissibility of the situation when the ruling party's newspapers and certain influential officials "are in full cry against the evils of capitalism and economic exploitation by the imperialists, including the United States." Flake made clear that there was no point in relying on American investments against such an unfavorable background: "If he [Nkrumah] and his supporters did not want private enterprise to undertake the Volta or some other project for the purpose of making a profit, he should say so at this time and the American companies would go elsewhere; but if the President wanted the consortium to proceed under conditions mutually agreed upon, then it was the President's responsibility to stop some of his supporters from their campaign of hate against American and other 'economic imperialists.'" Nkrumah assured Flake that "private enterprises which if invited into Ghana would be fully protected by the Government of Ghana and hecklers silenced." The American diplomat expressed dissatisfaction with the fact that "the USSR and Chinese Communist embassies here are distributing publications containing anti-American material." Nkrumah declared that "he would not permit Ghana being used as a cockpit to fight the Cold War."[269]

The Soviet-U.S. Propaganda Contest

Nkrumah could not prevent the launching of a propaganda war in Ghana between the USSR and the United States. The work of the "dissemination of the truth" about the Soviet Union carried out by the Soviet Embassy in Accra was far from efficient. The embassy's film collection in 1960 consisted of a few old documentaries, and new items were delivered only on rare occasions. The embassy had to show the same films many times. There were no cinema vans, and films were shown only in cities with an electricity supply.[270]

Defying a formal ban, Soviet diplomats freely distributed literature to libraries, organizations, educational institutions, and citizens. The first secretary of the embassy, V. Studenov, noted that "almost every" visitor to the embassy asked for works by Marx and Lenin and for books on socialism.[271]

The leaders of the Convention People's Party also showed an interest in Marxist literature. The party's secretary for ideology, Kweku Akwei, when in Moscow from September to October 1960, informed I. Pomelov, the deputy chief editor of the journal *Communist*, that "the [party's] aim is to build a society based on socialist principles, and it lays stress upon training the cadres in socialist spirit." Akwei lamented that there were no "works by Lenin and Marxian schoolbooks on social science in English in his country" and expressed a wish to receive these books.[272] Pomelov informed the CC CPSU about this request, and it adopted a resolution that charged the State Committee for Cultural Relations with Foreign Countries (Gosudastvennyi komitet po kul'turnym svyazyam s zarubeznymi stranami) with "picking over the works by the greats of Marxism-Leninism, sociopolitical and imaginative literature."[273] Formally, the decree was implemented, but the needs of Ghanaian general readers were not met. It was difficult for them to comprehend *Das Kapital* and similar writings by the greats of Marxism-Leninism that made up the majority of the books sent to Ghana.[274]

The bulk of the printed materials sent from the Soviet Union for dissemination through the Ghanaian press could hardly attract the attention of local readers, who were bored by long articles about the economic achievements of the USSR, overloaded with data put in Russian units of measure (puds, the traditional Russian weight measure, equivalent to 16 kilograms; rubles; etc.). Materials on topics of primary interest in Ghana (Soviet youth, high school, the religious situation) were rare.[275]

In November 1960, the Telegraph Agency of the Soviet Union (Telegrafnoye Agentstvo Sovetskogo Soyuza, TASS) opened a bureau in Accra

European education and was a poet and philosopher who was proficient in the arts. Kéi'ta, a descendant of the last ruling dynasty of the Mali Empire, was an orthodox Muslim trained as a teacher.

The two leaderships maintained basically incompatible political views. Senghor's party, the Progressive Union, advocated preserving close ties with France and saw the union with Mali as a loose one based on confederative principles. Senghor's conception of African socialism allowed for the development of a market-based economy and multiparty system. Kéi'ta's party, the Sudanese Union, professed a more rigorous socialism with slogans advocating accelerated industrialization, planned economics, a one-party system, democratic centralism, and the like. Its platform was to carry out a nonaligned policy and establish full-fledged relations with the East.[293]

A one-party regime was established in Sudan. "There is a single political party, the Sudanese Union, in Sudan," Ivanisov wrote, "that is highly organized and exerts influence on the masses through youth and women's organizations and trade unions. There is no organized opposition in the country."[294]

From the first days of the Mali Federation's existence, conflict erupted between the leaders of Senegal and Sudan regarding the filling of key posts. This strife came to a head in the middle of August 1960, when the Sudanese proposed replacing Senghor as president of the Federal Assembly with a prominent Senegalese politician, Lamine Guèye, a native of Mali.

In the nighttime of August 19, Kéi'ta hastily called a meeting of the Council of Ministers and summoned the chief of the Senegalese gendarmerie, a French lieutenant colonel. Neither he nor the Senegalese ministers attended the meeting. Then Kéi'ta imposed a state of emergency and dismissed Senghor's supporter, Mamadou Dia, from the post of minister of defense. Kéi'ta also asked the French chief representative in Mali to put troops at his disposal in accordance with an agreement between the Mali Federation and France. The latter not only did not do so but immediately informed Senghor and Dia. The Senegalese gendarmerie arrested the chief of the General Staff, a Colonel Soumarou, Kéi'ta's henchman, and all the Sudanese politicians who happened to be in Dakar. On August 21, they were sent in a sealed carriage and escorted by gendarmes to Bamako, the capital of Sudan.[295]

After only two months of existence, the Mali Federation disintegrated. The Senegalese leaders interpreted Kéi'ta's actions as an attempt at a coup d'état. They declared Senegal's withdrawal from the federation and pro-

151

claimed its independence. On August 20, Mamadou Dia dispatched to "the president of the USSR Republic" a telegram that partly read: "In consequence of the plot against internal security of the state of Senegal, organized by the Chairman of the Mali Government and some federal ministers, the Legislative Assembly of Senegal in August 1960 abrogated the law that passed some powers to the Mali Federation. . . . The Federation has been dissolved and hereafter cannot act on behalf of Senegal. The Senegalese government hopes and wishes your country will recognize an independent Republic of Senegal."[296] On September 15, the CC CPSU Presidium decided "to leave an appeal without an answer before ascertaining the situation in the Mali Federation."[297]

This decision resulted from the position of the Sudanese leaders. They perceived the collapse of the federation as a personal humiliation, for which they blamed France, along with the Senegalese who followed its instructions. On returning from Dakar, Kéi'ta stated that he would maintain the federation and sever diplomatic relations with the countries that recognized Senegal.[298] His emissaries applied to the USSR through diplomatic channels. On September 4, a Sudanese goodwill mission headed by the chairman of the Parliament, M. Haidara, met with the Soviet and Czechoslovakian ambassadors. "The essence of the position of this group," Solod informed Moscow, "is to make maximal efforts to reestablish the Mali Federation, even retaining the existing relations with France, with further struggle for the liberation of Mali from French domination in mind. If the restoration of the Federation proves to be impossible, they are going to declare Sudan independent, to dismantle French military bases on Sudanese territory, and to enter into cooperation with Guinea and socialist countries, primarily with the Soviet Union."[299]

It did not take long to make sure that there were no chances for the restoration of the federation. On September 22, 1960, Sudan was proclaimed the independent Republic of Mali.[300] On October 5, the CC CPSU Presidium, at the suggestion of the MID, decided to recognize the Republic of Mali and the Republic of Senegal as independent states.[301] On October 8, Khrushchev dispatched telegrams to both Kéi'ta and Dia, informing them about the Soviet Union's readiness to establish diplomatic relations and exchange diplomatic missions.[302] In reply, Kéi'ta assured the Soviet leader that the Malian government "gladly" consented to this suggestion.[303] Diplomatic relations between the Soviet Union and Mali were established on December 14, 1960.

A special congress of the Sudanese Union on September 22, 1960, repudiated all obligations to France and the French Community, terminated all the agreements with them, condemned "imperialist wars against the national liberation movement," and recommended that the government recall all Malians from French military units deployed in Algeria and Cameroon. The congress set about pursuing three main tasks: to carry out economic decolonization, to create a new economic structure "within the framework of socialist planning based on African reality," and to establish effective state control over the economy by developing the public and cooperative sectors of the economy.[304]

The similarity of the decolonization processes in Mali and Guinea was obvious for contemporaries. It became commonplace to call Mali "another Guinea." However, archival documents show a more complicated picture.

Externally, the events in Mali resembled what happened in Guinea when it became independent. In a telegram, American observers described the situation in Mali as follows: "Strange atmosphere pervades Bamako. Strong leftist movement exists in GOM [the government of Mali]. Police methods adopted. Increasing GOM pressure to provoke French to get out. French Army forced out of Bamako 1 Oct., now concentrated at Kati (1,500 men). GOM requested France return all Mali personnel from French Algerian Forces. All French advisers to Mali constabulary, and police as well as Special French Intelligence forces removed."[305]

But France had no intention of imposing sanctions on Mali "to punish" it. On the contrary, the French attempted to avoid an exodus of their nationals, dealt gently with Mali, continued economic assistance, and made concessions to hold on.

The splitting up of the Mali Federation did not catch the U.S. administration unawares. Diplomats predicted the "Guineaization" of the situation and proposed measures to prevent it. Donald Dumont warned of a "'positive neutralist' trend in Mali's government (especially its Sudanese elements), which is worrisomely reminiscent of Guinean experience." He believed that the "West in general and the U.S. in particular must be alert to this trend and show enough imagination to be a few steps ahead of it to the extent that we preclude repetition of Guinean fiasco."[306]

When Senegal and Mali proclaimed their independence, the U.S. Embassy in Paris provided more detailed recommendations. The recognition of Senegal, the embassy noted, should not be "precipitate," in order not to look like "closely coordinated action by three major Western powers regarding Senegal that might weaken its international position rather than strengthen it." During the brief interim period between the collapse of the Mali Federation and the recognition of Senegal, the embassy suggested in a telegram to the secretary of state that the United States approach Kéi'ta and make these points:

> (A) US greatly regretting events that took place Dakar Aug 19–20 and their aftermath. (B) US continues [to] hope that independent African states will find ways of drawing together in closer association, in accordance with freely expressed will of peoples directly involved. We are opposed to "balkanization" of Africa. . . . (D) US has friendliest feelings toward Sudan people and government. We look forward to close relations with it and also wish particularly to play a part in assisting the Sudanese in their economic and social development. . . . (F) We recognize that recent events have gravely shocked Sudanese leadership and people. Nevertheless, we express hope that wise and experienced Sudanese leaders will not waste efforts in dwelling on past and thinking in terms of reprisals or counter-humiliation. We are convinced that a moderate course based on a desire to preserve past fruitful relationships will prove best suited to promote the interests of Sudanese people and to hasten the realization of our common interest in a free and prosperous Sudan in association with a number of closely related African states.[307]

Thus, despite Malian anti-French rhetoric and actions, the United States' position toward Mali was far more flexible than it had been toward Guinea.

With French-Malian relations strained, Mali applied for economic and military assistance everywhere. In late September 1960, a Malian government delegation headed by the minister of labor, Ousmane Ba, visited Moscow "to elucidate the situation in the Mali Federation after Senegal's withdrawal and to discuss the issues of the Soviet aid to Mali." Ba assured his Soviet interlocutors that "the Sudanese do not want to ask Americans for aid, for they love their motherland too much to give it away for dollars."[308]

Almost simultaneously, Mali sent to Washington a confidential request for American assistance. The deputy undersecretary of state for administration, Loy Henderson, who arrived in Bamako in October 1960, assured both President Modibo Kéi'ta and the minister of the interior and defense, Madéïra Kéïta, that Mali's request for aid would be given "sympathetic consideration."[309] Henderson found out that there was no unity concerning foreign policy steps. Modibo Kéi'ta was "a moderate" who "would like leave the door open to the West," but Madéïra Kéïta was a "strong advocate of [the Soviet] Bloc." Henderson believed that an "orientation visit to Madéïra Kéïta with special treatment might change or modify his leanings."[310]

When in Bamako, Henderson and his entourage stayed at the Grand Hotel. In the dining room, he saw members of the Soviet delegation and the Czechoslovakian delegation sitting at a long table. Henderson had an impression that they were "in a triumphant mood," for "within the last week the Communist Bloc had scored some victories in Bamako."[311]

The Soviet delegation that Henderson watched at the Grand Hotel consisted of the representatives of the Ministry of Foreign Trade (Ministerstvo vneshnei torgovli) and the State Committee for Foreign Economic Relations, under the USSR Council of Ministers (Gosudarstvennyi komitet po vneshneeconomitcheskim svyazyam'). It concluded a trade agreement that allowed Mali 8 million rubles in credit to develop bilateral trade and pay for 25 percent of Malian exports in hard currency.[312]

In a confidential letter to Khrushchev dated November 24, 1960, Modibo Kéi'ta extended thanks for promptly meeting Mali's request for assistance and explained his intention to "accomplish a true economic and social revolution" on the basis of industrialization.[313] The Soviet Union seemed to be a few steps ahead of the United States in winning influence over Mali.

The United States drew a lesson from the Guinean fiasco. It did not intend to give the Communists a free hand in Mali. On November 1, 1960, President Eisenhower held a meeting of representatives of the State Department, the Bureau of the Budget, and the International Cooperation Administration. They decided to grant Mali $2.8 million. Because it was agreed that the proposed aid to Mali should be given quickly, the president suggested that "the necessary clearances be obtained by telephone and the document reach him as soon as possible."[314] In explaining the necessity to move quickly in assisting Mali, the acting secretary of state, Douglas Dillon, wrote in a telegram to the U.S. Mission to the United Nations:

> Our Mali aid effort based calculation that by responding rapidly to what Malians regard as crisis situation we can strengthen the hands of moderate elements and help create internal political atmosphere conductive maintenance important Western and French influence Mali. If we stand aside, danger exists left-

ists would gain undisputed ascendancy Mali internal politics and take hasty ill-considered actions which would push Mali irreversibly down path taken by Guinea. Dept cannot lightly contemplate possibility two West African states almost exclusively dependent Soviet Bloc for technical and advisory personnel, economic assistance, export markets.[315]

"Over longer terms," Dillon expressed a hope for "moderate Mali foreign policy behavior."[316] This prediction proved to be correct.

3. Seeking More Pragmatic Approaches, 1961–1962

The "Year of Africa," 1960, did not meet Soviet optimistic expectations. The West was about to win the battle for the Congo, and it enjoyed the support of a considerable number of African countries in the Congolese crisis. Yet it became obvious that the nations of Africa were deeply divided over key international issues and had conflicting judgments about the proper relations between newly independent states and former colonial powers.

In the years 1961 and 1962, the tone of Soviet publications changed. The euphoria of the early 1960s gave way to more guarded and realistic assessments. For instance, the leading Soviet Africanist, Ivan Potekhin, stressed that obtaining independence was only the first and not the most important stage of the anti-imperialist revolution: "Sometimes we say that this or that country has liberated itself from colonialism. It would be more correct to say that these countries have set themselves free from the direct political ascendancy of the imperialist powers. But this is not yet the decisive victory." And Potekhin had many arguments to illustrate this thesis. The African economy's commanding heights were occupied, as before, by moneyed, monopolistic corporations that "were owned by foreigners," no nation had its own sea fleet, and so on. "An economic dependence on the imperialist powers" made formally independent countries "look back to their old masters." And worst of all, in some African states "the colonizers have put in office specially selected puppet governments that are faithful to the former rulers with their minds and bodies."[1]

The different approaches of African states to international and domestic issues were manifested in the establishment of various interstate unions.

In December 1960, the Brazzaville Group was established, which consisted of twelve French-speaking countries, including five in West Africa—Côte d'Ivoire, Dahomey, Niger, Senegal, and Upper Volta. In January 1961, the Casablanca Group was formed, composed of Ghana, Guinea, Mali, Morocco, and the United Arab Republic. In April 1961, the presidents of Ghana, Guinea, and Mali met in Accra to found the Union of African States, which was open for membership by any African state. The Afro-Malagasy Union grew out of subsequent meetings of the Brazzaville Group, and at a May 1961 conference in Monrovia, seven nations— Ethiopia, Liberia, Libya, Nigeria, Sierra Leone, Togo, and Tunisia— formed the Monrovia Group.

The Soviet response to the fragmentation of Africa's continental politics was predictable. Potekhin endorsed the members of the Ghana-Guinea-Mali Union as genuine revolutionaries: "These three states coherently carry out an anti-imperialist, anticolonial policy. They defend the most progressive resolutions on the Congolese and the Algerian issues as well as those on all the other issues that concern the independence of African countries. On short notice, they achieved important successes in the struggle for economic independence and to strengthen national sovereignty."[2] But he harshly criticized the members of the Afro-Malagasy Union: "The foreign and domestic policy of the states of the Afro-Malagasy Union differs sharply from that of the Ghana-Guinea-Mali Union. Dealing with the Congolese and Algerian issues, they are trying to find a compromise solution that does not preclude the imperialists from perpetrating their black deeds or support the imperialist states openly. . . . The domestic policies of these countries are characterized by the stimulation of capitalist private enterprise and a curtailing of the democratic rights of working people."[3]

Ghana, Guinea, and Mali were considered the most promising countries for spreading Soviet influence in Sub-Saharan Africa. Boris Ponomarev, the chief of the International Department of the Central Committee of the Communist Party of the Soviet Union (CC CPSU), mentioned them among the other "national democratic states."[4]

The Soviet strategists also had to take into consideration such fundamental factors as the rise to power of the new U.S. president, John Kennedy. The African strategy of the previous U.S. administration had been defensive; Dwight Eisenhower had feared that "premature independence" and "irresponsible nationalism" would make Africa vulnerable to Communist penetration. He had considered the collapse of the colonial system a "destructive hurricane" and "viewed the proper American role in Africa's transition from colonialism as one that supported the European powers."[5] Now, however, Kennedy admitted that decolonization was important in world politics. He recognized that mostly decolonized Africa required a new American policy, one less identified with European powers and more tolerant of neutralism and nonalignment. And to achieve such "flexibility and freedom of action," it was indispensable to consult the former colonial powers and the NATO allies about their interests, but not to make them the cornerstone.[6]

Kennedy could not tolerate a supposed "neutralism" that in reality disguised partiality toward the Soviet Union and Marxism. But he believed that "true," "real," or "objective" neutralism was not detrimental to the United States' interests and could be used against its Cold War adversaries. For him, the goal of American policy in Africa should not be "winning the African states to capitalism or military alliance" but merely "to prevent the dominance of the continent by the Communist Bloc."[7] And the containment of Communism should remain the cornerstone of U.S. strategy in Africa. Like his predecessor, the new president was convinced that the Cold War should be "total," a "battle of minds and souls as well as lives and territories."[8]

By early 1961, the Congo remained the most problematic territory in Sub-Saharan Africa for both the USSR and the United States. In the next section, we consider the final acts of the Congolese tragedy—continuing from where the story left off in chapter 2.

The Final Acts of the Congolese Tragedy

The United States outplayed the USSR in the Congo by encouraging President Joseph Kasavubu's ousting of Prime Minister Patrice Lumumba and supporting the coup by Colonel Joseph Mobutu. And with its embassy expelled from the Congo and Lumumba in prison, the USSR's only leverage to influence the Congo's internal situation was providing support for the Lumumbists' regime in Orientale Province.

The Soviet Union Provides Aid to Gizenga, but Its African Allies Refuse
The Lumumbists, led by Antoine Gizenga, managed to consolidate their control over the Congo's Orientale Province and to achieve military successes in moving out into neighboring areas. On December 25, 1960, sixty soldiers from Stanleyville arrived in a column of Jeeps in Bukavu, the capital of Kivu Province (south of Orientale Province), and arrested its governor, several of his ministers, and the commander of the Bukavu gar-

rison, whose soldiers preferred to join the attackers rather than fight. The UN troops in the area remained neutral, and Kivu was captured without firing a shot. On December 30, an attempt by Joseph Mobutu to retake Bukavu failed. Gizenga's troops opened fire, and Mobutu's soldiers retreated or surrendered. Meanwhile, other troops loyal to Stanleyville easily took over northern Katanga, supported by members of the Baluba tribe who were against Moise Tshombe, and entered Equateur Province, west of Kivu. By mid-January 1961, pro-Lumumba forces controlled almost half the Congo's territory.[9]

The U.S. intelligence agencies saw this event as a demonstration of the fact that there was "a good deal of vitality" in the Gizenga regime. It would be greatly strengthened "if Lumumba should escape to Stanleyville to direct it and rally additional support."[10] Americans had no opinion about the fighting efficiency of Mobutu's forces and believed they had little chance of defeating the Lumumbists. "I am genuinely alarmed," Ambassador Clare Timberlake cabled to the Department of State on January 10, 1961, "at the direction in which military developments are going and I am increasingly skeptical of capacity of Mobutu or [the Government of the Congo] to arrest, let alone reverse, it. Loyalists of ANC [Armée Nationale Congolaise] units have always been tenuous and fluid; they go along with their paymasters, they do not like to fight and they like to be on winning side. It will not be at all surprising if ANC troops now in this area were to interpret present or further advances of Gizenga's troops as the wave of the immediate future and decide to join them." Timberlake warned that "it is therefore not exaggerating to say we may now be very close to a takeover by Lumumba."[11]

Gizenga kept on dispatching telegrams to the Kremlin, imploring it to provide assistance. On January 4, 1961, he informed the Soviet premier, Nikita Khrushchev, that "Belgian troops and Mobutu's soldiers are attacking our units in Bukavu," and "on behalf of the Congolese people," he requested "direct and immediate military intervention."[12] There was no reply, for the Kremlin had no plans to interfere "directly and military" in the Congo. However, Gizenga's military successes encouraged the Soviet leaders to extend him financial aid, and $500,000 was granted to his representatives in Cairo in two equal payments.[13]

The U.S. and British pressure on the Sudanese government was strong enough to frustrate attempts by Soviet diplomats to negotiate an agreement on transporting consignments through Sudanese territory.[14] Sudan even refused to allow humanitarian aid organized by the Soviet Red Cross to pass through to Stanleyville.[15]

The USSR lacked the ability to influence Sudan. On January 31, 1961, during his talk with Egyptian president Gamal Abdel Nasser in Cairo, the deputy foreign minister of the USSR, Vladimir Semenov, asked what measures could be taken "to press the Government of Sudan to agree to transport consignments through Sudanese territory." Nasser replied that "the safest way to deliver Soviet aid to Stanleyville is to parachute it in without warning the Sudanese authorities; however, this operation is risky and might have international consequences."[16]

Khrushchev did not want to take the risk of using guerrilla methods to deliver Soviet aid. The USSR thus made every diplomatic effort to persuade its allies to run the blockade of Orientale Province and thus avoid overt Soviet involvement in the Congo.

On December 22, 1960, Ghanaian president Kwame Nkrumah wrote to the Sudanese leader, General Ibrahim Aboud, and asked him "to secure refueling and staging rights in Khartoum for Ghana Government planes proceeding to the Congo from Accra."[17] His appeal was turned down. The Sudanese government refused to grant transit rights to anyone other than the UN force.

At their formative conference from January 3 to 7, 1961, the leaders of the Casablanca Group—again, Ghana, Guinea, Mali, Morocco, and the United Arab Republic—failed to agree on measures to assist Lumumba and Gizenga. Nasser, Guinean president Sékou Touré, and Malian president Modibo Kéi'ta were ready to withdraw their troops from the UN force, but Nkrumah "spoke strongly in favor of allowing African troops to remain in the Congo."[18] The conference declared "the intention and determination to withdraw their troops and other military personnel placed under the United Nations Operational Command in the Congo." It urged the UN to "disarm and disband the lawless bands of Mobutu," but decided against a public commitment to provide aid to the Stanleyville regime. Gizenga's name was not even mentioned in the final communiqué.[19]

At the initiative of the Soviet Union, an extraordinary session of the Council of Afro-Asian Solidarity was held in Cairo on January 21, 1961, but the Soviet representatives failed to secure a decision to send the council's representatives "to negotiate with national and international organizations the issue of providing comprehensive aid to the legitimate government of the Republic of the Congo, including sending to the Congo volunteers, armaments, and other materials needed for the defense of the Republic and also the issue of mobilizing world public opinion in favor of the Congolese people's struggle against the colonizers."[20] Nobody rushed to help Gizenga.

The State Department welcomed the decision of the United Arab Republic, Guinea, and Mali to withdraw their troops from the Congo and instructed the U.S. delegation to the UN to propose that the secretary-general replace these units with "troops from more reliable countries, African, Latin American, etc."[21]

Egyptian officials showed no inclination to follow Soviet recommendations to take the lead in supplying aid to Gizenga, and instead preferred to play their own game. After a conversation with Nasser on September 30, 1960, the UN secretary-general, Dag Hammarskjöld, concluded: "My guest of honor at dinner tonight obviously has been vaccinated against Lumumbism. All he now wants is a strong government without East or West influence, irrespective of who the top man is."[22] Nasser had high hopes of improving relations with the United States, where newly elected president John Kennedy was about to take office.

The volume and character of Egyptian aid to Gizenga were specified by President Nasser in his talk with Soviet deputy foreign minister Semenov on January 31, 1961: "The United Arab Republic battalion that is to leave the Congo was ordered to leave half its weapons (light mortars, small arms, and ammunition) to Gizenga's troops." Nasser admitted that "this wouldn't save the situation."[23] Semenov tried to find out whether Egypt was ready to send military advisers to help Gizenga. "We've made up our minds," he informed Nasser, "to send to Stanleyville an experienced person, and we are going to send a group of diplomats there, including the military, but we haven't had an opportunity to transfer them yet." He suggested sending Gizenga some Egyptians who had combat experience in Algeria. Nasser dismissed the matter with a joke, saying that parachuting in Soviet diplomats seemed to be the only way to guarantee that they would reach Stanleyville.[24] The United Arab Republic refused to let several Czechoslovakian planes fly over its territory, so the Czechoslovaks planned to ferry the planes to Stanleyville.[25]

The other African states on which the USSR meant to rely also did not show themselves firm partisans of the Gizenga regime. At the end of the year, Soviet arms and ammunition were delivered to Ghana so they could be passed on to the Gizenga regime.[26] Nkrumah, however, chose to improve relations with the United States, with dubious results, rather than provide military aid to Gizenga. In March 1961, he visited Washington, and President Kennedy declared that the U.S. government would fulfill its commitments to finance the hydroelectric initiative known as the Volta River Project. Nkrumah, in return, had changed his position on the Congo to match the U.S. line (see below in this chapter). The Soviet arms and ammunition had not been delivered from Ghana to the Congo.

Transcripts of talks from December 1960 to March 1961 between Richard Dvořák, the Czechoslovakian ambassador in Moscow, and Yakov Malik[27] and Arkadey Sobolev,[28] both deputies of the USSR's foreign minister, reveal that Czechoslovakia unsuccessfully tried to establish an airline route from Prague to Stanleyville via Cairo and Khartoum. Czechoslovakia gave £25,000 to its embassy in Cairo for the Gizenga government,[29] but it is doubtful whether the money ever reached Stanleyville. On March 9, 1961, Dvořák told the Soviet deputy minister of foreign affairs, Nikolai Firubin, that money allocated for Gizenga had not been handed to his representative in Cairo, Pierre Mulele. The ambassador hinted that Mulele was corrupt and unreliable: "It is known that Mulele lives in Cairo in luxury and is surrounded by the company of very dubious people. Agents of intelligence services of imperialist states might be among them."[30]

The USSR failed to establish an international coalition to counteract the actions of the UN troops that supported the pro-Western Congolese forces. Khrushchev used blustery rhetoric on the Congo, but he avoided steps that could have strained relations with the Western powers.

Lumumba's Assassination and the Aftermath
Even isolated in a cell, Lumumba remained dangerous for his enemies. The U.S. Central Intelligence Agency (CIA) admitted that, "as the new year began, the stock of Lumumba and Gizenga had perceptibly risen and that of Kasavubu and Mobutu perceptibly dropped—in spite of the UN resolution which seemed to support Kasavubu and indeed partly because of that Pyrrhic victory."[31] On January 13, the CIA's station chief in the Congo, Lawrence Devlin, cabled to Washington: "Station and embassy believe present government may fall within few days. Result would almost certainly be chaos and return [Lumumba] to power."[32] The cable's alarming tone could be explained by the news that the troops in the garrison at Thysville, the town 90 miles from Leopoldville where Lumumba was being held prisoner, had mutinied and were about to release him.

On January 17, Lumumba, Maurice Mpolo, the former youth minister, and Josef Okito, the head of the Senate, were airlifted to Elisabethville. In early February, Radio Katanga announced that they had escaped from prison. On February 13, the interior minister of Katanga, Godefroid Munongo, said during a press conference that the three escapees had fallen into the hands of bush villagers and had been immediately killed.[33]

Few, if any, believed this story. The Soviet government, in a special statement, called the assassination of Lumumba and his comrades "an international crime committed by the colonizers, primarily Belgian colonizers."[34] In the Soviet Union, elsewhere in the Eastern Bloc, and in many developing countries, Lumumba's death became a cause célèbre. There were mass demonstrations and carefully staged propaganda campaigns aimed at the United States; at its NATO allies, particularly Belgium; and at Hammarskjöld.[35] Friendship University in Moscow (see chapter 4) was renamed Lumumba University.

Time has affirmed the truth of the Soviet statement on Lumumba's assassination. A Belgian sociologist and writer, Ludo de Witte, using a huge array of official sources as well as personal testimony from many of those in the Congo at the time, proved what had been suspected for more than forty years—that clear responsibility for the murder of Lumumba lies with the Belgian government, among many other accomplices.[36]

De Witte's book on the event, *The Assassination of Lumumba*, was translated from Flemish into four languages and made a stir. Debates were held in the Belgian Parliament, which in 2000 finally decided to create a parliamentary investigation committee, whose main purpose was to reach "conclusions about Belgian responsibilities in the murder of the first prime minister of the Congo, Patrice Lumumba (and his fellow victims, Okito and Mpolo)." The commission included representatives of all the parliamentary parties and was assisted by "a number of experts who were responsible for content-related and historic-scientific work."[37]

In its report, the Belgian parliamentary investigation committee found that the murder was a premeditated one, the result of collusion between the Congolese authorities in Leopoldville and Katanga. The main conclusion was that "certain members of the Belgian government and other Belgian participants were morally responsible for the circumstances leading to the death of Lumumba." The facts given in the report referred to evidence directly implicating Belgium in the murder: "The Belgian government tried to take Lumumba prisoner and transfer him to Katanga"; "although Lumumba was arrested following an arraignment order dated September 1960 and based on precise charges, . . . the Belgian government authorities never insisted on a trial"; "on at least one occasion, the Head of State received an indication that the life of Lumumba was in danger; in a letter from Major Weber, a retired major of the Belgian army, Tshombe's military adviser, to the head of the King's Cabinet, [and] it has been proven that the King was aware of this letter"; "the transfer of Lumumba to Katanga was organized by the Congolese authorities in Leopoldville, supported by Belgian government authorities, especially the foreign minister (Pierre Wigny), the minister of African affairs (Harold d'Aspremont Lynden), and their colleagues, [and] Belgian advisers in

Leopoldville collaborated with the organization of the transfer"; and finally, "the execution occurred in the presence of Katangan ministers [the president of Katanga Moise Tshombe, and his ministers Jean-Batiste Kibwe, Gabriel Kitenge, and Godefroid Munongo] and was carried out by Katangan gendarmes or police officers, in the presence, though, of a Belgian police commissioner, Frans Vercheure, and three Belgian officers [Lieutenant Gabriel Michels, Captain Julien Gat, and Sergeant François Son] who were under the authority, leadership and supervision of the Katangan authorities."[38]

The CIA's involvement in the assassination plot has also been documented. The available documents "have revealed that it was not for want of trying that the CIA failed to assassinate Lumumba and left the job, in the end, to the Belgians and Katangans. A review of the evidence leaves little doubt that U.S. officials encouraged Lumumba's Congolese opponents to eliminate him at a time when it appeared that he might resume his position as prime minister and turn the clock back to the summer of 1960, with the Russians restored to a position of influence."[39] This conclusion, reached by the journalist and scholar Madeleine Kalb, is confirmed by the facts that Devlin, the former CIA station chief, mentioned in his memoirs.[40]

Beginning on February 14, Mulele from Cairo and Gizenga from Stanleyville kept on dispatching to the Kremlin urgent, almost desperate, requests for support. On February 14, Mulele cabled that "two companies of American rangers" were ready "to kill the members of Gizenga's government" and requested "to counter an imperialist subversion." He was aware of the consequences of complying with his request: "The legitimate government prefers the world war to begin rather than being meanly killed off."[41] On February 21, Gizenga informed Khrushchev about the danger of the enemy's invasion and solicited help, arguing that "a moral support only is insufficient."[42]

The assassination of Lumumba was a heavy blow to the prestige of the Soviet Union. Various passages in the Soviet government's special statement gave Gizenga hope: "The prime minister of the Congo died, but the legitimate government of the Republic of Congo, headed by his deputy, Antoine Gizenga, continues to function. Located in Stanleyville, provisional capital of the Republic, it controls over the half of the Congo's territory and enjoys peoples' support. . . . It is necessary to give utmost aid to the national government of the Congo in Stanleyville."[43]

On March 7, 1961, Mulele arrived in Moscow for an unofficial visit and spent a week there conducting negotiations with the Soviet deputy minister of foreign affairs, Vasilyi Kuznetsov, and other Soviet high officials. Mulele lamented that Soviet aid was insufficient and pushed for it to be increased and to become more comprehensive. According to Mulele, "We failed to transfer the second portion of your financial aid ($250,000) from Cairo to Stanleyville, because Sudan refused to grant a visa to our trusted person."[44]

This sum had never reached Gizenga. Devlin recounted that the CIA had an agent in Mulele's circle who was used as a contact with the Soviets and accompanied Mulele to Moscow. After the agent left the Soviet capital, "he told us the color of the suitcase containing the money and provided us with the man's return travel plans." Devlin organized an operation to distract the courier carrying the money from Cairo to Stanleyville and to snatch the suitcase with the $250,000 in the Khartoum airport.[45]

Mulele tried to convince his Soviet interlocutors that Gizenga's troops were suffering from a shortage of vehicles, fuel, and arms. He said: "Of course material difficulties badly affect the morale of our soldiers, especially when they meet face to face with Mobutu's troops and find out that the latter have everything, including modern arms."[46]

Mulele was not dramatizing the situation. According to other sources, it was even worse than the picture he presented. Polish newsmen in Stanleyville informed their foreign minister that the Gizenga government had no finances whatsoever. The economy was about to collapse, because stocks of goods and foodstuffs had been exhausted.[47] A Czechoslovakian newsman, Dushan Provarnik, reported that that Gizenga's army numbered 8,000 to 9,000 soldiers, armed with "relatively modern" Belgian weapons. The army was loyal to the Stanleyville government and obeyed its orders. The problem, however, was that this was a professional army and its fighting capacity depended on financing: "It is clear that if the army doesn't receive wages, it will refuse to fight. The Gizenga government has to pay its soldiers at least the same money that Mobutu gives his own soldiers— that is, 2,000 to 6,000 Congolese francs, depending on their grade. Under the existing circumstances, when the government has no revenues, as taxes have not been raised, these expenses are a heavy financial burden."[48] The army suffered from an acute shortage of ammunition, each Gizenga soldier had only ten cartridges to combat the enemy, and the units were not mobile due to the shortage of gas.[49]

Mulele called for urgent aid, especially military supplies. He was told that Soviet consignments were ready, and after the assassination of Lumumba new opportunities emerged for cooperation in arranging aid deliveries to Stanleyville. Mulele proposed creating a Congolese airline made up of Soviet civil planes with Congolese wing markings. Two possible air routes were discussed: Cairo to Stanleyville, and Accra to the mouth of the Congo River. Only long-range planes could cover the second route, and Mulele raised the issue "of buying in the Soviet Union 2-3 IL-18 [Ilyushin-18] planes."[50]

The Soviet reaction shattered Gizenga's hopes for increased aid. Vladimir Brykhin, the head of African Department II of the Ministry of Foreign Affairs of the USSR (Ministerstvo inostrannykh del, MID), said, "The problem of using our planes, especially the IL-18, is very complicated. It is necessary to also take into account the political dimensions. We think it is better to negotiate this with African countries, as the UN would not grant Soviet planes the right to fly to the Republic of the Congo."[51] The Soviet defense minister, R. Y. Malinovskyi, put it straight: "The UN position is quite clear for us: It will shoot down these planes."[52]

American sources do not confirm whether the UN had such intentions. At the meeting of the National Security Council on January 5, 1961, President Eisenhower asked the director of central intelligence, Allen Dulles, "whether the UN forces in Congo had any combat planes which could interrupt the Soviet airlift." Dulles replied, "The UN forces would not use planes against a Soviet airlift even if such planes were available."[53]

Nevertheless, Mulele was told that "flying of Soviet planes with Congolese wing markings over African countries, and especially Sudan, without their permission is fraught with international conflict, which might develop into world war, and this cannot be allowed."[54] The Soviet side made it clear that it would refrain from handling supplying problems. "The UN," Brykhin noted, "is not able to fight against all African states. If the heads of independent African states wish, they will decide the matter. The main thing is to reach an agreement with them. We are giving you all possible material and diplomatic support. We are doing everything that depends on us. However, the problem of communications should be solved by the African countries."[55] This sounded like an excuse for a rebuff, for it was clear to both sides that the African countries would never manage this problem. It was obvious that the Soviet Union had decided not to provide substantial material aid to the Stanleyville regime.

Soviet policy in the Congo had suffered serious setbacks. Despite his harsh anti-Western rhetoric and optimistic declarations, Khrushchev felt that the West had outplayed him in this distant and unknown heart of Africa. He was inclined to back off, to remove to some extent the Congo affair from the East/West conflict, and to reduce the Cold War danger in Africa. Global strategic concerns pushed the Congo below Europe, Asia, and North Africa on the Soviet list of priorities. The Soviet leader also wanted to disengage from the crisis because of the nature of the Gizenga regime. The USSR had never treated Gizenga as a reliable ally, and his leadership in opposition to the Leopoldville regime had not been consolidated. Moreover, the pro-Lumumba forces remained fatally divided after his death.

Mulele had every reason to inform Gizenga that long-awaited Soviet aid would not come. Not only the leadership of Orientale Province but also ordinary people lived with the hope of receiving this aid. According to Provarnik, "from the first day of our staying in Stanleyville, each Congolese asked us why we did not provide the aid they needed so badly. It became more and more difficult for us to explain them the situation, the reasons for not granting the material aid, to plead the position of Sudan and other African countries." After the assassination of Lumumba, it became dangerous for any white person to stay in Stanleyville. During a meeting with the chief of staff, a Major Losso, newsmen from socialist countries heard that "if aid from your countries was not provided, it would be regarded as a betrayal." Georgiy Fedyashin, a correspondent for the Telegraph Agency of the Soviet Union (Telegrafnoye Agentstvo Sovetskogo Soyuza, TASS) and an intelligence officer, made a pessimistic prognosis: "If our aid does not arrive here within a week, the Congolese will come and beat us like enemies."[56] Fedyashin's opinion was particularly authoritative, because he had regular private talks with Gizenga and was considered to be well-informed. On February 27, 1961, the Czechoslovakian correspondents left the Congo by plane.

The Adoula Government, U.S. Initiatives, and the Soviet Defeat
Stung by the absence of aid from the USSR and its allies, Gizenga began to search for other sources of support. On March 10, 1961, Frank Carlucci, an officer of the U.S. Embassy in Leopoldville, visited Stanleyville at Gizenga's invitation and enjoyed an unexpectedly warm reception. A telegram sent to the Department of State by the U.S. ambassador to the Congo, Clare Timberlake, on March 12 partly read: "Most amazing change is attitude toward the United States. Carlucci who three weeks ago was labeled a spy was given red carpet treatment. . . . Gizenga saw him privately for over hour and organized reception in his house attended by General Lundula, six key members Gizenga Government and two members of provincial Government." The Congolese appealed for U.S. "understanding and

aid," emphasizing that they were "not Communists" but neutrals trying to restore order and would accept aid from anyone.[57]

On March 31, 1961, U.S. assistant secretary of state G. Mennen Williams announced that Gizenga should be represented in a federal government.[58] Carlucci headed the U.S. consulate that had been established in Stanleyville. Under the circumstances, the absence of the USSR's official representatives might have been interpreted as a sign of having entirely surrendered the initiative in the Congo.

The USSR sent its diplomatic mission to the capital of Orientale Province "to maintain contacts with Gizenga and to lend him consulting assistance." Leonid Podgornov, who had been the chief of the station of the Komityet Gosudarstvennoy Bezopasnosti (KGB, Committee for State Security of the USSR) in Leopoldville, was appointed the chief of the mission. His group included two "external intelligence officers" (Podgornov and Oleg Nazhestkin); two military officers; one diplomat, who represented the MID; and three radio operatives–coders. In Jeeps left over from World War II that were meant for tourists, they advanced from one village to another through the equatorial forest in the Congo's northeastern region and reached Polis, an administrative center halfway to Stanleyville, where there was an airfield with Belgian pilots who agreed to take them to Stanleyville "for a considerable fee." But the Belgian officials, with reason, suspected that the Soviets were not diplomats. The Belgians then got the Congolese soldiers who guarded the airfield drunk with a "delicious Belgian beer" and told them, pointing at the group's bulky luggage, that it was "Russian spies' equipment." The Belgians asked to open the valises and the sealed diplomatic bags, which were protected by diplomatic immunity. Because this "diplomatic luggage" contained "secret ciphers, money, radio facilities," it might have cost Podgornov and his people their lives. As Nazhestkin recounted, "For more than two hours, Leonid Gavrilovich conducted painstaking negotiations with the pilots and Congolese soldiers. Little by little the tension relaxed; the soldiers put aside their automatic rifles and began to smile. At last, the loading permit was received," and two hours later, an airplane with the Soviet mission onboard safely reached its destination.[59]

In Stanleyville, the mission's radio station was set up right in the hotel room, protected by bedsheets from the eyes of occasional visitors. On July 6, 1961, Moscow heard the station's call sign on the air.[60]

The composition of a new government was endorsed by the Congolese Parliament on August 2, 1961. Cyrille Adoula became prime minister, and

Gizenga was appointed deputy prime minister. Adoula had led one of the three Congolese trade union federations and had been a senator, in which capacity he had helped the Americans when they "tried to remove Lumumba by means of a no-confidence vote in early September 1960."[61]

It was Gizenga's decision to participate in a united government and to formally reconcile with his enemies in Leopoldville. In reality, however, he had little choice about whether to join the Adoula government. If he had continued to refuse cooperation with Leopoldville, he would have invited action against secession like that taken by Moise Tshombe, the leader of Katanga. Meanwhile, the Soviet Union recognized the Adoula government, as it "received a vote of confidence from the Parliament, . . . as the legitimate successor of the government headed by Lumumba, and followers of Lumumba and Gizenga hold the majority of posts in it."[62]

The Adoula government was also recognized by the international community, including the Afro-Asian Bloc of states. On August 31, 1961, Khrushchev sent Adoula a telegram that read: "Taking note of the will of the Parliament, the highest legislative authority of the Republic of Congo, which decided that your government is the successor of the first federal Congolese government headed by the great patriot Patrice Lumumba, the Soviet government declares that it will continue to maintain diplomatic relations with the Republic of Congo and to make efforts to develop the relations of friendship and mutual understanding between our countries based on equality, respect for sovereignty, and noninterference in internal affairs."[63]

On September 24, 1961, the Soviet diplomatic mission, accredited in Stanleyville, arrived in Leopoldville. The staff could not resume full-scale activity, for "the Congolese figures connected with imperialist circles had thrown obstacles in the Embassy's way for a long time."[64] Oleg Nazhestkin gave the details of this story in his memoir:

> A few days after the mission removed to Leopoldville, Podgornov was summoned to the Congolese Foreign Ministry, where a petty official declared on behalf of the foreign minister, Justin Bomboko, "You have entered the Congo through the back door, without asking the hosts' permission, so you should leave the country." The right wing of Adoula's government—headed by Bomboko, the chief of the security service [Victor] Nendaka, and the chief of the General Staff, Mobutu—refused to implement the decision of the Congolese Parliament on the recognition of the diplomatic missions accredited in Stanleyville when

Gizenga was in power. The "ousting" of the Soviet mission had begun. Podgornov tried to set up a meeting with Bomboko and requested accreditation, but he was persistently told that his group did not have diplomatic status or the right to use its radio station, to receive or send diplomatic mail, and did not enjoy diplomatic immunity.[65]

The CIA's station chief, Lawrence Devlin, also arranged a "warm welcome" for the Soviet diplomats in Leopoldville. With the help of his agent "Jacques," Devlin had bugged as many of the apartments as possible in a large, ten-story apartment building that the Russians were going to buy and use as their embassy. His primary targets were the apartments on the top floors, where he believed "the ambassador's office, the communications center, and the offices of the senior KGB and GRU [Glavnoe Razvedyvatel'noe Upravlenie, the Main Intelligence Directorate of the General Staff of the Armed Forces] officers would be located." And the CIA did not only use sophisticated equipment "to make life difficult" for the inhabitants of the embassy building. As Devlin recounts, "We contacted a *feticheur* through Jacques and paid the man to place a curse on the embassy and anyone who entered the property. In order to ensure that his curse became well-known in the community, Jacques had him dance in front of the embassy for hours chanting the curse."[66]

The MID sent an inquiry to Podgornov on the practicability of the Soviet mission's staying in Leopoldville. The mission, however, replied that it had not exhausted its ability to influence the course of events and looked forward to a favorable decision on its accreditation. These were no idle words. According to Nazhestkin, "Using our contacts, we had initiated Parliamentary debates on fulfilling the decision to accredit the Stanleyville's diplomatic corps by the government. Tempestuous debates on this issue took place in the government. Our friends there, particularly the minister of the interior, [Christophe] Gbenye, supported our position."[67]

On December 2, 1961, "after protracted delays," the Congolese Ministry of Foreign Affairs did recognize the full powers of Podgornov as the Soviet chargé d'affaires ad interim.[68] In a short time, he was received by Bomboko. The minister declared that "the Congolese government, nevertheless, took the decision to accredit the Soviet diplomatic mission as a full embassy, and it was ready to examine the question of affording the USSR ambassador an agreement."[69] In January 1962, the Soviet ambassador, Sergei Nemchina, arrived in Leopoldville.

Soviet analysts believed that the Adoula government would pursue an appropriate "neutralist" policy. They reasoned that "Lumumba's followers" held twenty-three of forty-two posts in the government, including such key offices such as deputy prime minister and ministers of the interior, justice, the economy, agriculture, mining, and foreign trade.[70]

The White House had a different opinion. As Secretary of State Dean Rusk wrote to President Kennedy on August 3, 1961, "We considered that the risks of Gizenga's inclusion in the government in a minority position and controlling no politically sensitive ministries would be less of a risk than leaving Gizenga in his Orientale redoubt, where he is a standing invitation to Communist penetration and where his isolation tends to drive him closer to the Soviet Bloc." Rusk expressed the hope that Gbenye, "the most powerful of Gizenga's lieutenants," would not long continue to hold the Ministry of the Interior. The secretary of state believed that the establishment of the Adoula government was the heaviest blow to the Soviet positions in the Congo after the ousting of Lumumba: "Adoula's victory removes any legal basis for Gizenga to claim that his regime is the legal government of the Congo. It is the second Soviet defeat in the Congo."[71]

The American prognoses proved to be far more accurate. The Mobutu-Kasavubu tandem controlled the power structure, the bulk of the army, and the bankroll. It enjoyed the support of the Western powers and the UN staff in the Congo. And Adoula was not going to meet the conditions under which Gizenga's group agreed to participate in the government— "punishment of Lumumba's assassins and their accomplices; pursuing Lumumba's policy; Gizengists should hold the posts of Minister of Defense, Commander in Chief, and the Congo's representative in the UN; liquidation within the shortest time of the separatist regimes in Katanga and southern Kasai; and setting the time for the withdrawal of UN troops from the Congo." Instead, the Gizengists in the government were reduced to the role of "mere administrators."[72] Adoula kept "a sharp eye" on the "Gizenga menace" and launched a "psychological campaign" against Gizenga that resulted in the deputy prime minister's losing ground to his former allies, particularly Gbenye.[73] The relations between Adoula and Gizenga deteriorated to the extent that the latter, not feeling safe, left the capital for Stanleyville, his stronghold.

A document prepared by the MID characterized Gizenga's activity there as "rallying national democratic forces for maintaining the independence and territorial integrity of the Congo." Gizenga managed to replace the pro-Western president of Orientale Province with one of his own supporters. His troops took control of the town of Kindu in Kivu Province and created "the government of Maniema area" as a "counterweight to Adoula's henchman Mirukho," who controlled the town of Bukavu and adjacent areas. Gizenga began to organize a "united nationalist party, 'Pan-Lumumba.'" The Third Army group, dislocated in the eastern part of the country, remained loyal to him, and on his orders, it launched an offensive against Tshombe's troops in northern Katanga at the beginning of November. All these activities gave the MID's African Department II grounds to conclude that "the influence of Gizenga in the country has not decreased but continues to increase."[74]

U.S. officials described Gizenga's actions as an attempt "to restore his political power by returning to Stanleyville and creating a radical separatist movement."[75] They were determined to prevent the fall of the Adoula government because it is "generally recognized as being pro-American and following the policy of reconciliation, which the West has developed and supported; any new government would have an anti-Western bias." The best way to strengthen Adoula's position was to end the Katanga secession, so that the prime minister would gain victorious laurels in the fight for the united Congo. "If Western powers failed to act," Devlin admitted, "it was feared that Adoula would be replaced by Gizenga or another leftist, who would then turn to the Soviets for help defeating Tshombe and reintegrating Katanga into the Congo."[76]

On November 24, 1961, the UN Security Council adopted a resolution deploring "all armed action in opposition to the authority of the Government of the Republic of Congo, specially secessionist activities and armed action now being carried on by the Provincial Administration of Katanga with the aid of external resources and foreign mercenaries." The council authorized the new UN secretary-general, U Thant, to take vigorous action, including the use of a requisite measure of force, if necessary, for the immediate apprehension and detention, pending legal action and/or the deportation of all foreign military and paramilitary personnel and political advisers not under the UN command.[77] (On September 18, 1961, Secretary-General Dag Hammarskjöld had died in a plane crash near Ndola in Northern Rhodesia, now Zambia, where he was to have a meeting with Tshombe.) The USSR and the United States voted for the resolution; France and the United Kingdom abstained.

On December 3, after Tshombe's gendarmes set up roadblocks and fired on UN troops in Elisabethville, Thant ordered his representatives in Katanga to "act vigorously to reestablish law and order."[78] On December 5, clashes began between the central government and Tshombe's troops.

The United States succeeded in resolving the situation in its favor. It provided the UN forces in the Congo—the Organisation des Nations Unies au Congo (see chapter 2)—with aircraft, transport planes, antiaircraft guns, and armored cars. When the United Nations was close to achieving control of Katanga, the United States, under the threat of depriving the UN troops of tactical transport, arranged a cease-fire, compelled Adoula and Tshombe to begin negotiations, and supervised them closely to achieve an advantageous result. On December 21, at the Kitona Military Base, Adoula and Tshombe signed the Kitona Agreement—whereby Tshombe recognized the unity of the Congo, with Kasavubu as chief of state; agreed to place the Katangan military under central government control; and promised to send Katanga's deputies and senators to the Parliament in Leopoldville.[79] Rusk cabled Kennedy on December 23, 1961: "Agreement between Tshombe and Adoula based on results Kitona talks would be fully satisfactory to the United States and could make possible fulfillment major U.S. and UN objectives in Congo."[80]

However, the euphoria in Washington was short-lived. As soon as Tshombe returned to Elisabethville, he began to renege on the Kitona Agreement. His ministers charged that Edmund Gullion, the U.S. ambassador to the Congo, had forced Tshombe to sign it. The Katangan leader's commitment to the Kitona Agreement was uncertain; his real aim was to stall UN military operations.[81]

The main problem with which the United States had to deal in connection with the settling of the Katangan issue was reconciling differences with its NATO allies—Belgium, Great Britain, and France—which publicly required stopping the UN's military operation. The USSR watched these events from the sidelines. The Soviet diplomats in the Congo had nothing to do but to state that the Tshombe delegation in Kitona "was followed by the U.S. Ambassador and also by the British, French, and Belgian consuls in Elisabethville. And the delegation of prime minister Adoula was followed by Americans Bunche and Gardiner (UN representatives)." The diplomats reached the conclusion that "the way the negotiations in Kitona were conducted and their course had shown once again that Adoula's government was not free in its actions and that Adoula himself did not make any decisions without consultations with the United States and the UN mission in the Congo."[82]

Adoula promised Ambassador Gullion that after signing the Kitona Agreement, Gizenga would be removed from his post as deputy premier. Because Adoula's government remained weak and Gizenga held control over vast Congolese territories, the United States believed that the latter remained a dangerous nuisance. On January 8, 1962, the Chamber of Deputies voted that Gizenga should return to Leopoldville. When he refused, the Parliament voted his censure. On January 12, fighting broke out between his troops and soldiers loyal to the central government. Adoula immediately requested UN help in quelling the outbreak. U Thant ordered his forces to "exert all possible effort to restore and maintain law and order in Stanleyville and avert civil war there." The following day, Gizenga surrendered. On January 20, he was returned to Leopoldville on a UN plane.[83] Adoula assured Gullion that Gizenga "would continue to be excluded from public life and would be punished."[84] Gizenga was put under house arrest and eventually imprisoned for two and half years on the island of Bula Bemba off the coast near Leopoldville.

Gizenga's imprisonment placed the Soviet Union in a quandary. It was clear that Gizenga "lacked Lumumba's political popularity, his charisma and the ability to move quickly to exploit the situation."[85] Conversely, "as Lumumba's heir, Gizenga represented Congolese nationalism, and if Khrushchev wanted to keep his radical reputation and confound his domestic and foreign critics on the left, he could not let Gizenga languish in captivity without saying a word in his defense."[86]

On the international stage, Khrushchev instructed Valerian Zorin, the Soviet representative to the United Nations, to request a Security Council meeting, ostensibly to discuss the United Nations' failure to remove mercenaries from Katanga by force. It was generally assumed that the matter of Gizenga would be raised at the meeting. On January 30, the Security Council met in response to the Soviet request but voted to adjourn before adopting an agenda.

The Soviets invited Adoula to Moscow, but the offer was declined. Adoula instead visited the United States in February.

In the USSR, a prolonged protest campaign was launched. Soviet academics, including the doyen of African studies, Dmitryi Ol'derogge, made special pleas for Gizenga's life. Soviet and African students marched in front of Friendship University in Moscow in his support.[87]

On May 16, 1962, the CC CPSU International Department considered it "expedient to organize some additional measures to denounce intrigues of reactionary forces in the Congo and to defend Antoine Gizenga."[88] The CC CPSU approved a plan that envisaged, in particular, continuing to publish and broadcast materials showing that "the accusations submitted against Antoine Gizenga, the leader of Congolese national liberation movement, are groundless and that foreign imperialists and their Congolese minions are the real organizers of the reprisals against Gizenga." It was also planned to hold "rallies in defense of A. Gizenga in some plants of Moscow, Leningrad, and Tashkent and at Patrice Lumumba Peoples'

Friendship University."[89] A solidarity campaign was not supported by the Soviet actions inside the Congo, for the USSR was deprived of leverage and influence inside the country.

Devlin assumed that the Soviet chargé d'affaires, Leonid Podgornov, "got down to business immediately and started passing out money a bit too obviously to Adoula's opponents" to woo the leftist opposition.[90] But there is no evidence of such payments in the available Soviet archival documents. Yet even if Pogornov did pay, the money would have been frittered away.

Dealing with Joseph Kasongo, president of the Assembly and one of the leaders of the Stanleyville group, Podgornov faced a typical situation. Talking with Kasongo in January 1962, he concluded that "Kasongo is not a nationalist leader yet, he is a professed agent of Belgian-American imperialists." This uncomplimentary assessment was grounded in Kasongo's words that the arrest of Gizenga was justified because he "attempted to unleash a civil war." Podgornov was of the opinion that "it would not be amiss for us to divest Kasongo of authority and to lobby for nomination to his post Boshele, a first-string leader of the MNC [Mouvement National Congolais]–Lumumba." Podgornov argued that "Boshele himself is an obtuse person, but he is dedicated to the ideas of Lumumba and Gizenga and if he has good advisers, he will be a good president of the Assembly." The comment on the document, signed illegibly, read: "Not bad! But how can we do it?"[91] There was nothing the Soviet Union would do about it.

As Rusk predicted, Gbenye did not keep his post for long. Shortly after Gizenga's arrest, Gbenye was dismissed, for he did not desert the Lumumbist cause. Without Gizenga, the opposition suffered a crisis. The second secretary of the Soviet Embassy, Yuri Sidel'nikov, found that "national patriotic forces" were "fragmented and not organized," and that their actions were "spontaneous, scattered, and not enforced by mass protests." The rank and file had left the political parties headed by Lumumba's followers; only their leaders remained. Attempts to establish a new Lumumbist nationalist party had led nowhere. The MNC-Lumumba "crawled away to the provinces." The Parti Solidarité Africain "was split." The Centre de Regroupement Africaine (Center of African Grouping) and Balubakat were "being torn apart by intraparty strife." The opposition "does not have any newspaper" and "has lost serious positions in the Parliament."[92]

The USSR had to restrict its activity in the Congo to routine diplomacy and "covert and tentative encouragement of radical parliamentarians and potential ANC dissidents." Soviet efforts to scuttle the UN's sponsorship of training the Congolese army by offering to provide everything it needed were frustrated. The suggestion to extend Soviet economic aid to the Congo was not heard. According to the U.S. Department of State, the principal obstacle to Soviet attempts to achieve something in the Congo was "the strong pro-Western sentiment of Prime Minister Adoula and his small circle of advisors."[93]

The Soviets watched from the sidelines as events in the Congo unfolded according to the U.S. scenario. In October 1962, while Adoula was on a visit to the United States, the right-wing, pro-Western Binza Group led by Mobutu took full control of the nation (see chapter 2). Adoula formally remained prime minister, "but he no longer had any influence over major government decisions."[94]

Devlin assumed that the CIA "picked up intelligence that the Soviets had told Adoula that, after the UN's withdrawal from the country, Moscow would provide sufficient military equipment to enable the government to end Katanga's secession within a few months."[95] Adoula did not need Soviet assistance, and the Katanga problem was resolved by the UN forces, which received military equipment and aircraft from the United States and several other Western countries.

On Christmas Eve 1962, Katangan troops shot down a UN helicopter and wounded several UN soldiers. These incidents precipitated a sharp clash between the gendarmerie and UN forces, signaling the end of the Katangan secession. On December 29, troops from the UN forces attacked targets in Elisabethville and seized control of the city. They took Kipushi, a key border town, two days later. A formal Katanga surrender agreement was signed in Elisabethville on January 17. Tshombe acknowledged the defeat and pledged an end to Katangan secessionism. He then left the Congo to go into exile to Europe.

The reintegration of Katanga happened even without the Soviet Union being consulted, and thus this was the Soviet Union's conclusive setback in the Congo, depriving it of the last trump card. Madeleine Kalb noted that "the issue they [the Russians] had counted on for two and a half years to rally radical African support both inside and outside the Congo had suddenly vanished."[96] Likewise, the CIA acknowledged that "the combination of increased United States support for the United Nations and decisive events of late December . . . nipped a growing opportunity for Soviet penetration."[97]

On May 19, 1963, General Mobutu arrived in the United States for a two-week visit as a guest of the U.S. Army. On May 31, he was received by President Kennedy, who expressed his great appreciation for Mobutu's contribution to the success of American policy in the Congo. As Kennedy invited his guest to move into the Rose Garden for pictures, he said, "General, if it hadn't been for you, the whole thing would have collapsed and the Communists would have taken over." Mobutu replied with unusual modesty, "I do what I am able to do."[98]

When Mobutu was back home in the Congo, he and the Binza Group appeared to take full control and pushed Adoula to the sidelines. To demonstrate its power, the Binza Group resorted to a tried-and-true measure: the expulsion of all the Communist Bloc diplomats. The warnings of U.S. ambassador Gullion that such a drastic measure would "destroy Adoula's nonaligned image and damage American reputation in Africa" did not help.[99]

After Ambassador Nemchina entered office, there were staff changes in the Leopoldville KGB station. In particular, instead of the "completely knackered" Podgornov, a new chief, Boris Voronin, was appointed, and his official title was "counselor of the embassy." Before leaving for the Congo, Voronin was invited to visit the CC CPSU International Department, where he was told, per the Instantsiya (the highest authority, the CPSU leadership), that "under the existing situation in the Congo its opposition national patriotic parties probably would be banned and go underground." The CC CPSU therefore was ordering external intelligence officers to maintain secret contacts with these parties' leaders. According to Nazhestkin, "Voronin was consumed with the premonition that this would lead to no good. In addition, the Instantsiya's orders distracted the KGB station from its main work of dealing with agents among the Western countries' representatives and obtaining information about their activities in the Congo. The parties were poorly organized and had no experience with clandestine work. It was difficult to maintain secret contacts with them, and the bust-up was fraught with a major international scandal, perhaps even the severance of diplomatic relations, as had happened in September 1960."[100]

Voronin's fears turned out to be justified. In the summer of 1963, the opposition parties were banned and went underground. Those of their leaders who managed to escape arrest fled to Brazzaville, where the regime of Fulbert Youlou was ousted by the left. They established the Conseil National de Libération (National Liberation Committee), in which Gbenye played first fiddle, and began to call for a general strike and the overthrow of Adoula's government. The Instantsiya in Moscow kept asking to maintain contacts with the now-illicit parties, and the Soviet intelligence officers had to meet with Gbenye and his associates in Brazzaville.

178

For the Soviet diplomats in Leopoldville, life was not easy. As the embassy's second secretary, Yuri Viktorov, who arrived in the Congolese capital in mid-July 1962, recounted, "We immediately faced the problems of food, clothing, and service. Shops were empty; all that we could buy there were American chickens, which seemed to have been frozen during World War II, and sometimes fish. At the local markets, there were a lot of tropical fruit at a very low price—bananas, pineapples, papaya, mangos, etc. But there were no fruits to which we were accustomed—apples, pears, plums, etc. Only occasionally could one buy meat, and what was especially bad, there was almost no milk or other diary products.[101]

To do their shopping, embassy personnel regularly drove to Brazzaville, the capital of a neighboring country, where the supply of goods was more or less normal. That was easy. Crossing the Congo River by ferry took 10 minutes. Diplomats were not required to have visas or even passports to cross the border; it was enough to show their diplomatic cards, which had been issued by the Congolese Foreign Ministry.

On November 19, 1963, Voronin and the embassy's press attaché, Yuri Myakotnykh, drove to Brazzaville, but not to do shopping. There they met with members of the banned opposition parties, who provided them with policy documents. When the ferry approached the Leopoldville shore, the car was surrounded by gendarmes and plainclothes police. Voronin immediately sized up the situation. He managed to block the car's doors and raise its windows, and he began to tear up the documents. Myakotnykh helped him. But the gendarmes knocked out the car doors with the butts of their rifles and pulled the diplomats out by their legs and beat them severely there on the pier, then threw them in the back of a police pickup truck and drove away. Voronin lost consciousness. The Congolese, who had no respect for the sanctity of the diplomatic pouch, tore it open and seized the documents inside.[102]

A British diplomat who had happened to be on the ferry immediately drove to the Soviet Embassy and told about the incident. Ambassador Nemchina tried to make an appointment with President Kasavubu, but was refused by members of his staff. Finally, at about 2 AM, the embassy's limousine, with Nemchina inside, nearly rammed the guards at the gates of the president's residence, and the Soviets forced their way in. A sleepy Kasavubu, dressed in a robe, promised to give the appropriate order to have the Soviet diplomats released by morning. But it was clear that he was not master of the situation.[103]

Meanwhile, Voronin and Myakotnykh were taken to the lockup of the Congolese security service and put in separate rooms. As Nazhestkin recounted,

Interrogation began. Voronin said all that was customary in such cases—he protested against the violation of diplomatic immunity, and requested the arrival of the Soviet consul. Questions continued to hail, despite the protests. By the nature of the questions, Voronin realized that a major provocation had been imagined. Everything was intended to prove the existence of a conspiracy directed from the Soviet Embassy to overthrow the Congolese government. The idea was primitive, but the connections with the banned parties of Lumumba and Gizenga were obvious. There was no one to explain that such contacts, and even on the territory of a third country, are common in diplomatic practice.[104]

In the evening, the Soviet diplomats were taken to Ndola Prison, which was located in a military camp. This was the "kingdom of Mobutu": drunken soldiers, beatings, humiliation, and more interrogation. Mobutu showed himself to be a "jesting fellow":

In the night, a group of drunken soldiers rushed into the cell where Voronin and Myakotnykh were detained. They were under Mobutu's personal command. He was exhilarated. [The Soviet] diplomats were again beaten and dragged into the prison yard. They were put against the wall. Mobutu thickly stated that it was their last chance to confess to involvement in the antiauthority Communist conspiracy. Otherwise—shooting. Then Mobutu gave the command to his soldiers, who raised their rifles. This was a terrible moment. But then entered Nendaka, who had long been persuasive with Mobutu. After a very emotional conversation with Nendaka, Mobutu ordered the prisoners to be marched back to their cell.[105]

The next morning, Voronin and Myakotnykh were taken to the airport. A Soviet plane that was ready to take off stood there with women and children on board—after the Soviet Embassy had had its electricity and telephone cut off, and been surrounded by Mobutu's paratroopers, it had been decided to evacuate them home. However, representatives of the Congolese authorities stated that they should all get out of the plane, and only Voronin and Myakotnykh would fly. The Soviets were compelled to submit.[106] Voronin and Myakotnykh were bruised, their clothing was torn, and Voronin was barefoot. Before their expulsion, they rejected the proposal of an American, "who suddenly appeared," to exchange "Siberian exile" for a comfortable life in the West.[107]

On November 21, 1963, Adoula announced that he was breaking relations with the USSR and expelling the entire 100-member Soviet Embassy staff. The prime minister said that the papers found in the Soviet diplomats' car indicated that the Russians were working with a National Liberation Committee that had been formed in Brazzaville by Gbenye to overthrow the ruling regime. Despite Ambassador Nemchina's protests, the Soviet Embassy personnel were forced to leave Leopoldville.[108] The expulsion of the embassy staff, for the second time in a little more than two years, meant the end of even a formal Soviet presence in "the heart of Africa."

So crushing and humiliating was the Soviet defeat in the Congo that the USSR hesitated for a long time about supporting an armed rebellion that was spreading like a forest fire. The revolt was headed by Lumumba's close associates—Pierre Mulele, Gaston Soumialot, and Christophe Gbenye—"whose vague ideology was coached in Marxist jargon."[109] They had launched a wide-scale guerilla war, and by the summer of 1964, the Conseil National de Libération controlled the eastern part of the country, where the People's Republic of the Congo was proclaimed, with Stanleyville as its capital. In November 1964, the United States directly interfered with combat operations in the Congo to rescue American hostages in Stanleyville who had been captured by the rebels, and this galvanized the Soviet Union to provide military aid to the rebel movement.[110] But the revolt was suppressed, and the United States ended up with a monopoly on influence in the Congo.

Mobutu, who seized power in 1965, would be a staunch ally of the West for more than thirty years. Only when the Cold War was over did the Western powers let explosive Congolese internal discontent erupt and destroy Mobutu's regime.

The USSR also suffered a setback in West Africa when Guinea, a promising ally, turned to the West. We explore this development in the next section.

The Guinean Turn to the West

The Soviet Union kept investing heavily in the "Guinean experiment" to ensure Guinea's orientation toward the East. So great was the confidence in Guinean president Sékou Touré that the Kremlin did not consider as threats the danger signals—the "antisocialist" revision of the development plan, a refusal to establish diplomatic relations with East Germany, and so on.

Soviet-Guinean cooperation was developing and strengthening. On February 11–16, 1961, the first high-ranking Soviet delegation, headed by Leonid Brezhnev, chairman of the Presidium of the Supreme Soviet, visited Guinea. Brezhnev, who liked courtesies, noted with satisfaction in his report the solemnity and friendliness of the reception rendered to him "with all the honours necessary in such cases": participation of the top Guinean leaders in meeting the delegation at the airport, a salute of twenty-one guns, the playing of the national anthems. On February 12, a "great demonstration of youth" took place in honor of the distinguished Soviet guest, whereupon Touré and Brezhnev delivered their speeches and then Brezhnev was awarded the Order of Independence.[111]

The trip to Guinea convinced Brezhnev that Africans, for the time being, could not see the life of which they dreamed in the "Guinean window": "There are a goods famine and a shortage of industrial machinery here. Economic measures of the government aimed at alleviating poverty have not yet yielded results. . . . Economically, Guinea is a backward and poor country with very low living standards and cultural level of the people."[112]

To improve the situation, Brezhnev suggested that "examining the question of providing extensive and comprehensive economic and technical aid for the Guinean Republic, taking into account its complicated domestic and international situation, the specific character of its friendly and trusting relations with the Soviet Union, and our interest that Guinea as one of the most democratic states in Africa should withstand an onslaught of the colonizers and be strengthened economically and politically." Brezhnev considered it "expedient to take measures to increase the efficiency of the aid provided by the Soviet Union in accordance with existing agreements and give positive consideration to the new Guinean requests."[113]

These Guinean requests were not modest. In a confidential conversation with Brezhnev, Touré asked to increase Soviet purchases of Guinean "coffee, bananas, pineapples to balance trade with the USSR," "to allow new $8 million credit," and "to supply urgently thousand of trucks as an additional credit."[114] In the Soviet-Guinean communiqué, the Soviet side expressed its readiness "to expand supplies to the Guinean Republic of the needed goods, in particular machinery and equipment, petroleum products, [and] consumer goods and increase purchases of traditional goods of Guinean export."[115]

Soviet-Guinean Trade and Aid

Brezhnev and Touré did not discuss the effectiveness of economic and trade cooperation between their two states, though this was the problem that deserved their attention. Soviet-Guinean trade was being driven according to a principle that was accurately expressed by a Radio Moscow correspondent in a private talk with a U.S. Information Service officer in 1962: "We gave them what they wanted, and they didn't know what to do with it."[116] Soviet trade organizations worked in Guinea with little regard for reality. As William Attwood, Kennedy's ambassador to Guinea, put it, "The Guineans, meeting Santa Claus for the first time, accepted everything he brought in his bag. The presents looked so dazzling that no one paused to consider whether Guinea needed or could afford them."[117] When he visited warehouses in the port of Conakry, he was greatly impressed:

> Soviet and Chinese credits for commodity purchases brought a weird hodgepodge of articles into Conakry. Some were ordered by inexperienced clerks in the anarchic state trading organization; one, told to buy some corrugated-iron sheets for new housing, ordered enough to roof over the entire population of Guinea. We found warehouses piled high with Chinese oriental rugs and embroidered handbags. Other warehouses contained innumerable toilet bowls—with no bathrooms to put them in—enough canned Russian crabmeat to last fifty years and six tons of quill pens. Exotic-looking machinery rusted on the docks, and vacant lots were filled with broken-down and abandoned trucks and buses. The trucks were mostly Russian and the buses Hungarian. But they were turned over to Guinean drivers who had no notions of maintenance and in any case could probably not read the service manuals—even if they had been printed in French. When the vehicles ground to a stop for lack of lubrication or spare parts, the Guineans just shoved them into the ditch and complained that they were junk.[118]

Due to the inefficiency of Soviet trade organizations, there were often big losses of soon-rotting bananas, the major export item of Guinea. Soviet vehicles and machinery grew rusty and broke down, and bananas intended for export to the Soviet Union rotted in the port of Conakry.[119]

Not only bananas rotted. In his speech on March 3, 1961, President Touré admitted that the state-controlled trade system had collapsed: "Tons of butter, onions, potatoes and other perishables that had rotted in storage

183

had to be dumped into the sea." Corruption and theft became common. Goods to be sold in shops at fixed prices were smuggled into neighboring countries and sold at market prices.[120] In the capital, "some fruits and vegetables could be found in the open-air markets, but shop counters were usually bare except for odd items like canned Russian crabmeat or Bulgarian brandy."[121]

The domestic trade agency was unable to effectively distribute goods to the nation's interior, and as a result there were no supplies in rural areas. Shortages of burning oil, groundnut oil, salt, and matches were acute. "People on the spot began to reason that salt and burning oil were always available in villages before independence, but now, under the new independent regime, they disappeared," Minister of Culture Jean Faragué Tounkara lamented to the Soviet Embassy's second secretary, S. M. Kirsanov, on March 1961.[122]

To prevent mass protests, the Guinean authorities liberalized commercial policy. Normal conditions for the functioning of the private sector in wholesale and retail trade were created.

The effectiveness of Soviet economic aid was limited, primarily because much of it was channeled toward big "prestige" projects, or "white elephants," that were excessive for African needs, poorly conceived, or at times altogether unnecessary.

The Guinean leaders had peculiar conceptions of the essential needs of their people. When Guinea faced economic difficulties in April 1960, a Czechoslovakian economic adviser proposed that the Guinean minister of planning, N'Famara Kéi'ta, "see again whether it is efficient or not to spend the Soviet credit on building residencies for the president, ministries, and National Assembly, and that maybe it is better to abandon one of these projects and to spend uncommitted funds more rationally." Kéi'ta answered that the adviser did not understand the "African mentality" and that his proposal was unacceptable, for it was necessary in the nearest future to build in Guinea a number of buildings that would "impress the Africans."[123]

Attwood presents a vivid picture of failed or money-wasting Soviet construction projects in the country:

> By 1961 Conakry was swarming with Soviet Bloc technicians and engineers occupied with building a Polytechnic Institute for sixteen hundred students (though there were not more than fifty Guineans qualified to attend); a printing plant that eventually operated at less than 5 percent of capacity; a 100-kilowatt

184

radio station for external transmission (which never worked properly since it was erected over a vein of iron ore); a million-dollar outdoor theater (half completed and abandoned); the city public address system (switched off); a seafront hotel (still under construction three years after groundbreaking); a 25,000-seat sports stadium (for a city of 100,000 people); and a national airline equipped with nine Ilyushins (usually grounded), pilots who couldn't speak French and sophisticated radar equipment (there were no fogs) that slowly deteriorated in the damp heat. . . . The Russians often plunged into projects that fizzled out but still cost money—such as an unsuccessful experimental rice plantation ($4 million) and a railroad survey (nearly $1 million), which only proved the inadaptability of Russian rolling stock to Guinean track beds. A Soviet tomato cannery up in Mamou was constructed without regard to the absence of tomatoes or water in the area.[124]

The Guinean "window" turned into a "black hole" that absorbed considerable Soviet resources.

Touré Shifts to the West

Touré, who was dissatisfied with the volume and quality of aid provided by the USSR, decided to progressively distance Guinea from the senior partner's tutelage. He began with ideology, the most guarded from alien influence. The Guinean government did not allow a permanent Soviet cultural exhibition to open in Conakry, and it restricted existing opportunities for Soviet ideological penetration. In December 1961, the Guinean Foreign Ministry prohibited the Soviet Embassy from distributing propaganda materials. Kamara Dauda, a member of the Political Bureau of the Parti Démocratique de Guinée (PDG), explained that the majority of Guineans did not have "proper training" to "comprehend Marxian literature properly." He told the first secretary of the Soviet Embassy, G. V. Rykov, that the embassy should pass the Soviet literature to the PDG Secretariat, which would "distribute it among the party leadership and through local branches of the party." It was clear what would happen with this literature from the experience of 1960, when the embassy passed 3,000 volumes on to the Secretariat. At the end of 1961, these books were still boxed at the National Research Institute.[125] From the spring of 1961 onward, in accordance with a personal and secret directive from Touré, the most capable students were sent to study not in the USSR but in France, the United States, and the Federal Republic of Germany (West Germany).[126]

Guinean officials began to criticize the assistance rendered by the USSR and the work of its specialists. On August 22, 1961, Touré declared that he was "seriously discontented with the Soviet specialists engaged in the construction of a rice-producing state farm."[127] In a session held by the chief of Kankan District in September 1961, "it was declared that the Russians wanted to force Guinea to spend a lot of money on this farm so as to use it as an instrument of political pressure on the country—to compel it, for example, to support the Soviet line in the Berlin crisis. The Russians allegedly acted the same way while constructing the Aswan Dam."[128]

Starting in the summer of 1961, Senegalese living in Conakry—who were members of the Parti Africain de l'Indépendance, a Senegalese left-wing opposition party that had been banned in 1960—warned the Soviet Embassy of a possible changing of Guinean policy toward the USSR and of a turning to the West. Amessata Sarr, an assistant secretary-general of the government, and Will MacLorin, a professor at the lycée in Donka, told the Soviet Embassy's second secretary, Kirsanov, that the "pro-Western group in Guinean governmental and party circles had become active" and that the president's brother, Ismaël Touré, had joined it. According to them, this group and Western diplomacy "bear constant pressure upon President Sékou Touré trying to persuade him to turn from friendship and cooperation with socialist countries and follow the capitalist way of development." Kirsanov assured them that "for the present there are no reasons to suppose that Guinea will change its foreign and domestic policy."[129]

There is no evidence in the available Soviet archival documents that the MID or the CC CPSU worked out actions to prevent a Guinean shift to the West. Guinea was considered "the most progressive state" in Sub-Saharan Africa.[130] It was necessary to carry out commitments, for the "Guinean Republic is being carefully watched by many African countries, which still have close connections with the West and seek to liberate themselves from this dependence. Our nonfulfillment of contractual obligations on time in Guinea makes an unfavorable impression on them and is widely exploited by Western propaganda."[131]

The Kennedy administration was concerned with the attention that African "intellectuals and officials" paid to "Guinea's effort to build an authoritarian Marxist state with [Soviet] Bloc assistance."[132] On March 17, 1961, George Ball, U.S. undersecretary of state for economic affairs, proposed allocating $400 to $500 million for the construction of the Kon-kouré Dam, a smelter in Boké, and related industrial facilities. President Kennedy expressed doubt that the United States should put so much money into Guinea, which was "too small a country" and "far down the road to Soviet commitment." He decided to do nothing before receiving a report from his new ambassador to Guinea, Attwood, on the situation in the country.[133] But Attwood's reports, with an eye to Communists' mistakes, did not change this wait-and-see policy.

The Expulsion of the Soviet Ambassador

In November 1961, Guinea faced a political crisis when the country's Teachers' Union submitted a memorandum to the PDG Politburo demanding an increase in wages and certain fringe benefits, such as a housing allowance and overtime pay. The memorandum was also sent to some foreign embassies, including that of the USSR. The secretary of the Teachers Union, Koumandian Kéi'ta, addressing the conference of the National Confederation of Workers of Guinea in Conakry on November 16 to 19, "pointed to the benefits allegedly lost and contrasted the conditions of the workers with the benefits of the ruling elite." Kéi'ta was "enthusiastically applauded."[134]

The leaders of the Teachers Union, including Kéi'ta, were arrested. Two of them were sentenced to ten years in prison, and three were sentenced to five years.[135] The severity of the sentence could be explained by the authorities' fear that teachers might have led spontaneous protest actions against shortages of food, inadequate supplies of necessities, and a great deal of bureaucratic incompetence and corruption.

The repressions provoked students' indignation. On November 24, students at almost all secondary schools and lyceums went on strike. A students' meeting in Conakry ended in clashes with the police, who employed weapons and killed several students.[136]

The Guinean media insisted that intrigues orchestrated by external forces were responsible for these events. Initially, the government asserted that the teachers "were part of a worldwide imperialist plot." The U.S. Embassy considered these charges absurd, especially "in view of the known Marxist and anti-Western orientation of the principal defendants."[137] On December 11, Touré called the teachers, who had already been sentenced, "spies" and "saboteurs" and referred to contacts maintained by them with "certain Eastern embassies" and "certain ambassadors." These types of accusations were a novelty for Guinean officials hitherto used to accusing neocolonialists, imperialists, French agents, the Catholic Church, and Freemasons. The counselor at the U.S. Embassy in Conakry, Claude Ross, speculated that this speech "may, indeed, herald the beginning of Guinea's shift to a more truly neutral ground."[138]

On December 16, Soviet ambassador Daniel Solod unexpectedly left Guinea. There were no official statements from either side, but there were rumors that he had been expelled. On December 18, Attwood asked Touré about Solod and received this answer: "All I can tell you is that we caught him red-handed."[139] Attwood, however, did not believe that his Soviet colleague had been implicated in subversive activity. He reported to Washington that "it is more likely that Russians and Czechs, as individuals, were meeting with and encouraging dissident Marxist intellectuals as a matter of course—in a sense, as Communist missionaries—rather than as part of a master plan inspired by Solod."[140]

On December 26, at the opening of the national PDG conference in Labé, Touré "stated flatly that 'anti-national' elements among teachers, trade unions and youth organizations motivated by personal ambition and 'inspired by Marxism-Leninism' had been conspiring for two years to overthrow [the] government."[141] The documents that were disclosed at the conference did not seem cogent to Americans: "The 'documentary evidence' presented to the Conference showed no intent of violence and only the shadow of potential opposition. . . . The 'plot' is a manifestation of usual bloc activities, which Guinea probably knew of for some time, and conveniently put to use, as it did the 'imperialist plot' of April 1960, to exterminate any criticism or opposition."[142]

Later, Touré himself confirmed this indirectly. In the autumn of 1962, he explained the reasons for Solod's expulsion to a French journalist, Ike-Jerard Shalian, who told the Soviet attaché that, according to Touré, "the USSR tended to treat Guinea with paternalism. The Soviet Union, the president said, apparently had the impression that Guinea itself was incapable of differentiating good and evil and therefore it should be patronized and 'headed off from the wrong way.'" Attempts "to educate" the Guineans using the illegal dissemination of propagandistic literature had resulted in conflict with Ambassador Solod, who was expelled.[143]

There were no grounds for the expulsion insofar as attempts "to educate," if any, did not mean participation in an antigovernment plot. As for the literature, the embassy had disseminated it legally and openly. In fact, Touré had exploited what became known as the "Teachers' Plot" to turn to the West.

The Guinean president did again calculate everything to a dot. The Soviet Union, which had invested heavily in the Guinean "showcase window," did not adopt retaliatory measures to avoid being discredited elsewhere among the African and Asian countries, tried to minimize the damage to its international prestige, and outwardly acted as if nothing had happened.

At the time, a Soviet trade exhibition was being erected at the Conakry fairgrounds. It was to be opened on January 6, 1962, and a Soviet delegation headed by the first deputy chairman of the USSR Council of Ministers, Anastas Mikoyan, arrived in Conakry the day before—ostensibly for the fair but actually to patch up relations. Speaking at the ceremony for the opening of the exhibition, Mikoyan mentioned "the Soviet miracle," "which is based not on witchcraft but on our socialist social order."[144]

Touré, on the contrary, tried to show that the relationship between the two countries had changed, and not for the better. There was none of the usual fanfare about Mikoyan's visit—the president did not meet him at the airport and refused to receive him on arrival. Touré said that "we are against paternalism in any form and give priority to the dignity of our people over any aid, except completely disinterested one," and noted that "revolutions can neither be imported nor exported." As for Guinea's domestic policy, it would "correspond to our special conditions, our means and the humane character of our struggle."[145]

Touré finally received Mikoyan at his palace. According to Attwood, "Mikoyan left after a reception at the palace, where he was subjected to nearly four hours of Guinean drumming and dances. [U.S. Information Agency director Ed] Murrow, who came along with us, called it 'Sékou's revenge.'"[146]

Before leaving Guinea on January 10, Mikoyan declared that "the Soviet Union is not looking for his own benefit; it did not make political or any other conditions and has no intention to interfere in domestic affairs of Guinea as well as of any other country or to peddle its ideology."[147] This meant that the USSR had abandoned its plans to turn Guinea into an African Communist showcase, the outpost of Soviet influence in the continent, and it set mutual relations on a pragmatic base. The new Soviet ambassador, Dmitri Degtyar, who arrived with Mikoyan, was an economist. Participation in working out Soviet-Guinean economic agreements might have helped him salvage what was possible to save from the two nations' joint projects and to reduce Soviet losses.

Touré kept Degtyar waiting seven weeks before letting him present his credentials. At the ceremony of presentation, the president said that "misunderstanding" between the USSR and Guinea was in the past and that his country "was ready not only to reestablish but to strengthen our kind relations."[148]

Guinea Strengthens Its Relations with the West

Actually, Guinea strengthened its relations with Western countries, first of all with the United States. The U.S. Embassy deemed that the Teachers' Plot and its consequences could be counted "as a gain for U.S. objectives in Africa."[149] Attwood cabled U.S. secretary of state Rusk: "We now have an opportunity through aid programs to show that cooperation with the West can be fruitful and sensible in contrast with three years' experience with [Soviet] Bloc aid."[150]

The U.S. administration did not rush; it took a reserved attitude. "Any Western propaganda hailing Guinea events as smashing victory for West could boomerang if, as likely, it forced Touré to soft-pedal or stop present attacks on Marxist-Leninists," according to Rusk's cabled instructions to Attwood. But Rusk did not exclude the possibility that Touré would reestablish relations with the USSR, especially because there was no evidence that the Russians would be "kicked out of Guinea."[151]

On February 1, the Guinean ambassador to the United States, Seydou Conté, told President Kennedy that the Guinean government would like to broaden the base of its economic cooperation with Washington and "to have the United States augment the assistance it is giving to Guinea." The ambassador informed the president that Touré "would like to send an economic and trade mission to the United States." Kennedy replied that his country "would be pleased to welcome such a mission from Guinea" and "he would like to see the delegates personally during their stay."[152]

The Americans were not sure that Touré's turn to the West was irreversible. "Do you think this request [for additional U.S. economic assistance] opens opportunity for the U.S. and possibly West as a whole to reorient significantly Guinea away from the Soviet Bloc, or is this merely Government of Guinea's effort to obtain greater U.S. aid while it maintains political and economic alignments basically unchanged?" Rusk asked Attwood in a telegram.[153] The White House did not consider the expulsion of the Soviet ambassador to be sufficient ground for increasing economic aid, much less for heavy investments. "Unless Guinean leaders take necessary corrective steps, additional U.S. aid might fail to achieve demonstrable degree of progress," Rusk telegraphed Attwood.[154] What measures the Guinean leaders were expected to take was clear from the questions Rusk raised in the same telegram: "Would GOG [Government of Guinea]

mation supplied to McGeorge Bundy, Kennedy's special assistant for national security affairs, suggested that Kennedy "respond affirmatively" to Touré's plea, for it would "mark a turning point in Guinea's relations with the United States and the West generally" and would "culminate our efforts to decrease Guinea's reliance on the Soviet Bloc."[175]

However, the final U.S. position was different. On September 12, Conté told Henry Tasca, deputy assistant secretary of state for African affairs, that "Guinea is facing economic problems largely because the Soviet Bloc had stopped economic assistance and is pressing for repayment previous credits." The ambassador also mentioned the "exodus" of bloc technicians as contracts were not renewed by Guinea's government. This did not impress Tasca. He informed Conté that the U.S. government "could give no assurance about the loan" and that "Touré probably should not come if he feels an aid commitment is essential."[176]

Nevertheless, Touré decided to come to the United States, and he met with Kennedy on October 10, 1962. The American president repeated the negative position about additional loans, citing the United States' "efforts to aid the African countries within the limits of our own resources."[177] Touré recounted the economic difficulties that his country was enduring and called for "assistance to small firms and enterprises which do not require large capital." He noted that "this kind of assistance would have considerable impact, not only in Guinea but also in other parts of Africa, for the latter would see themselves that Guinea does not permit 'certain nations' to introduce systems it does not wish." It was clear that he meant the Soviet Bloc. As for the Konkouré Dam project, Guinea decided not to cooperate with the USSR and asked the United States to take charge of it. Kennedy replied that "the amount of funds in our disposal for foreign aid" was limited due to "a heavy international financial burden."[178]

Analyzing the results of Touré's visit, U.S. secretary of state Rusk stressed that it "served to consolidate his recent reorientation from the Soviet Bloc toward the United States and the West generally" and "to confirm that Touré sincerely desires to improve his relations with the United States."[179] Another confirmation was the position of Guinea on the Cuban missile crisis. In August 1962, an all-service runway constructed by the Soviet Union was put into operation at Conakry airport. At the time, the USSR deployed intermediate-range missiles in Cuba to defend the regime of Fidel Castro from a potential U.S. military attack. The Soviet leadership planned to use the Conakry airport as an intermediate airport for a Moscow-Havana airlift to be established if a naval quarantine was imposed by the United States to prevent the arrival of more Soviet offensive weapons on the Cuban island.[180] On October 24, two days after Kennedy announced the discovery of the missile installations to the public and his decision to quarantine Cuba, acting Guinean foreign minister Alpha Diallo told Attwood that "the Russians had requested landing rights in Conakry for long-range jets" to make a refueling stop, but "Touré himself had made the decision to refuse the Soviet request."[181] Formally, the use of the runway was denied "on the ground that no fuel was available." Privately, the Guinean government informed the U.S. Embassy that "to assist a Soviet military buildup in Cuba would be incompatible with 'positive neutralism.'"[182] The Soviet Union thus failed to arrange a Moscow-Havana airlift.

The Kremlin decided to expel Touré's Guinea from the list of recipients of Soviet aid. At the CC CPSU Presidium meeting on September 10, 1963, speaking about Touré's request to provide the Guinean army with military outfits, Khrushchev remarked: "This president behaves like a boor; don't give him any assistance."[183]

American analysts did not consider the Guinean leadership's line to rapprochement with the West irreversible. A memorandum prepared for Sargent Shriver read: "If Guinea does not feel that the West is responsive to its needs or threatens its independence or dignity, it may feel that it has no alternative but to swing back toward the Soviet orbit." The dangers for the West were also behind the country's internal situation, especially "excessive Guinean expectations and limited absorptive capacity for external aid" and a "failure to appreciate the procedures for U.S. assistance as well as its quantitative limitations."[184]

The U.S. administration was guided by the principle that aid to African countries should be "within the limits of our own resources" and did not make an exception for Guinea. American aid remained modest, "designed to meet some of Guinea's most pressing needs for equipment and basic articles for consumption."[185] Touré expected a more sizable reward, but in vain. He did not "swing back toward the Soviet orbit" but acted more resourcefully. In 1966, the American ambassador in Conakry shared the same lot as his Soviet counterpart of 1961, yet Touré managed to find new and more generous sponsors among Arab oil-producing countries. Guinean foreign policy under Touré was a distinguished example of flexibility, pragmatism, and balanced neutrality.

The only positive result of the "Guinean experiment" for the Soviet Union was that the Soviet leaders saw in the "Guinean window" their own miscalculations and mistakes. What I would call the Guinean syndrome made them thenceforth adopt a more pragmatic policy toward "progressive" African countries and be less inclined to invest heavily when there were dubious prospects for receiving both economic and political dividends.

The failure in Guinea forced the USSR to seek another ally in Sub-Saharan Africa. Ghana came to be seen by the Soviet leadership as the most promising contender.

Ghana, the New "Leading Light of African Freedom"

The murder of Patrice Lumumba had caused anti-American riots in Accra and convinced Ghanaian president Kwame Nkrumah that he might become the next target. On February 14, 1961, when the news of the murder reached the world, he dispatched a telegram to the chairman of the Soviet Supreme Soviet, Leonid Brezhnev, inviting him to Ghana.

Brezhnev in Accra

On February 16, Brezhnev arrived in Accra. The situation in the Congo was the highest-priority subject for Brezhnev's talks with Nkrumah. The Ghanaian president kept holding onto his fanciful scheme to exchange the UN troops in the Congo for forces of African states under a unified Afri-, can command. Nkrumah's position toward UN secretary-general Dag Hammarskjöld had changed; he said he would not call into question "taking measures to dismiss Hammarskjöld from handling Congolese affairs." Brezhnev and Nkrumah visited the building of the Central Committee of the Convention People's Party (CPP), which was decorated with placards, one of them reading: "Hammarskjöld is Judas."[186]

Nkrumah tried to portray himself as a down-the-line Marxist. He told Brezhnev that he admired the USSR's achievements, which had "inspired Ghanaians to build a Socialist society"; he called Vladimir Lenin his teacher; and he expressed the hope that the "African future would inevitably be connected with socialism." Brezhnev, however, did not receive Nkrumah as a true Marxist, for he had heard Nkrumah speak at the opening ceremony of the CPP Winneba Ideological Institute about "specific African socialism" and using "nonviolent positive actions" in the African liberation movement.[187]

The Ghanaian president tried to convince Brezhnev that Ghana had no choice but to establish close relations with the Soviet Union. In his report on their meeting, Brezhnev wrote: "Nkrumah alleged that the relations of his country with the West, the United States, and England and France in

197

particular, as well as his personal relations, had been spoiled for good and well. These countries would like to dispose of him, but being unable to do this, they did lose an opportunity. This does not mean, however, Nkrumah stressed, that they do not intrigue against him." That is why he "ostensibly intends to rely on Soviet support and aid increasingly in the future." Brezhnev did not take Nkrumah's allegations about his confrontation with the West at face value, explaining Nkrumah's interest in rapprochement with the USSR in relation to pan-African ambitions and his competition with Sékou Touré for Soviet aid: "Pretending to the role of the leader of Africa and trying to make an impression that he intends to sever ties with England and the United States in the future, Nkrumah keeps a jealous eye on the policy of his rival Sékou Touré and has an interest in maintaining relations with the Soviet Union as well as Guinea."[188]

Nkrumah Zigzags under U.S. Pressure

The U.S. administration was anxious about Ghana's courtship with the Soviet Union and the aggressive anti-American propaganda in the Ghanaian government press.[189] The United States used the financing for the Volta River Project (also see chapter 2), on which Nkrumah had staked his domestic and international reputation, to pressure him to alter his policy. The newly appointed U.S. ambassador to Ghana, Francis Russell, wrote to Rusk on January 20, 1961: "If the present virulent anti-American campaign . . . plus growing rapprochement with the Soviet bloc should continue, it would be self-defeating for the West to proceed with the financing of the Volta project." He advised President Kennedy to "wait and see" if Nkrumah continued "to follow the Soviet line" before making a decision on the financing of the project.[190] This advice was heard. The investors did not begin the construction, under the guise of needing new expert estimates and verifying technical details.

This made Nkrumah zigzag in his permanent maneuvering between the West and the East. At the end of February 1961, he applied for a personal meeting with President Kennedy, who agreed to receive him on March 8. The day before, Rusk warned the president: "Nkrumah should depart with no misconceptions on our firm support of the UN in the Congo, and with the clear understanding that while we are prepared to cooperate in every possible way to assist Ghana in its development we expect equitable treatment in return. . . . Our past experience with Nkrumah has been that in private meetings with U.S. officials, he adopts a conciliatory and receptive posture; but, all too frequently, he subsequently reverses himself and speaks critically of the West."[191]

This time, however, Nkrumah could not afford to criticize the West. One day earlier, on March 7, 1961, addressing the resumed session of the Fifteenth General Assembly of the United Nations, he expressed support for the UN mission in the Congo as well as Hammarskjöld's actions, and urged it to take "speedy and effective" measures to regain "that prestige and moral backing which it must have if it is to tackle other even graver world problems." Nkrumah proposed establishing "a new strengthened United Nations civil and military command." As for the command's composition, it should be "primarily," not completely, African, as he had previously argued. He did not call the Gizenga government "the only legitimate" one in the Congo, and he proposed holding a new general election under the UN's supervision.[192] In a secret memo, a Soviet journalist and diplomat in Accra called Nkrumah's speech "lengthy and entangled" and concluded that he had radically changed his former position on the Congo to match the U.S. line.[193]

The next day, talking with Kennedy, the Ghanaian president continued to minimize the difference between his and the United States' views on the situation in the Congo. He recounted that in September 1960, he had told Soviet foreign minister Andrei Gromyko that "the Soviets should give up their campaign to force" Hammarskjöld out. He also reminded Kennedy that "he had stood alone in the Casablanca conference [see above] against withdrawing troops from the UN force and had finally succeeded in forcing a compromise under which the participants agreed to await developments for a month before making a decision on withdrawing their contingents." Nkrumah did not want his succumbing to look like a deal. He "exhibited no desire to talk about U.S.-Ghana bilateral relations and at one point turned off the Secretary's attempt to bring up the Volta project."[194] It was stressed in a joint communiqué that the two presidents "are convinced of the need for unflagging and genuine support, both moral and material, of United Nations efforts to bring peace to the people of the Congo." The Volta project was not mentioned; it was only pointed out that "economic and political problems of common interest" were reviewed.[195]

After his meeting with Kennedy, Nkrumah held a news conference in a White House conference room. One of the reporters asked him this question: "Mr. President, you said you received some encouragement from President Kennedy on your proposals for the Congo. Does that mean that perhaps the United States will join your country in sponsoring some of these proposals or supporting them?" Nkrumah replied: "Yes, but there is a concrete example—the United States of America is helping us with the Volta River Project." But the reporter pressed: "I am talking now specifically on proposals for bringing peace to the Congo."[196] And then Nkrumah began to talk of the Congo. He deliberately mentioned the Volta project, but not to the point of letting the world think that he had reached an agreement on U.S. assistance. A Soviet diplomat in Washington expressed typical international opinion, reporting to Moscow that "Kennedy assured Nkrumah that the U.S. government and American companies in the immediate future would allocate to Ghana the resources needed for the construction of the water power station and smelter."[197]

Soviet diplomats in Accra noted that "criticism of imperialist policy had disappeared almost completely" from the Ghanaian government press and that the right-wing forces in the Parliament, the government, and the CPP had become active, concluding that "recently the Ghanaian line of policy had altered appreciably, creating favorable conditions for rapprochement with the United States and American penetration into Ghana."[198] They had strong grounds for such an evaluation.

Important staff changes now took place. Tawia Adamafio was dismissed from the post of general secretary of the CPP's Central Committee. According to the Soviet ambassador, M. Sytenko, he "was the most coherent and active in pressing for consolidating the relations with the USSR and socialist way of development." Nkrumah decided to hold this post himself and announced his decision during Yugoslav president Josip Broz Tito's visit to Ghana from February 28 to March 11, 1961. Sytenko did not consider it a mere coincidence, for he was informed that "Tito gave Nkrumah to understand that there is no reason to stretch a point in relations with socialist countries and to irritate the Westerners, the United States in particular; Ghana should follow its own way as Yugoslavia does, seeking aid in the East as well as in the West, using contradictions between the two camps."[199] Nkrumah hardly needed such advice, for the principle formulated by Tito was already the keystone of Ghanaian foreign policy.

Several actions were organized to demonstrate the warming in U.S.-Ghanaian relations. The whole staff of the U.S. Embassy donated blood to a hospital in Accra without compensation, with the ambassador at the head of the line. The U.S. ship *Hermitage* delivered medicines and books for hospitals and schools to the port of Tema. Ghanaians received an opportunity to visit the ship, and "six helicopters plying between the ship and Accra were carrying high-ranking officials."[200]

The signs of Nkrumah's tilt toward the West provided influential American business and political circles advocating an undelayable implementation of the Volta River Project with additional arguments. Its active lobbyist was Chad Calhoun, vice president of Kaiser Aluminum & Chemical Corporation, who initiated the establishment of Valco (the Volta Aluminum Company). In a memo sent to leading U.S. politicians, Calhoun argued in favor of "prompt, immediate and effective action" to start the construction of the project's dam and smelter. He stressed that the project, "unlike many economic projects of the underdeveloped nations," was economically feasible and sound. It involved political risks and "would go forward if the U.S. government took effective steps to cover these risks." We must not, Calhoun insisted, let the project be delayed, for "Ghana is a decisive battlefield [of the Cold War in Africa], where the issue still hangs in the balance." He warned that if the project fell into Soviet hands, the West would face acute economic problems: "If the West declines to build the Volta River dam and the aluminum smelter, the story of the Aswan Dam may repeat itself. If the Soviets again seize such a golden political opportunity, the political and economic consequences will be felt far beyond the shores of Africa. A Soviet-controlled aluminum smelter in Ghana, exporting its output to Western markets, at times and prices that suit Soviet political purposes, could have a disastrous effect on the entire Western aluminum industry and, indeed, on the underlying private enterprise economy of the Atlantic Alliance."[201]

Kennedy did not make the final decision concerning the U.S. commitment, waiting for the results of Nkrumah's lengthy tour of the Communist world (see below). On June 29, he wrote the Ghanaian president: "I am delighted to be able to advise you that all major issues involved in negotiations for the United States Government's share of the financing of the dam and smelter have been resolved. The United States Government representatives are now working with your representatives here to develop the necessary documentation for signature and final closing."[202] This sounded like diplomatic advice to Nkrumah to keep to "true neutralism" when in Communist countries. But he did not follow this advice.

*Nkrumah Adopts the Lessons of the Soviet Experience—
and U.S. Reactions*
On July 10, 1961, Nkrumah arrived in Moscow and said at the airport that he was eager "to see the great achievements of the Soviet people, which we have heard so much about, and the glorious results of the Communist revolution and reconstruction."[203] More evidence of his intention was the

duration of his visit, or more properly several visits—from July 10 to 25, the Ghanaian delegation visited Moscow, Irkutsk, Tashkent, Kiev, and Leningrad; from August 12 and 14, Nkrumah was in Moscow on his way from Tirana to Beijing; and from August 20 to 31 and September 8 to 15, he vacationed in the Crimea.

Nkrumah gave ample praise to the USSR and the CPSU. He went far along lines presumably calculated to please his hosts. Addressing a friendship rally in Moscow, he said: "Your tremendous successes in industrial and agricultural development and the organization that helped to achieve them are now an important lesson not only for us, Ghanaians, but for the whole Africa."[204] While in Irkutsk, Nkrumah noted that the Soviet achievements were thanks to the CPSU's leading role and stressed that "the CPSU is a party that knows where it should guide the people." The Ghanaian president showed special interest in the CPSU's experience of ruling a multinational country, and he linked it to his own pan-African ambitions. Delivering a speech at a ceremonial dinner in Bratsk, he declared that he would "work for the 'Leninization' of Africa."[205] Afterward, the Western press labeled him a politician who wanted to "Leninize" Africa. ·

During the flight from Tashkent to Kiev and from Kiev to Leningrad, Nkrumah asked about "the methods and measures taken by the CPSU to mobilize and organize people for the fulfillment of the plans adopted by the Soviet government." He remarked that in Ghana "they don't always succeed in mobilizing and organizing the people, and good decisions of the government frequently remain unrealized."[206] Nkrumah wanted his country to "take off" from a basis of poverty toward growth and prosperity, and he believed that he had found in the USSR a sacramental formula for accelerated development.

He could not resist admiring the scales and rates of the construction of the Bratskaya hydroelectric power station on the Angara River in Siberia and drawing a parallel with the Volta River Project. The Soviet officials who accompanied him reported to the MID: "Nkrumah said he regretted that he consorted with the United States in the construction of the dam and smelter and they had been delaying it for eight years. After visiting the Bratskaya hydroelectric power station, he is sure that if the Soviet Union assists Ghana in implementing the Volta River Project, construction will be completed within two to three years."[207]

Economic issues took an important place in Soviet-Ghanaian negotiations. Nkrumah gave the Soviet government a note containing Ghanaian proposals on the development of trade relations. He suggested concluding a long-term trade agreement and increasing annual sales to 100 million rubles. The USSR would purchase not less than 100,000 tons of cocoa beans annually, paying in goods and in hard currency. The share of hard currency would decrease from 55 percent in 1961–62 to 20 percent in 1965–66. And the Soviet Union would be banned from reexporting cocoa beans to overseas markets, excluding socialist countries.[208]

In convincing Khrushchev to accept these favorable conditions for Ghana, Nkrumah "appealed to the specific position of his country on the African continent as the vanguard of socialism in Africa."[209] The Soviet side agreed to purchase cocoa beans "in accordance with the scheme proposed by the Ghanaian side."[210]

Nkrumah altered his position on major international issues to match the Soviet line. In a joint communiqué issued July 24, 1961, the governments expressed their "unanimous support for the legitimate Government of the Congo with Antoine Gizenga at its head" and their shared feeling regarding "the UN's existing structure, which does not match the new world lineup and does not reflect the historical shifts that have occurred within fifteen years of the organization's existence."[211] Ghana "appreciated the proposals of the Soviet Government concerning a peace treaty with Germany and the settlement of the West Berlin issue on the basis of that treaty."[212]

Nkrumah's approval of the Soviet position on Berlin, the hottest spot of the Cold War at that time, disturbed Western governments and made them consider Ghana's stance a poor example of nonalignment. Ghanaian foreign minister Ako Adjei, who had briefly joined Nkrumah's trip, "related how he tried to explain to Dean Rusk at a later date that the key word, *appreciate*, was used in its strict sense, derived from Latin, to establish that Ghana had taken note of the Russian position."[213] The communiqué published in Russian said that Ghana "*viewed with understanding* [s poni-maniem otneslos'] the Soviet government's proposals concerning a peace treaty with Germany."[214] Nkrumah himself made it clear in all quarters that he sympathized with the Russian position on Berlin. Thus, in September 1961, when addressing the Conference of Heads of State and Governments in Belgrade—at which the Non-Aligned Movement was founded—he called on the great powers to conclude a peace treaty with Germany and to "recognize the existence of two sovereign states: West Germany and East Germany."[215]

Nkrumah's order to select as early as possible 400 Ghanaian officer cadets for training in the USSR for the "African High Command" was appraised by the West as another indication of Ghana's move away from a position of nonalignment. British general H. T. Alexander, the chief of staff of Ghana's armed forces, sent his emissary to Yalta to talk Nkrumah out of doing this. Nkrumah acknowledged that it would be difficult to recruit 400 cadets but insisted that he intended to send "some" cadets. Walt Rostow, a deputy of McGeorge Bundy, wrote Kennedy on September 13, 1961: "It appears that the situation is not as bad as we suspected. However, as an officer in the British Embassy here [in Washington] has indicated, even 50 or 60 cadets indoctrinated in the USSR for 5 years would create serious problems in the Ghanaian armed forces."[216] In the event, seventy-one cadets were sent to the USSR for training in the spring of 1962.[217]

Nkrumah intended to change Ghana's domestic policy in a way that seemed to the Soviet leaders very promising. While on vacation in the Crimea, he had talks with the USSR's minister of culture, Ekaterina Furtseva. He said that "on returning to Ghana, he would immediately get down to elaborating a new program of Ghana's development." He promised "to take drastic measures to squeeze out foreign companies from the country," to establish "a number of new national organizations managing some or other industries," and to adopt a new economic plan, taking into consideration "the experience of the USSR and other socialist countries." He believed that these measures "would allow Ghana to follow the way of building socialism irreversibly."[218]

The fact was that Nkrumah's promise to build socialism stood for something more than a hackneyed aspiration to gain aid, thus convincing a potential donor of his ideological affinity. On this point, the U.S. government prepared a document titled "Kwame Nkrumah: A Psychological Study." This study's anonymous author(s), who obviously had been trained in psychology, succeeded in dissecting Nkrumah's domestic and foreign policy, and in doing an in-depth analysis of the psychological and ideological aspects of his zigzags between East and West.

According to this study, Nkrumah possessed "a remarkable gift of vision which enables him to see over the mass or mess" and to mobilize his intellectual and physical resources for achieving a lofty goal. He dreamed of "a harmoniously organized free and independent Africa, possessed of its own unique personality which stands in equality before the rest of the world, accepted, honored, and respected." It was the only passion with which he was obsessed: "This vision is, to Nkrumah, the 'ultimate reality'; all other things—politics, economics, people, lesser goals and ideas—are less real, less important, transient, expendable. Whatever he does, whatever he achieves, whatever he thinks is related to and subordinate to this ultimate goal. Power, to this uniquely ideological leader, is less an end than a means by which to achieve his end. Money, status, possessions, prestige are not ends and goals, but again are agencies which enable him to achieve his true goal."[219]

The study defined Nkrumah's political credo as "pragmatism": He "may look like a Communist, a tyrant, a dictator, a left-winger or right-winger" and "can be all of these, and at the same time be none of these." Nkrumah was ready "to adopt and to endorse any approach (and anyone's approach) which will fit into the scheme of things, as defined by his aspirations and willingness to lend his support to the approach, the person, or the group insofar as these are demonstrably goal-fulfilling."[220]

Nkrumah had received a reasonably good legacy from the British. By African standards, Ghana had developed a sound, cash-based economy, as the world's largest producer of cocoa beans with a modern mining industry and a well-developed transport infrastructure. Ghana's per capita income was the highest in Tropical Africa. In March 1957, when it achieved independence, the country had a cash reserve of $200 million and a well-trained civil service. But in all measures of external well-being, Ghana's economy was peripheral, with its vulnerability to the vagaries of the world market, a lack of processing industries, the loose interconnectivity of sectors, and the like. In the early 1960s, the country faced the problem of industrialization and—more globally—changing the paradigm of modernization.

Nkrumah dreamed of a rapid modernization, believing that Ghana would be able to gain truly cosmic speed. At first he figured that economic liberalism and Western investments would become the very booster stages of the rocket that would launch Ghana into the orbit of industrial countries, with himself on top of the pan-African political Olympus. But this did not happen. The available foreign capital and internal financial resources were not enough for the industrialization Nkrumah conceived, world cocoa prices were dropping, and currency reserves were running low. Compulsory savings, new sources of foreign investment, and new overseas market outlets were needed. A new ideology and instruments of development were in demand. And Nkrumah found all these in socialism.

Characteristically, Nkrumah treated socialism pragmatically. For him, socialism provided "precisely the kind of model he can use for organization and for action." He was "too independent and self-oriented to deliver Ghana into 'the Soviet camp,' or anyone else's camp." The anonymous authors of the U.S. government study made this prognosis concerning Soviet-Ghanaian relations: "As a pragmatic politician, Nkrumah will milk the Soviets for all he can get, and 'play the role' as necessary to pay the bill—so long as he feels that his independence is not in jeopardy. . . . The greatest error the Soviets can make is to over-evaluate his commitment to them, and try to 'bend' his independence without being strong enough, locally, to wrest it from him. He can become just as independent, as he has been independent against the West."[221]

Nkrumaism, the theory elaborated by Nkrumah, included three constituent parts: his conception of African personality, Pan-Africanism, and socialism. The first two parts were sacred constants, symbolizing African identity. The third was variable and became "African" or "scientific," depending on the circumstances.

During his second visit to the Crimea, from September 8 to 15, 1961, Nkrumah demonstrated physical well-being, and he took to the sea onboard a Soviet warship and submarine. But his mood was hardly undisturbed, due to events back in Ghana.

Ghana was engulfed in strikes and antigovernment demonstrations. The immediate cause was the promulgation of a new budget designed to raise additional revenue for Nkrumah's ambitious development plans. In addition to freezing salaries and raising taxes, this budget introduced a compulsory savings scheme, whereby 5 percent of all wages and salaries would go toward the purchase of nontransferable ten-year National Development Bonds. By the beginning of September, the Ghanaian economy was virtually paralyzed with many strikes. The U.S. Embassy in Accra reported that the people "are 'fed up' with the Ghana Government and President Nkrumah. . . . The strike is complete and well-organized. Unidentified leaders are remaining carefully underground."[222] The Soviet Embassy reported that "imperialist agents were becoming active" and that a coup was being planned.[223]

The information on the coup was accurate. According to Richard Mahoney, the CIA station in Accra received word of a plot among senior Ghanaian officers. It collapsed after the chief conspirator, Brigadier General Joseph Michel, was killed in an airplane crash in Ghana on September 3. Former finance minister Komla Gbdemah also weaved a plot to seize power. He "had no problem in obtaining CIA backing for his conspiracy, but he wanted an official assurance of American support. He approached Ambassador Russell on September 6 and told him of his plans. Would the U.S. support him? Washington gave an unequivocal yes."[224]

Talking in the Crimea with the first deputy chairman of the USSR Council of Ministers, Anastas Mikoyan, and a deputy USSR foreign minister, Yakov Malik, Nkrumah blamed the strikes on "the underhanded plotting of the imperialists and colonialists." Leaving the USSR for Ghana on September 15, he said that "the situation in Ghana had become normal."[225] But the way he departed showed that the situation was far from stable. Initially, he had planned to sail from Yalta on the Ghanaian ship *Prah-River*, which was to call at Alexandria and Casablanca en route to Accra. But on September 9, a counselor in the MID's African Department II, S. Petrov, reported to Malik that Nkrumah "intends to fly to Accra on September 15 and requested to send to Simferopol for a Ghanaian IL-18 now in Moscow."[226] On September 16, the Ghanaian president's plane landed at the Accra airport.

On returning to Ghana, Nkrumah acted decisively. He twice appealed to the strikers to return to work, and they obeyed. He relieved all 230 British officers, including General Alexander, of their command positions in the Ghanaian army. He dismissed four Cabinet ministers, including Gbdemah, who were the CPP right-wingers and represented the "old guard." The key posts were filled with CPP left-wingers; Adamafio was appointed minister of information. Talking with Sytenko on October 3, Nkrumah characterized the reorganization of the government as a measure "of purging state machinery of obviously reactionary elements."[227] Soon Nkrumah ordered the arrest of forty-eight persons, including members of the Parliament, under the Preventive Detention Act. On October 31, at the request of the president, the Parliament passed a bill "to establish special, nonjury courts that could order the death sentence for political offenses with no right to appeal."[228] By then, Gbdemah had already fled the country.

Nkrumah's new lurch to the East caused discontent in the White House. Walt Rostow told M. Smirnovskyi, the minister counselor of the USSR's Embassy in Washington, that "Kennedy 'grew irritated' by Nkrumah's behavior at the Belgrade conference." He added that the U.S. government "was annoyed to hear 'pieces of advice' from personalities who receive American aid but subsist to support the USSR on the German question, for example, simultaneously." On October 5, the U.S. administration repelled a Ghanaian offer to sign the final agreement on U.S. participation in the Volta River Project. Instead, the State Department's representative declared that "additional study" of the project was necessary.[229]

This additional study lasted for two months. Thomas Noer has argued that the June letter to Nkrumah informing him about the U.S. agreement to fund the Volta River Project had "trapped" Kennedy (see above). According to Noer, Nkrumah "wrote the President threatening to make public Kennedy's letter if America reneged."[230] I did not find Nkrumah's letter in the archives, but its contents were widely known, including by the Soviet Embassy in Washington,[231] and thus could hardly become the theme of threats and blackmail. In the U.S. administration, the viewpoint prevailed that it would be counterproductive to cancel the project. An American withdrawal might have placed "extremely heavy pressure on Nkrumah to make any terms with Moscow he can get to build this dam."[232] And Kennedy wanted to avoid being faced "with something a bit like the Aswan Dam situation."[233]

On December 12, the president formally approved a $37 million loan to Ghana and $97 million in loan guarantees to the American consortium engaged in the Volta River Project.[234] A few days later, he commented in a private letter that "we have put quite a few chips on a very dark horse, but I believe the gamble is worthwhile."[235]

"Nkrumaism Based on Scientific Socialism"

On returning to Ghana, Nkrumah got down to work transforming the Ghanaian economy according to socialist principles. He set up a Planning Committee to elaborate the Seven-Year Plan and called upon a Hungarian economist to help with its formulation. The emphasis was on state-operated enterprises in industry and large-scale state farms in agriculture. On December 1, 1961, state control was introduced over export and import operations. However, these reforms did not affect foreign enterprises and investments. As the authors of the State Department's analytical memorandum on the situation in Ghana pointed out, "Ghanaian economic policy continues to be directed along pragmatic lines, and in this important field the West retains its ability to influence the orientation of Ghanaian society."[236]

In international affairs, Ghana's policies were consistently more favorable to the East than to the West, but Nkrumah did not prove himself to be a Soviet proxy. During the second week of the Cuban missile crisis, West African airports assumed vital importance as the only places where the Russians could refuel their aircraft should they decide to relieve the quarantined Cuba. In October 1962, William Mahoney, the U.S. ambassador to Ghana since June, armed with photographs of the Soviet missile launchers, met with Nkrumah and "asked him to deny the Soviet Union all overflight and landing rights in Ghana." The president "acceded categorically to the request, despite the fact that he had signed a major aviation assistance agreement with the Russians only three months earlier."[237]

The development of an economic foundation for socialism was complemented with corresponding political measures. In October 1961, Nkrumah took a symbolically important step by sending his representative to the Twenty-Second CPSU Congress in Moscow. In a month, copying the CPSU experience, the CPP's Central Committee decided to organize the party primary organizations in all labor collectives and to enforce propaganda activity. In July 1962, the CPP congress adopted a new program, which aimed to produce a socialist society by changing the nation's social and economic structure. "Nkrumaism based on scientific socialism" was declared to be the CPP's ideology.[238]

Staff changes in the Ghanaian government were also made with the goal of strengthening economic ties with the Soviet Union. On November 4, 1961, agreements on the extension of economic and technical cooperation between the USSR and Ghana and long-term trade were signed in Moscow. The latter made provisions for the realization of the scheme proposed by the Ghanaian side concerning payment for cocoa beans in hard currency—in 1962, to the tune of 55 percent; in 1963, 50 percent; in 1964, 40 percent; in 1965, 30 percent; and in 1966, 20 percent.[239]

In accordance with the agreement on technical cooperation, the Soviet Union assumed the obligation to provide Ghana with 38 million rubles in credit to pay for "design and exploration work and for supplies and materials for building projects."[240] Among the projects mentioned in a published text were a block-making plant, a gold refinery, and a cotton mill. There was also a secret supplement containing a reference to an Army ammunition plant.[241]

In January 1962, Mikoyan paid an official visit to Ghana. He arrived from Guinea, where he had tried to settle the problems deriving from the expulsion of the Soviet ambassador, and the Guinean syndrome was felt in his speeches. He did not emphasize the "similarity" between postrevolutionary Russia and the newly independent African states; he spoke of their self-dependence and originality. In Accra on January 12, at a dinner given by Nkrumah in his honor, he declared: "Of course, our way and our conditions differ significantly from your way and your conditions. I'd like to make it absolutely clear that being faithful to the principles of respecting the sovereignty of the other countries and of noninterference in their internal affairs, we are far from judging what you are doing right and what you are doing wrong. All this is within your purview, only your purview." Speaking about the CPP, he mentioned its intention to build socialism "in Africa, taking into account its national traditions and historical conditions." He accorded Ghana a new status. Mentioning "the leading lights" that "set the pattern in the fight for freedom for the other African nations," he called Ghana "the first among these leading lights."[242] This remark indicated not only the shift of the Soviet Union's preferences from Guinea to Ghana but also its special interest in Ghana.

U.S. Efforts to Neutralize the Soviet Bloc's Influence in Ghana
The White House reacted quickly to this shift in the Soviet Union's African preferences. The State Department elaborated a comprehensive program aimed at halting "the dangerous drift of Ghana toward the [Soviet] Bloc,"[243] and achieving "a genuine position of nonalignment in East/West issues, coupled with a realization that Ghana is a part of the Free World in the sense that only the Free World has an interest in true Ghanaian independence."[244]

Iron-fisted methods of pressure on Nkrumah and his encirclement were unacceptable: "The greatest error the West can make is to over-provoke Nkrumah, arousing his petulance and negativism to the degree that he 'independently' moves into the Soviet camp."[245] Any attempt "to write off Nkrumah as an African Castro" may have been precisely such a mistake.[246] It was argued that the main threat to Western interest in Ghana came from young, "vigorous Marxist-oriented officials in key positions, who tend to identify the West with 'imperialism' and reaction, and to see in the Soviet Bloc the embodiment of true socialism, democracy and progress." It was necessary to work with this group patiently, widening "the appreciation of these 'African Marxists' for many different forms of political organization which exist, e.g., in the United States, Scandinavia, Israel, and India," working "within the framework of the policies of 'socialism' and neutrality which Ghana has chosen."[247] The matter of principle that should not be the subject of compromise was a postulate "that 'socialism' in the sense professed by Ghana is not, and cannot be, identical with the kind of 'socialism' practiced by the Communist states and that the basic differences between Ghana and the Communist countries are greater than between Ghana and the West."[248] Not only ideological methods were meaningful in trying to win the sympathies of officials opposed to close ties with the West: "Anti-Western officials are more likely to cooperate with U.S. programs, and to approve their continuation, if they can see some personal political or economic benefit to be derived from them."[249]

One of the program divisions dealt with "neutralizing Bloc influence." The authors conceived that "specific projects and policies in the economic and technical assistance fields designed to minimize the Soviet Bloc and build up U.S. influence in sensitive ministries, sectors of the economy, and regions of the country" were to become the main instrument of neutralization.[250] The Volta River Project was considered the most important effort, "the focal point of the U.S. aid program in Ghana": "By associating itself with Ghana's efforts to develop the Volta Valley, the West will be in a position to bring the concept of 'scientific planning' down from the realm of Marxist slogans, where the Bloc excels, to the practical ground of organization and technical efficiency, where the West can compete effectively." The United States, therefore, should cherish the project like the apple of its eye, guarding it from even hypothetical threats. The main task was to deprive the USSR of an opportunity to prove to the Ghanaians that it was able to cope with an analogous project. It was necessary to charge the World Bank with delaying "the construction of the Bui Dam for as long as possible, e.g., on the grounds of its impact on the Okosombo [Volta River] project, and flooding of Ivory Coast land, etc." Even the far-fetched possibilities that the leftist trade union leader John Tettegah "and the Soviet Bloc might try to disrupt construction of Volta" through organizing labor disturbances were anticipated.[251]

The program called for a better use of UN programs in Ghana to strengthen Western influence: "Steps should be taken through [the U.S. Mission to the United Nations] in New York to ensure that U.S. nationals, or at least Western-oriented officials, hold the more sensitive jobs; i.e., organizer of an economic research unit, adviser in the field of industrial development and civil service training, and analyst of the second development plan."[252] Time-tested methods of competitive struggle were also considered worthy of attention. The program recommended "bringing home to Ghanaian officials the weakness in existing Bloc programs or equipment, or in projects proposed by the Bloc, by the timely display of U.S. equipment or brochures, discussion between Western-oriented officials and U.S. technicians, etc."[253]

The Americans hardly needed to underline the "weakness" of Soviet products, because the Soviets themselves unwittingly helped them. The quality of Soviet-made goods to be bartered for raw materials remained poor. The trade counselor of the Soviet Embassy in Ghana, V. Myshkov, described a typical situation. Many sacks of cement were lighter than they should have been. Because pieces of sugar were different sizes and weights, it was impossible to sell sugar through Ghanaian retail traders. Textiles were not delivered in time and did not match the customers' request. Soap arrived in time but not in boxes. It was unloaded from the ship by buckets and piled up at the port.[254] It was impossible to improve this situation radically within the tenets of a totally planned economy. Soviet producers turned a deaf ear to the entreaties of Soviet trade missions in West African countries. When Mikoyan visited Ghana in January 1962, the mission's staff asked him, among other things, to convince manufacturers back home to produce fabric 48 inches wide, which was "in great demand among native population," and to export Soviet goods "in packaging matching the conditions of tropical climate."[255]

Myshkov concluded that the fulfillment of the Soviet-Ghanaian trade protocol of April 18, 1962, "is under the threat of failure, mainly due to the fault of the Soviet side."[256] The volume of trade between the two countries was decreasing. In 1960, the value of Soviet imports from Ghana was 1.4 million rubles; in 1961, 5.5 million; and in 1962, 3.2 million. And the value of exports to Ghana was respectively 18.4, 7.7, and 9.7 million rubles.[257] Under the swing credit of $11 million provided for by the 1961 trade agreement, the Soviet Union at the end of 1964 owed Ghana $10.6 million, as Ghana's private traders "scorned Soviet products for English goods."[258] The Soviet Union had to renege on the graduated purchasing quotas to which it had agreed under the 1961 trade protocols. But it did meet its obligations to purchase fixed portions of Ghana's cocoa in a freely convertible currency.

The USSR Shares the Financial Burden of Nkrumah's Rapid Modernization

Efforts to implement Soviet-Ghanaian projects faced substantial difficulties. Since 1960, Ghana had been living beyond its income. The volume of investments, poured mainly into relatively unproductive prestige projects, was not harmonized with the country's financial capacity. Ghana ran a heavy and increasing deficit in its balance of payments. At the end of 1960, its foreign exchange reserve was 148 million Ghanaian pounds, and in June 1962, only 10 million pounds, "the equivalent of one month's supply of imports."[259] To cover expenses, the government strengthened foreign exchange restrictions and increased taxes and dues and fees, but these measures did not have sufficient effect. Nkrumah sought new loans and aid from Western countries and the International Monetary Fund but received only promises. Compulsory savings also affected Soviet-Ghanaian projects. Ghana had "to ground 6 of the 8 Soviet Ilyushins of her prestige Ghana Airlines due to their prohibitive operating cost."[260]

Nkrumah wanted the USSR to take up a considerable part of the financial burden imposed by rapid modernization. He hoped that increasing Soviet aid would force the Western countries to grant loans. And thus he appealed to Khrushchev with a request to free Ghana from paying Soviet specialists their salaries, accident benefits, transport expenses, and "installation" allowances.[261] Khrushchev replied: "The Soviet Government, being guided by the interests of furthering the friendship and cooperation . . . has given favorable consideration to the ideas set out in your letter and has found it possible to meet your wishes halfway. . . . The Soviet Side expressed its consent to 50 percent average decreases in the salaries, . . . and it also agrees to the Ghana side bearing no expenses in respect for granting 'installation' allowances to the experts, of paying their insurance and for the transportation of their luggage."[262] A protocol to this effect was signed in Accra on January 15, 1962, during Mikoyan's visit.[263]

In July 1962, the Ghanaian minister of industry, Krobo Edusei, pleading his nation's financial hardships, requested that the Soviet side finance the turnkey construction of joint projects. The Soviets refused. In October, the deputy chairman of the State Committee of Ministers of the USSR of Foreign Economic Relations, A. I. Alikhanov, explained to the Ghanaians "the principles of Soviet economic and technical assistance."[264] They withdrew the request.

The lack of funds compelled the Ghanaians to invent new schemes to free themselves from expenses on the construction of joint projects. On November 6, 1962, Nkrumah's economic adviser, Emmanuel Ayeh-Kumi, asked the Soviet Embassy in Accra for a "grant . . . to cover domestic expenses on the construction of the projects mentioned in Soviet-Ghanaian agreements."[265] The Soviet Union agreed to extend a commodity credit to cover the expenses.[266]

Sometimes the Soviets succeeded in concluding contracts that were lucrative for them but not for their partners. On studying the contract for the construction of state-owned collective farms, the Ghanaians "were not happy" to find that the Soviet contract "dealt almost exclusively with the sale and delivery of Soviet machinery and equipment, and very little with the organization, establishment, and management of the State Farms."[267] The Ghanaian negotiators proposed that the manager of each state farm should be "a Russian specialist, with full responsibility for three years, after which time a trained Ghanaian would replace him." They also demanded that the Soviet Union "guarantee the quality and smooth operation of the equipment and machines delivered."[268] The Soviets did not agree, for both proposals were impracticable. If approximately half the Soviet state farms were unprofitable, how could Russian managers make them profitable in Ghana? Soviet tractors could not work properly on fuel delivered to Ghana by Western companies.[269] Ambassador Sytenko did convince Nkrumah that if the Soviet Union were to be given responsibility not only for the "productive aspect" of the farms but also for their "efficient management," it would mean Soviet "interference in Ghana's internal affairs."[270] The Ghanaian state farms did not become profitable and were abolished after Nkrumah was ousted in 1966.

After its failure in Guinea, the Soviet Union opened its purse more cautiously to feed its African allies. The policy of establishing Soviet strongholds in Africa regardless of the cost gave way to a more pragmatic approach based on operational capabilities.

Nkrumah Zigzags Again

The Soviets were more modest than Nkrumah believed. Starting in the spring of 1962, American analysts noted that Ghana "is becoming increasingly disillusioned with Soviet Bloc assistance."[271] And this helped promote U.S. efforts to bring Ghana back to a "true neutralism."

Another obstacle to Ghana's "drifting to the East" became the Volta River Project. A paper prepared by the U.S. National Security Council stated: "Unquestionably, our decision to give assistance on the Volta project changed the atmosphere from one of acrimony to one of guarded cordiality." This did not bring about any fundamental change in Nkrumah's foreign or domestic policies, but "hopeful developments" (e.g., cooperation with "more moderate neighbors," the recognition of Adoula's government in the Congo) were visible.[272] The U.S. State Department regarded Nkrumah's recent staff appointments with approval. It called the individuals appointed to significant positions in the Ministry of Foreign Affairs "strongly pro-Western civil servants," and Ayeh-Kumi was seen as "a staunch friend of the West."[273] Having bypassed his left-wing associates entirely, Nkrumah appointed "conservative, Western-oriented persons" to all eight positions on the important Board of the Volta River Authority.[274]

In another development, Nkrumah had to cancel the contract with the Soviet Union for the design and exploration work for the construction of the Bui Dam. He told Chad Calhoun that the construction should not be undertaken, in view of the adequacy of the power to be supplied from the Volta River Dam. However, on July 14, 1962, the *Ghanaian Times* announced that "work on building a hydro-electric power station at Bunda— the Bui Dam site—will start by Monday. Customary rites have been performed on the site to mark the commencement of constructional work at the dam site. Nana Kofi Dwuru, Omanhene of Banda, slaughtered a cow and poured libation as part of the ceremony. About 300 Ghanaians and 60 Soviets will work on the project. Already about 60 bungalows and staff quarters have been completed for occupation by the workers."[275] Under pressure from the U.S. Embassy in Accra, the Ghanaian government, in defiance of previous agreements, proposed that the Soviet side "reassess the feasibility of the construction of the Bui Dam." But the design and exploration work was "temporarily postponed" and never resumed.[276]

The USSR was also deprived of its Ghanaian propaganda headquarters, the Soviet cultural center in Accra, which had been opened in May 1962 for "the popularization of the USSR's achievements in the building of Communism among the Ghanaian general public." The center disseminated Soviet printed publications, organized film exhibitions, hosted lectures, sponsored Soviet-Ghanaian friendship events, offered Russian language courses, and the like. But on November 25, Ghana's Ministry of Foreign Affairs informed the Soviet Embassy "about the decision of the Ghanaian Government to close all foreign cultural centers" and requested that the Soviet center cease activity within a month.[277] However, the American and British information centers escaped closure, because the United States threatened to "withdraw its entire aid mission were the American [U.S. Information Service] library closed."[278]

The Americans were also more successful than the Russians in propagandizing their achievements in space exploration. In June 1962, "enthusiastic attendance at the three-day Glenn Space Capsule Exhibit in Accra reached 50,000, exceeding attendance at the same exhibit in London, Paris, and Madrid, and evoked numerous comments doubting that the Russians, who have not publicly exhibited a space capsule, have actually sent a man into space."[279] The new U.S. ambassador to Ghana, William Mahoney, after two months on the job, gained the impression that, "despite the socialist litanies," Nkrumah "very strongly wants to be accepted by the West and particularly President Kennedy; and that he leans heavily on our continued support."[280]

The Assassination Attempt on Nkrumah and the Deterioration of U.S.-Ghanaian Relations

Events in Ghana in the summer and autumn of 1962 forced President Nkrumah to doubt his ability to "lean heavily" on Western support. On August 1, he barely escaped death in an assassination attempt. The presidential motorcade stopped on the outskirts of the village of Kulungugu, where the schoolmaster had assembled his schoolchildren to greet the president. When Nkrumah dismounted from a car to receive a bouquet, a hand grenade was thrown at him. The explosion killed the little boy who was presenting the bouquet, and several persons were injured. Nkrumah was hit by shrapnel but was not seriously wounded.[281]

At first Nkrumah was sure that the attackers were Ghanaians connected with the opposition United Party. According to Tawia Adamafio, while Nkrumah was lying on a hospital table waiting for a doctor to extract the pellets from his back, he exclaimed: "Tawia, these [United Party] men are wicked. They nearly got me."[282]

However, at the end of August, three officials—Adamafio, then the minister of information and broadcasting; Ako Adjei, the foreign minister; and Kofi Crabbe, the CPP's executive secretary—were detained for their alleged connections to the assassination attempt. Terrorist bombings swept Ghana, and by late September 1962, the toll of dead and wounded exceeded three hundred.[283] In October, the CIA prepared "The Outlook for Ghana," considering likely developments if Nkrumah were to be assassinated.[284]

In his memoirs, Adamafio swears that he was innocent and explains his arrest as resulting from the intrigues of his "party enemies": "My fall brought back to power the national capitalists and compradors in the party who paid lip service to socialism and Nkrumaism and set in the rot which maintained a steady decline in the party until the inevitable crash in 1966."[285] Taking into account Adamafio's habit of exaggerating his political influence, it is necessary to note the obvious fact that one of the leading CPP left-wingers had been removed from the political scene. Adamafio was released in 1966 after Nkrumah was ousted.

Attorney General Geoffrey Bing, a British national and former left-wing Labour Party member of the Parliament, was placed in charge of the Kulungugu bombing investigation. He was the most influential expatriate in Nkrumah's immediate entourage. The State Department characterized Bing as a "highly intelligent, articulate, and unscrupulous" person holding "pronounced anti-U.S. views."[286] General Alexander described him as "the most evil man in this country." Bing's provocative "overinvolvement during the initial stages of the Congo affair" aroused the general's suspicion that Bing "was a paid Soviet agent." Trying to get rid of Bing, Alexander informed the British MI-5 (which was equivalent to the CIA) about his suspicions. MI-5 replied that "about six months ago they had, in fact, initiated precisely this type of investigation. However, they have been instructed (no indication of by whom) to drop the investigation."[287]

The leftists around Nkrumah held strong positions in the Ghanaian state-controlled media, and their reaction to the arrest of Adamafio was predictable. Criticism of the United States increased markedly. Articles

216

appeared charging that the CIA was implicated in the bombings, and attacks were made on the United States' policy toward the Congo, its actions in the Cuban missile crisis, and the Peace Corps.[288] In a reference to his Arizona origins, Ambassador Mahoney was identified as "the cowboy nuclear imperialist." On September 22, he visited Nkrumah and lodged a protest against these press attacks. Mahoney found Nkrumah willing to issue a formal retraction of the press charges on the basis of his "trust" in President Kennedy.[289] After Mahoney's protest, the anti-American media campaign subsided.

Kennedy requested a review of U.S. relations with Ghana, with which he wanted to deal more harshly. But his deputy special assistant for national security affairs, Carl Kaysen, spoke against a harder policy toward Ghana in a memorandum dated October 29, 1962: "There are signs that Nkrumah is turning away from the Bloc and that his neutralism is moving from neutralism against us to neutralism for us."[290]

Kaysen was too optimistic. Obsessed with the CIA, Nkrumah was convinced that it was conspiring with the United Party opposition in Togo and acted accordingly. On December 27, the Ghanaian Ministry of Foreign Affairs officially requested that the United States withdraw two embassy officials, William Davis and Carl Nydell, who were charged with being CIA agents involved in the Togo-Ghana arms traffic to arm the Ghanaian terrorist underworld.[291]

The Ghanaian government delivered a note stating that Davis and Nydell would be declared personae non gratae if they were not immediately transferred. The State Department immediately took reciprocal action and declared the second secretary of the Ghanaian Embassy in Washington persona non grata. Nkrumah suspended the procedure, and the incident was settled.[292]

Following his logic to counteract Western intelligence services, Nkrumah decided in September 1962 to sever Ghana's intelligence and security relationship with the British and called in the Russians to replace them. When Edgar Kaiser came by the Oval Office on January 23, 1963, to discuss the current crisis in U.S.-Ghanaian relations, the president inquired: "What is this guy—some kind of a nut?"[293] Kennedy meant Nkrumah.

After the setback in Guinea, the USSR abandoned its practice of providing assistance in advance, believing only words about the "socialist choice." Only after Ghanaian president Nkrumah had altered his position on major international issues to match the Soviet line and had revised his domestic policy according to socialist formulas did the Soviet Union agree to share the financial burden of his accelerated modernization. The Guinean syndrome also affected Soviet-Malian relations, and not only in the economic sphere. Khrushchev demanded more ideological purity from Malian president Modibo Kéi'ta, who championed his unique conception of socialism.

Debates over African Socialism—and Soviet-Malian Relations

The Soviet leaders had strongly approved Mali's first demonstration of independence, which in their opinion revealed the "progressive" nature of the Malian government. Within the proclaimed "economic decolonization," measures were taken to establish a planned economy, to expand the state-owned sector, and to promote the spread of cooperatives in agriculture. Mali's foreign policy had an evident socialist, Eastern vector. In February 1961, it recognized the Algerian Provisional Government and the Gizenga regime in the Congo. On September 5, 1961, the last French soldier left Mali. Its position on the key international issues were similar or "very close" to the Soviet Bloc line.[294] In July 1961, Mali joined the Ghana-Guinea Union, which was renamed the Union of African States.

Soviet propaganda alleged that it was "the choice of development" dictated by fundamental ideological factors. But the U.S. assistant secretary of state for African affairs, G. Mennen Williams, differed. He believed that the two factors that had "the greatest influence on the foreign policy of Mali" were "hatred for the French and for Senegal" and the Congo crisis. "Mali's leaders," he wrote, "compare the separatism of Katanga to the secession of Senegal that broke up the old Mali Federation, and they compare the Belgian role in Katanga with the French role in Senegal. The violence of their 'anti-colonial' sentiments—and a demagogic desire to place the greatest distance between themselves and the French—have led the Malians to vote more often with the [Soviet] Bloc in the UN than any other African country."[295]

The U.S. administration did not believe that "a generally radical and anti-Western posture since the breakup of the former Federation" would transform Mali into another Guinea. A State Department briefing paper saw "little tangible evidence that things are presently moving even further left." There were no "expulsions from the political bureau [of the Sudanese Union] of the moderate elements or changes in the Cabinet" that could give "any proof of a change in the internal power balance."[296] The United States should continue to support a moderate faction, led by President Modibo Kéi'ta, as a counterweight to "an extremist group of 'Young

Turks' led, by Madéïra Kéïta, which advocates alignment with the Communist Bloc."[297]

The United States regarded "a substantial French presence in Mali as necessary to the maintenance of the Western position there," and it had no desire "to displace the French." As French aid continued at its preindependence level (about $8–9 million annually), Eisenhower's directive to move quickly in assisting Mali was carried out in a slipshod manner. In November 1960, the United States committed to supply food assistance ($1.7 million) and vehicles for internal security purposes ($300,000); and in February 1961, it offered road-building equipment ($300,000). Yet by June 1961, "due to [International Cooperation Administration] procedural delays," no food assistance had been delivered, orders for the road building equipment "were only recently placed with manufacturers," and only the internal security vehicles (mainly Jeeps) were to arrive in Bamako "in a few days." These long delivery delays "had been a source of great annoyance to the Mali government."[298]

The United States began a military assistance program only after it became abundantly clear that Mali would not take additional aid from France in this sphere but was turning to other sources, mainly the Eastern Bloc. Following the breakup of the Mali Federation (see chapter 2), the Republic of Mali faced the problem of obtaining arms for its internal security forces. The Malians found it politically unacceptable to receive military equipment from France and turned to the United States and the Eastern Bloc. Having in mind the deterioration of French-Malian relations, the United States did not agree to deliver the arms requested, but Czechoslovakian armored cars and firearms were obtained. In May 1961, the Malian secretary of state for defense arrived in Washington with a "shopping list" to negotiate for immediate U.S. military assistance. This list was composed of items "such as parachutes and quartermaster and minor engineer equipment." No arms were requested. The negotiations were a success, and the United States allocated $1 million for military assistance to Mali—"primarily for political reasons to counter Soviet Bloc inroads in Malian security forces."[299]

Strengthening Economic and Cultural Ties
The Soviet Embassy in Bamako was opened on January 26, 1961. The very same day, Ambassador A. I. Loshakov presented President Modibo Kéï'ta with his credentials.[300]

In March 1961, a Malian delegation headed by Madéïra Kéïta paid a

219

visit to the USSR and signed three Soviet-Malian agreements (economic, trade, and cultural).[301] According to an economic agreement, the USSR committed itself to extending Mali $44 million in credits to assist with a broad range of development projects. A trade agreement set the bill of goods for mutual deliveries. The list of Soviet export goods included machinery and equipment, rolled metal, petroleum products, chemical fertilizers, paper, sugar, and food products. Mali made a commitment to export peanuts, cotton, wool, and oil seeds.[302]

Anastas Mikoyan addressed the Malian delegation in the Kremlin: "You are not alone in your struggle. You join hands with your neighbors Guinea and Ghana and other African nations that achieved independence."[303] On the Soviet list of strategic and geopolitical priorities, Mali took place, pari passu, with Guinea and Ghana.

In 1961, the USSR sold ten planes, seventy trucks, and other goods from the export list to Mali. Mali exported 20,000 tons of peanuts and received 40 percent of the payments in hard currencies. In December, the USSR's share of Mali's foreign trade reached 12 percent. The only problem was exceeding the terms for Soviet deliveries of sugar, which put Mali on the verge of a deficit.[304]

In January 1962, seventy-one Soviet technical experts (railwaymen, geologists, and river-transport workers) worked in Mali. They were accommodated in furnished apartments with refrigerators, gas stoves, and air conditioners.[305]

To implement a cultural exchange agreement, Malian students were sent to the USSR (in November 1961, there were "more than 90 of them"),[306] and Soviet teachers were sent to Mali. In January 1962, there were eighteen Soviet instructors of mathematics, physics, chemistry, and the Russian language.[307] They were good specialists in these subjects, but their French was so poor that their Malian pupils often could not understand them. The Malian minister of education, A. Singhare, on November 2, 1961, officially asked Ambassador Loshakov to make Soviet teachers improve their French or replace them with teachers "who can speak French much better."[308] To avoid a scandal, the Soviet side had to send interpreters to assist the teachers.

The Guinean Syndrome as Applied to Mali

A Soviet delegation headed by Mikoyan, which visited Mali from January 16 to 19, 1962, persuaded the USSR's Malian partners to drop large-scale and money-wasting projects that were destined to fail, as had happened in

Guinea. The sides agreed to cut down the financing of geological explorations. And the Soviets did not commit themselves to large-scale hydraulic works on the Senegal River or road building.[309]

During the period 1961–63, the USSR allotted Mali 55 million rubles in credits and paid for Malian peanuts in hard currency. In 1964, Soviet purchases increased by 19 percent in comparison with 1962, and they reached 34 percent of Mali's peanut exports.[310]

The setback in Guinea made the Soviet leadership update the correlation between ideological and security imperatives for its policy toward Ghana, Guinea, and Mali. The conceptions of African socialism, professed by Kwame Nkrumah, Sékou Touré, and Modibo Kéi'ta, did not vary from the "socialism of a national type," which the CPSU's 1961 program characterized as "one of the varieties of petty bourgeoisie's illusions about socialism deceiving people and slowing down the development of the national liberation movement."[311] There were a lot of brickbats about Nkrumaism and Malian socialism in Soviet secret materials. "Despite all socialist clothes," a Soviet diplomat in Accra wrote, Nkrumaism "is only one of the varieties of petty bourgeois nationalism and in no way can be chalked up as a Marxist theory."[312]

The "opportunism" of Nkrumah, Kéi'ta, and Touré did not preclude the Soviet Union from establishing allied relations with their regimes. Strong anti-Western trends in their policies made the Soviets tolerate the "drawbacks" of their "socialisms" and "unique ways of development." Ideological imperatives were of lesser importance than security considerations.

Touré's turn to the West led the USSR to seek more definite ideological eligibility criteria for procuring allies. It is commonplace to assert that Soviet scholars, under orders from above, "rehabilitated" African socialism, whereas Nkrumah and Kéi'ta reciprocally ceased underlining the difference between their socialisms and a "scientific" (i.e., Soviet-style) socialism.[313] However, new archival evidence reveals a more complicated and ambivalent situation.

Many newly independent African countries expressed an intention to build some type of "socialism." The deputy chairman of the board of the News Press Agency (Aghenstvo Petchati Novosti), Spartak Beglov, who toured eight African countries in November and December 1961, observed:

> Concerning *internal policy*, there is one issue that unifies most of these countries regardless of their differences and peculiarities: They wish to develop in *a noncapitalist way*. Only monar-

chic states like Ethiopia and Morocco, and also countries that are highly dependent on foreign monopolies like Togo, openly pronounce their adherence to private-ownership relationships. As for the rest of the countries, their leaders are not afraid of calling themselves "socialists," though the meaning and the interpretation of the idea of socialism varies depending on the quality of political training of the cadres, the character and ambitiousness of the leaders, and, of course, the level of economic development, or more exactly underdevelopment. . . . Thus, ideological perceptions of "socialisms" in Africa are as different as levels of development and traditions of African countries.[314]

The Malians perceived socialism in relation to the level of development of their country. They argued that classes of the Marxist type did not exist in Mali, as there were no exploiters. Talking with Ivan Potekhin, Modibo Kéi'ta dropped a hint of doubt "about the possibility of applying the principles of Marxism-Leninism to African reality." He said he had read some of the works by Lenin, but "they refer to Russia." Lenin wrote about "class struggle, capitalists and landlords, about revolution made by proletariat. But in the Republic of Mali, . . . there are neither landlords nor capitalists and therefore is no class struggle." Proletarian revolution "cannot happen in Mali," for there were few workers there and they are much better off than peasants.[315]

After the setback in Guinea, Khrushchev felt compelled to publicly demand more ideological purity of the leaders of the developing countries enjoying substantial Soviet aid. On May 19, 1962, speaking at a meeting in Sofia, he criticized them for their attempts to carry out policy that was not based on a class approach and ignoring the existing class structures of their countries.[316] He decided to demonstrate this new approach during Kéi'ta's official visit to the USSR starting May 21, 1962. Yet, as Robert Legvold rightly assumed, "because Mali's leadership boasted more than others about a program to build socialism, Soviet ideologists may have caused a certain irritation by contradicting its well-advertised claims."[317]

On May 30, 1962, when Kéi'ta was in Moscow, Khrushchev tried to give him a public lesson, saying: "It would be wrong to think that it is enough to proclaim the slogan, 'We are for socialism' and then lie in the shade of a tree waiting for everything to arrange itself. No, great energy, persistence, and labor are demanded of a people building socialism. . . . We would like our Malian friends to see and understand the complexity of the tasks which arise in the building of a new society."[318] Kéi'ta chose to ignore this humiliating observation. He reciprocated by saying that "the Great October Socialist Revolution of 1917 has brought us along, resolving the problems of the future of our Africa."[319]

The Malian president's major problem was to obtain additional Soviet financial and economic assistance. He managed to receive both. The USSR committed itself to render assistance in the construction of additional facilities in Mali and to implement educational and training projects there.[320]

Khrushchev argued in his memoirs that he dealt with the Malian president in the right way: "Visiting our country (and then in his country), he [Kéi'ta] loudly declared that Mali would develop according to the principles of a scientific socialism and that was the only right way for his Republic."[321] Archival materials put a different complexion on the matter. On returning to Mali, Kéi'ta wrote Khrushchev, admitting that his contacts in Moscow had convinced him of "the superiority and the inevitable victory of the socialism that the people of Mali had been building since September 22, 1960."[322] This unpublished letter is further evidence that Kéi'ta considered his unique concept of socialism, based on Malian history and tradition, to be the only one appropriate for Mali, and that he was not going to transform it according to Soviet recommendations.

Africans were eager to decipher the secret of the "Russian miracle" that had turned the Soviet Union into a superpower within one generation. Their interest in the Soviet experience was thus utilitarian. They wanted to know, as quickly as possible, how the USSR had tackled the practical problems it faced on the road to socialist modernization in order to overcome their own underdevelopment. According to Spartak Beglov:

> We should take into consideration that the African reader generally has already known much about the great achievements of the Soviet socialist system. Now he is greedily trying to find in each [Soviet medium] material answers to the question in *what practical way* did the Soviet Union achieve these results, what *specific knowledge* one can derive from the Soviet experience for building a new life in one or another country. Some African friends (in particular the director of the People's bookstore in Bamako) in the heat of frankness argued that big words and brilliant pictures showing the scope of Soviet achievements more irritate than convince some Malian readers. They react to advertising successes in the following way: "Well, you've got this and can enjoy creature comforts and even afford flying into

Space. But we are suffering poverty, we have no capital and skilled manpower, we don't know how to begin and what to do."[323]

Inferior Soviet Propaganda in Mali

Soviet-made media productions exported to Mali often were not adapted to local realities and mentalities. For instance, the USSR's ambassador to Mali, I. A. Mel'nik, lamented that the organizations responsible for circulating Soviet books in Africa "have little knowledge of the African market, its peculiarities and buyers' needs." Among the books delivered to Mali and to other West African countries from the Soviet Union, the predominant ones were complicated theoretical works on socialism and communism that an average reader could not comprehend.[324]

The propagandistic effectiveness of Radio Moscow broadcasting to Mali was low. Programs sent from Moscow to local radio stations often did not fit the requirements either thematically or professionally. In 1962, the State Committee for Radio and Television delivered thirty-two programs to Mali instead of the agreed-upon forty-eight. And those were mainly music programs, in spite of the fact that the Malians had asked the Soviets to send more informational materials.[325] The delivered programs had "little relevance to the life in Mali and other African countries." Within ten months, into 1963, there had been no radio interviews with Malian officials, though thirteen delegations from Mali had visited the USSR.[326]

Soviet films were rare birds in Mali's private cinemas, which were dominated by French productions. The state-owned movie theaters built by the Malian government were ready to begin showing Soviet films but could not function, because promised supplies of Soviet equipment (stationary film projectors, diesel generators, etc.) had been delayed.[327] One could see Soviet films in commercial cinemas only during the weeks when Soviet cinema was annually presented in the country. One such presentation was given in Bamako in March 1962, and in the opinion of the Soviet ambassador was a success, despite "certain shortcomings in organization, a lack of advertisements, the representative of Sovexportfilm being late, and obstacles put up by the owners of the movie houses."[328] The repertoire could also be a source of controversy. Two films shown in Bamako "offended the religious feelings of the Muslims."[329]

The Soviet Embassy counted on Russian-language courses as propaganda tools. The embassy took a lease on a good-size house in Bamako with a big classroom and rooms for a library, photography exhibitions, book storage, a film collection, and the like. The courses began in April 1962, but the Malian government prohibited foreign powers from disseminating literature and films through public organizations. The tutors had to combine Russian-language teaching with propagandistic activity. The chief of a Soviet tourist group that visited Mali in December 1962 observed: "The courses work well, enjoy popularity, and 140 students (5 study groups) attend them. There are a library and a reading room. The majority of books lent out are not returned. A large quantity of Soviet literature is being disseminated in such a way. Two teachers work to capacity and reasonably use lessons for carrying out a propagandistic work (answering numerous questions, talking about the Soviet reality, etc.)."[330]

Soviet ambassador Mel'nik admitted that the French propagandistic activity in Mali was far more large-scale and effective. Twenty titles of French periodicals were available in store chains all through the country. "Almost all national intelligentsia, civil servants and secondary school students" regularly bought or subscribed to them. In bookstores, one could find modern French imaginative, reference, and scientific literature, along with schoolbooks.[331] Mel'nik observed that French periodicals specially oriented toward Africans were popular among educated Malians. These periodicals, "under the guise of objectivity, coherently propagandize a capitalist way of development (frequently in the form of 'an African socialism'), show the impossibility of implementing a scientific socialism in Africa, write about the assistance that the capitalist countries render to African states, and discreetly denote the ineffectiveness and costliness of the aid from the Soviet Union and the other socialist countries."[332] French radio broadcasting in Mali excelled in the "variety of themes covered, simplicity of expounding materials, and regular inclusion of Africans in the programs"[333]—that is, precisely the issues that the Soviet materials designed for the Malian radio lacked.

The Soviet leaders did not support one project that could have met a major U.S. challenge in West Africa. In the summer of 1961, Sergey Pavlov, the leader of the CPSU youth organization Komsomol (its full name, for which Komsomol is the acronym, is Vsesoyuznyi Leninskyi Kommunistitcheskyi Soyuz Molodezhi, i.e., the All-Union Leninist Communist Youth Union), approached the CC CPSU with a plan to create a counterweight to the U.S. Peace Corps. He proposed sending specially trained groups of young Soviet volunteers to Ghana, Guinea, and Mali to spread propaganda about Soviet achievements; to help with the construction of industrial installations, schools, and hospitals; and to assist with teaching, medical treatment, and sports training for the indigenous population.[334]

225

The idea was approved, and the Secretariat of the CC CPSU adopted a resolution that permitted Komsomol to negotiate with the youth organizations of Ghana, Guinea, and Mali about sending Soviet young specialists there.[335] The leaders of the three countries' youth organizations agreed to receive the Soviet groups and even promised to pay for their accommodations and cover their commuting expenses. The Malians, in particular, wanted "three medical practitioners, a doctor in sports medicine, an obstetrician, a veterinarian, three zoological technicians, a projectionist, an engineer on the road construction and an agricultural engineer."[336] But Pavlov's plan was eventually turned down, because the estimated Soviet expenses of $200,000 were deemed prohibitive.[337]

4. The Struggle for the Souls of the West African Elite, 1963–1964

As Cold War adversaries, the USSR and the United States particularly aspired to win the goodwill of the educated elite in the developing world. This elite was the main target of the two sides' propaganda efforts in West Africa.

With the Sino-Soviet split deepening, moreover, the USSR acquired another ideological foe and faced a dual competition in West Africa. As Robert Legvold expressed it, "On the one hand, [the] capitalist powers possess[ed] the advantages of large economic resources and a long-established presence in the developing nations, and, on the other, . . . the Chinese . . . could offer the impatient nationalists of Asia and Africa a more revolutionary approach to the problem of decolonization and the tasks of political and economic modernization."[1]

The October 1962 Cuban missile crisis had brought the United States and the USSR to the verge of a nuclear exchange and demonstrated the danger of an uncontrolled arms race. After the crisis, there was a short period of détente. In August 1963, the superpowers signed a limited test ban treaty and established a "hot line" to enable instant, direct telephone contact between Washington and Moscow.

The Sino-Soviet Split and West Africa
The signs of détente between America and the USSR incurred sharp criticism from the Chinese leadership, which had decried Nikita Khrushchev for backing down in the Cuban missile crisis, for negotiating a test ban treaty, and for pursuing "peaceful coexistence." Since 1961, the Soviet Union's most galling preoccupation had been the challenge thrown down

by China. By 1963, Chinese attacks on the Kremlin's strategy and tactics had degenerated into a harsh, open feud that engulfed all Soviet relations, particularly with the countries of the developing world. The Chinese accused Khrushchev of betraying the national liberation movement and denounced him for ideological heresies.

Addressing the Plenum of the Central Committee of the Communist Party of the Soviet Union (CC CPSU) in December 1963, Secretary Boris Ponomarev admitted that the "Chinese threat" to Soviet interests in the developing world existed: "Chinese representatives seek to bring the national liberation movement under their control. At all crossroads, they depict themselves as true friends of Asian, African, and Latin American countries. But now it is evident to all that the Chinese leaders have no positive program to assist the people of these areas achieve actual results in their revolutionary struggle."[2]

China ridiculed Soviet priorities for other than ideological reasons. Nuclear war was the only real threat to the existence of the Soviet state. Recognizing that local crises in faraway places might escalate and even lead to a nuclear exchange, the Soviets were not willing to indulge in "direct action." Their response to the Congolese crisis clearly demonstrated this. Conversely, the Chinese leaders considered a new world war inevitable. And because they had no nuclear weapons, they sought to secure their country by involving their main enemy, the United States, in local armed conflicts as far away as possible from China's borders.

The thesis of the primacy of force in national liberation movements became an ideological background for this strategic Chinese task. The Chinese declared that armed struggles, "just wars," were the most effective path to national liberation, and hence it appeared that Khrushchev had subordinated the national liberation struggle to the struggle for peace. Chinese propaganda alleged that by betraying revolutionary movements in colonies (and former colonies) for the sake of peaceful coexistence, the USSR had brought itself into line with the West (which epitomized "the rich against the poor"), analogously (but with pure motives) to the way in which the West rendered aid to newly independent nations "with mercenary motives" and nursed expansionist schemes toward them (resulting in "Soviet imperialism").

Communist China, a poor and underdeveloped country in the process of modernization, by presenting itself as a fellow former victim of colonial oppression that had triumphantly achieved national liberation, appeared more attractive to many Africans than the socialist regimes in Europe.

Exploiting these advantages, the Chinese suggested that African elites consider Communist China's own ostensibly universal prescriptions for national liberation and overcoming backwardness. In particular, the Chinese insisted on the leading role of the working class led by a communist party in a bourgeois-democratic revolution and showed preference for liberation through armed struggle derived from the Chinese Communists' own revolutionary experience.

The keystone of the Chinese strategy in Africa was nourishing "militant liberation movements" engaged in armed struggle. The original basis for Chinese activity in Africa had been Egypt. By 1959, relations between Gamal Abdel Nasser and the Communist powers had deteriorated, and Guinea had become a new stronghold.[3] In West Africa, China supported small radical groups of minor political significance, such as the National Liberation Committee of the Ivory Coast. The only influential communist party, the Parti Africain de l'Indépendance, showed no desire to follow the Chinese line. The Chinese tried to discredit Soviet policy in international forums in which African representatives participated, including the conferences of the Afro-Asian Peoples' Solidarity Organization and meetings of the World Federation of Trade Unions' World Peace Council.[4] In 1960, China established diplomatic relations with Ghana, Guinea, and Mali.

The USSR's rivalry with China was one of the factors that made Khrushchev upgrade the ideological standing of the left-wing regimes in the developing world. He abandoned the criticism he made in his Sofia speech in May 1962 for carrying out a policy not based on a class approach. In a December 1963 interview with foreign reporters, a Ghanaian among them, Khrushchev said that he approved the declarations of those revolutionary democratic political leaders who "sincerely advocate noncapitalist methods for the solution of national problems and declare their determination to build socialism."[5] This interview was published in the heat of Chinese premier Zhou Enlai's African tour, which marked a new Chinese attempt to enlarge contacts in Africa.[6] He was to visit Ghana, Guinea, and Mali. Khrushchev admonished these nations' leaders "that it is impossible to decree socialism, to leap the stage of democratic changes, to implement measures without the socioeconomic conditions and mass support required."[7] Legvold was right to decipher this message as follows: "Rather than exhorting the Africans to make the revolution, as the Chinese were doing, he was toying with the idea of telling them that they had already made the revolution and could now go forward, arm in arm, with the most advanced socialist society."[8]

The Soviet response to the new Chinese initiative in Africa was well timed. Modibo Kéï'ta of Mali was the only African head of state to agree with Zhou's thesis of "old and new imperialism."[9]

Malian-Chinese relations were good, and there was a strong pro-China lobby in high Malian circles. The language used by Modibo Kéï'ta and his associates in many pronouncements was highly reminiscent of Chinese usage. Soviet diplomats in Bamako reported that the Chinese Embassy was very active in making propaganda, and that "Chinese magazines, pamphlets, and books appear in abundance." The daily bulletins of the Xinhua News Agency included "materials of an anti-Soviet character" and tried "to persuade readers that China is the only true friend of newly independent nations of African and Asian nations and also of all states and people fighting for national liberation—that it is a coherent enemy of American imperialism."[10]

The Soviets retaliated with counterpropaganda measures. They disseminated 400 brochures with materials on the CC CPSU Plenum held in February 1964 that openly condemned Chinese "splitting actions" among high-ranking Malian officials, libraries, media, and foreign embassies in Bamako. A lecture, "Fight for the Unity of All Contemporary Progressive Forces and Chinese Policy Aimed at the Isolation of the National Liberation Movement from the International Labor Movement," was delivered to Soviet Embassy personnel.[11]

The Soviet ambassador, I. A. Mel'nik, and other diplomats met with Modibo Kéï'ta and his associates "to explain the position of the CPSU and other communist parties and to underline the splitting activity of the Chinese leaders." The talks revealed that the Malians took a neutral position: "The party [Union Soudanaise] is alarmed by existing friction, seeks to settle differences, but for the sake of friendly relations with all socialist countries prefers to sit on the fence." Malian neutrality was intuitional rather than calibrated: "Malians have not comprehended the essence of differences, and furthermore they are of the opinion that the theoretical level of the Union Soudanaise is not high enough to do it. Not thinking over complicated theoretical problems, they saw the main danger in the threat of the split of the international communist movement and in the Chinese aspiration to rend the struggle for national liberation from the other progressive forces of modernity." Madéïra Kéïta and Ousmane Ba, two influential Politburo members of the Union Soudanaise, told Mel'nik that a book by Mamadou Gologo, the state secretary of information—*China, Giant Nation with a Promising Future*, which contained covert invectives against the Soviet Union and communist parties—was a mistake and not in accord with the official line.[12]

Mel'nik admitted that "demagogic Chinese propaganda" had found some success in Mali. Summing up the explanations he had received from Malians, he mentioned two main reasons for this. The thesis about the "rich" and "poor" nations was attractive to many of them. Though Chinese economic aid to Mali was much smaller in volume than that of the USSR and other socialist countries, it was granted on more favorable conditions for the recipients (i.e., the low wages of Chinese technicians and turnkey construction), and Chinese propaganda effectively exploited these facts.[13]

Most Africans refused to tie themselves firmly to either the Soviet or Chinese in the dispute. In the months after Zhou's African visit, the Chinese position had lost ground (except in Mali), and therefore China scarcely created a serious challenge for the Soviets.

The Cold War adversaries were still eager to reach the educated elite in Africa. This eagerness of course involved conflict, and so we next consider the USSR's attempts in this "struggle for the very soul of mankind" to reach the West African elite, particularly students.[14]

To Train "People with Progressive Views, Sincere Friends of the Soviet Union"

Researchers who attempt to explore without bias the position of African students in the USSR will get into difficulty. It was one of the salient issues of ideological competition during the Cold War and was treated by both sides from politically loaded positions. Soviet propaganda coherently portrayed a typical African student as a person who was eager to acquire knowledge, did not face racial discrimination, admired the achievements of the Soviet Union, and was grateful for its care. With no less persistence, the Western media described the life of Africans in the USSR as an endless nightmare of routine racial attacks and public insults, poor living circumstances and housing, brainwashing and indoctrination to carry Communist ideas to their homeland, and shadowing and provocations by secret services.

The documents that I discovered in Russian archives were designed for internal use within government and Communist Party structures. They present an all-embracing and unvarnished picture of African students' presence in the USSR.

During the early 1960s, hundreds of young people from West Africa were enrolled in Soviet institutions of higher education. In May 1961, there were 9 students and postgraduate students from Côte d'Ivoire, 108 from Ghana, 69 from the Republic of Guinea, 2 from Portuguese Guinea, 1 from Dahomey, 1 from Liberia, 20 from Mali, 1 from Niger, 27 from Nigeria, 7 from Senegal, 22 from Sierra Leone, and 20 from Togo.[15] (These data are incomplete because they do not cover cadets.)

The most important Soviet educational training institution accommodating students from Africa was the Peoples' Friendship University (Universitet Druzhby Narodov, UDN, also known as Patrice Lumumba Friendship University). It was established in Moscow in February 1960, at Khrushchev's personal initiative. In a published resolution of the CC CPSU and the USSR Council of Ministers, the UDN's stated goal was "to train national cadres from Asian, African, and Latin American countries."[16] Yet archival materials reveal that its true goals were far more ambitious: "to prepare specialists capable of outclassing graduates from Western universities both in knowledge and general cultural outlook." The UDN was thus conceived as a first-rate (judging by world standards) educational institution, "excellently organized, with experienced teaching staff, equipped with modern facilities, and having high scientific and sociopolitical authority."[17] It opened its doors in the fall of 1960.

Speaking at the UDN's inauguration ceremony in November, Khrushchev denied that its educational program would be ideologically biased: "Naturally, we shall not force our ideas, our ideology on any student. World outlook is an absolutely voluntary affair. If you wish to know my political convictions, I will not conceal the fact that I am a Communist and firmly believe that the most advanced ideology is the Marxist-Leninist ideology. If any of you comes to the conclusion that this ideology is acceptable to him, we shall bear him no grudge. However, neither shall we be disconcerted if you do not become Communists."[18]

This public proclamation differed markedly from the secret decisions and directives of the party and government apparatus. A special resolution of the CC CPSU Secretariat provided measures ensuring that students from the developing world leave the USSR "not only as qualified specialists but also as people with progressive views, the Soviet Union's sincere friends."[19] The Ministry of Higher and Specialized Secondary Education saw its mission as the "indoctrination of students from 'less developed countries' with a socialist ideology."[20] The ministerial staff was instructed "to explain to the students circumstantially that the modern age is the time of the destruction and the collapse of the capitalist system, the time of the emergence and the rise of economic and political relations of a socialist type that existed, for example, between countries of a people's democracy and with many Asian and African countries."[21] Minister Vyacheslav Elyutin gave directions "to propagandize intelligibly the achievements of the Soviet Union in internal and foreign policy, its struggle for peace," to teach foreign students "the history of the CPSU and of our country, the basics of Marxism-Leninism, philosophy, and political economy."[22] Although these social science courses, which were compulsory for Soviet students, were elective for foreign students, the educational process was interwoven with Communist indoctrination, beginning with preparatory studies, from which enrollees received "a basic, general view of world history and geography, and of the tenor of life in the Soviet society."[23]

The Soviet authorities did their best to provide attractive living conditions for students from the countries of the developing world. They received stipends that were liberal compared with those received by even the most capable Soviet students. And the Soviet government covered the costs of tuition, housing, clothing, medical care, and transportation to and from the students' homelands.[24]

But the Soviet reality sometimes caused disillusionment, even among the "sincere friends." Some African students in the USSR complained that living conditions were unsatisfactory, that their allowances were inadequate, that their personal movement and social intercourse with local populations were restricted, that they encountered racial discrimination, and that they were exploited for propaganda purposes. Some students were upset by the Russian style of living, which seemed depressing to them. "No cars, no cafés, no good clothes or good food," a Nigerian student in Moscow lamented, "nothing to buy or inspect in the stores, no splash of color to relieve Moscow's damp gray. Nothing but shortages and restrictions. No opportunity to let go normally, breathe easily, and enjoy some harmless student fun. Not a trace of the civilized pleasures of Paris—or even Dakar."[25]

Many such complaints were justified. In confidential documents, Soviet officials admitted that there were crowded living conditions, a lack of privacy, inadequate sanitary facilities, and a monotonous diet uncustomary for Africans.[26]

Most of the African students enrolled in various Soviet institutions of higher learning came from positions of relative privilege in their home countries and did not match the image of Africans prevalent in the Soviet media and literature—poor, oppressed, unselfish, simple-hearted, virtuous people. Racial incidents were numerous, and they compelled African students to form unauthorized organizations to defend their rights. One of these organizations, the Black African Students' Union in the USSR, in March 1960 mailed Khrushchev a private letter that partly read: "To prevent as much as possible what we do not wish to call 'racial discrimination,' we feel that something ought to be done by the government of this country to ensure that the repetition of such incidents does not jeopardize our future friendship. . . . Like many other African students in other parts of the world, we have come to this country to study, not as refugees. Therefore we consider it right that we should be accorded normal human respect, which is the right of everyone in this country."[27] The letter was signed by a Guinean student, Khila Deys, the chairman of the union's Executive Committee. Among "its chief organizers" was a Nigerian, Theophilus Okonkwo.[28]

The pathos of the letter was not in accord with the facts of "racial discrimination" to which it referred. The most serious incident described in the letter involved a student from Somalia who was allegedly "attacked, beaten, and left unconscious by four Russian students" at Moscow University. The CC CPSU established several commissions to verify the letter's claims. They found out that there was a brawl between Somalian students and Russian students, which allegedly had been provoked by a Somali who publicly spat in the face of a Russian girl because she refused to dance with him.[29]

The conclusions reached by Soviet officials about the roots of this incident were very representative. The chief of the Komityet Gosudarstvennoy Bezopasnosti (KGB, Committee for State Security of the USSR), Alexander Shelepin, was sure that Khila Deys had only signed the letter but that its true authors were "Negro students . . . suspected of collaboration with foreign intelligence departments. All of them are hostile to the Soviet Union and repeatedly solicited students from African countries to acts of provocation."[30] The chief of the Foreign Department of Moscow State University, Nikiforov, saw the source of the trouble in the social backgrounds and morals of some African students. He wrote to the Ministry of Foreign Affairs of the USSR (Ministerstvo inostrannykh del, MID): "In our opinion, the choice of some African students to study at Moscow University is poor. Some of them belonged to the feudal and merchant noble classes of their countries. They arrived in the Soviet Union not from their native countries but from Western Europe and North America, where they used to study and therefore were corrupted by bourgeois morals." Nikiforov was alarmed that some African students kept constant contacts with British and U.S. embassies and that one of them had served in the Canadian navy.[31] The deputy minister of higher and specialized secondary education, Mikhail Prokofiev, considered it necessary to radically alter attitudes toward African students and treat them according to their "social background, political commitments, and life experience." He urged those involved to drop the "naive approach when we look upon all of them like representatives of oppressed or formerly oppressed nations. We leave out of our account that many of these students, if not the majority, belong to the bourgeoisie and feudal nobility and that they are infected with bourgeois ideology."[32]

The measures taken in connection with the letter were evidence that this recommendation was accepted. The two students, Somalian and Russian, who had come to blows were given admonitions. But the three students from Nigeria (Theophilus Okonkwo), Togo (Michel Ayih), and Uganda (Andrew Amar), whom Shelepin had said were being hostile to the Soviet Union, were expelled—ostensibly for academic failure. After the Soviet authorities disbanded the Black African Students' Union in the USSR, Okonkwo sent an open letter to all African governments "condemning the Soviet Union for its inability to provide adequate education to foreign students."[33]

Soviet officials were governed by the postulate that there was no racism in their country of proletarian internationalism, where Africans should be considered "younger siblings" of the socialist brotherhood. But in reality, there was racial tension, and they had to seek external enemies and class-determined aliens among Africans to blame.

There was a sphere where any African—irrespective of his or her social position, wealth, or political commitments—could not avoid feeling denigrated. The African student population sent to Russia was disproportionately male. In the eyes of the majority of Soviet people, including the ruling leadership, to be next to a black was immoral. The Soviet authorities discouraged miscegenation. Press campaigns openly condemned mixed marriages involving Russian women and men from the developing world, particularly Africans. Archival documents reveal how one such campaign affected interracial relations in the Soviet Union.

On September 27, 1962, the Soviet youth newspaper *Komsomol'skaya Pravda* published an article titled "Regret Was Too Late." It was, its author asserted, the true story of a woman student from Moscow. Her name was Larisa, and she was a beauty of a girl with golden hair. Seeking a better life in the capitalist world, she could not resist wooing a certain Makhmud, an Eastern beauty with a "hard and avid eye," and she left her Russian boyfriend to marry him. He took Larisa away to his native Muslim country, which was unnamed but resembled Egypt. As a Soviet citizen, Larisa faced many problems there. She failed to get a job that fit her line of work. Reluctantly, she agreed to be naturalized, and the penalty followed immediately: The foul rogue Makhmud deceived gullible Larisa and sold her to a rich old man. The author described her first morning in a new place:

> Larisa turned gray overnight. She was able to move only after doctors massaged her body. But her brains did not work well. Other wives of the old man watched her suffering. They felt pity for Larisa and consoled her. She will be the favorite wife for their master. He did pay a world of money for her anyway. It is good that he is not too old; he has not reached his sixties. She should not feel nervous about the future, for she is the only blonde with blue eyes in the country. The master might be fed up with her not very soon, in two or three years. And at the proper time, he will sell her not to a peasant, as he usually does with his aged wives, but to a man of family, as such a pretty white woman will always be in great demand. As for gray hair, they will paint them today to return their golden color. . . . And what a good life Larisa might have had, indeed.[34]

This article led to increasing racial animosity toward Africans and Arabs, who considered its publication a demonstration of official support for racism. A month passed, and the UDN's leadership had to sound the alarm. Its rector, S. M. Rumyantsev, wrote to the CC CPSU that the article, "Regret Was Too Late," had aroused indignation among foreign students. In meetings of students from Arab countries, they claimed that the author's views "expressed the policy aimed at discrimination of foreign students, especially of Arabs and Africans." They also "referred to many cases of growing hostility toward Arabs (taunting, abuses, harassments)," under the influence of the article. Arab Communist students managed to reduce the decisions of the meetings to the election of delegates with full powers to make an oral protest to the editorial board of *Komsomol'skaya Pravda*. Negotiations between the delegates and members of the editorial board resulted in "the declaration that the cases mentioned in the article did not concern Arab countries."[35]

But this did not satisfy the Arab students, and in fact it caused "a new wave of protest among African students." If the article did not concern Arab countries, it was obvious that the cunning seducer Makhmud, who cruelly deceived Larisa, was an African. At the meeting with the deputy editor in chief of *Komsomol'skaya Pravda*, African students asked him to publish an elucidation that the author did not mean African countries. But the newspaper refused to publish this, and the African students became so irritated that the UDN's rector had to hold a special meeting to calm them down. At the meeting, the students stigmatized the article as racist and complained that since its publication, Muscovites had begun to treat Africans poorly.[36]

This complaint was not groundless. Memoranda delivered to the CC CPSU by four deputy chiefs of its departments referred to many cases of anti-African violence. In Moscow, students from the Congo, Mali, and Sierra Leone suffered racial assaults and harassments. Bokuma Muhuma, the son of the Malian foreign minister, was beaten badly. Racist slurs like "monkeys," "darkies," and "idlers" were hurled at Africans everywhere. The authors of the memoranda admitted that the general public in the USSR would not condemn the majority of these facts, which were not investigated by the police.[37]

Communist Party officials were anxious about the fact that Cold War foes exploited these incidents in propaganda campaigns against the Soviet Union. "Reactionary elements among foreigners, some embassies of capitalist countries, try to drive anti-Soviet sentiments among immature foreign students and make them leave the USSR and organize unfriendly acts against the Soviet Union," they wrote. The measures they suggested to improve the situation were representative for Soviet bureaucracy in their window-dressing, counterpropagandistic character:

> The newspaper *Vechernyaya Moskva* should describe one of the cases when criminal proceedings were instituted against hooligans for beating up foreign students. The Novosti News Agency within two months should prepare and publish in foreign languages a booklet under the title *We Study in the USSR* composed of articles written by foreign students who study in the Soviet Union and disseminate it abroad. The booklet should show the assistance that the Soviet Union is rendering to underdeveloped countries in training highly knowledgeable specialists. It is necessary to demonstrate shining, actual examples of how successfully foreign students acquire contemporary knowledge, how they enhance their standard of culture, and how their progressive world outlook is being formed.[38]

However, there was a less expensive, faster, and certainly more efficient way to counteract the "generating of anti-Soviet sentiments" among foreign students. And the UDN's rector did suggest that the CC CPSU "give the directive to publish in the press perhaps a very short explanation of the fallaciousness of the article 'Regret Was Too Late.'" But the CC CPSU Department of Propaganda and Agitation rejected this idea.[39]

African Students in the Cold War Competition

African students in the USSR became an important instrument for both sides in the Cold War ideological competition. The United States was quick to take advantage of Soviet difficulties by providing disillusioned African students with lucrative opportunities to study in the West.[40] And the Western media argued that African students were not only indoctrinated with Communism but also trained for terrorism and subversive activity.

On July 16, 1961, under the screaming headline "Moscow Trained Me for Revolt in Africa," the *Sunday Telegraph* of London published the story of a Nigerian, Anthony Okotcha, who had studied at the UDN from October 1960 to January 1961. Okotcha had arrived in Moscow from London. In the article, he asserted that the second secretary of the Soviet Embassy had enabled him and his wife to enroll at the UDN because he was married to Obiamaka Azikiwe, a sister of Nnamdi Azikiwe, then the governor-general of Nigeria.[41]

The Nigerian couple's first impressions of Moscow and the UDN were favorable. They were given a "not luxurious but comfortable" dormitory room, while other students "slept five in a room, with one Russian student in each party." The lectures surprised Okotcha; he apparently sincerely described his impression of the first lecture on political science, as follows:

> A fat, middle-aged professor stood on the rostrum. In rather broken English, he congratulated us on having come to the happiest and most progressive land on Earth. Than he began to abuse the British Commonwealth and all it stood for and to argue that Western democracy had outlived its usefulness. He went on to expound Marxist-Leninist philosophy and launch a vitriolic attack on Christianity. He declared that our duty in Africa was to learn how to organize a popular front and drive the plundering imperialists into the ocean.

Thus, Okotcha disliked the lecture, particularly the attack on Christianity.[42] However, according to Okotcha, even such a primitive level of political education was allegedly effective. Within eight weeks of their arrival, he and his wife "were ready to declare all-out war on Western democracy. We had learned the Marxist-Leninist fundamentals by heart. We had learned to hate what the Russians hated and to love what they loved."[43]

The continuation of the Okotcha tale resembled a tabloid detective story full of fantasies that, according to the scholar Maxim Matusevich, "bordered on utter nonsense."[44] Okotcha asserted that one day he attended a "class for self-defense," where about two hundred students from various African, Central American, and Asian countries gathered. It was an espionage school for special training in sabotage and assassination techniques. The students were instructed "by serious-faced military men in uniform in target practice with pistols, rifles and sub-machine guns," and they were shown "how to dynamite a bridge, a railway train, a house and many other objectives," "how to throw a hand-grenade into a crowd, how to kill a man quickly with a dagger, and how to make surprise attacks at night." Okotcha fortunately escaped training in this class. "You will be more of a planner, along with your wife," he was supposedly told by the university authorities.[45]

"Planners" were also supposed to deal with many interesting things, particularly "occult science," taught by a Professor Safronchuk, "an expert in African affairs who spoke Swahili perfectly." He, Okotcha narrated, began his first lesson by saying: "As you know, in certain underdeveloped parts of Africa, the people are highly superstitious, and it is only by playing on their superstition that they can be won over for political ends. Hence, there is a need to adopt a system similar to that which sparked the Mau-Mau rebellion in Kenya. One witch doctor operating among primitive people can do more than a dozen political lecturers. He can move the masses in any way he chooses. Well, then, suppose he is a Communist."

The professor proceeded to demonstrate his art. He placed a skull on the table and caused it to issue commands such as these:

> I am your ancestor speaking. I command you to go tonight, kill the British governor and bring his head and hands to me. If you fail, I will cast evil spells on you and your family. . . . I am the spirit of God. I command you to burn that Englishman's house and rape his wife and daughter. If you don't, you and all your family will be under the earth within seven days. . . . I am Shango from the deep waters. I will fetch you if you refuse to join the Communist Party and do whatever its leader tells you.

The professor showed how these voices were produced by radio microphones. Okotcha explained that "he then taught us how to simulate spirit rappings, cause a phantom to appear in a cloud of smoke, produce weird sounds in boxes, make a skeleton walk into dark rooms, haunt the houses of enemies, and pretend we were possessed by spirits."[46]

In January 1961, the UDN administration sent Okotcha and his wife to London "to recruit African and Asian students for the University." He fulfilled this mission in good faith and discharged commissions of Soviet diplomats and "agents." Afterward, he was ordered to Nigeria "to reorganize the two disguised Communist movements there." On May 30, he came to the Soviet Embassy to receive instructions and was introduced to two members of these movements who were preparing to go to Moscow. They told Okotcha that "with the assistance of the Soviet Union, it was only a question of time before Nigeria would become a Communist state." They had a "political blueprint in the form of a typed booklet," and their plans included "assassinations, terrorism, arson, intimidation and all imaginable social unrest." In this blueprint, Okotcha saw "how the disguised Communist movements would come to power, how their leaders would proclaim a state of emergency over the entire country, suspend Parliament, and, if necessary, invite the assistance of Russian troops, and how they would deprive chiefs and emirs of their thrones and abolish the Constitution." The wicked designs impressed Okotcha, and he "suddenly realized that not for all the gold in Russia would he agree to send his country into a bloodbath." He left the embassy and decided to "sever all connection with Communism" and never to have "anything more to do with the Russians who were privy to such ghastly plans."[47]

The Soviet authorities asserted that Okotcha's interview had been arranged by the British Intelligence Service. UDN rector Rumyantsev asked the editor of the *Sunday Telegraph* to publish the letter that Okotcha allegedly brought to the Soviet Embassy in London on February 20, 1961. This letter read that Okotcha had left Moscow for London, where people from the British Intelligence Service compelled him to make anti-Soviet statements, proposing to solve his financial and housing problems in return. He wrote that he refused to do it and wanted to return to Moscow, but the Nigerian mission in Moscow refused to issue his passport. Rumyantsev questioned the veracity of Okotcha's interview and assured the *Telegraph* editor that the UDN "does not pursue any aim other than providing disinterested aid to the people of Asia, Africa, and Latin America and has no intention to conspire or to organize uprisings."[48]

The CC CPSU charged the MID and the KGB to take measures to publish Rumyantsev's letter to the editor of the *Sunday Telegraph* and a photocopy of Okotcha's letter to Rumyantsev in the foreign press. Other counterpropagandistic steps were also taken. The chairman of the State Committee for Cultural Relations with Foreign Countries, Georgii Zhukov, informed the CC CPSU secretary, Nuritdin Mukhitdinov, on October 14, 1961, that

> all students of Friendship University [i.e., the UDN] were acquainted with a publication of Okotcha's story, and they deprecated his calumny. After that, many African students wrote articles on their studies at Friendship University in newspapers issued in their native countries, and now they are receiving favorable responses from their young compatriots. Nowadays Friendship University is preparing a handbook on the University. Shortly, this handbook will be edited and a large number of copies will be printed in English, French, and Spanish, partly in Moscow and partly by the offices of the Novosti News Agency abroad, and will be dispersed in the countries of Asia, Africa, and Latin America.[49]

Okotcha's story is a prime example of the use of African students as an instrument of the Cold War.

Political Indoctrination on the Spot

The Soviets did not confine their work with West African elites to indoctrinating students in the USSR. They also tried to reach the ruling circles of the "progressive countries." Particular attention was paid to the political formation of future and acting leaders.

In Ghana, Soviet lectures helped with the curriculum of the Kwame Nkrumah Ideological Institute at Winneba, which was established in 1961 to train the Convention People's Party (CPP) workers in socialist ideology.[50] From July to August 1963, at the invitation of the CC CPSU, a CPP delegation, headed by Executive Secretary Nathaniel Welbeck, visited the Soviet Union. The delegation got acquainted with "the system of training of ideological and propagandist cadres of the CPSU," noting its "role in directing a national economy and the country's political life" and "the methods of affecting the party's leading role in social organizations."[51] In October 1963, a second CPP delegation, led by Kweku Akwei, the ideological secretary of the party, arrived in the Soviet Union. These Ghanaians studied the CPSU's propaganda work and visited the Soviet Higher Party School.[52]

Two teachers of political economy and philosophy, Yuryi Popov and

Gennadyi Predvechnyi, were sent to the National Administrative School of Mali "to counter bourgeois training and influence." They delivered lectures on the same subjects as French teachers did. The impossibility of "peaceful coexistence" between the two ideologies quickly became evident, and the administration of the school had to change the curriculum, so that beginning on January 1, 1964, "all the students began to study Marxism-Leninism." Up to that time, they "had been almost completely under bourgeois influence," but "the lack of proper academic training was compensated for by a fierce desire to learn the ideology of anti-imperialist and anticolonial revolution." Popov and Predvechnyi organized a presentation of Soviet films at the school, and they regularly disseminated Marxist literature there.[53]

Popov and Predvechnyi also criticized the "Chinese splitters." As they expressed it, "while lecturing on philosophy and political economy, it was necessary to pay special attention to the problems being interpreted dogmatically by the Chinese Communist Party's leadership. G. P. Predvechnyi delivered lectures on the problems of war and peace in the modern age, the conjunction of national liberation, and the world communist movement. Much attention was paid to the basic contradiction of the modern age: the contradiction between socialist and imperialist camps."[54]

Popov and Predvechnyi believed that they succeeded in "transforming the ideology of the students." The teachers quoted "numerous statements" of their pupils that "while learning Marxism-Leninism, they comprehended the substance of the process of social development, the reactionary and class character of bourgeois ideology." Popov and Predvechnyi considered it their achievement when students "bewildered" the French teachers, asking them questions "from the point of view of Marxism-Leninism," and spoke ironically of the Chinese Great Leap Forward and communes when a Malian recounted his impressions on staying in China.[55]

The talks of Popov and Predvechnyi with high-ranking Malian officials revealed that their prior perception of socialism was far from a "scientific" (i.e., Soviet) conception of socialism. A member of the Politburo of the Sudanese Union, Seydou Kouyaté, felt that Soviet scientists, and I. I. Potekhin in particular, did not properly appreciate the Malian distinctiveness, for "classes and class struggle do not exist there." Kouyaté dissented from the Soviet postulate of the noncapitalist way of development. He was of the opinion that this formula "meant implicit recognition of the third way." Meanwhile, "the creation of conditions for building socialism" is actually "building socialism itself."[56]

Soviet representatives did not achieve much in disseminating socialist ideas in Ghana. As N. Torocheshnikov—an expert on an international commission on developing Ghanaian education, who worked in Ghana from December 1960 to January 1961—observed: "One of my strongest impressions in Ghana was the fact of a deep British penetration of the educational system at all levels. The British sensitively influence the native population through their instructional staff. This influence is exerted with the help of the apologists of bourgeois, idealistic philosophy."[57]

Little or nothing had changed within the four years when, in February 1965, F. Kurnikov, an adviser to Ghana's Plan Commission, stressed in his memorandum to the MID that Ghanaian libraries contained no Soviet books on economics but were full of books by Western authors on economic topics. There was only one Soviet book in the Plan Commission library, a statistical data collection titled *The USSR in 1963*. It was in Russian and of no use to Ghanaians. Talks with Ghanaian civil servants convinced Kurnikov that their knowledge of the Soviet Union came almost entirely from Western sources. He proposed that his colleagues select, translate into English and French, and edit for circulation throughout Africa Soviet works on economics "that might be of interest for developing countries."[58]

The deputy minister of foreign affairs, Y. A. Malik, sent Kurnikov's memorandum to the CC CPSU Ideological Department. In his reply to an inquiry made by the CC CPSU, V. Tret'yakov, deputy chairman of the State Committee for the Coordination of Scientific Research, noted that "the study of economic literature edited in the USSR revealed that this literature with the rare exception shouldn't be advised for translation, as it mainly concerns general problems and there is no concrete analysis of economic processes of interest to developing countries." Tret'yakov proposed producing the literature needed in the period 1966–68.[59] Soon the committee was disbanded, and this proposal was not implemented.

In February 1964, Ghanaian president Kwame Nkrumah informed the Soviet ambassador to Ghana, G. M. Rodionov, that he intended "to begin teaching the theory of scientific socialism in universities and colleges" and asked for assistance in producing textbooks on the CPP's history and on the problems of socialism. On March 17, the CPSU Secretariat approved the text of a telegram to the ambassador in Accra that partly read: "We are ready to receive in Moscow two Ghanaian comrades to let them work in one of the Soviet scientific establishments, for example in the Academy of Social Sciences attached to the CC CPSU, where they will receive comprehensive aid in producing textbooks."[60] But they did not manage to produce the textbooks before Nkrumah was ousted in 1966.

Against this background, the achievements of the USSR's adversaries in spreading Western values in Ghana looked much weightier. A paper prepared in the U.S. State Department for the visit to Ghana by the assistant secretary of state for African affairs, G. Mennen Williams, from June 22 to 26, 1963, enumerated "favorable conditions for U.S.-Ghanaian relations":

> The United States and the West generally continue to enjoy the basic goodwill of the Ghanaian people. Ghana's governmental system and judiciary have been influenced by the British constitution and common law. . . . The civil service is good and, along with the armed forces and the police, is predominantly Western trained. The academic staff in the universities and secondary schools are also the products of Western education, and nearly 80 percent of Ghanaian students studying overseas are in Western institutions. . . . Most of the senior officials in the Government Planning Commission, the Bank of Ghana, the Volta River Authority and Ghanaian Investment Bank are pro-Western. U.S. aid programs and the Peace Corps efforts in Ghana have been noteworthy successes. Both activities have enabled Americans to meet and work with a wide range of Ghanaians throughout the country.[61]

U.S. ambassador William Mahoney reported to Williams that "after hundreds of calls, receptions, and exchanges with Ghanaians of every walk of life, I am getting to feel at home in the job."[62]

Archival documents that might shed light on the efforts of Soviet diplomats and other officials to influence Ghanaian political leaders remain classified. However, there are many declassified U.S. materials on American contacts with Ghanaian politicians, including the president. This evidence mirrors the problems that the Soviets faced dealing with Ghanaians. According to these documents, Nkrumah was really "some kind of a nut," and the Americans experienced difficulties trying to transform his "neutralism against us" into "neutralism for us."

The year 1963 did not bring relaxation of the tension in bilateral Ghanaian-U.S. relations. In Ghana, the leftist press and radio continued the anti-American campaign launched in the autumn of 1962. The attacks ranged from "general accusations of American colonialist-imperialist ambitions and attacks on policies of the United States through personal attacks on our Ambassador and the Attorney General to charges of official American involvement in the assassination attempt against Nkrumah on August 1, 1962."[63]

This assassination attempt had been a severe shock to Nkrumah, and, in fear for his life, he had since largely isolated himself in his well-guarded Flagstaff House residence. He distrusted Ghanaians and chose mainly leftist foreigners for his immediate entourage, with Geoffrey Bing playing first fiddle.[64] Nkrumah became suspicious, and because he sincerely believed that that the U.S. Central Intelligence Agency (CIA) was hunting for him, he was determined "to fight with the CIA, which is a menace, particularly to small nations."[65] The Ghanaian government intended to try the nation's former foreign minister, Ako Adjei, as a CIA agent in the conspiracy trial.[66] Ghana refused to withdraw its demand to expel the American diplomats William Davis and Carl Nydell from the country. And there were repeated incidents of harassment of American personnel in Ghana.

In keeping with the Department of State's instructions, Ambassador Mahoney met Nkrumah on February 1 and told him that "(a) all action regarding the two embassy officials must be stopped; (b) harassment of American personnel should cease; (c) continued strident anti–United States attacks in the Ghanaian press will inevitably lead to a serious deterioration in our relations; the use of Soviet material in the local press was to be deplored; and (d) in view of the many reports we have received on the Bui Dam [with the USSR's assistance], the United States would like to know the Ghanaian intentions on this project." This sounded like an ultimatum but did not have an effect; Nkrumah gave the ambassador no assurances.[67]

The only effective remedy to influence Nkrumah left in the U.S. diplomatic arsenal was to cut off financing for the Volta River Project (see the chapters above, especially chapter 3). U.S. president John Kennedy decided that no Volta aid would be disbursed unless Ghana withdrew its demand that Nydell and Davis be removed from the country. In January 1963, two major private investors in the Volta project, Edgar Kaiser and Chad Calhoun, arrived in Accra "to deliver a message of a general character" to Nkrumah from Kennedy. They "immediately pointed out to Nkrumah the dangerous implications of the contemplated expulsion action."[68] After six weeks of pressure "at all levels," the Ghanaian government backed away from the idea of expelling Nydell and Davis.[69] The anti-American campaign in the Ghanaian media declined. Adjei was freed from the charge of being a CIA agent, but he was not released from prison. Kennedy ordered a resumption of the financing for the Volta project but directed the State Department to provide him with detailed information on the situation in Ghana.

Talking with Kaiser and Calhoun shortly after their visit to Ghana, Kennedy asked Kaiser "to explain Nkrumah's behavior." The president could understand "his trying to deal with both the U.S. and the Soviet Union," but he was amazed at "the lack of subtlety and balance" in maneuvering between the two superpowers. Kaiser mentioned two reasons: "the influence of Bing and others in Nkrumah's immediate entourage, and the desire of Nkrumah to respond favorably to everybody who saw him frequently."[70]

One person who contacted Nkrumah frequently, U.S. ambassador Mahoney, also noticed Nkrumah's "highly personal approach to all things, programs and ideas, as well as people."[71] In his letters to Williams, Mahoney recounted the difficulties he faced while trying to achieve his main objective—"to steer Nkrumah and Ghana in our direction." He called Nkrumah "a fortress," and in besieging it, he believed, "we have achieved some small victories." Nkrumah, Mahoney noted, "is so essentially the political animal and so self-centered a person that to expect him to surrender his contrived spot on the world stage (as by calming down the press or voting more moderately in the UN) is expecting him to change his very nature." Old methods to influence Nkrumah—verbal persuasion, official representations, and ultimatums—were "fruitless" and "counterproductive" and had run dry: "The new and serious element is that he no longer seems to feel the need to do anything about our protests, no matter how friendly he feels toward me personally, since we never do anything but talk." The ambassador suggested adopting a "siege" tactic. He believed that acting with intelligence and firmness rather than exhorting would make Nkrumah come to terms. It was necessary to withdraw from "activities that are peripheral to our real purpose here" and to retain those that "directly benefit the U.S. and Western position here": to complete the Volta River complex, and to continue the Peace Corps program, "our small [Agency for International Development] program," and "our Food for Peace program."[72]

Mahoney's recommendations for a "siege" tactic were not accepted, however, because U.S.-Ghanaian relations improved without the need to toughen the American line. The anti-American campaign in the Ghanaian press ceased, laws favorable for increasing foreign direct investment were passed, and Nkrumah made some friendly gestures—such as throwing a reception for the Peace Corps.[73]

President Kennedy followed the events in Ghana closely, personally monitoring the cable traffic. At one point, the State Department's desk officer was amazed to receive "a call from the President asking him for the details about Ghana's problem controlling the capsid, a parasite that was ruining the cocoa crop."[74]

In early November 1963, Kennedy signed a document on state guarantees of U.S. investments in the construction of the Volta River complex. Construction began. Kennedy concerned himself with the situation in Ghana shortly before his tragic death. On November 19, he talked with Mahoney. The president asked what Mahoney thought of Nkrumah's ideas, "specifically whether he is a Marxist." Mahoney assured Kennedy that Nkrumah's "Marxist bark was worse than his bite": "I replied that Nkrumah is a badly confused and immature person who is not quite sure of what he wants except that he wants to lead all of Africa. I said he has much Marxism in his makeup but that his performance, as in the development of Ghana's domestic economy, was mixed and that internally there was promise of Ghana's being at least partially Western. I said that in the field of foreign relations, Nkrumah frequently serves the purposes of Mao and Khrushchev but that he was too much of an egoist ever willingly to be their pawn."[75]

Nkrumah was not a governable figure for the Soviets either. He bore good feelings for Khrushchev; "he treats me like a brother," he said, remembering their vacations together in the Crimea.[76] But this did not prevent Nkrumah from protecting his own interests when dealing with the Soviets. The essence of Ghanaian policy toward both the East and the West was explicated in a secret aide-memoire prepared by Nkrumah's assistants for his talks with Averell Harriman, the U.S. undersecretary of state, and "delivered" to the U.S. ambassador on March 21, 1964, a few hours before Harriman's arrival in Accra: "We have socialism and anti-imperialism in common with the Communists, which makes us travel with them on many paths which you will not tread. On the other hand, we have economic, cultural, intellectual and moral ties with the West which the Communists do not share, and which take us along paths in company with the West."[77] The authors of the aide-memoire believed that to develop full-scale relations with Ghana, both socialist and capitalist countries should follow these principles: "no interference in our internal politics, no transmission of cultural ideas which we find degrading, no economic ties which limit our independence."[78]

Harriman Tests Nkrumah

After Kennedy's assassination, the new U.S. president, Lyndon Johnson, sent Harriman to Accra to save U.S.-Ghanaian relations, which were in "grave condition."[79] On January 2, 1964, another attempt was made on Nkrumah's life. A guard fired several shots at Nkrumah before he was overpowered. Nkrumah was convinced that the CIA was behind the plot, and his attitude toward the United States changed from suspicion to hostility. The Ghanaian press launched a new round of attacks against "American imperialism" and the CIA. On February 3, a mass anti-American demonstration was held near the U.S. Embassy. The demonstrators, not content to chant slogans, pulled down the U.S. flag. Four American professors at the University at Legon were dismissed on the charge that they were CIA agents, despite the rector's objections. On February 26, 1964, in a letter to Johnson, Nkrumah characterized the CIA as an organization that "seems to devote all its attention to fomenting ill-will, misunderstanding and even clandestine and subversive activities among our people, to the impairment of the good relations which exist between our two Governments."[80]

During Harriman's visit to Accra, he had two long talks with Nkrumah, on March 22 and 23. Ambassador Mahoney, who was present at these conversations, cabled a record of them to Washington. Harriman "took the offensive" from the beginning and did not grope for antiseptic formulations to express discontent with the Soviet policy and the rapprochement between the USSR and Ghana.

Johnson's envoy "said that it is not the fact that Russia is Communist that disturbs" Washington, but "what we object to is Russia's imperialism; . . . Khrushchev's methods have changed from Stalin's, [but] he is still out to communize the world." Nkrumah reacted, "saying it is not true, that in the modern world it is no longer possible for one nation to force its ideas upon another; . . . this was an aspect of international Communism that died with Trotsky."[81]

Harriman noted the fact that Nkrumah "had asked the Russians to establish state farms in Ghana." Indeed, the USSR has enjoyed success in industry and science, but its "agricultural program had been a constant failure." Nkrumah responded "lamely": "I need the machinery."[82] To illustrate his thesis, Harriman tore a page of analysis from an American document on the Soviet economy and showed it to the Ghanaian president. The page was full of graphs showing that in the USSR, approximately 50 percent of all animal products and vegetables were produced on small, individually operated plots, on only 3 percent of the country's arable land. "This, Harriman was trying to make his interlocutor to understand, proved that if Khrushchev wished to solve his food products problem, all he had to do was to give land back to farmers and abandon this ideological nonsense." According to Mahoney, "Nkrumah seemed impressed."[83]

Exploiting this success, Harriman mounted another attack against "Russian imperialism." He agreed that there had been a small change in Khrushchev's methods vis-à-vis the Stalinist background, but "he still had not given up his imperialism and aggressive Communist objectives." Nkrumah disagreed.[84]

Nkrumah withstood Harriman's sophisticated pressure and did not share his anti-Soviet stance. Back in Washington, Harriman informed a National Security Council meeting on April 13, 1964, that Nkrumah was "moving to the left," "turning to the East in an effort to gain support," is "afraid of assassination," and "blames the U.S. and U.K. for his troubles." However, Harriman recommended following through on the Volta River Project to avoid the "loss of our standing and of the money so far invested."[85] His recommendations were accepted.

Nkrumah resisted Western pressure, and this brought him political dividends in his nation's relations with the East. But in Ghana, his power and prestige had eroded. Socialism as an instrument of an accelerated modernization and pan-African ambitions seemed at best only a name but more often a dangerous chimera to the majority of Ghanaian politicians and officials. The USSR had lost the struggle for their souls.

Regimes Destined to Fall

The regimes in Ghana, Mali, and Guinea were destined to fall. Nkrumah, Kéi'ta, and Touré suppressed opposition, and without viable opposition parties, the mass democratic organizations of the nationalist period were rapidly transformed into top-down centralized parties that valued loyalty above all else. The three leaders succumbed to the temptation of ultimate power and of personality cults, and they became authoritarian rulers at the apexes of huge bureaucratic pyramids that had no positive feedback from common people. In Ghana, approximately half of all employees worked for the state or the Convention People's Party apparatus. These nations' bureaucracies, which were mostly apolitical or pro-Western, were the locus for the most influential social class, with articulate corporative interests that differed greatly from officially proclaimed goals. Officialdom, deaf to the calls to mobilize the masses for the building of socialism, chiefly concerned itself with personal enrichment and the conversion of power into property, and it thus lived in luxury, benefiting from corruption and party patronage. And all this brought such regimes predictable and universal economic results: loss-making state-owned enterprises, fiascos with compulsory established state farms, wasteful big "prestige" projects of doubtful feasibility, shortages of goods, rises in the cost of living, supplementary taxation, and the depreciation of the national currency.

Many ordinary people associated the socialism professed by Nkrumah, Kéi'ta, and Touré with destitution, frustrated hopes, arbitrary rule, and a trampling of civil liberties. As the gap between the highest ranks and the rank and file of the ruling parties grew, people's enthusiasm vanished, replaced by apathy and passive or active resistance.

In February 1966, a coup by members of the Ghanaian army and police overthrew Nkrumah's regime. Nkrumah went into exile in Guinea, where he received a hero's welcome and was named copresident. He died in 1972, without ever returning to his homeland. In Mali, Kéi'ta was ousted by the army in November 1968. He was put in prison, where he died in 1977. In Guinea, a military coup followed Touré's death in March 1984. The new military government proclaimed a policy of "desekoutarization" of all spheres of life, which buried Touré's deeds and ideas.

Conclusion

The main factor that determined the making of Soviet policy toward West Africa and the Congo in the late 1950s and early 1960s was the global confrontation between the USSR and the West, in which the strengthening of either side's position in any part of the world was believed to result in the weakening of the adversary's. The era's sweeping decolonization of Africa so impressed the Soviet leaders that they decided to penetrate the continent, the former preserve of European colonial powers, and thus deliver a blow to "the soft underbelly of imperialism" that would undermine Western interests. For these purposes, the Congo, a huge territory strategically located in the heart of Africa and richly endowed with mineral resources, was particularly attractive.

It has been argued that Soviet actions in West Africa and the Congo were a part of the Kremlin's global strategy to take over Africa. However, the archives on which much of this book is based have revealed that there was no document specifying an established Soviet African blueprint per se, only some drafts of it. The Soviet analysts who planned to strengthen the USSR's influence on "the Negro peoples of Africa" had a flawed knowledge of Africa and Africans, and they proceeded from general assumptions based on Marxism-Leninism. As the Soviet expert Karen Brutents recalled, the later USSR policy toward Africa similarly "lacked any coherent single concept; there existed only some general—too general—principle: 'to help the national liberation movement,' which in effect concealed 'superpower' logic. Many things—and sometimes everything—were determined by momentary circumstances, by the impulses coming from the African leaders, by whom we frequently let ourselves be led, and finally, by the arbitrary and sometimes ill-conceived decisions of the Soviet leaders."[1]

The archives contradict the prevailing opinion that West Africa was a mere backwater of the Cold War. Though the region was never an arena of East/West confrontation causing international crises and direct super-power involvement, it was a revealing exemplar of the implicit, less-explored dimensions of the Cold War, especially propaganda and economic rivalry. The struggle for the souls of Ghanaians, Guineans, and Malians was as acute as the propaganda wars in hotter Cold War spots. The financial burdens were also considerable—especially the Guinean experiment financed by the Soviet Union and the Volta River Project in Ghana, for which the United States paid dearly.

Western historians have tended to have few disagreements about the ideological and security imperatives for Soviet policy toward West Africa. It has been argued that Soviet policy toward Ghana, Guinea, and Mali was a model of ideology-dominated policy when the national interest had to be sacrificed for the support of ideologically close regimes, whereas policy toward "moderate" states (i.e., states oriented toward the West) was pragmatic and based on the national interest. Yet this dichotomy seems to be artificial. Considerations of security and ideology had to be more balanced. Ghana, Guinea, and Mali attracted the attention of the Soviet leadership as promising allies primarily because of their anti-Western rhetoric and deeds. Sékou Touré of Guinea became the Soviet favorite as the leader of the only French territory to opt for immediate independence in the 1958 referendum. The Guinean political elite, having been seriously affected by the severing of economic and other ties with the West, at first regarded all Western countries as potential or actual conspirators against Guinean independence. With respect to Ghana, the real rapprochement between Moscow and Accra began after Kwame Nkrumah had adopted his own line in the Congo crisis, which hampered the United States' efforts to resolve it and in some aspects coincided with the USSR's position. And Mali became the third Soviet ally in West Africa following the break-up of the Mali Federation in August 1960, which was initiated by Senegal with apparent French backing. This the Malian leaders saw as a profound humiliation, which further alienated them from France and pushed them closer toward joining the Guinea-Ghana Union.

The confrontation with the West was the chief criterion for procuring Soviet allies in West Africa and elsewhere, but the ideological aspect did play an important role. The ideological eligibility criteria were not rigid. The conceptions of African socialism—as professed by Nkrumah, Touré, and Kéi'ta—were far from being "scientific" from the Soviet perspective.

After the setback in Guinea, Nikita Khrushchev demanded more ideological purity from the leaders of the developing world who were enjoying substantial Soviet aid. However, his chief purpose was not to convert them to "scientific" socialism but to counter growing Chinese activity in the developing world and to pacify orthodox figures in high Soviet circles who were disgruntled with the wasting of money on countries like Guinea. The conception of the "noncapitalist path of development," articulated by Soviet scholars at the direct request of the Kremlin,[2] gave Khrushchev the ideological flexibility to choose whom he wanted to support, as long as the sponsored nation indicated a desire to avoid reliance on the "imperialist powers."

Khrushchev's attitude toward "moderate" states was also predicated on a mixture of security and ideological considerations. From a security point of view, it made sense to establish healthy relations with all West African countries, and especially with those of geopolitical value. Soviet diplomacy sought contacts with all regimes, including that of the Ivorian leader Félix Houphouët-Boigny, a convinced anticommunist, whom the Soviet press routinely described as being "an African only in color."[3]

Ideological tribute was paid to upholding the "worldwide revolutionary process" by providing financial and other aid to indigenous Marxist organizations, some of them clandestine. The Soviet authorities were fastidious in choosing proper partners among the numerous claimants for assistance, as the Jan Tamraro story highlighted (see chapter 1).

In Western historiography, two approaches to Khrushchev's policy in the Congo prevail. One sees him as engaging in "adventurism," with his emotional reaction to the events based on ideology; the other sees him as fighting with one hand for the sake of national interests, exemplified by his cynical treatment of the Congolese leftist nationalists as "throwaway items." Both approaches follow a rigid division between security and ideology. Instead, I have argued in this book that Khrushchev, despite his flamboyant style, adopted the principle that policy is the art of the possible, and thus his way of dealing with the Congolese crisis was another demonstration of the flexible balance of security and ideology imperatives in Soviet foreign policy. The USSR's leverage vis-à-vis the Congo was rather limited, and was inferior in comparison with that of the United States. The Soviet Union could not sustain the military challenge of the Western powers. Its naval capacity was rather limited, and it lacked aircraft carriers and the airlift capability to transport and supply forces thousands of miles from home. But the United States succeeded in making the

UN forces in the Congo an effective instrument to secure Western interests. This left the Soviet Union no choice but to influence events mainly through its allies, thus avoiding overt involvement and a possible armed clash with another superpower.

The role of the Soviet Union in the Congo crisis was ambivalent. Its involvement in the Congo was paltry compared with that of the United States, but the supplies it sent to the Lumumba government contributed to the escalation of the crisis. However, the Soviet Union also played a decisive role in the deescalation of the crisis when, at several key moments, Khrushchev declined to provide significant aid to the government of Antoine Gizenga, despite a reasonable chance that such aid might have resulted in a victory for its recipients. The USSR failed to create an international coalition as a counterweight to the UN forces supporting the pro-Western circles in the Congo. This was partly due to Khrushchev's miscalculations. The Soviet leader made a strategic mistake in trying to use the ousting and assassination of Lumumba in his attack against the UN secretary-general, Dag Hammarskjöld. Khrushchev proposed dismissing Hammarskjöld, abolishing the post of secretary-general, and switching to a so-called troika of three elected leaders. This troika plan was advertised by Soviet propaganda as a "reform" of the United Nations, but it would have inevitably destroyed the organization's usefulness. One of the troika members was to represent the Afro-Asian Bloc of countries, and Khrushchev thereby hoped to secure the bloc's greater support for his policy in the Congo. But the result turned out to be contrary to his expectations. The Afro-Asian Bloc did not support his troika plan, considering it nothing more than the diplomatic maneuvering and propaganda that it actually was. In the end, the Soviet Union lost the battle for the Congo, but it also avoided an escalation of a conflict that would have had very doubtful results for boosting revolutionary processes and would have guaranteed a harsh confrontation with the West in a region where it had neither sufficient resources nor allies.

Soviet policy toward West Africa and the Congo was a complicated synthesis of ideological and security considerations. It was motivated by ideals and factors affecting the USSR's national interests, power, and prestige. The correlation between them was flexible, depending on specific undertakings, but in comparison with the quest for security, the lure of revolution was always secondary.

The Western—primarily American—factor also contributed to shaping Soviet attitudes. Before the opening of the Eastern Bloc's archives, there was little agreement among historians over this issue. Soviet scholars used to blame "imperialist intrigues" for all Soviet setbacks in Africa. W. Scott Thompson expressed the typical Western position: "Soviet African policy has in every major way unfolded [in response] to opportunities created by its own ideological limbering and by what the Soviets would call 'objective conditions' in Africa, and these American-offered opportunities have at best been short term, a dimple on the face of a very tall body of policy development."[4]

The reality lay between these two extremes. The archival documents that have been brought to light show that the United States developed a comprehensive and subtle strategy to counter the "Communist penetration" of Africa. In West Africa and the Congo, the Americans challenged the Soviets in every sphere—political, diplomatic, economic, social, and military—and their countermeasures and preemptive steps helped to frustrate Soviet plans. Moreover, the Soviet plans were poorly conceived and unrealistic, and their implementation failed, mainly due to Soviet miscalculations.

The Soviet Union was entering Africa enjoying a serious advantage over the West. It was a newcomer that did not have colonies, it advocated the decolonization of the African continent in the shortest possible time, and it defended Africans' civil rights and economic interests. Also, a considerable number of educated Africans saw socialist administrative and economic models as useful guides and felt a sympathy for the USSR. For instance, 300 students from ten French-speaking African countries were polled in Paris in 1962. When asked about "the country they admired most," 25 percent mentioned the USSR; 20 percent, China; 12.4 percent, Israel; 12 percent, Cuba; 8 percent, France; 6 percent, Switzerland; and 3.3 percent, the United States. A total of 37.8 percent preferred "integral socialism, as in the USSR or China," for their country; 29.3 percent wanted "personalist Socialism"; 19.7 percent chose "liberal Socialism, as in Scandinavia"; and 6.8 percent preferred a liberal economy.[5] However, the results of this poll reflected expectations of the part of African elites that were not fulfilled. The leg up that history initially gave the USSR quickly disappeared. The Soviet Union tried to meet the challenges from the United States and its allies, but it failed to compete with the West head to head.

As the poorest of the donor nations, the USSR could not replace the West economically. The effectiveness of Soviet economic aid was limited, primarily because much of it was channeled toward large and prestigious projects, which proved to be white elephants that were either excessive for African needs or poorly conceived. Also, such "little things" as the poor quality of Soviet export goods and a lack of entrepreneurial market skills within the Soviet establishment hampered the development of Soviet-African trade relations and compelled indigenous African entrepreneurs to shun the Soviet trade organizations.

The Soviet Union also lost the battle for the souls of the West Africans and the Congolese. Soviet propaganda was not free of blunders and was generally inferior to that of the United States, and thus its effectiveness left much to be desired. Soviet-made media productions exported to West Africa and the Congo were not adapted to local realities and attitudes, and the Africans could not find in the Soviet literature the formulas to solve their urgent economic problems. Radio Moscow's foreign broadcasts and the programs it sent to local radio stations in African countries often did not fit the requirements either thematically or professionally and had little relevance to life in these countries. Soviet films were rare birds in private cinemas that were dominated by American, French, and British productions. Attempts to indoctrinate African students in the USSR with the Communist ideology were hampered by the daily reality the students faced in "the country of a victorious socialism," with unexpected and unpleasant consequences for the Soviet authorities—including racial conflicts, "anti-Soviet sentiments," and unauthorized student organizations.

Most researchers examining Soviet policy toward West Africa and the Congo have concentrated largely on the interests and actions of the great powers and on East/West confrontation. Recently, however, studies have appeared showing that Africans were not passive witnesses or victims in the Cold War contest.[6] Thus, in dealing with the USSR and the United States, the leaders of Ghana, Guinea, Mali, and the Congo showed themselves to be historical actors with their own agendas, not mere pawns of the superpowers.

In turning to the Soviet Union for help, these Africans were guided mainly by pragmatic considerations. Guinea's independence was followed by the abrupt withdrawal of French economic, technical, and administrative assistance. Sékou Touré badly needed Soviet aid to maintain Guinea as an independent country as well as to ensure his own political survival. Guinea itself lacked both trained personnel and sufficient economic resources. The first country Touré turned to for help was the United States; the first head of state to be invited to Guinea was President Dwight Eisenhower. But Touré's overtures were rejected, because the U.S. government had to support its ally, France. The USSR was more responsive to Guinean appeals, and Guinea received extensive Soviet aid to fill the void left by the French. Soviet aid projects, however, turned out to be disappointing to Touré, both in quality and in quantity. In December 1961, the Soviet ambassador was expelled from Conakry. Guinea swung away from economic dependence on the Soviet Bloc and sought friendlier relations with the West, without burning its bridges to the East. As time went by, Touré became dissatisfied with American assistance. In 1966, the American ambassador in Conakry shared the same lot as his Soviet counterpart of 1961, yet Touré again managed to find new sponsors among the Arab oil-producing countries. Guinean foreign policy under Touré was a distinguished example of flexibility, pragmatism, and balanced neutrality.

The fate of another West African leader, Kwame Nkrumah, demonstrates what consequences an African politician might encounter after taking the East's side in the Cold War. Nkrumah dreamed of becoming the foremost leader of the United States of Africa, which would be independent and free of the continent's colonial legacy. Relationships with great powers were for him no more than a channel for his zealous drive toward this ambitious goal of African unification and prosperity. He wanted the USSR or the United States to be the rocket that would launch Ghana into the orbit of industrial countries, with himself on top of the pan-African political Olympus. He did manage to retain power while skillfully maneuvering between the two camps, but he lost it after finally opting for the USSR. He made his choice for two major reasons. First, the Soviets had always impressed him more with their development model, whose ruthless application in the USSR had turned a backward and economically devastated nation into an industrial giant. Second, he became convinced that his aspirations to play a dominant role in Africa had been frustrated by the opposition of "imperialist and neocolonialist forces," as he called them. He was ousted in 1966 as a result of a military coup.

Modibo Kéi'ta preferred the USSR to France as a donor because of the latter's role in the secession of Senegal and the breakup of the Mali Federation. Patrice Lumumba applied for Soviet assistance when the dissolution of the Congo became a reality and his power hung by a single thread.

Africans sought to suck advantage out of the Cold War confrontation, to become the third force, the only winning party in a zero-sum game. Touré, Nkrumah, and Kéi'ta all demonstrated considerable capacity as diplomats in inventing arguments to persuade their Soviet partners that Guinea, Ghana, and Mali would be able to cope with the "imperialist threat"—that is, contingent on receiving additional aid from the USSR. But they always kept their distance from the premises of Soviet ideology. Lumumba clumsily maneuvered, looking to both the West and the East for help, and trying to play the USSR and the United States against each other. He made his choice in favor of the Soviet Union because it supplied his government with the limited military aid he badly needed to crush the separatism of Katanga Province, to get the Congo under control, and to survive politically and even physically. The danger of a direct military conflict between superpowers was not a restrictive imperative for the leftist Congolese nationalists. As Pierre Mulele, the representative of the Gizenga government in Cairo, cabled Khrushchev on February 14, 1961: "The legitimate government prefers the world war to begin rather than being meanly killed off."[7]

The impact of Africans on the development of Soviet policy in West Africa and the Congo was considerable. Chistopher Stevens' witty one-liner—"The Soviet Union proposes, Africa disposes"—seems quite to the point.[8]

After Khrushchev's ouster in 1964, Soviet policy in West Africa became more pragmatic. Military coups in Ghana (1966) and in Mali (1968) deprived the Soviet Union of West African allies to showcase Soviet policy in the developing world. The "leading lights" intended to show the rest of Africa the superiority of the Kremlin-sponsored developmental path had now been extinguished. Security considerations based on a sober assessment of the geopolitical value of individual countries became the chief determinants of Soviet intentions and actions in West Africa. The USSR's support of the federal government in Nigeria during the civil war from 1967 to 1970 is a good illustration of this.[9] Generally speaking, West Africa slipped off the list of Soviet foreign policy priorities and would remain peripheral for decades to come, while Soviet attention was shifting to the Horn of Africa and Southern Africa.

The Congo crisis ended up with the West having a monopoly of influence in the Congo. Joseph Mobutu seized power in 1965 and remained a staunch U.S. ally for more than thirty years. Only when the Cold War was over did the Western powers let explosive Congolese internal discontent erupt and destroy Mobutu's regime.

Soviet policy toward West Africa and the Congo is not only an issue of purely scientific and academic interest. The USSR, together with the Western powers, contributed to the creation of today's West Africa and the Congo by fueling many of the processes, movements, and ideologies that exist there now. It is impossible to understand the contemporary situation of West Africa and the Congo and to find effective ways to meet the severe and protracted crisis that has swept across Sub-Saharan Africa without taking into account the experience of the period from 1956 to 1964.

Notes

These abbreviations are used throughout the Notes:

AVP RF   Archiv vneshnei politiki Rossyiskoi Federatsii (Archive of Foreign Policy of the Russian Federation)
CC CPSU   Central Committee of the Communist Party of the Soviet Union
FRUS   U.S. Department of State, *Foreign Relations of the United States*
GRDS   General Records of the U.S. Department of State
NA   National Archives of the United States
RG   Record Group
RGANI   Rossyiskyi gosudarstvennyi archiv noveisheyi istorii (Russian State Archive of Contemporary History)

Russian archival notation follows the accepted form of abbreviation:

f.   *fond* (collection)
op.   *opis'* (inventory)
p.   *papka* (folder)
d.   *delo* (file)
l., ll.   *list, listy* (page, pages—literally, leaf, leaves)

Notes to the Introduction

1. Robert Legvold, *Soviet Policy in West Africa* (Cambridge, Mass.: Harvard University Press, 1970), 347.

2. A. B. Davidson and S. V. Mazov, eds., *Rossiya i Afrika: Dokumenty i materially, Tom. II, 1918–1960* (Russia and Africa: Documents and materials, Vol. 2, 1918–1960) (Moscow: IVI RAN, 1999).

3. John Gaddis, *We Now Know: Rethinking Cold War History* (Oxford: Clarendon Press, 1997).

4. Christopher Stevens, *The Soviet Union and Black Africa* (London: Macmillan, 1976), 102, 103.

5. Madeleine Kalb, *The Congo Cables: The Cold War in Africa from Eisenhower to Kennedy* (New York: Macmillan, 1982), xiv.

6. Lise Namikas, "Battleground Africa: The Cold War and the Congo Crisis, 1960–1965," PhD dissertation, University of Southern California, 2002; Apollon Davidson, Sergey Mazov, and Georgiy Tsypkin, *SSSR i Afrika 1918–1960: Dokumetntirovannaya istoriya vzaimootnosheniyi (*USSR and Africa 1918–1960: Documentary history of relations) (Moscow: IVI RAN, 2002), 251–304; Aleksandr Fursenko and Timothy Naftali, *Khrushchev's Cold War: The Inside Story of an American Adversary* (New York: W. W. Norton, 2006); Sergey Mazov, "Soviet Aid to the Gizenga Government in the former Belgian Congo (1960–1961) as Reflected in Russian Archives," *Cold War History* 7, no. 3 (2007).

7. *FRUS, 1958–1960, Volume 14, Africa* (Washington, D.C.: U.S. Government Printing Office, 1992); *FRUS, 1961–1963, Volume 20, Congo Crisis* (Washington, D.C.: U.S. Government Printing Office, 1994).

8. Lise Namikas and Sergey Mazov, eds., *CWIHP Conference Reader Compiled for the International Conference on the Congo Crisis, 1960–1961, Washington, D.C., September 23–24, 2004, Organized by the Woodrow Wilson Center's Cold War International History Project and the Africa Program* (Washington, D.C.: Cold War International History Project, Woodrow Wilson International Center for Scholars, 2004).

9. Kevin C. Dunn, *Imagining the Congo: The International Relations of Identity* (New York: Palgrave Macmillan, 2003), 5.

10. Ibid., 8.

11. Ibid., 10.

12. Kwame Nkrumah, *Challenge of the Congo: A Case Study of Foreign Pressures in an Independent State* (New York: International Publishers, 1967).

13. S. V. Mazov, *Paradoksi "obraztsovoi" kolonii: Stanovlenie colonial'nogo obshestva Gany, 1900–1957* (The paradoxes of a "model colony": The shaping of colonial society in Ghana, 1900–1957) (Moscow: Nauka, 1993), 153–88; S. V. Mazov, "Soviet Scholar Comments on Nkrumah's 70th Birthday Anniversary," *Echo,* September 30, 1979; S. V. Mazov, "'Tsarstvo' Kvame Nkrumy" ("'The kingdom' of Kwame Nkruman"), *Vostok,* no. 1 (2010): 62–72.

14. Basil Davidson, *Black Star: A View of the Life and Times of Kwame Nkrumah* (New York: Praeger, 1974); David Birmingham, *Kwame Nkrumah: The Father of African Nationalism* (Athens: Ohio University Press, 1998); Ahmad A. Rahman, *The Regime Change of Kwame Nkrumah: Epic Heroism in Africa and the Diaspora* (New York: Palgrave, 2007).

15. Henry L. Bretton, *The Rise and Fall of Kwame Nkrumah: A Study of Personal Rule in Africa* (New York: Praeger, 1966); Ali Mazrui, "Nkrumah: The Leninist Czar," in *On Heroes and Uhuru-Worship: Essays of Independent Africa,* ed. Ali Mazrui (London: Longmans, 1967), 113–34; Peter P. Omari,

Kwame Nkrumah: The Anatomy of an African Dictatorship (New York: Africana, 1972).

16. Stephen Weissman, *American Foreign Policy in the Congo, 1960–1964* (Ithaca, N.Y.: Cornell University Press, 1974); Kalb, *Congo Cables*; Richard D. Mahoney, *JFK: Ordeal in Africa* (New York: Oxford University Press, 1983).

17. "Telegram from the Department of State to the Embassy in Ghana, October 13, 1960," in *FRUS, 1958–1960, Volume 14, Africa*, 668.

18. Melvyn P. Leffler, *For the Soul of Mankind: The United States, the Soviet Union, and the Cold War* (New York: Hill and Wang, 2007), 3.

Notes to Chapter 1

1. Quoted by A. N. Porter and A. J. Stockwell, *British Imperial Policy and Decolonization, 1938–64, Volume 1, 1938–51* (New York: St. Martin's Press, 1987), 357–58.

2. AVP RF, f. 431/1, op. 1, p. 5, d. 33, ll. 2–13.

3. AVP RF, f. 6, op. 7, p. 17, d. 174, l. 60.

4. Sergey Mazov, "The USSR and the Former Italian Colonies, 1945–1950," *Cold War History* 3, no. 3 (2003): 49–78.

5. Quoted by Vladimir O. Pechatnov, *"The Allies Are Pressing on You to Break Your Will": Foreign Policy Correspondence between Stalin and Molotov and Other Politburo Members, September 1945–December 1946*, CWIHP Working Paper 26 (Washington, D.C.: Cold War International History Project, Woodrow Wilson International Center for Scholars, 1999), 22.

6. For more information on Potekhin, see Apollon Davidson, "Osnovatel' Instituta Afriki (I. I. Potekhin)" [The Founder of the Institute for African Studies (I. I. Potekhin)], in *Stanoveniye otechestvennoi afrikanistiki, 1920-e–nachalo 1960-kh* (The Formative Years of African Studies in Russia: The 1920s–Early 1960s), ed. A. B. Davidson (Moscow: Nauka, 2003), 116–35.

7. Ivan Potekhin, "Etnicheskyi i klassovyi sostav naseleniya Zolotogo Berega" (The ethnic and class structure of the population of the Gold Coast), *Sovetskaya Etnografiya*, no. 3 (1953): 113.

8. See Guy Laron, *Cutting the Gordian Knot: The Post–WW II Egyptian Quest for Arms and the 1955 Czechoslovak Arms Deal*, CWIHP Working Paper 55 (Washington, D.C.: Cold War International History Project, Woodrow Wilson International Center for Scholars, 2007).

9. RGANI, f. 5, op. 30, d. 161, l. 1.

10. Ivan Potekhin, "Politicheskoe polozhenie v stranakh Afriki" (The political situation in African countries), *Sovetskoe Vostokovedinie*, no. 1 (1956): 25.

11. Ibid., 28.

12. Zbigniew Brzezinski, "Conclusion: The African Challenge," in *Africa and the Communist World*, ed. Zbigniew Brzezinski (Stanford, Calif.: Stanford University Press, 1963), 208–10, 212.

13. Colin Legum, "USSR Policy in Sub-Saharan Africa," in *The Soviet Union and the Third World: The Last Three Decades*, ed. Andrzei Karbonsky and Francis Fukuyama (Ithaca, N.Y.: Cornell University Press, 1987), 229.

14. Jiri Valenta, "Soviet Decision-Making on the Intervention in Angola," in *Communism in Africa*, ed. David E. Albright (New York: Macmillan, 1980), 116; Richard E. Remnek, "The Significance of Soviet Strategic Military Interests in Sub-Saharan Africa," in *The Soviet Impact in Africa*, ed. Craig R. Nation and Mark V. Kauppi (Lexington, Mass.: D. C. Heath, 1984), 158.

15. Karen Brutents, *Tridtsat' let na Staroi Ploshadi* (Thirty years at the Staraya Ploshad') (Moscow: Mezhdunarodnye otnosheniya, 1998), 213.

16. RGANI, f. 4, op. 16, d. 469, ll. 73–75; resolution of the CC CPSU Secretariat "On the Measures for the Extension of Cultural and Public Relations with Asian and African Countries," Protocol 61, point 35-gs, of the CC CPSU Secretariat meeting (March 24, 1958). Ibid., f. 3, op. 14, d. 354, ll. 73–77; decree of the CC CPSU "On the Extension of Cultural and Public Relations with the Negro Peoples of Africa and the Strengthening of the Influence of the Soviet Union on These Peoples," from Protocol 260 of the CC CPSU Presidium of January 20, 1960.

17. RGANI, f. 5, op. 30, d. 273, ll. 177–93; "Recommendations of the Section for the Issues of Soviet Propaganda to the Countries of the Orient and Cultural Relations with These Countries," September 11, 1958. Ibid., op. 35, d. 79, l. 170–240; transcript of the Conference of Soviet Orientalists on the Problems of the Current Situation in the Countries of the Orient, October 30, 1958, morning session. Ibid., ll. 244–322; transcript of the Conference of Soviet Orientalists, evening session. Ibid., op. 30, d. 273, ll. 107–76; transcript of the meeting of the Section for the Issues of Soviet Propaganda to the Orient and Cultural Relations with the Countries of the Orient, October 31, 1958. Ibid., op. 3, d. 80, ll. 161–294; transcript of the Conference of Soviet Orientalists, November 1, 1958, plenary session.

18. RGANI, f. 3, op. 14, d. 354, l. 75; decree of the CC CPSU "On the Extension of Cultural and Public Relations with the Negro Peoples of Africa and the Strengthening of the Influence of the Soviet Union on These Peoples."

19. RGANI, f. 4, op. 16, d. 469, ll. 73, 74; decree of the CC CPSU Secretariat "On the Measures for the Extension of Cultural and Public Relations with Asian and African Countries."

20. RGANI, f. 5, op. 30, d. 273, l. 185; "Recommendations of the Section for the Issues of Soviet Propaganda to the Countries of the Orient and Cultural Relations with These Countries."

21. RGANI, f. 4, op. 16, d. 469, l. 74; decree of the CC CPSU Secretariat "On the Measures for the Extension of Cultural and Public Relations with Asian and African Countries."

22. RGANI, f. 3, op. 14, d. 354, ll. 76–77; decree of the CC CPSU "On the Extension of Cultural and Public Relations with the Negro Peoples of Africa and the Strengthening of the Influence of the Soviet Union on These Peoples."

23. Ibid., l. 73.

24. Ibid., l. 75.

25. RGANI, f. 5, op. 35, d. 79, ll. 200–201; transcripts of the Conference of Soviet Orientalists, October 30, 1958, morning session.

26. RGANI, f. 4, op. 16, d. 469, l. 73; decree of the CC CPSU Secretariat "On the Measures for Extension of Cultural and Public Relations with Asian and African Countries."

27. RGANI, f. 5, op. 35, d. 79, l. 202; transcripts of the Conference of Soviet Orientalists, October 30, 1958, morning session.

28. RGANI, f. 3, op. 14, d. 354, l. 76; decree of the CC CPSU "On the Extension of Cultural and Public Relations with the Negro Peoples of Africa."

29. Brzezinski, "Conclusion," 205.

30. Ibid., 226.

31. Pieter Lessing, *Africa's Red Harvest: An Account of Communism in Africa* (London: Michael Joseph, 1962), 120–22.

32. V. V. Laptukhin, "Nebyvalyi fenomen Hausa" (The unprecedented phenomenon of the Hausa), in *Pod nebom Afriki moei: Istoriya, yazyki, kul'tura narodov Afriki* (Under my Africa's sky: The history, languages, and culture of African Peoples), vol. 2 (Moscow: Muravei, 2003), 97.

33. RGANI, f. 4, op. 16, d. 1033, ll. 149–50, 151, 152; "On the Expansion of Soviet Broadcasting to African Countries," extract from Protocol 338 of the CC CPSU Presidium meeting, July 20, 1961.

34. Laptukhin, "Nebyvalyi fenomen Hausa," 98.

35. AVP RF, f. 0601, op. 2, p. 5, d. 15, ll. 10, 11; deputy chairman of the State Committee for Cultural Relations with Foreign Countries S. K. Romanovskii to deputy minister of foreign relations V. V. Kuznetsov, "Implementation of the decisions of the policy-making agencies [direktivnikh organov] 'On the Extension of Cultural and Public Relations with the Negro Peoples of Africa and the Strengthening of the Influence of the Soviet Union on These Peoples' and 'On Sending Soviet Teachers and Specialists for Work in Educational Institutions of the Republic of Mali and the Implementation of the Plans of Cultural Exchange with African Countries in 1961," August 24, 1961.

36. RGANI, f. 11, op. 1, d. 40, ll. 128–29; decree of the CC CPSU Commission on the Issues of Ideology, Culture, and the Party's International Relations, "On the Work of the Publishing House 'Inostrannaya Literatura,'" Protocol 30, point 81, of the meeting of the CC CPSU Commission on the Issues of Ideology, Culture, and the Party's International Relations, June 4, 1959.

37. RGANI, f. 3, op. 12, d. 639, l. 57; chief of the CC CPSU Department of Propaganda and Agitation in Union Republics L. Il'itchev and chief of the Bureau of the CC CPSU Department of Propaganda and Agitation in Union Republics K. Bogolubov, memoranda to the CC CPSU, December 9, 1959.

38. RGANI, f. 5, op. 35, d. 79, l. 273; transcripts of the Conference of Soviet Orientalists, October 30, 1958, evening session.

39. RGANI, f. 3, op. 12, d. 639, l. 57; memoranda to the CC CPSU by L. Il'itchev and K. Bogolubov, December 9, 1959.

40. RGANI, f. 5, op. 35, d. 180, ll. 12–77; deputy minister of higher and specialized secondary education of the USSR, M. Prokof'ev to the CC CPSU, "Statistical Materials on Foreign Students and Post-Graduate Students Being Educated in the Higher Educational Establishments of the USSR," February 17, 1961.

41. S. V. Mazov, "Neizvestnaya istoriya sozdaniya Instituta Afriki AN SSSR" (The Institute for African Studies of the Academy of Sciences of the USSR: The unknown history of its creation), *Vostok*, no. 1 (1999): 80–88.

42. RGANI, f. 11, op. 1, d. 39, ll. 105–6; resolution of the CC CPSU Commission on the Issues of Ideology, Culture, and the Party's International Relations, "Improvement of African Studies," Protocol 29, point 48, of the meeting of the CC CPSU Commission on the Issues of Ideology, Culture, and the Party's International Relations, May 18, 1959.

43. RGANI, f. 11, op. 1, d. 42, ll. 75–76; resolution of the CC CPSU Commission on the Issues of Ideology, Culture, and the Party's International Relations, "On the Establishment of the Institute for African Studies in the USSR Academy of Sciences," Protocol 32, point 48, of the meeting of the CC CPSU Commission on the Issues of Ideology, Culture, and the Party's International Relations, June 29, 1959.

44. RGANI, f. 3, op. 14, d. 304, ll. 12–13; decree of the CC CPSU "On the Establishment of the Institute for African Studies in the USSR Academy of Sciences," Protocol 226, point 22, of the CC CPSU Presidium meeting, July 2, 1960.

45. A. B. Davidson, "I. I. Potekhin i sovetskaya afrikanistika" (I. I. Potekhin and Soviet African Studies), *Sovetskaya etnografiya*, no. 3 (1974): 83.

46. Brutents, *Tridtsat' let na Staroi Ploshadi*, 168.

47. RGANI, f. 4, op. 16, d. 929, l. 208.

48. Ibid., l. 209. V. Kuznetsov; memoranda to the CC CPSU, February 1, 1961.

49. RGANI, f. 4, op. 16, d. 929, ll. 209–10, 212, 213.

50. Ibid., ll. 210, 211.

51. Ibid., l. 199; "On the Personnel Arrangement of the USSR Embassy in the Central African Republic," extract from Protocol no 317 of the CC CPSU Presidium meeting, March 2, 1961.

52. Brutents, *Tridtsat' let na Staroi Ploshadi*, 303.

53. RGANI, f. 3, op. 14, d. 105, l. 63; decree of the CC CPSU "On the Measures for the Improvement of Soviet Foreign Policy Propaganda," Protocol 80, point 15, of the CC CPSU Presidium meeting, March 4, 1957.

54. RGANI, f. 5, op. 30, d. 273, l. 110; transcripts of the meeting of the Section for the Issues of Soviet Propaganda to the Orient and Cultural Relations with the Countries of the Orient, October 31, 1958.

55. RGANI, f. 4, op. 16, d. 377, ll. 29, 30; resolution of the CC CPSU Secretariat "On the Reorganization of the All-Union Society of Cultural Relations with Foreign Countries," extract from Protocol 48, point 180-gs, September 5, 1957.

56. RGANI, f. 4, op. 16, d. 624, l. 52; "The Issue of the All-Union Society of Cultural Relations with Foreign Countries," extract from Protocol 214 of the CC CPSU Presidium meeting, April 15, 1959.

57. RGANI, f. 4, op. 16, d. 469, ll. 73–75; resolution of the CC CPSU Secretariat "On the Measures for the Extension of Cultural and Public Relations with Asian and African Countries."

58. RGANI, f. 4, op. 16, d. 937, l. 148; G. Abdurashidov, memo to the CC CPSU "On the Measures for Improving the Working Conditions of the Soviet Representatives in the Permanent Secretariat of the Afro-Asian Peoples' Solidarity Organization," October 27, 1960.

59. Ibid., ll. 148–53.

60. Ibid., ll. 153–54.

61. Ibid., l. 154.

62. RGANI, f. 4, op. 16, d. 937, l. 142; proposals of the Soviet Afro-Asian Solidarity Committee, Protocol 171, point 13c, of the CC CPSU Secretariat meeting, January 13, 1961.

63. Soviet Bloc Challengers in Sub-Saharan Africa and Certain Implications on U.S. Policy, March 22, 1960, file FW 770.5-MSP/3-3060, GRDS, Central Decimal File, RG 59, NA, pp. 1, 4.

64. Ibid., 2, 4.

65. "Memorandum of Conversation, April 16, 1959, First Tripartite Talks on Africa," in *FRUS, 1958–1960, Volume 14, Africa* (Washington, D.C.: U.S. Government Printing Office, 1992), 48.

66. "Statement of U.S. Policy toward Africa South of the Sahara Prior to Calendar Year 1960," in *FRUS, 1955–1957, Volume 18, Africa* (Washington, D.C.: U.S. Government Printing Office, 1989), 77.

67. "Communist Penetration in Africa," United States Draft Paper on Africa CA-57-21, January 8, 1959, Department of State Instruction, file 770.001/1-859, GRDS, Central Decimal File, RG 59, NA, pp. 4–5.

68. George W. Shephard Jr., Saint Olaf College, "The Conflict of Interests in American Policy on Africa," paper presented to the African Studies Association First Annual Meeting, Northwestern University, Evanston, Ill., September 8–10, 1958, file 611.70/10-158, GRDS, Central Decimal File, RG 59, NA, p. 1.

69. "The United States in Africa South of the Sahara, Memorandum Prepared in the Office of African Affairs. Washington, August 4, 1955," in *FRUS, 1955–1957, Volume 18, Africa*, 14.

70. Odd Arne Westad, *The Global Cold War: Third World Interventions and the Making of Our Times* (New York: Cambridge University Press, 2006), 132.

71. Papers for Tripartite Talks on Africa, April 16, 1959, Introduction by Mr. Murphy, GRDS, Bureau of African Affairs, RG 59, NA, p. 5.

72. Ibid., p. 3.

73. *FRUS, 1955–1957, Volume 18, Africa*, 18.

74. Thomas J. Noer, *Cold War and Black Liberation: The United States and*

White Rule in Africa, 1948–1968 (Columbia: University of Missouri Press, 1985), 35–36.

75. *FRUS, 1955–1957, Volume 18, Africa,* 47.

76. United States Draft Paper on Africa, CA-57-21, January 8, 1959, p. 5.

77. Ibid., p. 6.

78. Cited by Fred Marte, *Political Cycles in International Relations: The Cold War and Africa 1945–1990* (Amsterdam: VU Press, 1994), 79.

79. *FRUS, 1955–1957, Volume 18, Africa,* 65.

80. Department of State Press Release, August 20, 1958, no. 478, Department of State Establishes New Bureau of African Affairs, GRDS, Bureau of African Affairs, RG 59, NA, p. 1.

81. Remarks for Use in Presenting S 1832, July 9, 1958, ibid., p. 5.

82. Office Memorandum, United States Government, Mr. Mallory Browne to AF–Mr. Dolgin, Suggestions to Help Counteract Communist Penetration in Africa, April 2, 1958, file 770.001/4-258, GRDS, Central Decimal File, RG 59, NA, p. 1.

83. AVP RF, f. 105, op. 1, p. 1, d. 1, ll. 1–2.

84. Boima H. Fahnbulleh Jr., *The Diplomacy of Prejudice: Liberia in International Politics, 1945–1970* (New York: Vantage Press, 1985), 68.

85. S. V. Mazov, "Diplomatchicheskyi debut SSSR v Tropicheskoi Afrike: Iz istorii sovetsko-liberyiskikh otnoshenyi, 1945–1960 gg." (The diplomatic debut of the USSR in Tropical Africa: An episode from the history of Soviet-Liberian relations, 1945–1960), *Vostok,* no. 6 (2000): 37–40.

86. AVP RF, f. 105, op. 1, p. 1, d. 1, ll. 1–2; acting secretary of state of Liberia George Padmore to first deputy chairman of the USSR Council of Ministers and foreign minister V. V. Molotov, July 16, 1955.

87. RGANI, f. 5, op. 28, d. 446, l. 9; T. Kuprikov, "Contemporary Africa (Memorandum)," December 31, 1955.

88. Fahnbulleh, *Diplomacy of Prejudice,* 75.

89. AVP RF, f. 105, op. 1, p. 1, d. 1, l. 4.

90. AVP RF, f. 0105, op. 3, p. 1, d. 1, l. 20; A. P. Volkov and V. I. Bazyhkin, "Memo on the Process of Negotiations between the Soviet Government Delegation and the Liberian Government on the Establishment of Diplomatic Relations between the USSR and Liberia," January 24, 1956.

91. AVP RF, f. 0105, op. 3, p. 1, d. 1, ll. 12–13; A. P. Volkov and V. I. Bazyhkin, "Report on the Visit of the Soviet Delegation to Liberia," January 24, 1956.

92. Ibid., l. 21; Volkov and Bazyhkin, "Memo on the Process of Negotiations."

93. *FRUS, 1955–1957, Volume 18, Africa,* 389.

94. Ibid., 390, 391.

95. AVP RF, f. 0105, op. 3, p. 1, d. 1, ll. 21–23; Volkov and Bazyhkin, "Memo on the Process of Negotiations."

96. *FRUS, 1955–1957, Volume 18, Africa,* 392.

97. Ibid., 393.

98. AVP RF, f. 0105, op. 3, p. 1, d. 1, l. 23; Volkov and Bazyhkin, "Memo on the Process of Negotiations."

99. Ibid., l. 24.

100. Fahnbulleh, *Diplomacy of Prejudice*, 59.

101. AVP RF, f. 0105, op. 2, p. 1, d. 2, l. 6; "Joint Communiqué on the Negotiations between the USSR Government Delegation and the Government of the Republic of Liberia on the Issue of the Establishment of Diplomatic Relations between the USSR and the Republic of Liberia."

102. AVP RF, f. 0105, op. 2, p. 1, d. 2, ll. 14, 15; Volkov and Bazyhkin, "Report on the Visit of the Soviet Delegation to Liberia."

103. AVP RF, f. 0105, op. 3, p. 1, d. 1, l. 26; Volkov and Bazyhkin, "Memo on the Process of Negotiations."

104. Ibid., ll. 26, 27.

105. *FRUS, 1955–1957, Volume 18, Africa*, 396.

106. Ibid., 396, 397.

107. AVP RF, f. 0105, op. 3, p. 1, d. 1, l. 28.

108. AVP RF, f. 0105, op. 6, d. 2, l. 15; Department of African Countries of the USSR MID, "Soviet-Liberian Relations (Memorandum)," December 23, 1959.

109. AVP RF, f. 105, op. 3, p. 1, d. 1, ll. 2–3; G. N. Zarubin, "Memo on the Conversation with the Liberian Ambassador to the USA Padmore," April 20, 1956.

110. AVP RF, f. 0105, op. 3, p. 1, d. 1, ll. 35, 39–40.

111. AVP RF, f. 0105, op. 6, p. 1, d. 2, l. 1; V. S. Semenov to M. A. Men'shikov, January 28, 1959.

112. Ibid., l. 2; M. N. Smirnovskii to V. S. Semenov, March 10, 1959.

113. Ibid., l. 7, 9, 10; USSR MID African Department II, "Soviet-Liberian Relations (Memorandum)," December 23, 1959.

114. N. A. Mukhitdinov, *Reka vremeni (ot Stalina do Gorbatcheva): Vospominaniya* [The River of Time (from Stalin to Gorbachev): Memoirs] (Moscow: Rusti-Rusti, 1995), 468.

115. AVP RF, f. 0105, op. 7, p. 1, d. 2, l. 1.

116. Mukhitdinov, *Reka vremeni*, 466.

117. Ibid., 469.

118. Ibid., 467.

119. AVP RF, f. 0105, op. 7, p. 1, d. 2, l. 1, 2.

120. Ibid., ll. 7, 8, 15; counselor of the USSR Embassy in Guinea I. I. Marchuk, "Report on the Visit to Guinea 18–25 February, 1960," March 9, 1960.

121. Ibid., ll. 11, 12.

122. *SSSR i strany Afriki 1946–1962 gg: Dokumenty i materially, Tom. I (1946g.–sentyabr' 1960g.)* [USSR and African countries 1946–1962: Documents and materials, Vol. 1 (1946–September 1962)] (Moscow: Gosudarstvennoe izdatel'stvo politicheskoi literatury, 1963), 533.

123. AVP RF, f. 0105, op. 7, p. 1, d. 2, l. 20; II African Department of the USSR MID, "The Issues of Soviet-Liberian Relations (Regarding the Meeting with the Delegation of the Municipality of Monrovia), 29 November 1960."

124. Ibid., l. 22.

125. Fahnbulleh, *Diplomacy of Prejudice*, 91.

126. American Consulate General, Accra, to the Department of State, Dispatch 149, January 23, 1956, "Alleged Contacts between the Gold Coast and Russian Delegates at the Inauguration of President Tubman of Liberia," file 645.61/1-2356, GRDS, Central Decimal Files, RG 59, NA.

127. Department of State Instruction to the American Consulate General, Accra, CA-6355, February 20, 1956, "Department's Views on Prospect of USSR Establishing Diplomatic Relations with the Gold Coast," file 645.61/2-2056, ibid., p. 1.

128. Dispatch from American Consul General in Accra to the Department of State, 140, December 5, 1956, "Reported Liberian Decision to Exchange Diplomatic Representations with Russia, Communist China and Egypt," file 645K.61/12-556, GRDS, ibid., p. 1.

129. Ibid., 2.

130. Ibid.

131. AVP RF, f. 573, op. 1, p. 1, d. 1, l. 1, 3.

132. *FRUS, 1955–1957, Volume 18, Africa*, 372–73.

133. Department of State Instruction to American Embassy, Monrovia, A-50, February 27, 1957, "Possible Liberian Talk with Ghana Officials on Soviet Mission," file 645K.61/2-2157, GRDS, Central Decimal Files, NA.

134. Telegram from the Embassy in Monrovia to Secretary of State, 181, February 27, 1957, file 645K.61/2-2757, ibid.

135. Telegram from the Embassy in Monrovia to Secretary of State, 183, February 23, 1957, file 645K.61/2-2857, ibid.

136. I. I. Potekhin, *Stanovleniye novoi Gany* (The emergence of New Ghana) (Moscow: Nauka, 1965), 273.

137. *Pravda,* March 4, 1957.

138. *Novoye vremya*, no. 11 (1957): 31.

139. AVP RF, f. 573, op. 2, d. 6, l. 49; attaché of the USSR Embassy in Great Britain N. A. Makarov, "Ghana (Survey Memorandum)," June 11, 1958.

140. *Pravda*, April 17, 1957.

141. Dispatch from American Embassy in Accra to the Department of State, 258, March 23, 1957, "Conversation with Minister of Finance Gbdemah," file 745J.13/3-2357, GRDS, Central Decimal Files, RG 59, NA, p. 1.

142. *FRUS, 1955–1957, Volume 18, Africa*, 374–78.

143. "Report to the President on Vice-President's Visit to Africa (February 28–March 21, 1957): Political Conclusions and Recommendations," April 15, 1957, GRDS, RG 59, NA, p. 4.

144. W. S. Thompson, *Ghana's Foreign Policy 1957–1966: Diplomacy, Ideology, and the New State* (Princeton, N.J.: Princeton University Press, 1969), 14.

145. Telegram from American Embassy in Accra to Secretary of State, 152, October 12, 1957, file 745J.13/10-1257, GRDS, Central Decimal Files, NA, pp. 1–2.

146. Telegram from American Embassy in Accra to Secretary of State, 182, November 4, 1957, file 645J.61/11-457, GRDS, Central Decimal Files, RG 59, NA, p. 1.

147. Telegram from American Embassy in Accra to Secretary of State, 152, p. 2.

148. *Manchester Guardian*, April 4, 1957.

149. *FRUS, 1955–1957, Volume 18, Africa*, 381–83.

150. Ibid., 386.

151. D. F. Safonov, *A dughi gnut terpen'em . . . (Kak ya stal diplomatom-afrikanistom)* [And they sweep by patience . . . (How I became a diplomat-Africanist)] (Moscow: Institut Afriki RAN, Sovet veteranov MID RF, 2002), 147.

152. Ibid., 148, 149.

153. Ibid., 148.

154. Dispatch from American Embassy in Accra to the Department of State, 200, December 12, 1957, "Views of United Party Leaders," file 745J.00/12-1257, GRDS, Central Decimal Files, RG 59, NA, p. 4.

155. AVP RF, f. 573, op. 2, d. 6, ll. 49–51; Makarov, "Ghana."

156. Dispatch from American Embassy in Accra to the Department of State, 492, June 17, 1958, "Some Political Developments in Ghana During Its First 15 Months as an Independent State," file 745J.00/6-1758, GRDS, Central Decimal Files, RG 59, NA, p. 6.

157. Ibid., p. 1.

158. Dispatch from American Embassy in Accra to the Department of State, 200, p. 1.

159. RGANI, f. 4, op. 16, d. 441, ll. 80–81; Central Committee of Jan Tamraro to the minister of state farms of the USSR, March 9, 1957.

160. Ibid., ll. 74–76; Memorandum by chief of the CC CPSU International Department B. N. Ponomarev to the CC CPSU, December 25, 1957.

161. Ibid., ll. 69–73; regarding the talk with chairman of the Jan Tamraro Party F. M. Alale, draft.

162. AVP RF, f. 573, op. 2, p. 1, d. 8, ll. 4–5; I. Potekhin, "My Meetings with Ghanaian Politicians," January 31, 1958.

163. *FRUS, 1958–1960, Volume 14, Africa*, 648, 649.

164. Kwame Nkrumah, *I Speak of Freedom: A Statement of African Ideology* (London: Heinemann, 1961), 145.

165. Memorandum of conversation, July 24, 1958, "Discussion of Ghana's

Various Diplomatic Problems, Including Exchange of Missions with USSR and Recognition of Communist China," file 745J.00/7-2458, GRDS, Central Decimal Files, RG 59, NA, p. 2.

166. Dispatch from American Embassy in Accra to the Department of State, 388, December 18, 1958, "Ghana Today: An Analytical Survey," file 745J.00/12-1858, ibid., p. 11.

167. Quoted by Basil Davidson, *Black Star: A View of the Life and Times of Kwame Nkrumah* (New York: Praeger, 1974), 164.

168. Nkrumah, *I Speak of Freedom*, 107.

169. Thomas A. Howell and Jeffrey P. Rajasooria, eds., *Ghana & Nkrumah* (New York: Facts on File, 1972), 52.

170. Michael Dei-Anang, *The Administration of Ghana's Foreign Relations, 1957–1965: A Personal Memoir* (London: Athlone, 1975), 1.

171. On George Padmore, see, e.g., James R. Hooker, *Black Revolutionary: George Padmore's Path from Communism to Pan-Africanism* (London: Praeger, 1967).

172. All-African People's Conference: Resolution on Imperialism and Colonialism, Accra, December 5–13, 1958; http://www.fordham.edu/halsall/mod1958-aapc-res1.html.

173. RGANI, f. 5, op. 30, d. 336, l. 69; deputy chief of the MID African Department I. Kolosovskyi, "Ghana (Short Information)," April 30, 1960.

174. *Pravda*, June 12, 1958.

175. AVP RF, f. 0573, op. 3, p. 1, d. 10, l. 1; deputy chief of the MID Department of African Countries A. V. Budakov to USSR ambassador in Ghana M. D. Sytenko, July 20, 1959.

176. RGANI, f. 5, op. 30, d. 336, l. 69; Kolosovskyi, "Ghana."

177. AVP RF, f. 0573, op. 3, p. 1, d. 10, l. 5; trade counselor in Ghana V. Myshkov, memorandum "On the Situation in Trade between the USSR and Ghana," November 27, 1959.

178. AVP RF, f. 0573, op. 4, p. 6, d. 30, ll. 23–25; V. M. Studyenov, first secretary of the Embassy of the USSR in Ghana, to V. Matveev, chief of the Department of the Middle Eastern Countries and Africa of the Union of Soviet Societies for Friendship and Cultural Relations with Foreign Countries, February 15, 1960.

179. Dispatch from American Embassy in Accra to the Department of State, 388, p. 19.

180. Marte, *Political Cycles*, 148.

181. Lanciné Kaba, "From Colonialism to Autocracy: Guinea under Sékou Touré, 1957–1984," in *Decolonization and African Independence: The Transfers of Power, 1960–1980*, ed. Prosser Gifford and William Roger Louis (New Haven, Conn.: Yale University Press, 1988), 228.

182. Brutents, *Tridtsat' let na Staroi Ploshadi*, 288.

183. G. I. Mirskii, "Polveka v mire vostokovedeniya" (Half a century in the world of Oriental studies), *Vostok*, no. 6 (1996): 130.

184. AVP RF, f. 0136, op. 42, p. 75, d. 23, l. 69.

185. Ruth Shachter Morgenthau, *Political Parties in French-Speaking West Africa* (Oxford: Clarendon Press, 1964), 219–54; Elizabeth Schmidt, *Cold War and Decolonization in Guinea, 1946–1958* (Athens: Ohio University Press, 2007).

186. Elizabeth Schmidt, "Cold War in Guinea: The Rassemblement Démocratique Africain and the Struggle over Communism, 1950–1958," *Journal of African History* 48, no. 1 (2007): 97–98, 116, 120–21.

187. AVP RF, f. 0575, op. 1, p. 1, d. 2, l. 19; acting chief of the USSR MID Board of Foreign Policy Information S. Kudryavtsev, memorandum, "The Guinean Republic," October 6, 1958.

188. Ibid., l. 1; V. V. Kuznetsov to CC CPSU, October 3, 1958.

189. *SSSR i strany Afriki*, vol. 1, 382.

190. Office memorandum, U.S. Government, October 13, 1958, "Present Status of French Guinea," file 770B.00/10-1358, GRDS, Central Decimal File, RG 59, NA, p. 1.

191. *FRUS, 1958–1960, Volume 14, Africa*, 672.

192. Department of State, telegram from Dakar to secretary of state, 97, October 6, 1958, file 770B.02/10-658, GRDS, Central Decimal File, RG 59, NA, p. 1.

193. "United States Recognition of Guinea," October 9, 1958, GRDS, Bureau of African Affairs, RG 59, NA, p. 3.

194. Department of State, outgoing telegram, October 10, 1958, file 770B.02/10-858, GRDS, Central Decimal File, RG 59, NA, pp. 1–2.

195. "United States Recognition of Guinea," pp. 1–2.

196. *FRUS, 1958–1960, Volume 14, Africa*, 674.

197. Department of State, telegram from Dakar to secretary of state, 115, October 13, 1958, file 770B.02/10-1358, GRDS, Central Decimal File, RG 59, NA, p. 2.

198. *FRUS, 1958–1960, Volume 14, Africa*, 674.

199. Ibid., 675, 676.

200. Ibid., 675.

201. Ibid., 675–77.

202. Department of State, telegram from Paris to secretary of state, 1481, October 22, 1958, file 770B.02/10-2258, GRDS, Central Decimal File, RG 59, NA.

203. *FRUS, 1958–1960, Volume 14, Africa*, 675; dispatch from Amcongen, Dakar, F.W.A. to the Department of State, Washington, 99, October 24, 1958, "Premature Announcement at Conakry of U.S. Recognition of Government of Guinea," file 770B.02/10-2458, GRDS, Central Decimal File, RG 59, NA, p. 1.

204. Dispatch from Amcongen, Dakar, F.W.A. to the Department of State, Washington, 100, October 27, 1958, "Further Comment on My October 22 Visit to Conakry and Impressions of Prime Minister Sékou Touré," file 770B.02/10-2758, ibid., p. 2.

205. *FRUS, 1958–1960, Volume 14, Africa*, 680.

206. White House, telegram to Sékou Touré, prime minister of the Republic of Guinea, Conakry, November 1, 1958, file 870B.47411/11-158, GRDS, Central Decimal File, RG 59, NA.

207. "Further Comment on My October 22 Visit to Conakry," pp. 1–3.

208. Ibid., pp. 3–4.

209. Ibid., p. 4.

210. AVP RF, f. 0575, op. 1, p. 1, d. 2, l. 8; USSR minister of foreign affairs A. A. Gromyko, memo to the CC CPSU "On the Measures Aimed at Establishing Contacts with the Guinean Republic," November 8, 1958.

211. Edward Mortimer, *France and the Africans 1944–1960: A Political History* (New York: Walker, 1969), 311–12.

212. Sékou Touré, *Nezavisimaya Gvineya: Stat'i i rechi* (Independent Guinea: Articles and speeches). (Moscow: Izdatel'stvo inostrannoi literatury, 1960), 73.

213. William Attwood, *The Reds and the Blacks: A Personal Adventure—Two Tours on Duty in Revolutionary Africa as Kennedy's Ambassador to Guinea and Johnson's to Kenya* (New York: Harper & Row, 1967), 21.

214. Memorandum of conversation; participants: Sékou Touré, president of Guinea, Saifoulaye Diallo, president of National Assembly of Guinea, and William Attwood, American ambassador to Guinea, May 3, 1961; GRDS, Bureau of African Affairs, RG 59, NA, p. 4.

215. Touré, *Nezavisimaya Gvineya*, 123–51.

216. Memorandum of conversation, November 24, 1958, "Liberia: Ghana-Guinea Relations—Guinean Request for Arms and Ammunition," file 670B.76/11-2458, GRDS, Central Decimal File, RG 59, NA, p. 1.

217. Dispatch from American Embassy, Monrovia, to the Department of State, Washington, 134, October 27, 1958, "Enclosure of President Tubman's Cable to Ambassador Padmore," file 770B.02/10-2758, ibid., p. 1.

218. Howell and Rajasooria, *Ghana & Nkrumah*, 53–54.

219. Memorandum of conversation, November 24, 1958, "Liberia," pp. 1–2.

220. Memorandum, December 17, 1958, GRDS, Bureau of African Affairs, RG 59, NA, pp. 2–3.

221. John H. Morrow, *First American Ambassador to Guinea* (New Brunswick, N.J.: Rutgers University Press, 1968), 62.

222. AVP RF, f. 0575, op. 1, p. 1, d. 2, l. 8; Gromyko, Memo to the CC CPSU "On the Measures."

223. Ibid., l. 32; counselor of the USSR Embassy in Guinean Republic P. I. Gerasimov, report on the visit to the Guinean Republic, December 20, 1958.

224. Ibid., l. 33.

225. Ibid., l. 35.

226. Ibid., l. 26.

227. Ibid., ll. 37–39.

228. Ibid., ll. 12–13.

229. RGANI, f. 4, op. 16, d. 583, l. 91; materials for Protocol 89, point 5c, of the CC CPSU Presidium meeting, December 30, 1958.

230. AVP RF, f. 575, op. 2, p. 1, d. 10, l. 1; deputy head of Office of African Countries of Ministry of Foreign Trade of the USSR L. Ezhov, information on the Soviet trade delegation's stay in the Guinean Republic, March 5, 1959.

231. Ibid, ll. 2–3.

232. Ibid., l. 6.

233. *SSSR i strany Afriki*, vol. 1, 421–24.

234. AVP RF, f. 0575, op. 2, p.1, d. 6, ll. 3–5; second secretary of the USSR Embassy in the Guinean Republic S. M. Kirsanov, the arrival in Conakry of USSR ambassador to the Guinean Republic P. I. Gerasimov and the presentation of his credentials to President Sékou Touré (brief reference), May 12, 1959.

235. "Czech Shipments of Arms to Guinea," March 30, 1959, GRDS, Bureau of African Affairs, RG 59, NA.

236. Dispatch from Embassy, Conakry to the Department of State, Washington, 64, May 5, 1959, "May Day in Conakry," file 770B.00–May Day / 4-559, GRDS, Central Decimal File, RG 59, NA, pp. 1–2.

237. Memorandum for the president, April 22, 1959, "Tripartite Talks on Africa," GRDS, Bureau of African Affairs, RG 59, NA, p. 4.

238. *FRUS, 1958–1960, Volume 14, Africa*, 685–87.

239. Ibid., 687–89.

240. To Mr. Dillon from J. S. Satterthwaite, April 27, 1958, "Assistance for the Republic of Guinea," GRDS, Bureau of African Affairs, RG 59, NA, pp. 1–2.

241. Dispatch from Embassy, Conakry, to the Department of State, Washington, 71, May 18, 1959, "Sensitivity of Sékou Touré to U.S. End-Use Checks on Aid Program," file 870.49/5-1859, GRDS, Central Decimal File, RG 59, NA, pp. 1–4.

242. Telegram from Conakry to secretary of state, 84, June 17, file 670B.49/6-1759, GRDS, Central Decimal File, RG 59, NA.

243. *SSSR i strany Afriki*, vol. 1, 460.

244. RGANI, f. 5, op. 30, d. 309, ll. 86, 87, 88, 89; M. Yakovlev, A. Shvedov, and L. Ezhov, CC CPSU, to comrade A. I. Mikoyan, telephone message, August 25, 1959.

245. Ibid, d. 305, ll. 290–91; D. Degtyar', information on Soviet-Guinean cooperation, December 26, 1959.

246. AVP RF, f. 575, op. 2, p. 1, d. 2, ll. 66–67; I. I. Marchuk, memo on the conversation with state secretary for national defense N'Famara Kéi'ta, October 18, 1959.

247. Ibid, l. 67.

248. RGANI, f. 4, op. 16, d. 937, l. 103.

249. RGANI, f. 4, op. 16, d. 761, ll. 145–46; "On the Gratuitous Training of Guinean Military Personnel in the USSR," extract from Protocol 261 of the CC CPSU Presidium meeting, January 25, 1960.

250. "Memorandum from the Assistant Secretary of State for African Affairs (Satterthwaite) to the Under Secretary of State (Dillon), October 6, 1959," in *FRUS, 1958–1960, Volume 14, Africa*, 694.

251. Ibid., 693.

252. Ibid., 694.

253. Ibid.

254. Morrow, *First American Ambassador*, 30.

255. *FRUS, 1958–1960, Volume 14, Africa*, 698–702.

256. Ibid., 702–6.

257. To Mr. Cassilly from Arva C. Floyd, no date, "Impressions of the Visit of Sékou Touré and his Party to the United States," GRDS, Records of Component Offices of the Bureau of Intelligence and Research, lot 65D350, RG 59, NA.

258. Dispatch from American Embassy, Conakry, to the Department of State, Washington, 141. December 21, 1959; "Fodéba Kéi'ta, Minister of Interior and Security, Calls upon Ambassador Morrow and Also Attends a Reception for Senator Stuart Symington," file 611.70B/12-2159, GRDS, Central Decimal File, RG 59, NA.

259. *SSSR i strany Afriki*, vol. 1, 503–7.

260. Touré, *Nezavisimaya Gvineya*, 170; *SSSR i strany Afriki*, vol. 1, 501.

261. N. S. Khrushchev, *Vremya, Lyudi, Vlast' (Vospominaniya: v 4 knigah)* [Time, People, Power (Memoirs in four volumes)] (Moscow: IIK Moskovskie Novosti, 1999), vol. 3, 449.

262. *SSSR i strany Afriki*, vol. 1, 493.

263. Ibid., 495–96.

Notes to Chapter 2

1. V. Kudryavtsev, "Afrika shagaet vpered" (Africa moves ahead), *Sovremennyi Vostok*, no. 4 (1960): 45.

2. "Pod znamenem bor'by za svobodu" (Under the banner of national liberation), *Sovremennyi Vostok*, no. 1 (1960): 21.

3. Contacts between Africa and Sino-Soviet Bloc, January 21, 1960, GRDS, Bureau of African Affairs, RG 59, NA, p. 2.

4. Position Paper on "Soviet Penetration of Africa," April 18, 1960, ibid., p. 3.

5. *FRUS, 1958–1960, Volume 14, Africa* (Washington, D.C.: U.S. Government Printing Office, 1992), 120.

6. Stephen Weissman, *American Foreign Policy in the Congo, 1960–1964* (Ithaca, N.Y.: Cornell University Press, 1974); Madeleine Kalb, *The Congo Cables: The Cold War in Africa—From Eisenhower to Kennedy* (New York: Macmillan, 1982); Richard D. Mahoney, *JFK: Ordeal in Africa* (New York: Oxford University Press, 1983).

7. Ludo de Witte, *The Assassination of Lumumba* (London: Verso, 2001), xvi, xvii.

8. Lise A. Namikas, "Battleground Africa: The Cold War and the Congo Crisis, 1960–1965," PhD dissertation, University of Southern California, 2002.

9. National Security Council Briefing "Belgian Congo," May 4, 1960, in *CWIHP Conference Reader Compiled for the International Conference on the Congo Crisis, 1960–1961, Washington, D.C., September 23–24, 2004, Organized by the Woodrow Wilson Center's Cold War International History Project and the Africa Program*, ed. Lise Namikas and Sergey Mazov (Washington, D.C.: Cold War International History Project, Woodrow Wilson International Center for Scholars, 2004).

10. Ian Scott, *Tumbled House: The Congo at Independence* (London: Oxford University Press, 1969), 11.

11. Ibid., 26.

12. Alan P. Merriam, *Congo: Background of Conflict* (Evanston, Ill.: Northwestern University Press, 1961), 196–201; Scott, *Tumbled House*, 10, 17–18, 22–23.

13. Namikas, "Battleground Africa," 32.

14. Catherine Hoskyns, *The Congo since Independence: January 1960–December 1961* (London: Oxford University Press, 1965), 72–78.

15. Ibid., 14.

16. Weissman, *American Foreign Policy*, 29.

17. *FRUS, 1958–1960, Volume 14, Africa*, 262.

18. V. M. Lesiovskyi, *Taina ghibeli Hammarshel'da* (The secret of Hammarskjöld's death) (Moscow: Mysl', 1985), 82.

19. Kalb, *Congo Cables*, 4.

20. Lawrence Devlin, *Chief of Station, Congo: A Memoir of 1960–67* (New York: PublicAffairs, 2007), 9.

21. Lesiovskyi, *Taina ghibeli Hammarshel'da*, 83–87.

22. AVP RF, f. 590, op. 2, p. 1, d. 5, l. 63.

23. Ibid., ll. 1, 2, 3; Yu. N. Rakhmaninov, "About the January Events in the Belgian Congo," January 25, 1959.

24. Ibid., l. 60; M. Sytenko to deputy minister of foreign affairs of the USSR V. S. Semenov, February 19, 1959.

25. AVP RF, f. 0590, op. 1, p. 1, d. 1, l. 5; USSR ambassador to the Guinean Republic P. I. Gerasimov, notes of conversation with the representative of the Mouvement National Congolais, Patrice Lumumba, April 18, 1959.

26. RGANI, f. 11, op. 1, d. 427, ll. 47–48.

27. RGANI, f. 11, op. 1, d. 372, l. 30.

28. Ibid., l. 31.

29. RGANI, f. 5, op. 50, d. 257, ll. 22–25; adviser of the Soviet Embassy in Belgium B. A. Savinov, memo of conversation with the leader of the National Congolese Movement, Patrice Lumumba, February 19, 1960. (This document was obtained and translated into English by Lise Namikas.)

30. Ibid.

31. Namikas, "Battleground Africa," 104.

32. Ibid., 106–7.

33. Memorandum of conversation (Victor Nendaka, ex–vice president of MNC [Lumumba Wing]; Robert A. McKinnon, second secretary; Lawrence R. Devlin, attaché), March 25, in *CWIHP Conference Reader Compiled for the International Conference on the Congo Crisis.*

34. RGANI, f. 5, op. 50, d. 257, ll. 47–50; translators of the USSR Embassy in Belgium A. Ustinov and G. Uranov, memo of conversation between Philippe Kanza and Thomas Kanza, publisher and editor, respectively, of the weekly *Congo*, May 7, 1960. (This document was obtained and translated into English by Lise Namikas.)

35. AVP RF, f. 0575, op. 2, d. 2, ll. 105, 106; USSR chargé d'affaires in the Guinean Republic, notes of conversation with Pierre Mulele, Antoine Kingotolo, and Raphael Kinki, December 28, 1959.

36. RGANI, f. 11, op. 1, d. 474, l. 3.

37. *SSSR i strany Afriki 1946–1962 gg.: Dokumenty i materially, Tom. I (1946g.–sentyabr' 1960g.)* [USSR and African countries 1946–1962: Documents and materials, Vol. 1 (1946–September 1960)] (Moscow: Gosudarstvennoe izdatel'stvo politicheskoi literatury, 1963), 549–50.

38. Thomas Kanza, *The Rise and Fall of Patrice Lumumba: Conflict in the Congo* (London: Rex Collins, 1978), 155–64.

39. Weissman, *American Foreign Policy*, 55.

40. Kanza, *Rise and Fall of Patrice Lumumba*, 187.

41. Devlin, *Chief of Station, Congo*, x–xi.

42. Ibid., 10; *FRUS, 1958–1960, Volume 14, Africa*, 282.

43. *SSSR i strany Afriki*, vol. 1, 552.

44. M. Rakhmatov, *Afrika idet k svobode* (Africa goes toward freedom) (Moscow: Gospolitizdat, 1961), 69–73.

45. Kanza, *Rise and Fall of Patrice Lumumba*, 189.

46. Ibid., 189–90.

47. Weissman, *American Foreign Policy*, 56–57.

48. *SSSR i strany Afriki*, vol. 1, 553.

49. Hoskyns, *Congo since Independence*, 98.

50. Ibid.

51. Kanza, *Rise and Fall of Patrice Lumumba*, 198–200.

52. "Zayavleniye Sovetskogo Pravitel'stva v svyazi s imperialisticheskoi interventsiey v otnoshenii nezavisimoi Respubliki Kongo" (Statement of the Soviet government in connection with imperialist aggression against the Republic of the Congo, July 13, 1960), in *SSSR i strany Afriki*, vol. 1, 557.

53. AVP RF, f. 590, op. 3, p. 2, l. 34.

54. Ian Colvin, *The Rise and Fall of Moise Tshombe* (London: Leslie Frewin, 1968), 28.

55. "Analytical Chronology" [January 1961], in *CWIHP Conference Reader Compiled for the International Conference on the Congo Crisis.*

56. Kalb, *Congo Cables*, 7.

57. "Analytical Chronology," 7.

58. Quoted by Weissman, *American Foreign Policy*, 59.

59. Kanza, *Rise and Fall of Patrice Lumumba*, 206.

60. *SSSR i strany Afriki,* vol. 1, 553–54.

61. Ibid., 558.

62. Hoskyns, *Congo since Independence*, 112–13.

63. Conor Cruise O'Brien, *To Katanga and Back: A UN Case History* (London: Hutchinson, 1962), 49–52. A high-ranking British official of the UN Secretariat, Brian Urquhart, asserts that the Congo Club was nothing more than a group that gathered in Hammarskjöld's office, "for convenience," to deal with the Congo crisis. He calls "meretricious nonsense" allegations that the club was "a conspiracy by the United States to take over the UN Congo operation" for Hammarskjöld and notes Bunche's "continuous disagreements with the United States and their strong reaction to *any* government which attempted to tell them what to do." Brian Urquhart, *A Life in Peace and War* (New York: Harper & Row, 1987), 174.

64. Urquhart, *Life in Peace and War*, 56–57.

65. Ibid., p. 57.

66. Kalb, *Congo Cables*, 21.

67. "Resolution Adopted by the Security Council at its 873rd Meeting on July 14 1960 (S/4387)," quoted by Hoskyns, *Congo since Independence*, 484.

68. AVP RF, f. 590, op. 4, p. 6, d. 16, ll. 9–10; first secretary of the USSR MID Department of International Organizations V. Polyakov, "The UN Debate on the Situation in the Congo from July 1960 to April 1961," April 25, 1961.

69. Kwame Nkrumah, *Challenge of the Congo: A Case Study of Foreign Pressures in an Independent State* (New York: International Publishers, 1967), 20–21.

70. Kanza, *Rise and Fall of Patrice Lumumba*, 207.

71. Ibid.

72. *SSSR i strany Afriki,* vol. 1, 562.

73. Quoted by Merriam, *Congo*, 309.

74. Urquhart, *Life in Peace and War*, 147.

75. Hoskyns, *Congo since Independence*, 133–34.

76. *SSSR i strany Afriki,* vol. 1, 563.

77. *Izvestiya*, July 22, 1960.

78. W. Scott Thompson, *Ghana's Foreign Policy 1957–1966: Diplomacy, Ideology and the New State* (Princeton, N.J.: Princeton University Press, 1969), 131–32.

79. AVP RF, f. 590, op. 36, p. 4, d. 1, l. 23.

80. Ibid., l. 275.

81. This means that the corresponding decision was made by the Presidium of the CC CPSU, the party's highest organ, on July 30, 1960.

82. AVP RF, f. 0601, op. 1, p. 1, d. 6, l. 1.

83. Kalb, *Congo Cables*, 19.

84. K. Nepomnyashyi, "Spasibo sovetskim lyetchikam" (Thanks to Soviet pilots), *Pravda*, July 31, 1960.

85. "Analytical Chronology," 11.

86. AVP RF, f. 590, op. 36, p. 4, d. 1, l. 145.

87. Merriam, *Congo*, 309.

88. *FRUS, 1958–1960, Volume 14, Africa*, 330.

89. Ibid., 338, 339.

90. Ibid., 347.

91. Dwight D. Eisenhower, *Waging Peace 1956–1961: The White House Years* (Garden City, N.Y.: Doubleday, 1965), 575.

92. *FRUS, 1958–1960, Volume 14, Africa*, 354.

93. Devlin, *Chief of Station, Congo*, 48.

94. Ibid.

95. *SSSR i strany Afriki*, vol. 1, 566, 567, 571.

96. "Analytical Chronology," 15; AVP RF, f. 590, op. 4, p. 6, d. 16, l. 11; Polyakov, "UN Debate."

97. "Resolution Adopted by the Security Council at Its 879th Meeting on 22 July 1960 (S/4405)," quoted by Hoskyns, *Congo since Independence*, 484–85.

98. Quoted by Hoskyns, *Congo since Independence*, 156.

99. Kanza, *Rise and Fall of Patrice Lumumba*, 238.

100. Ibid., 243.

101. *FRUS, 1958–1960, Volume 14, Africa*, 358–64.

102. Kalb, *Congo Cables*, 37.

103. Intelligence Directorate, "Sino-Soviet Bloc Aid to the Republic of Congo," September 9, 1960, in *CWIHP Conference Reader Compiled for the International Conference on the Congo Crisis*.

104. *SSSR i strany Afriki*, vol. 1, 577.

105. "Analytical Chronology," 18.

106. Quoted by Merriam, *Congo*, 232–33.

107. "Analytical Chronology," 30–31.

108. Urquhart, *Life in Peace and War*, 158.

109. "Analytical Chronology," 22.

110. *SSSR i strany Afriki*, vol. 1, 590, 592.

111. AVP RF, f. 0573, op. 4, p. 2 d. 9, l. 1; USSR minister of foreign affairs A. A. Gromyko to the CC CPSU, "The Possibility of Soviet Aid to Ghana in Connection with the Events in the Congo," August 9, 1960.

112. Nkrumah, *Challenge of the Congo*, 30–31.

113. AVP RF, f. 0573, op. 4, p. 2, d. 9, l. 3; USSR MID to the CC CPSU, draft instruction to the USSR chargé d'affaires in Ghana, August 9, 1960.

114. AVP RF, f. 0601, op. 2, p. 4, d. 9, l. 6; L. I. Brezhnev, "On the Trip of L. I. Brezhnev to Guinean Republic, Ghana and Morocco," February 24, 1961.

115. United Nations, Security Council, "Fifteenth Year, 885th Meeting, 8 August 1960," in *Official Records* (New York: United Nations, 1960–64), 21.

116. Ibid., 18.

117. Ibid., 21.

118. "Resolution Adopted by the Security Council at its 886th Meeting on August 9, 1960 (S/4426)," quoted by Hoskyns, *Congo since Independence*, 485–86.

119. Hoskyns, *Congo since Independence*, 171; Charlie Simon, *Dag Hammarskjöld* (New York: Dutton, 1967), 146.

120. "Analytical Chronology," 24.

121. AVP RF, f. 590, op. 36, p. 4, d. 1, ll. 37–38, 39–40.

122. AVP RF, f. 0590, op. 2, p. 2, d. 17, ll. 6, 7.

123. Devlin, *Chief of Station, Congo*, 25.

124. Ibid., 24.

125. Vadim A. Kirpichenko, *Iz arkhiva razvedchika* (From a secret service man's archive) (Moscow: Mezhdunaroddnye Otnosheniya, 1993), 87.

126. O. I. Nazhestkin, "Gogy kongolezkogo krizisa (1960–1963 gg.): Zapiski razvedchika" (The years of the Congolese crisis, 1960–1963: A secret service man's memoirs), *Novaya i noveishaya istortiya*, no. 6 (2003): 155.

127. Ibid.

128. Ibid., 155–56.

129. AVP RF, f. 590, op. 3, p. 3, d. 22, l. 14.

130. Quoted by Christopher Stevens, *The Soviet Union and Black Africa* (London: Macmillan, 1976), 17.

131. Kalb, *Congo Cables*, 56.

132. Vladimir Ronin, *"Russkoye Kongo": Knigha-memorial* (The "Russian Congo": A book-memorial), 2 vols. (Moscow: Dom Russkogo Zarubezhya imeni Aleksandra Solzhenitsina: Russkyi Put', 2009), vol. 2, 406.

133. "Bloc Personnel in the Congo," September 9, 1960, in *CWIHP Conference Reader Compiled for the International Conference on the Congo Crisis*.

134. Devlin, *Chief of Station, Congo*, 66.

135. "Analytical Chronology," 30.

136. *FRUS, 1958–1960, Volume 14, Africa*, 441.

137. Devlin, *Chief of Station, Congo*, 66–67.

138. "Analytical Chronology," 32.

139. Devlin, *Chief of Station, Congo*, 67.

140. H. M. Epstein, ed., *Revolt in the Congo 1960–64* (New York: Facts on File, 1965), 37.

141. Devlin, *Chief of Station, Congo*, 67.
142. Kanza, *Rise and Fall of Patrice Lumumba*, 287–88.
143. "Analytical Chronology," 33; Epstein, *Revolt in the Congo*, 38–39.
144. Urquhart, *Life in Peace and War*, 166–67.
145. Epstein, *Revolt in the Congo*, 41.
146. Kalb, *Congo Cables*, 79.
147. Nazhestkin, "Gody kongolezkogo krizisa," 156–57.
148. Kalb, *Congo Cables*, 79–80.
149. Nazhestkin, "Gody kongolezkogo krizisa," 157.
150. *SSSR i strany Afriki,* vol. 1, 633–35.
151. AVP RF, f. 0590, op. 2, p. 1, d. 8, l. 56.
152. V. A. Subbotin, "Kongo: Leopool'dvil' v 1960" (Congo: Leopoldville in 1960), in *Afrika v vospominaniyah veteranov diplomaticheskoi sluzhby* (Africa in the memoirs of veterans of the Foreign Service), vol. 5 (of 12 vols.). (Moscow: Institut Afriki RAN, Sovet veteranov MID RF, 2004), 284.
153. Epstein, *Revolt in the Congo*, 39.
154. Kalb, *Congo Cables*, 77.
155. Devlin, *Chief of Station, Congo*, 76–80.
156. Kanza, *Rise and Fall of Patrice Lumumba*, 304.
157. Rajeshwar Dayal, *Mission for Hammarskjöld: The Congo Crisis* (Princeton, N.J.: Princeton University Press, 1976), 69–74.
158. Namikas, "Battleground Africa," 202; de Witte, *Assassination of Lumumba*, 27–28.
159. Dayal, *Mission for Hammarskjöld*, 75–76.
160. Nazhestkin, "Gody kongolezkogo krizisa," 157.
161. Ibid., 75.
162. Devlin, *Chief of Station, Congo*, 26.
163. Dayal, *Mission for Hammarskjöld*, 75.
164. AVP RF, f. 590, op. 4, p. 6, d. 19, l. 94.
165. Oleg Grinevskyi, *Tysyacha i odin den' Nikity Serggevicha* (A thousand and one days in the life of Nikita Sergeevich) (Moscow: Vagrius, 1998), 336–37.
166. Epstein, *Revolt in the Congo*, 44.
167. Ibid., 44–45.
168. Quoted by Hoskyns, *Congo since Independence*, 234.
169. Quoted in "Analytical Chronology," 40.
170. Epstein, *Revolt in the Congo*, 45.
171. "Resolution Adopted by the Fourth Emergency Session of the General Assembly on 20 September 1960 (A/RES/1474/Rev. 1 (E.S.IV)," quoted by Hoskyns, *Congo since Independence*, 486–88.
172. Epstein, *Revolt in the Congo*, 46–47.
173. Kalb, *Congo Cables*, 105.

174. United Nations, "Official Records of the General Assembly, Fifteenth Session (Part I), Plenary Meetings, Volume I, Verbatim Records of Meetings 20 September–17 October 1960," in *Official Records*, 71–72.

175. Ibid., 82–83.

176. Ibid., 95.

177. Ibid., 318–19.

178. Ibid., 332.

179. Kalb, *Congo Cables*, 106.

180. *FRUS, 1958–1960, Volume 14, Africa*, 501.

181. Originally, the College of High Commissioners was called the "College of Commissars," but the State Department found it "too Russian, too Communist" and Devlin convinced Mobutu to change "Commissars" to "Commissioners." Devlin, *Chief of Station, Congo*, 87, 88.

182. Ibid., 98–99.

183. "Analytical Chronology," 49.

184. Epstein, *Revolt in the Congo*, 51.

185. Devlin, *Chief of Station, Congo*, 107.

186. "Analytical Chronology," 46.

187. See U.S. Congress, Senate, Select Committee to Study Government Operations with Respect to Intelligence Activities, *Alleged Assassination Plots Involving Foreign Leaders*, Senate Report 94-465, 94th Congress, 1st Session (Washington, D.C.: U.S. Government Printing Office, 1975).

188. Devlin, *Chief of Station, Congo*, 94–97.

189. Dayal, *Mission for Hammarskjöld*, 132–33.

190. Epstein, *Revolt in the Congo*, 59.

191. *SSSR i strany Afriki 1946–1962 gg.: Dokumenty i materially, Tom. II (Sentyabr' 1960g.–1962g.)* [USSR and African countries 1946–1962: Documents and materials, Vol. 2 (September 1960–1962)] (Moscow: Gosudarstvennoe izdatel'stvo politicheskoi literatury, 1963), 95–100.

192. Ibid., 132.

193. Devlin, *Chief of Station, Congo*, 99.

194. AVP RF, f. 590, op. 4, p. 6, d. 19, l. 12.

195. AVP RF, f. 590, op. 3, p. 1, d. 11, l. 5.

196. *SSSR i strany Afriki*, vol. 2, 141.

197. Kalb, *Congo Cables*, 172.

198. AVP RF, f. 0590, op. 2, p. 1, d. 2, ll. 2–4.

199. "Memorandum from the Department of State to Certain Diplomatic Missions, December 15, 1960," in *FRUS, 1958–1960, Volume 14, Africa*, 630.

200. Kalb, *Congo Cables*, 169–70.

201. AVP RF, f. 0590, op. 3, p. 4, d. 1, l. 33.

202. AVP RF, f. 0590, op. 2, d. 9, ll. 62–63.

203. AVP RF, f. 590, op. 3, p. 2, d. 9, l. 38.

204. *SSSR i strany Afriki*, vol. 2, 507.

205. Fritz Schatten, *Communism in Africa* (London: George Allen & Unwin, 1966), 136–38.

206. John H. Morrow, *First American Ambassador to Guinea* (New Brunswick, N.J.: Rutgers University Press, 1968), 135.

207. AVP RF, f. 0575, op. 3, p. 3, d. 7, l. 8; counselor of Embassy of the USSR in Guinean Republic I. I. Marchuk, memorandum of conversation with Czechoslovakian experts Goushka and Svoboda, March 7, 1960.

208. Ibid., l. 23; counselor of the USSR Embassy in Guinean Republic I. I. Marchuk, memorandum of conversation with the first secretary of Czechoslovakian Embassy V. Juck, April 11, 1960.

209. AVP RF, f. 575, op. 4, p. 6, d. 6, l. 15.

210. Jean Suret-Canale, *Gvineyskaya Respublika (Guinean Republic)* (Moscow: Progress, 1973), 196.

211. Embassy Conakry to the Department of State, Dispatch 276, May 5, 1960, Guinea Food Crisis Alleviated by Bloc Aid, file 870/B.03/5-560, GRDS, Central Decimal File, RG 59, NA, p. 1.

212. Ibid., 2.

213. *SSSR i strany Afriki*, vol. 1, 620–21.

214. Ibid., 628.

215. AVP RF, f. 0575, op. 4, p. 6, d. 6, l. 15; assistant secretary of the USSR Embassy to Guinea S. M. Kirsanov, memorandum of conversation with counselor of the Ministry of Economy of Guinea Jerar Kaye, January 11, 1961.

216. *SSSR i strany Afriki*, vol. 1, 622–27.

217. AVP RF, f. 0575, op. 3, p. 5, d. 23, l. 55; Department of African Countries of the USSR Foreign Ministry, Guinean Republic (short information), August 29, 1960.

218. American Embassy, Monrovia, to the Department of State, Dispatch 531, June 6, 1960, Bloc Aid to Guinea, file 870B.0061/6-660, GRDS, Central Decimal File, RG 59, NA, p. 1.

219. Department of State, Memorandum of Conversation, April 23, 1960, Situation in Guinea, file 770B.00/4-2360, ibid., p. 2.

220. Incoming Telegram, Department of State, no. 165, October 9, 1960, file 770B.00/10-960, ibid., p. 2.

221. Touré-Eisenhower, Conakry, July 19, 1960, unnumbered file, ibid., p. 3.

222. File 870B.00/8-1260, ibid., p. 1.

223. *FRUS, 1958–1960, Volume 14, Africa*, 717.

224. U.S. Programs in Guinea, May 1961, GRDS, Bureau of African Affairs, RG 59, NA, p. 10.

225. AVP RF, f. 0575, op. 3, p. 3, d. 7, ll. 24, 36.

226. *Izvestiya*, March 11, 1960.

227. Incoming Telegram, Department of State, no. 2329, March 15, 1960, file 601.70B62B/3-1560, GRDS, Central Decimal File, RG 59, NA, p. 1.

228. Morrow, *First American Ambassador*, 143–47.

229. Schatten, *Communism*, 134.

230. AVP RF, f. 0575, op. 2, p. 1, d. 8, ll. 88–89; first secretary of the Soviet Embassy in Guinean Republic V. I. Ivanisov, information on a trip around the country (November 24–30, 1959), December 24, 1959.

231. American Embassy, Conakry, to the Department of State, Dispatch 135, December 10, 1959, impressions from a nine-day trip through Guinea, file 770B.00/12-1059, GRDS, Central Decimal File, RG 59, NA, p. 6.

232. American Embassy, Conakry, to the Department of State, Dispatch 62, August 24, 1959, observations of American documentary film photographer on interior of Guinea, file 770B.00/8-2459, GRDS, Central Decimal File, RG 59, NA, p. 2.

233. AVP RF, f. 0575, op. 3, p. 3, d. 25, ll. 8, 9–10.

234. Ibid., d. 7, ll. 46, 47; first secretary of the USSR Embassy in Guinean Republic V. I. Ivanisov, memorandum of conversation with Guinean general secretary of foreign affairs Alpha Diallo, August, 15, 1960.

235. John H. Morrow to C. Vaughan Ferguson Jr., director, Office of Middle and Southern African Affairs, Department of State, April 12, 1960, GRDS, Bureau of African Affairs, RG 59, NA, pp. 1–2.

236. American Embassy, Conakry, to the Department of State, Dispatch 116, November 10, 1959, celebration of 42nd Anniversary of Russian Revolution in Guinea, file 870B.48661/11-1059, GRDS, Central Decimal File, RG 59, NA, pp. 2–3.

237. Tawia Adamafio, *By Nkrumah's Side: The Labour and the Wounds* (Accra and London: Westcoast Publishing House and Rex Collins, 1982), 87–89.

238. AVP RF, f. 0573, op. 5, p. 8, d. 10, l. 60; memoranda of the USSR MID African Department II "On the Construction of the Complex of Installations on the Volta River in Ghana," October 4, 1961; Volta River Hydroelectric Project and Valco Smelter Project in Ghana. January 30, 1961, Papers of W. Averell Harriman, container 464, Collections of the Manuscript Division, Library of Congress; David Rooney, *Kwame Nkrumah: The Political Kingdom in the Third World* (London: I. B. Tauris, 1988), 154–57.

239. AVP RF, f. 0573, op. 4, p. 3, d. 12, l. 9; deputy chief of the USSR MID African Department I. Kolosovskyi, instruction sheet for talk with Ghanaian parliamentary delegation, April 30, 1960.

240. Thompson, *Ghana's Foreign Policy*, 105.

241. Ibid., 102.

242. AVP RF, f. 0573, op. 4, p. 3, d. 12, l. 4; minister of foreign affairs of the USSR A. A. Gromyko to CC CPSU, April 29, 1960.

243. Ibid., l. 23; Kwame Nkrumah's letter to N. S. Khrushchev, delivered by Embassy of Ghana in USSR to MID on May 3, 1960.

244. Ibid., l. 49; N. Patolitchev, S. Skatchkov, Y. Ushin, and V. Myshkov, memorandum report to CC CPSU on talk with Ghanaian parliamentary delegation.

245. Ibid., ll. 49–50.

246. Ibid., l. 51; deputy of the USSR Supreme Soviet N. A. Dygai, information on the stay of the Ghanaian parliamentary delegation in Moscow on May 5–6, May 26, 1960.

247. Ibid., ll. 51, 52.

248. Ibid., ll. 80–81; deputy of the USSR Supreme Soviet N. A. Dygai, information on the stay of Ghanaian parliamentary delegation in Moscow on May 13–17, May 26, 1960.

249. Thompson, *Ghana's Foreign Policy*, 164–65.

250. *SSSR i strany Afriki,* vol. 1, 580–82.

251. Adamafio, *By Nkrumah's Side*, 90.

252. *Pravda*, August 6, 1960.

253. Adamafio, *By Nkrumah's Side*, 90.

254. Thompson, *Ghana's Foreign Policy*, 164.

255. Ibid.

256. *Izvestiya*, August 29, 1960.

257. H. T. Alexander, *African Tightrope: My Two Years as Nkrumah's Chief of Staff* (New York: Frederick A. Praeger, 1965), 34.

258. *FRUS, 1958–1960, Volume 14, Africa*, 658, 659.

259. Ibid., 660.

260. Ibid., 661, 662.

261. Nkrumah, *Challenge of the Congo*, 70–71.

262. Ibid., 71.

263. *Pravda*, September 25, 1960.

264. *FRUS, 1958–1960, Volume 14, Africa*, 664.

265. Ibid., 668.

266. *Prezidium TsK KPSS 1954–1964, Tom. I: Tchernovye protokol'nye zapisi zasedaniei—Stenogrammy* (Presidium of the CC CPSU 1954–1964, Vol. 1: Draft protocol sentences of meetings—Verbatim reports), ed. A. A. Fursenko (Moscow: Rosspan, 2003), 445.

267. Mahoney, *JFK*, 158.

268. *FRUS, 1958–1960, Volume 14, Africa*, 668.

269. Ibid., 666–67.

270. AVP RF, f. 0573 op. 5, p. 9, d. 17, ll. 8–10; Soyuz sovetskikh obshestv druzby (Union of Soviet Societies of Friendship and Cultural Relations with Foreign Countries) representative in Ghana, first secretary of the Embassy V. Studenov, report on developing cultural relations with Ghana in 1960, March 14, 1961.

271. Ibid., 6.

272. RGANI, f. 11, op. 1, d. 561, l. 115; memo to the CC CPSU by I. Pomelov, deputy editor in chief of the journal *Communist*, October 1, 1960.

273. Ibid., l. 112; "On Transferring Literature to Public Organizations of Ghana," Protocol 52, point 237-gs, of the CC CPSU Commission on Ideology, Culture, and International Party Ties meeting, December 12, 1960.

274. Ibid., 113; memo to the CC CPSU by deputy chief of the CC CPSU Department of Agitation and Propaganda in the Union Republics A. Romanov and

deputy of chief of the CC CPSU International Department V. Tereshkin, December 6, 1960.

275. AVP RF, f. 0573, op. 5, p. 8, d. 13, ll. 1–3; second secretary of the Embassy of the USSR in Ghana V. Kodakov, "On Dissemination of the Truth about the Soviet Union in the Local Press," March 15, 1961.

276. Ibid., pp. 4–5.

277. Ibid., p. 9, d. 16, ll. 1–3; first secretary of the Embassy of the USSR in Ghana V. Studenov, "Information on American Activity to Disseminate Anti-Soviet Propaganda in Ghana," March 16, 1961.

278. AVP RF, f. 0607, op. 1a, p. 1a, d. 9, l. 2; first secretary of the USSR Embassy in the Guinean Republic V. I. Ivanisov, memo "On Internal Political and Economic Situation in the Mali Federation," February 18, 1960.

279. Airgram from Amcongen, Dakar, Senegal, to secretary of state, no. G-33, December 3, 1959, file 751T.00/12-359 EMW, GRDS, Central Decimal File, RG 59, NA, p. 3.

280. Airgram from Amcogen, Dakar, Senegal, to secretary of state, no. G-54, October 16, 1959, file 751T.00/10-1659, EMW, ibid., p. 1.

281. Airgram from Amcogen, Dakar, Senegal, to secretary of state, no. G-56, October 19, 1959, file 751T.00/10-1959, EMW, ibid., p. 2.

282. Ibid.

283. Airgram from Amcongen, Dakar, Senegal, to secretary of state, no. G-33, December 3, 1959, p. 4.

284. AVP RF, f. 0607, op. 1a, p. 1a, d. 9, ll. 5, 6, 7; first secretary of the USSR Embassy in the Guinean Republic V. I. Ivanisov, memo.

285. Ibid., l. 12.

286. *SSSR i strany Afriki*, vol. 1, 547.

287. Ibid., 548.

288. S. Volk, "Perevorot v Mali" (The Mali Coup), *Novoe vremya*, no 36 (1960): 18.

289. AVP RF, f. 0607, op. 1a, p. 1a, d. 9, l. 24; ambassador of the USSR in Guinean Republic D. S. Solod, memo "On the Events in Mali," September 18, 1960.

290. Ibid., 24, 27.

291. Ibid., 27.

292. D. M. Kurtz, "Political Integration in Africa: The Mali Federation," *Journal of Modern African Studies* 8, no. 3 (1970): 416, 417.

293. William J. Foltz, *From French West Africa to the Mali Federation* (New Haven, Conn.: Yale University Press, 1965), 129–87.

294. AVP RF, f. 0607, op. 1a, p. 1a, d. 9, ll. 10–11; first secretary of the USSR Embassy in the Guinean Republic V. I. Ivanisov, memo.

295. Ibid., ll. 31–32; ambassador of the USSR in Guinean Republic D. S. Solod, memo.

296. AVP RF, f. 0607, op. 1a, p. 1a, d. 6, l. 9.

297. Ibid., l. 5; deputy of the USSR foreign minister V. V. Kuznetsov, memo

to the CC CPSU "On the Recognition of the Republic Mali and the Republic of Senegal."

298. Volk, "Perevorot v Mali," 19.

299. AVP RF, f. 0607, op. 1a, p. 1a, d. 9, 1. 35; ambassador of the USSR in Guinean Republic D. S. Solod, memo.

300. AVP RF, f. 0607, op. 1a, p. 1a, d. 6, 1. 10.

301. Ibid., 1. 5; Kuznetsov, memo.

302. *SSSR i strany Afriki*, vol. 2, 36, 37.

303. Ibid., 36.

304. AVP RF, f. 607, op. 3, p. 3, d. 7, 1. 146; first secretary of the USSR Embassy in Mali Yu. I. Bel'skyi, "Short Data on the Internal Political Situation in the Republic of Mali," January 10, 1960.

305. Telegram from Deputy Undersecretary Loy W. Henderson to secretary of state, November 10, 1960, GRDS, Bureau of African Affairs, RG 59, NA, p. 2.

306. Telegram from Dakar to secretary of state, no. 349, May 18, 1960, file 751T.02/5-1860, GRDS, Central Decimal File, RG 59, NA, p. 1.

307. Telegram from Paris to secretary of state, no. 1022, September 10, 1960, file 751T.02/9-1060, ibid., p. 2.

308. AVP RF, f. 0607, op. 2, p. 2, d. 12, 1. 14; African Department I of the USSR MID, "Short Information on Ousmane Ba, Minister of Labor of the Republic of Mali," February 13, 1960.

309. Dispatch from American Embassy, Conakry, to the Department of State, no. 103, October 25, 1960, Deputy Undersecretary Henderson's call on president of Mali, GRDS, Bureau of African Affairs, RG 59, NA, p. 2.

310. Telegram from Henderson to secretary of state, November 10, 1960, p. 2.

311. Loy W. Henderson, deputy undersecretary of state for administration, to Joseph C. Satterthwaite, assistant secretary for African affairs, Department of State, Conakry, October 25, 1960, ibid., p. 2.

312. AVP RF, f. 0607, op. 2, p. 4, d. 11, 1. 47; third secretary of the USSR Embassy in Mali Yu. A. Timofeev, memo, "The Economy of the Mali Republic," July 8, 1961.

313. AVP RF, f. 607, op. 1, p. 1, d. 3, 1. 3.

314. Memorandum of conversation, November 1, 1960, aid for Mali, GRDS, Bureau of African Affairs, RG 59, NA, pp. 1, 2.

315. Telegram from Department of State to U.S. Mission to the United Nations, New York, November 30, 1960, file 770.5-MSP/11-2360, GRDS, Central Decimal File, RG 59, NA, p. 1.

316. Ibid., p. 2.

Notes to Chapter 3

1. I. Potekhin, "Africa: Itogi i perspectivy antiimperialisticheskoi revoltutsii" (Africa: The results of and prospects for the anti-imperialist revolution), *Aziya i Afrika segodnya*, no. 9 (1961): 11.

2. Ibid, 12.

3. Ibid., 13.

4. B. Ponomarev, "O gosudarstve natsional'noi demokratii" (On the national democratic state), *Kommunist*, no. 8 (1961): 37–38.

5. Richard D. Mahoney, *JFK: Ordeal in Africa* (New York: Oxford University Press, 1983), 35.

6. "Memorandum from Secretary of State Rusk to President Kennedy, February 15, 1961," in *FRUS, 1961–1963, Volume 21, Africa* (Washington, D.C.: U.S. Government Printing Office, 1995), 282.

7. "Report to the Honorable John F. Kennedy by the Task Force on Africa, December 31, 1960," cited by Thomas J. Noer, "New Frontiers and Old Priorities in Africa," in *Kennedy's Quest for Victory. American Foreign Policy, 1961–1963*, ed. Thomas G. Patterson (New York: Oxford University Press, 1989), 257.

8. "Special Message to the Congress on Urgent National Needs, May 25, 1961," available at http://www.cs.umb.edu/jfklibrary.

9. "Analytical Chronology [January 1961]," in *CWIHP Conference Reader Compiled for the International Conference on the Congo Crisis, 1960–1961, Washington, D.C., September 23–24, 2004, Organized by the Woodrow Wilson Center's Cold War International History Project and the Africa Program*, ed. Lise Namikas and Sergey Mazov (Washington, D.C.: Cold War International History Project, Woodrow Wilson International Center for Scholars, 2004), 57, 60; Madeleine Kalb, *The Congo Cables: The Cold War in Africa from Eisenhower to Kennedy* (New York: Macmillan, 1982), 175–76.

10. "Special National Intelligence Estimate: Main Elements in the Congo Situation, January 10, 1961," in *FRUS, 1961–1963, Volume 20, Congo Crisis* (Washington, D.C.: U.S. Government Printing Office, 1994), 5.

11. Ibid., 12, 13.

12. AVP RF, f. 590, op. 4, p. 5, d. 11, l. 130.

13. AVP RF, f. 0590, op. 3, p. 4, d. 1, l. 71; transcript of the talk between deputy foreign minister of the USSR V. V. Kuznetsov and minister of education and arts of the Republic of the Congo Pierre Mulele, March 8, 1961.

14. AVP RF, f. 0590, op. 4, p. 5, d. 12, l. 16; USSR MID African Department II, short memo, "Facts of Western Powers' Interference in the Congo's Internal Affairs."

15. AVP RF, f. 0590, op. 3, p. 4, d. 1, l. 33; transcript of talk between deputy foreign minister of the USSR V. S. Semenov and United Arab Republic president Gamal Abdel Nasser, January 31, 1961.

16. Ibid., l. 35.

17. Kwame Nkrumah, *Challenge of the Congo: A Case Study of Foreign Pressures in an Independent State* (New York: International Publishers, 1967), 116.

18. Ibid., 104.

19. Ibid., 105–6.

20. RGANI, f. 4, op. 16, d. 941, l. 150; resolution of the CC CPSU, "On the Soviet Delegation's Participation in an Extraordinary Session of the Council of

Afro-Asian Solidarity in Cairo," extract from Protocol 171, point 121-gs, January 16, 1961.

21. "Analytical Chronology," 72.

22. Kalb, *Congo Cables*, 119.

23. AVP RF, f. 0590, op. 3, p. 4, d. 1, l. 34.

24. Ibid., l. 36.

25. Ibid., l. 48; transcript of talk between deputy of foreign minister of the USSR A. A. Sobolev and ambassador of Czechoslovakia in Moscow G. R. Dvořák, March 9, 1961.

26. AVP RF, f. 0601, op. 2, p. 4, d. 9, l. 6; L. I. Brezhnev, "About the Trip of L. I. Brezhnev to the Republic of Guinea, Ghana and Morocco," February 24, 1961.

27. AVP RF, f. 0590, op. 3, p. 4, d. 1, ll. 18–20; transcript of talk between deputy foreign minister of the USSR Y. A. Malik and ambassador of Czechoslovakia in Moscow G. R. Dvořák, January 12, 1961. Ibid., ll. 57–59; transcript of talk between deputy foreign minister of the USSR Y. A. Malik and ambassador of Czechoslovakia in Moscow G. R. Dvořák, February 24, 1961.

28. Ibid., ll. 47–48; transcript of talk between deputy foreign minister of the USSR A. A. Sobolev and ambassador of Czechoslovakia in Moscow G. R. Dvořák, March 9, 1961.

29. Ibid.

30. Ibid., l. 76; transcript of talk between deputy foreign minister of the USSR N. P. Firubin and ambassador of Czechoslovakia in Moscow G. R. Dvořák, March 9, 1961.

31. "Analytical Chronology," 69.

32. Kalb, *Congo Cables*, 190.

33. Ludo de Witte, *The Assassination of Lumumba* (London: Verso, 2001), 143.

34. Zayavlenie Sovetskogo pravitel'stva v svyazi s ubiyistvom Patrisa Lumumbi (Statement of the Soviet government in connection with the assassination of Patrice Lumumba, February 14, 1961), in *SSSR i strany Afriki 1946–1962 gg.: Dokumenty i materially, Tom. II (Sentyabr' 1960g–1962g.)* [USSR and African countries 1946–1962: Documents and materials, Vol. 2 (September 1960–1962)] (Moscow: Gosudarstvennoe izdatel'stvo politicheskoi literatury, 1963), 195.

35. *Patris Lumumba: Pravda o tshudovishnom prestuplenii kolonizatorov* (Patrice Lumumba: The truth about the colonizers' monstrous crime) (Moscow: Izdaniye soyuza zhurnalistov SSSR, 1961).

36. De Witte, *Assassination of Lumumba*, 61–124.

37. "Parliamentary Committee of Enquiry in Charge of Determining the Exact Circumstances of the Assassination of Patrice Lumumba and the Possible Involvement of Belgian Politicians," in *CWIHP Conference Reader Compiled for the International Conference on the Congo Crisis*.

38. Ibid.

39. Kalb, *Congo Cables*, 189.

40. Lawrence Devlin, *Chief of Station, Congo: A Memoir of 1960–67* (New York: PublicAffairs, 2007), 94–97, 113–14.

41. AVP RF, f. 590, op. 4, p. 5, d. 11, l. 91.

42. Ibid., p. 133.

43. "Statement of the Soviet Government in Connection with the Assassination of Patrice Lumumba, February 14, 1961," in *SSSR i strany Afriki*, vol. 2, 197.

44. AVP RF, f. 0590, op. 3, p. 4, d. 2, l. 71; transcript of talk between V. V. Kuznetsov and Pierre Mulele, March 8, 1961.

45. Devlin, *Chief of Station, Congo*, 140–41.

46. AVP RF, f. 0590, op. 3, p. 4, d. 2, l. 71.

47. Ibid., l. 85; transcript of talk between deputy foreign minister of the USSR N. P. Firubin and ambassador of Poland in the USSR B. Yashuk, March 10, 1961.

48. AVP RF, f. 0590, op. 3, p. 6, d. 17, l. 3; Československá tisková kancelář (Czechoslovakian Telegraph Agency) special correspondent Dushan Provarnik, "Report on Staying in the Congo," March 6, 1961.

49. Ibid., l. 4.

50. AVP RF, f. 0590, op. 3, p. 4, d. 2, ll. 16, 19; transcript of talk with minister of education and arts of the Republic of Congo Pierre Mulele, March 9, 1961, participants: P. Mulele and A. Ponsele (Congolese side); and V. A. Brykhin, N. I. Gusev, and G. S. Sidorovich.

51. Ibid., l. 19.

52. AVP RF, f. 0590, op. 3, p. 4, d. 2, l. 73; transcript of the talk with Minister of Education and Arts of the Republic of Congo Pierre Mulele, March 8, 1961, participants: V. V. Kuznetsov, R. Y. Malinovskyi, S. A. Skatchkov, N. I. Gusev, V. A. Brykhin, G. S. Sidorovich.

53. *FRUS, 1961–1963, Volume 20, Congo Crisis*, 1.

54. AVP RF, f. 0590, op. 3, p. 4, d. 1, l. 64; transcript of talk with the minister of education and arts of the Republic of Congo Pierre Mulele at the breakfast, March 8, 1961, participants: V. V. Kuznetsov, R. Y. Malinovskyi, S. A. Skachkov, V. A. Brykhin, N. I. Gusev, G. S. Sidorovich.

55. AVP RF, f. 0590, op. 3, p. 4, d. 2, l. 20; transcript of talk with P. Mulele, March 9, 1961.

56. AVP RF, f. 0590, op. 3, p. 6, d. 17, ll. 8, 10, 11; Dushan Provarnik, "Report on Staying in the Congo."

57. *FRUS, 1961–1963, Volume 20, Congo Crisis*, 103.

58. Lise Namikas, "Battleground Africa: The Cold War and the Congo Crisis, 1960–1965," PhD dissertation, University of Southern California, 2002, 292.

59. O.I. Nazhestkin, "Gogy kongolezkogo krizisa (1960–1963 gg.): Zapiski razvedchika" (The years of the Congolese crisis, 1960–1963: A secret service man's memoirs), *Novaya i noveishaya istortiya*, no. 6 (2003): 157.

60. Ibid.

61. Devlin, *Chief of Station, Congo*, 155.
62. AVP RF, f. 0590, op. 4, p. 8, d. 18, l. 6; information from MID African Department II, "The Republic of Congo," January 8, 1962.
63. *SSSR i strany Afriki*, vol. 2, 401.
64. AVP RF, f. 0590, op. 4, p. 8, d. 18, l. 6.
65. Nazhestkin, "Gogy kongolezkogo krizisa," 159.
66. Devlin, *Chief of Station, Congo*, 194–95.
67. Nazhestkin, "Gogy kongolezkogo krizisa," 159.
68. AVP RF, f. 0590, op. 4, p. 8, d. 18, l. 6.
69. Nazhestkin, "Gogy kongolezkogo krizisa," 159.
70. AVP RF, f. 0590, op. 4, p. 6, d. 18, l. 38; memorandum by MID African Department II, "On the Situation in the Republic of Congo," October 14, 1961.
71. *FRUS, 1961–1963, Volume 20, Congo Crisis*, 185.
72. AVP RF, f. 0590, op. 4, p. 8, d. 18, l. 75; third secretary of the USSR Embassy in the Congo L. Petrov. "The Activity of the Adoula Government," May 28, 1962.
73. Kalb, *Congo Cables*, 304.
74. AVP RF, f. 0590, op. 4, p. 6, d. 17, ll. 67–68; MID African Department II, "The Situation in the Congo," May 28, 1962.
75. "Congo White Paper," n.d. [March 1963?], in *CWIHP Conference Reader Compiled for the International Conference on the Congo Crisis*, 39.
76. Devlin, *Chief of Station, Congo*, 187.
77. "Resolution Adopted by the Security Council on November 24, 1961 (S/5002)," quoted in Conor Cruise O'Brien, *To Katanga and Back: A UN Case History* (London: Hutchinson, 1962), 338–39.
78. Kalb, *Congo Cables*, 313.
79. Ibid., 321.
80. *FRUS, 1961–1963, Volume 20, Congo Crisis*, 344.
81. Kalb, *Congo Cables*, 322–23.
82. AVP RF, f. 0590, op. 3, p. 6, d. 17, l. 66; MID African Department II, "The Situation in the Congo," December 29, 1961.
83. Kalb, *Congo Cables*, 326–30.
84. *FRUS, 1961–1963, Volume 20, Congo Crisis*, 369.
85. Devlin, *Chief of Station, Congo*, 162.
86. Kalb, *Congo Cables*, 330.
87. *Pravda*, January 26–28, 1962.
88. RGANI, f. 4, op. 18, d. 145, l. 112; memo of the deputy chief of the CC CPSU International Department V. Korionov to the CC CPSU, May 16, 1962.
89. Ibid., ll. 110–11; resolution of the CC CPSU Secretariat "On the Measures to Defend Antoine Gizenga," Protocol 25, point 26g, of the CC CPSU Secretariat meeting, May 24, 1962.
90. Devlin, *Chief of Station, Congo*, 193.

91. AVP RF, f. 0590, op. 4, p. 7, d. 3, ll. 19, 20; chargé d'affaires ad interim L. Podgornov, transcript of talk with president of the Assembly Joseph Kasongo, January 22, 1962.

92. AVP RF, f. 0590, op. 4, p. 7, d. 8, ll. 72–73; second secretary of the USSR Embassy in the Republic of Congo Yu. Sidel'nikov, "Internal Situation in the Republic of Congo," May 28, 1962.

93. Bureau of Intelligence and Research, U.S. Department of State, Research Memorandum, "The Soviets, the UN and the Congo, March 29, 1963," in *CWIHP Conference Reader Compiled for the International Conference on the Congo Crisis.*

94. Kalb, *Congo Cables*, 377.

95. Devlin, *Chief of Station, Congo*, 203.

96. Kalb, *Congo Cables*, 371.

97. "Congo White Paper," 42.

98. *FRUS, 1961–1963, Volume 20, Congo Crisis*, 860.

99. Kalb, *Congo Cables*, 377.

100. Nazhestkin, "Gogy kongolezkogo krizisa," 160.,

101. Yu. P. Viktorov, "Moi afrikanskie epizody" (My African episodes), in *Afrika v vospominaniyah veteranov diplomaticheskoi sluzhby* (Africa in the memoirs of veterans of the Foreign Service), vol. 5 (of 12 vols.) (Moscow: Institut Afriki RAN, Sovet veteranov MID RF, 2004), 73–74.

102. Nazhestkin, "Gogy kongolezkogo krizisa," 161–62.

103. Ibid., 162.

104. Ibid.

105. Ibid., 163.

106. Viktorov, "Moi afrikanskie epizody," 79–80.

107. Nazhestkin, "Gogy kongolezkogo krizisa," 163–64.

108. H. M. Epstein, ed., *Revolt in the Congo 1960–64* (New York: Facts on File, 1965), 152; *Izvestiya*, November 26, 1963.

109. Piero Gleijeses, *Conflicting Missions: Havana, Washington and Africa, 1959–1976* (Chapel Hill: University of North Carolina Press, 2002), 63.

110. Ibid., chap. 3; Namikas, "Battleground Africa," chap. 13.

111. AVP RF, f. 0601, op. 2, p. 4, d. 9, ll. 1, 3; L. I. Brezhnev, "About the Trip of L. I. Brezhnev to the Republic of Guinea, Ghana and Morocco."

112. Ibid., ll. 6, 7, 15.

113. Ibid., ll. 10, 15.

114. Ibid., ll. 13, 14.

115. *SSSR i strany Afriki*, vol. 2, 204.

116. William Attwood, *The Reds and the Blacks: A Personal Adventure—Two Tours on Duty in Revolutionary Africa as Kennedy's Ambassador to Guinea and Johnson's to Kenya* (New York: Harper & Row, 1967), 72.

117. Ibid., 68.

118. Ibid., 69.

119. AVP RF, f. 0575, op. 4, p. 4, d. 8, ll. 10–11.

120. Dispatch from American Embassy in Conakry to the Department of State, March 23, 1961, no. 236, "Liberalization of Commerce in Guinea," file 870B.00/3-2361, GRDS, Central Decimal Files, RG 59, NA, 1–2.

121. Attwood, *Reds and the Blacks*, 31.

122. AVP RF, f. 0575, op. 4, p. 6, d. 6, l. 20.

123. AVP RF, f. 0575, op. 3, p. 3, d. 7, ll. 25–26.

124. Attwood, *Reds and the Blacks*, 68–69.

125. AVP RF, f. 0575, op. 4, p. 4, d. 9, ll. 94, 95.

126. AVP RF, f. 0575, op. 4, p. 6, d. 6, l. 45.

127. Ibid., l. 65.

128. Ibid., ll. 65, 71.

129. Ibid., l. 46.

130. AVP RF, f. 0601, op. 2, p. 5, d. 12, l. 49.

131. Ibid, l. 20.

132. U.S. Programs in Guinea, May 1961, GRDS, Bureau of African Affairs, RG 59, NA, p. 1.

133. Memorandum of conversation, March 17, 1961; participants: the president and George W. Ball, undersecretary of state for economic affairs; subject: Africa; file 870B.2614/3-1761, GRDS, Central Decimal Files, RG 59, NA.

134. Dispatch from American Embassy in Conakry to the Department of State, November 29, 1961, no. 123, "Five Teachers Imprisoned, Secondary School Strike Broken in Political Crisis in Guinea," file 770B.00/12-561, ibid., pp. 1–3.

135. Telegram from Conakry to Secretary of State, November 24, 1961, no. 297, file 870B.43/11-2461, ibid., p. 1; dispatch from American Embassy in Conakry to the Department of State, December 18, 1961, no. 132, "Personality Factors Underlying 'Teachers' Plot'"; A Tale of Three Comrades: Touré, Kéi'ta, and Autra, file 770B.00/12-1861, ibid., p. 1.

136. Dispatch from American Embassy in Conakry to the Department of State, November 29, 1961, no. 123, pp. 8–9; Robert Legvold, *Soviet Policy in West Africa* (Cambridge, Mass.: Harvard University Press, 1970), 125–27.

137. Dispatch from American Embassy in Conakry to the Department of State, November 29, 1961, no. 123, p. 1.

138. Dispatch from American Embassy in Conakry to the Department of State, December 18, 1961, no. 134, file 770B.00/12-1861, GRDS, Central Decimal Files, RG 59, NA, pp. 1, 6.

139. Attwood, *Reds and the Blacks*, 63.

140. Airgram A-57 from American Embassy in Conakry to Secretary of State, December 28, 1961, "Probable Consequences of Current Political Crisis in Guinea," file 770B.00/12-2861, GRDS, Central Decimal Files, RG 59, NA, p. 1.

141. Ibid.

142. Dispatch from American Embassy in Conakry to the Department of State, January 4, 1962, no. 148, "PDG National Conference: Calls for Death Penalty for Teachers' Union Leaders, Approves New 'Decentralization Plan,' Continues Attacks on Both East and West," file 770B.00/1-462, ibid., p. 13.

143. AVP RF, f. 0575, op. 5, p. 9, d. 5, l. 62; attaché of the Soviet Embassy in Guinean Republic A. Melik-Shakhnazarov, memorandum of conversation with French journalist Ike-Jerard Shalian, September 18–24, 1962.

144. *SSSR i strany Afriki*, vol. 2, 499.

145. Ibid., 504.

146. Attwood, *Reds and the Blacks*, 66.

147. *SSSR i strany Afriki*, vol. 2, 509.

148. AVP RF, f. 0575, op. 5, p. 6, d. 16, l. 4; ambassador of the USSR in Guinean Republic D. Degtyar, report on the Soviet ambassador's presentation of credentials to the president of Guinean Republic Sékou Touré, March 24, 1962.

149. Dispatch from American Embassy in Conakry to the Department of State. January 15, 1962, no. 163, "Appraisal of Significant Political Developments in Guinea October 1–December 31, 1961," file 770B.00/1-1562, GRDS, Central Decimal Files, RG 59, NA, p. 2.

150. Airgram A-57 from American Embassy in Conakry to secretary of state, December 28, 1961, p. 3.

151. Telegram from Department of State to certain American embassies, January 3, 1962, file 770B.00/1-362, ibid.

152. U.S. Trade and Economic Aid Relations with Guinea, February 1, 1962, file 411.20B41/2-162, ibid., pp. 1–2.

153. Telegram from Department of State to American Embassy in Conakry, February 7, 1962, file 870B.00/2-462, ibid., p. 1.

154. Ibid.

155. Ibid., pp. 1–2.

156. Memorandum from Donald Dumont to Mr. Tasca, March 12, 1962, "Responsibility of Proposed High-Level Guinean Aid and Trade Mission," Bureau of African Affairs, RG 59, NA, p. 1.

157. Memorandum to Mr. John Alexander, Peace Corps, Mr. Shriver's Trip to Guinea, April 29, 1963, ibid., p. 2.

158. Background Paper: Mr. Bowles' African Trip, October 15–November 6, October 9, 1962, ibid., p. 4.

159. Attwood, *Reds and the Blacks*, 66.

160. Background Paper: Mr. Bowles' African Trip, pp. 4–5.

161. AVP RF, f. 0575, op. 5, p. 9, d. 5, ll. 30, 31; attaché of USSR Embassy in Guinean Republic A. Melikh-Shachnazarov, memorandum of conversation with the owner of African bookshop, Mamadou Traoré, February 25 and 28, 1962.

162. Dispatch from American Embassy in Conakry to Department of State,

March 15, 1962, no. 214, "Marxist Bookshop in Conakry Closed," file 770B.001/3-1562, GRDS, Central Decimal Files, RG 59, NA, p. 1.

163. Dispatch from American Embassy in Conakry to the Department of State, March 8, 1962, no. 209, "Three High Officials Leave Conakry in Aftermath of Teachers' Crisis," file 770B.00/3-862, ibid., pp. 1, 2.

164. Attwood, *Reds and the Blacks*, 104.

165. AVP RF, f. 0575, op. 5, p. 9, d. 5, ll. 50, 51.

166. AVP RF, f. 0607, op. 3, p. 5, d. 16, ll. 50, 51.

167. W. Slater for L. D. Battle, executive secretary [U.S. Department of State], memorandum for McGeorge Bundy, White House, April 24, 1962, "Request for Appointment of High-Guinean Ministerial Delegation with the President," GRDS, Bureau of African Affairs, RG 59, NA, p. 2.

168. Dispatch from American Embassy in Conakry to Department of State. April 19, 1962, no. 254, "Appraisal of Significant Political Developments in Guinea, January 1–March 31, 1962," file 770B.00/4-1962, GRDS, Central Decimal Files, RG 59, NA, p. 2.

169. Williams G. Mennen to attorney general, Department of Justice, Washington, April 13, 1962, file 770B.11/4-1362, ibid., pp. 1–2.

170. Memorandum from Elbert G. Mathews to Mr. Fredericks, August 6, 1962, "Guinea Request for Peace Corps Program," GRDS, Bureau of African Affairs, RG 59, NA, p. 1.

171. Airgram A-52 from American Embassy in Conakry to the Department of State, August 8, 1962, "Semi-Annual Labor Report," file 870B.06/8-862, GRDS, Central Decimal Files, RG 59, NA, p. 2.

172. Dispatch from American Embassy in Conakry to the Department of State, June 5, 1962, no. 290, "Highlights of Motor Trip through Central and Eastern Guinea," file 123, William Attwood, xe770B.00, ibid., p. 2.

173. *FRUS, 1961–1963, Volume 21, Africa*, 407, 408.

174. Airgram A-52 from American Embassy in Conakry to Department of State, August 8, 1962, p. 3.

175. William H. Brubeck, executive secretary of the National Security Council, memorandum for Mr. McGeorge Bundy, White House, September 11, 1962, "Desire of President Touré to Discuss Guinea's Economic Plight with the President," file 770B.11/9-1162, GRDS, Central Decimal Files, RG 59, NA.

176. Telegram from the Department of State to American Embassy in Conakry, September 12, 1962, file 870 B.00/9-1262, ibid., p. 2.

177. *FRUS, 1961–1963, Volume 21, Africa*, 410.

178. Ibid., 413, 414.

179. Airgram CA-4755 from the Department of State, Circular, November 1, 1962, "President Touré's Visit to the United States," file 770B.11/11-162, GRDS, RG59, Central Decimal Files, NA, p. 4.

180. On the Cuban missile crisis, see, e.g., Aleksandr Fursenko and Timothy

Naftali, *"One Hell of a Gamble": The Secret History of the Cuban Missile Crisis* (New York: W. W. Norton, 1997).

181. Attwood, *Reds and the Blacks*, 109.

182. Airgram A-230 from American Embassy in Conakry to the Department of State, January 3, 1963, "Principal Officer's Personal Year-End Assessment of Problems and Prospects during 1963," file 770.00/1-363, GRDS, Central Decimal Files, RG 59, NA, p. 1.

183. *Prezidium TsK KPSS 1954–1964, Tom. I: Tchernovye protokol'nye zapisi zasedaniei—Stenogrammy* (Presidium of the CC CPSU 1954–1964, Vol. 1: Draft protocol sentences of meetings—Verbatim reports), ed. A. A. Fursenko (Moscow: Rosspan, 2003), 753.

184. Memorandum to Mr. John Alexander, Peace Corps, "Mr. Shriver's Trip to Guinea," April 29, 1963.

185. Guidelines for Policy and Operations, Guinea, April 1963, GRDS, Bureau of African Affairs, RG 59, NA, p. 2.

186. AVP RF, f. 0601, op. 2, p. 4, d. 9, ll. 8, 9, 4; L. I. Brezhnev, "About the Trip of L. I. Brezhnev to the Republic of Guinea, Ghana, and Morocco."

187. Ibid., l. 16.

188. Ibid., ll. 17, 7.

189. John T. Byrnes Jr., resident manager, West Africa, to George Wauchope, executive vice president, Farrel Lines Incorporated, "Report on Recent Political, Economic and General Developments Here in Ghana," January 18, 1961, GRDS, Bureau of African Affairs, RG 59, NA, pp. 1–2.

190. Cited by Noer, "New Frontiers and Old Priorities in Africa," 280.

191. *FRUS, 1961–1963, Volume 21, Africa*, 343–44.

192. Nkrumah, *Challenge of the Congo*, 139–42.

193. AVP RF, f. 0573, op. 5, p. 9, d. 16, ll. 23–24; first secretary of the USSR Embassy in Ghana V. Studenov and TASS correspondent I. Yanchenko, "On the Question of American-Ghanaian relations (Memo)," April 8, 1961.

194. *FRUS, 1961–1963, Volume 21, Africa*, 345, 346.

195. Joint Communiqué after the meeting between the president of the United States and president of the Republic of Ghana, Dr. Osagyefo Kwame Nkrumah, March 8, 1961, GRDS, Bureau of African Affairs, RG 59, NA.

196. Department of State, White House, News Conference, March 8, 1961, ibid., p. 3.

197. AVP RF, f. 0573, op. 5, p. 9, d. 16, l. 141; I. Azarov, "On the Question of American-Ghanaian Relations in 1961," memo, December 8, 1961.

198. Ibid., l. 26.

199. Ibid., l. 81; USSR ambassador to Ghana M. Sytenko, "President of Yugoslavia Tito's visit to Ghana" (February 28–March 11, 1961), April 10, 1961.

200. Ibid., l. 28.

201. Chad F. Calhoun, vice president of Kaiser Aluminum & Chemical Corp.,

to the Honorable Averell Harriman, Ambassador at Large, Memorandum, "The Volta River Hydroelectric Project and the Valco Aluminium Project in Ghana," January 30, 1961, Papers of W. Averell Harriman, container 464, Collections of the Manuscript Division, Library of Congress.

202. *FRUS, 1961–1963, Volume 21, Africa*, 349.

203. *Pravda*, July 11, 1961.

204. *SSSR i strany Afriki*, vol. 2, 358.

205. AVP RF, f. 573, op. 5, p. 7, d. 16, l. 72; Malik Arushunyan, telephone message to USSR MID, A. A. Gromyko, from Irkutsk, July 16, 1961.

206. Ibid., ll. 88–89; Malik Arushunyan, telephone message to the CC CPSU, from Leningrad, July 20, 1961.

207. Ibid., l. 73; Malik Arushunyan, telephone message to the USSR MID, July 16, 1961.

208. AVP RF, f. 0573, op. 5, p. 8, d. 10, ll. 30–31; chief of the Department of Trade with African Countries of the USSR Ministry of Foreign Trade V. Mordvinov, memo on trade relations between the USSR and Republic of Ghana, December 22, 1961.

209. AVP RF, f. 573, op. 5, p. 7, d. 16, l. 127; quotation from Nkrumah's personal message to Khrushchev, September 22, 1961.

210. AVP RF, f. 0573, op. 5, p. 8, d. 10, l. 31.

211. *SSSR i strany Afriki*, vol. 2, 364.

212. Joint communiqués issued during Osagyefo Kwame Nierumah's tours of Eastern European countries, Accra, 1961, 4; quoted by W. Scott Thompson, *Ghana's Foreign Policy 1957–1966: Diplomacy, Ideology and the New State* (Princeton, N.J.: Princeton University Press, 1969), 175.

213. Ibid.

214. *SSSR i strany Afriki*, vol. 2, 366; emphasis added.

215. *Pravda*, September 3, 1961.

216. *FRUS, 1961–1963, Volume 21, Africa*, 353.

217. (G. Mennen) Williams' European Talks, Position Paper, June 27, 1962, Ghana, GRDS, Bureau of African Affairs, RG 59, NA, p. 4.

218. AVP RF, f. 573, op. 5, p. 7, d. 16, l. 111; Vorob'ev, telephone message to the deputy foreign minister of the USSR Y. A. Malik, from Yalta, August 30, 1961.

219. "Kwame Nkrumah: A Psychological Study, General Assessment," June 1962, GRDS, Bureau of African Affairs, RG 59, NA, p. 1.

220. Ibid., p. 2.

221. "Kwame Nkrumah: A Psychological Study, Assessment Supplement—Communism," June 1962, GRDS, Bureau of African Affairs, RG 59, NA, pp. 1–3.

222. Memorandum from Donald Dumont to G. Mennen Williams, Status Report: Ghana, September 11, 1961, GRDS, Bureau of African Affairs, RG 59, NA, p. 1.

223. AVP RF, f. 0573, op. 5, p. 9, d. 14, l. 83; African Department II of the USSR MID, "On Strikes in Ghana," September 23, 1961.

224. Mahoney, *JFK*, 171, 172.

225. AVP RF, f. 0573, op. 5, p. 9, d. 14, l. 83; African Department II of the USSR MID, "On Strikes."

226. AVP RF, f. 573, op. 5, p. 7, d. 16, l. 96.

227. AVP RF, f. 0573, op. 5, p. 9, d. 14, l. 85; African Department II of the USSR MID, "On the Reorganization of the Ghanaian Government," short memo, October 18, 1961.

228. Mahoney, *JFK*, 174.

229. AVP RF, f. 0573, op. 5, p. 9, d. 16, l. 142; Azarov, "On the Question."

230. Noer, "New Frontiers and Old Priorities in Africa," 281.

231. AVP RF, f. 0573, op. 5, p. 9, d. 16, l. 141; Azarov, "On the Question."

232. "Memorandum from the President's Deputy Special Assistant for National Security Affairs (Rostow) to President Kennedy. October 2, 1961," in *FRUS, 1961–1963, Volume 21, Africa*, 359.

233. Memorandum of telephone conversation between President Kennedy and the acting undersecretary of state (Ball), September 21, 1961, ibid., 355.

234. Noer, "New Frontiers and Old Priorities in Africa," 282.

235. Mahoney, *JFK*, 179.

236. Information Memorandum on the Current Situation in Ghana, January 12, 1962, GRDS, Bureau of African Affairs, RG 59, NA, 3.

237. Mahoney, *JFK*, 181.

238. Convention People's Party, *Program of the Convention People's Party: "For Work and Happiness"* (Accra, n.d.).

239. AVP RF, f. 573, op. 5, p. 8, d. 19, l. 17; protocol to long-term agreement between the USSR and Ghana, November 4, 1961.

240. *SSSR i strany Afriki*, vol. 2, 442.

241. AVP RF, f. 0573, op. 5, p. 8, d. 10, ll. 18–19; supplement to Soviet-Ghanaian agreement on the extension of economic and technical cooperation, November 4, 1961.

242. *SSSR i strany Afriki*, vol. 2, 512, 513.

243. "U.S. Programs in Ghana, February 20, 1962," GRDS, Bureau of African Affairs, RG 59, NA, p. 1.

244. Ghana, "Guidelines for United States Policy and Operations," draft, March 12, 1962, GRDS, Bureau of African Affairs, RG 59, NA, 11.

245. "Kwame Nkrumah: A Psychological Study, Assessment Supplement—Communism," p. 3.

246. Ghana, "Guidelines for United States Policy and Operations," p. 2.

247. "U.S. Programs in Ghana," p. 1.

248. Ghana, "Guidelines for United States Policy and Operations," p. 12.

249. "U.S. Programs in Ghana," p. 2.

250. Ibid., p. 6.

251. Ibid., pp. 4, 5, 9.

252. Ibid., p. 6.

253. Ibid., p. 7.

254. AVP RF, f. 0573, op. 6, p. 10, d. 9, ll. 26–29; V. Myshkov, Memoranda to the Soviet Ambassador in Ghana M. D. Sytenko, June 12, 1962.

255. Ibid., ll. 1–4; senior reviewer Popyrin to Comrade A. I. Mikoyan, January 27, 1962.

256. Ibid., l. 28; Myshkov, Memoranda to the Soviet Ambassador.

257. AVP RF, f. 0573, op. 7, p. 13, d. 20, l. 59; USSR ambassador to Ghana G. M. Rodionov to USSR deputy foreign minister Y. A. Malik, "Materials on Foreign Economic and Technical Assistance to Ghana," January 25, 1963.

258. Legvold, *Soviet Policy*, 212.

259. Governor Williams' European Talks, Position Paper, June 27, 1962, Ghana, GRDS, Bureau of African Affairs, RG 59, NA, p. 5.

260. Ghana, June 8, 1962, GRDS, Bureau of African Affairs, RG 59, NA, p. 2.

261. AVP RF, f. 573, op. 5, p. 7, d. 16, l. 126; Nkrumah to Khrushchev, November 1, 1961.

262. Khrushchev to Nkrumah, December 2, 1961, quoted by Thompson, *Ghana's Foreign Policy*, 273–74.

263. AVP RF, f. 0573, op. 6, p. 10, d. 8, ll. 33–34; protocol on the conditions of sending Soviet specialists to the Republic of Ghana for rendering technical support and other services, January 15, 1962.

264. AVP RF, f. 0573, op. 6, p. 10, d. 9, ll. 41–42; USSR MID African Department II, on the question of Soviet-Ghanaian economic cooperation, November 26, 1962.

265. Ibid., ll. 42, 43.

266. AVP RF, f. 0573, op. 7, p. 13, d. 20, ll. 68–69; Rodionov to Malik, January 25, 1963.

267. Quoted by Thompson, *Ghana's Foreign Policy*, 274.

268. Ibid., 274.

269. AVP RF, f. 0573, op. 7, p. 13, d. 20, l. 73; Rodionov to Malik, January 25, 1963.

270. Thompson, *Ghana's Foreign Policy*, 274.

271. Ghana, June 8, 1962, p. 1.

272. *FRUS, 1961–1963, Volume 21, Africa*, 375, 376.

273. Governor Williams' European Talks, Position Paper, June 27, 1962, Ghana, p. 4.

274. Ghana, June 8, 1962, p. 2.

275. *Ghanaian Times*, July 14, 1962.

276. AVP RF, f. 0573, op. 6, p. 10, d. 9, ll. 41–42.

277. AVP RF, f. 0573, op. 6, p. 11, d. 15, ll. 44, 45; deputy chairman of the Soyuz sovetskikh obshestv druzby (Union of Soviet Societies of Friendship and Cultural Relations with Foreign Countries) Presidium E. Ivanov to the CC CPSU, letter on the cessation of the activity of the Soviet cultural center in Ghana, December 12, 1962.

278. Thompson, *Ghana's Foreign Policy*, 272.

279. Ghana, June 8, 1962, p. 3.

280. William P. Mahoney to G. Mennen Williams, August 9, 1962, GRDS, Bureau of African Affairs, RG 59, NA, p. 1.

281. Tawia Adamafio, *By Nkrumah's Side: The Labour and the Wounds* (Accra and London: Westcoast Publishing House and Rex Collins, 1982), 127.

282. Ibid., 127–28.

283. Mahoney, *JFK*, 183.

284. "The Outlook for Ghana," in *FRUS, 1961–1963, Volume 21, Africa*, 378–79.

285. Adamafio, *By Nkrumah's Side*, 132.

286. William C. Trimble to (G. Mennen) Williams, "Likely Motivations of Ghanaian Request for Withdrawal of Nydel and Davis," January 22, 1963, GRDS, Bureau of African Affairs, RG 59, NA, p. 1.

287. James Frederick Green, counselor of American Embassy in Accra to William D. Toomey, officer in charge, Ghana, Liberia, Sierra Leone affairs, Department of State, April 6, 1961, ibid., pp. 1, 2.

288. William C. Trimble to (G. Mennen) Williams, "Likely Motivations of Ghanaian Request," p. 1.

289. Mahoney, *JFK*, 183–84.

290. *FRUS, 1961–1963, Volume 21, Africa*, 382.

291. Mahoney, *JFK*, 186.

292. G. Mennen Williams to the acting secretary, "Strategic Study on Ghana, Draft Memorandum for the President, Possible United States Courses of Action in Ghana," April 3, 1963, GRDS, Bureau of African Affairs, RG 59, NA, pp. 1–2.

293. Mahoney, *JFK*, 186.

294. AVP RF, f. 607, op. 3, p. 4, d. 11, l. 46; V. Abarshalin, short memo, "Republic of Mali," November 28, 1962.

295. G. Mennen Williams to the undersecretary, April 18, 1961, "Briefing Paper for Your 5:30 Appointment with Mamadou Diakite, Secretary of State for Defense of the Republic of Mali," GRDS, Bureau of African Affairs, RG 59, NA, p. 2.

296. Wendell B. Coote to (G. Mennen) Williams, "Briefing Papers for Your Meeting with Joint Chiefs of Staff on Ghana-Guinea-Mali," January 4, 1962, tab C, ibid., p. 1.

297. (G. Mennen) Williams to the undersecretary, April 18, 1961, "Briefing Paper," p. 1.

298. U.S.-French Talks on Africa, Washington, June 28 and 29, 1961, GRDS, Bureau of African Affairs, RG 59, NA, pp. 3, 4.

299. "Briefing Paper for Assistant Secretary of State G. Mennen Williams, June 7, 1961, Military Assistance for the Republic of Mali," ibid, p. 1.

300. AVP RF, f. 0607, op. 2, d. 13, p. 2, l. 3.

301. *SSSR i strany Afriki*, vol. 2, 227–40.

302. AVP RF, f. 607, op. 3, p. 3, d. 7, ll. 13–14; A. Laptev, information on treaties and agreements concluded by the USSR Government with the Government of the Mali Republic, April 28, 1962.

303. *SSSR i strany Afriki*, vol. 2, 241.

304. AVP RF, f. 607, op. 3, p. 3, d. 9, ll. 12–13; "Memo on Trade Relations between the USSR and the Republic of Mali," January 26, 1962.

305. Ibid., l. 20; counselor on economic issues of the USSR Embassy in the Mali Republic P. Grushin, "Memo on a Course of the Implementation of the Soviet Obligations under the Soviet-Malian Agreement Signed on March 18, 1961," January 15, 1962.

306. AVP RF, f. 607, op. 12, p. 2, d. 14, l. 14; memorandum of conversation between the Gosudastvennyi komitet po kul'turnym svyazyam s zarubeznymi stranami (State Committee for Cultural Relations with Foreign Countries) chairman G. A. Zhukov with the counselor of the Embassy of the Republic of Mali in the USSR Abdoula Diallo, November 29, 1961.

307. AVP RF, f. 607, op. 3, p. 3, d. 9, l. 20; Grushin, "Memo on a Course of the Implementation of the Soviet Obligations."

308. AVP RF, f. 607, op. 2, p. 2, d. 9, ll. 80–81.

309. AVP RF, f. 607, op. 3, p. 3, d. 9, ll. 1–8; memorandum of conversation between the minister of public works and mining industry of the Republic of Mali Mamadou Av and the other Malian representatives and Soviet representatives comrades Orlov, Alikhanov, and Mordvinov, January 18, 1962.

310. AVP RF, f. 607, op. 4, p. 4, d. 4, l. 6; counselor on economic issues of the USSR Embassy in the Republic of Mali V. Mordvinov, "Memo on a Course of the Implementation of Agreements on Economic and Technical Cooperation between the USSR and the Republic of Mali (as of August 15, 1963)," August 25, 1963.

311. *Programma Kommunisticheskoi Partii Sovetskogo Soyuza, Prinyataya XXII Syezdom KPSS* (Program of the Communist Party of the Soviet Union, adopted by the 22nd Congress of the CPSU) (Moscow: Gospolitizdat, 1968), 54.

312. AVP RF, f. 0573, op. 5, p. 9, d. 14, ll. 59–60; third secretary of the USSR Embassy in Ghana Yu. Dedov, "Nkrumahism Revisited," June 1, 1961.

313. A. J. Klinghoffer, *Soviet Perspective on African Socialism* (Rutherford, N.J.: Farleigh Dickinson University Press, 1969), 60–118; N. S. MacFarlane, *Superpower Rivalry & 3rd World Radicalism: The Idea of National Liberation* (London and Baltimore: Croom Helm and Johns Hopkins University Press, 1985), 158–67.

314. RGANI, f. 5, op. 33, d. 181, ll. 98–99, 100; S. I. Beglov, "Report on African Trip (1 November–12 December 1961)," December 22, 1961; emphasis in original.

315. AVP RF, f. 607, op. 3, p. 3, d. 7, l. 99; memorandum of conversation between Professor Potekhin, director of the Institute for African Studies of the

USSR Academy of Sciences, and president of the Republic of Mali Modibo Kéi'ta, Institute for African Studies, May 30, 1962.

316. *Pravda*, May 20, 1962.

317. Legvold, *Soviet Policy*, 143.

318. *Pravda*, May 31, 1962.

319. *SSSR i strany Afriki*, vol. 2, 574.

320. Ibid., 582.

321. N. S. Khrushchev, *Vremya, Lyudi, Vlast' (Vospominaniya: v 4 knigah)* [Time, People, Power (Memoirs in four volumes)] (Moscow: IIK Moskovskie Novosti, 1999), vol. 3, 455.

322. AVP RF, f. 607, op. 3, p. 3, d.7, l. 107.

323. RGANI, f. 5, op. 33, d. 181, ll. 120–21; Beglov, "Report"'; emphasis in the original.

324. AVP RF, f. 0607, op. 4, p. 7, d. 18, l. 72; I. A. Mel'nik, "Information on Soviet Aid to the Sudanese Union for the Ideological Education of the Masses," November 20, 1963.

325. Ibid., l. 15; chief of the Department of African Countries of the State Committee for Cultural Relations with Foreign Countries V. S. Bogatyrev, "On Cultural Ties with Guinea and Mali," March 26, 1963.

326. Ibid., l. 73; Mel'nik, "Information on Soviet Aid."

327. Ibid., l. 74.

328. AVP RF, f. 0607, op. 3, p. 4, d. 15, l. 117; ambassador of the USSR in Mali A. I. Loshakov to deputy chairman of the State Committee for Cultural Relations with Foreign Countries A. I. Bol'shakov, "Soviet Films in Mali," December 14, 1962.

329. AVP RF, f. 0607, op. 4, p. 7, d. 18, l. 73; Mel'nik, "Information on Soviet Aid."

330. AVP RF, f. 0607, op. 3, p. 5, d. 16, l. 53; A. Rytchagov, report on the trip of a specialized tourist group to Guinea and Mali (December 11–28, 1962), January 28, 1963.

331. AVP RF, f. 0607, op. 4, p. 7, d. 18, l. 73; Mel'nik, "Information on Soviet Aid."

332. Ibid., ll. 60–61.

333. Ibid., l. 63.

334. RGANI, f. 4, op. 6, d. 1056, ll. 32–33; secretary of the Komsomol Central Committee S. Pavlov to the CC CPSU, July 12, 1961.

335. RGANI, f. 4, op. 17, d. 1, l. 12; "On Sending of Groups of Soviet Specialists to Ghana, Guinea, Mali," Protocol 1, p. 5-c, of the CC CPSU Secretariat meeting, November 3, 1961.

336. RGANI, f. 4, op. 18, d. 4, ll. 74–75; secretary of the Komsomol Central Committee V. Sayushev to the CC CPSU, June 26, 1962.

337. Ibid., l. 76; reviewer of the CC CPSU International Department E. Kuchughin, information, August 17, 1962.

Notes to Chapter 4

1. Robert Legvold, *Soviet Policy in West Africa* (Cambridge, Mass.: Harvard University Press, 1970), 81.

2. RGANI, f. 2, op. 1, d. 665, l. 15; speech of the CC CPSU secretary B. N. Ponomarev at the December (1963) Plenum of the CC CPSU, with corrections.

3. Richard Lowenthal, "China," in *Africa and the Communist World*, ed. Zbigniew Brzezinski (Stanford, Calif.: Stanford University Press, 1963), 164–67.

4. Legvold, *Soviet Policy*, 86–87.

5. "The Answers of N. S. Khrushchev to the Questions of the Newspapers *Ghanaian Times*, *Algérie Républicain*, *Peuple*, and *Botatown*," *Pravda*, December 22, 1963.

6. Ismael Y. Tareq, "The People's Republic of China and Africa," *Journal of Modern African Studies* 9, no. 4 (1971): 513–15.

7. "Answers of N. S. Khrushchev."

8. Legvold, *Soviet Policy*, 188.

9. Tareq, "People's Republic of China and Africa," 513–14.

10. AVP RF, f. 607, op. 4, p. 5, d. 5, l. 50; attaché of the USSR Embassy in the Republic of Mali A. Kotcheshkov and correspondent of the *Trud* newspaper·A. Rusakov, "National Union of Working People of Mali (Short Information)," October 16, 1963. Ibid., op. 3, p. 4, d.13, l. 38; third secretary of the USSR Embassy in the Republic of Mali Yu. Timofeev, "Informational Work of the (People's Republic of China, PRC) Embassy," January 27, 1962.

11. AVP RF, f. 607, op. 5, p. 9, d. 15, ll. 27–28; ambassador of the USSR in the Republic of Mali I. Mel'nik, "On the Work of Dissemination and Elucidation of the Materials of the CC CPSU February Plenum in the Republic of Mali in April–May 1964 (a Letter of Information)," May 18, 1964.

12. Ibid., ll. 29, 31–32.

13. Ibid., ll. 30–31.

14. Melvyn P. Leffler, *For the Soul of Mankind: The United States, the Soviet Union, and the Cold War* (New York: Hill and Wang, 2007), 3.

15. RGANI, f. 5, op. 35, d. 180, ll. 76, 77; minister of higher and specialized secondary education of the USSR V. Elyutin to the CC CPSU, "Information on Foreign Enrollees," May 22, 1961.

16. RGANI, f. 5, op. 35, d. 783, l. 13.

17. RGANI, f. 4, op. 16, d. 806, l. 19; minister of higher and specialized secondary education of the USSR V. P. Elyutin and rector of the Peoples' Friendship University S. M. Rumyantsev to first secretary of the CC CPSU and chairman of the Council of Ministers of the USSR N. S. Khrushchev, "Memoranda on Measures Dealing with Creation of the Peoples' Friendship University," April 12, 1960.

18. *Pravda*, November 18, 1960.

19. RGANI, f. 4, op. 16, d. 902, l. 30; CC CPSU Presidium resolution "On Measures to Improve the Work among Students, Post-Graduate Students, and Proba-

tioners from Countries of Asia, Africa, Latin America, and Certain Western Countries Studying in Institutions of Higher Learning of the USSR," Protocol 166, point 4-c, of the CC CPSU Secretariat meeting, October 29, 1960.

20. Ibid., l. 41; "Information on Educational Work with Foreign Students and Post-Graduate Students in Higher Educational Institutions of the USSR," September 28, 1960.

21. Ibid.

22. Ibid., l. 35; decree of minister of higher and specialized secondary education of the USSR no. 86, "On Educational Work with Students and Post-Graduate Students Who Arrived in the USSR from Economically Less-Developed Capitalist Countries," June 30, 1960.

23. RGANI, f. 5, op. 35, d. 180, l. 197; deputy minister of higher and specialized secondary education of the USSR M. Prokofiev to the CC CPSU, "Information on the Tuition of Foreign Students in Institutions of Higher Education of the USSR and on the State of Educational Work with Them," December 15, 1961.

24. RGANI, f. 4, op. 16, d. 902, l. 51; minister of higher and specialized secondary education of the USSR V. Elyutin and deputy minister of higher and specialized secondary education of the Russian Soviet Federal Socialist Republic N. Krasnov to the CC CPSU, "Information on Educational Work with Foreign Students and Post-Graduate Students in Higher Learning Institutions of the USSR," September 28, 1960.

25. Quoted in Maxim Matusevich, *No Easy Row for a Russian Hoe: Ideology and Pragmatism in Nigerian-Soviet Relations, 1960–1991* (Trenton, N.J.: Africa World Press, 2003), 84.

26. RGANI, f. 4, op. 16, d. 902, ll. 51–52.

27. RGANI, f. 5, op. 35, d. 144, l. 44.

28. RGANI, f. 5, op. 35, d. 149, l. 53; deputy chief of the CC CPSU Department of Science, Institutions of Higher Learning, and Schools D. Kukin and deputy chief of the CC CPSU International Department D. Shevlyaghin to the CC CPSU, May 10, 1960.

29. S. V. Mazov, "Afrikanskie studenty v God Afriki v Moskve" (African Students in Moscow in the Year of Africa), *Vostok*, no. 3 (1998): 90–92.

30. RGANI, f. 5, op. 35, d. 149, l. 54

31. AVP RF, f. 581, op. 4, p. 1, d. 6, ll. 10–11.

32. RGANI, f. 5, op. 35, d. 180, l. 197; Prokofiev, "Information on the Tuition of Foreign Students."

33. Matusevich, *No Easy Row*, 84.

34. Arkadiyi Sakhnin, "Raskayanyie zapozdalo" (Regret was too late), *Komsomol'skaya Pravda*, September 27, 1962.

35. RGANI, f. 5, op. 33, d. 202, l. 221; rector of the Universitet Druzhby Narodov S. Rumyantsev and Secretary of the CPSU Committee of the Universitet Druzhby Narodov A. Golubev to the CC CPSU, November 20, 1962.

36. Ibid., l. 222.

37. RGANI, f. 5, op. 33, d. 194, ll. 99–100; deputy chief of the CC CPSU Department of Science, Institutions of Higher Learning, and Schools V. Kirillin, deputy chief of the CC CPSU International Department V. Tereshkin, deputy chief of the CC CPSU Department Yu. Andropov, and deputy chief of the CC CPSU Department of Propaganda and Agitation in the Union Republics V. Snastin to the CC CPSU, November 16, 1962.

38. Ibid., ll. 100, 101.

39. Ibid., l. 223; chief of the CC CPSU Department of Propaganda and Agitation in the Union Republics A. Egorov to the CC CPSU, November 28, 1962.

40. "U.S. Assistance to Asian and African Students Disaffected from Soviet Bloc Schools," draft memorandum from Mr. Kohler to the Undersecretary, April 10, 1961, GRDS, Bureau of African Affairs, RG 59, NA.

41. *Sunday Telegraph*, July 16, 1961.

42. Ibid.

43. Ibid.

44. Matusevich, *No Easy Row*, 100.

45. *Sunday Telegraph*, July 16, 1961.

46. Ibid.

47. Ibid.

48. RGANI, f. 5, op. 35, d. 180, ll. 135–38.

49. Ibid., l. 153.

50. Legvold, *Soviet Policy*, 180.

51. *Pravda*, July 31 and August 20, 1963.

52. Legvold, *Soviet Policy*, 181.

53. AVP RF, f. 0607, op. 5, p. 9, d. 15, ll. 63, 68, 65; Yu. N. Popov and G. P. Predvechnyi, "Information on the Work of Soviet Teachers in National Administrative School of the Republic of Mali (November 1963–June 1964)," June 9, 1964.

54. Ibid., l. 71.

55. Ibid., ll. 71–72.

56. Ibid., ll. 38–41; teacher of political economy in National Administrative School of Mali Yu. Popov, "Memorandum of conversation with a member of the Politburo of Sudanese Union Seydou Badiyan Kouyaté," January 25, 1964.

57. RGANI, f. 5, op. 35, d. 180, l. 113; N. S. Torocheshnikov to minister of higher and specialized secondary education of the USSR V.P. Elyutin, "Information on the Work of N. S. Torocheshnikov in the Commission of Higher Education Attached to the Government of Ghana," March 25, 1961.

58. RGANI, f. 5, op. 35, d. 218, ll. 23–29; F. Kurnikov, "On the Necessity of the Improvement of Economic Information Coming from the Soviet Union to the Developing Countries," February 22, 1965.

59. Ibid., l. 90.

60. RGANI, f. 4, op. 18, d. 584, l. 80; "Request by K. Nkrumah to Assist with

Producing Textbooks on Scientific Socialism," Protocol 95, point 458g, of the CC CPSU Secretariat meeting, March 17, 1964.

61. Briefing Paper, (G. Mennen) Williams' African Trip (June 21–July 9, 1963), Ghana (June 22–26, 1963), June 10, 1963, GRDS, Bureau of African Affairs, RG 59, NA, pp. 1–2.

62. William P. Mahoney Jr., American Embassy, Accra, Ghana to the Honorable G. Mennen Williams, assistant secretary of state for African affairs, Department of State, August 9, 1962, ibid., p. 2.

63. G. Mennen Williams to the acting secretary of state, "Strategic Study on Ghana: Draft Memorandum for the President—Possible United States Courses of Action in Ghana," April 4, 1963, ibid., p. 1.

64. William Trimble to (G. Mennen) Williams, "Likely Motivation for Ghanaian Request for Withdrawal of Nadell and Davis," ibid., p. 1.

65. Williams, "Strategic Study on Ghana," p. 1.

66. Richard D. Mahoney, *JFK: Ordeal in Africa* (New York: Oxford University Press, 1983), 231.

67. Williams, "Strategic Study on Ghana," p. 3.

68. Ibid., p. 2.

69. Mahoney, *JFK*, 231.

70. *FRUS, 1961–1963, Volume 21, Africa* (Washington, D.C.: U.S. Government Printing Office, 1995), 384–85.

71. William P. Mahoney Jr., American ambassador, Accra, to G. Mennen Williams, assistant secretary for African affairs, Department of State, May 30, 1963, letter 1, GRDS, Bureau of African Affairs, RG 59, NA, p. 1.

72. Ibid., letter 2.

73. *FRUS, 1961–1963, Volume 21, Africa*, 389.

74. Mahoney *JFK*, 233.

75. *FRUS, 1961–1963, Volume 21, Africa*, 391.

76. Mahoney, *JFK*, 233.

77. Airgram A-499, from American Embassy, Accra, to Department of State, March 26, 1964, "Transmittal of Advance Aide-Memoire for Harriman-Nkrumah Talks," Papers of W. Averell Harriman, container 543, Collections of the Manuscript Division, Library of Congress, p. 2.

78. Ibid., p. 3.

79. *FRUS, 1964–1968, Volume 24, Africa* (Washington, D.C.: U.S. Government Printing Office, 1999), 428.

80. Ibid., 426.

81. Telegram from American Embassy in Accra to secretary of state, March 24, 1964, Papers of W. Averell Harriman, container 543, Collections of the Manuscript Division, Library of Congress, section I, pp. 2–3, and section II, p. 1.

82. Ibid., section II, pp. 3–4.

83. Ibid., section IV, p. 2.

84. Ibid., pp. 2–3.
85. *FRUS, 1964–1968, Volume 24, Africa,* 437.

Notes to the Conclusion

1. Karen Brutents, *Tridtsat' let na Staroi Ploshadi* (Thirty years at the Staraya Ploshad') (Moscow: Mezhdunarodnye Otnosheniya, 1998), 215.

2. G. I. Mirskii, "Polveka v mire vostokovedeniya," (Half a century in Oriental studies), *Vostok,* no. 6 (1996).

3. Miroslav Azembskyi, "Reportaj s Berega Slonovoi Kosti" (Reporting from the Ivory Coast), *Novoye vremya,* no. 40 (1968): 28. See Sergey Mazov, *Politika SSSR v Zapadnoi Afrike, 1956–1964: Neizvestnye stranitsy istorii kholodnoi voiny* (Policy of the USSR in West Africa, 1956–1964: Unknown Pages of Cold War History) (Moscow: Nauka, 2008), 132–45, 224–60.

4. W. Scott Thompson, "The African-American Nexus in Soviet Strategy," in *Africa and International Communism,* ed. David L. Albright (New York: Macmillan, 1980), 190.

5. Franz Ansprenger, "Communism in Tropical Africa," in *The Soviet Bloc, China and Africa,* ed. Sven Hamrell and Carl Gosta Widstrand (Uppsala: Pall Mall Press, 1964), 97.

6. See, e.g., Kevin C. Dunn, *Imagining the Congo: The International Relations of Identity* (New York: Palgrave Macmillan, 2003); and Elizabeth Schmidt, *Cold War and Decolonization in Guinea, 1946–1958* (Athens: Ohio University Press, 2007).

7. AVP RF, f. 590, op. 4, p. 5, d. 11, l. 91.

8. Christopher Stevens, *The Soviet Union and Black Africa* (London: Macmillan, 1976), 191.

9. Oye Ogunbadejo, "Nigerian-Soviet Relations, 1960–87," *African Affairs* 87, no. 346 (1988).

Bibliography

Archives

Archiv vneshnei politiki Rossyiskoi Federatsii (Archive of foreign policy
of the Russian Federation, AVP RF), Moscow.
Library of Congress, Manuscript Division, Washington.
National Archives of the United States, College Park, Maryland.
Rossyiskyi gosudarstvennyi archiv noveisheyi istorii (Russian State Ar-
chive of contemporary history, RGANI), Moscow.

Published Sources

Adamafio, Tawia. *By Nkrumah's Side: The Labour and the Wounds.* Accra
and London: Westcoast Publishing House and Rex Collins, 1982.
Alexander, H. T. *African Tightrope: My Two Years as Nkrumah's Chief of
Staff.* New York: Frederick A. Praeger, 1965.
All-African People's Conference. Resolution on Imperialism and Colo-
nialism, Accra, December 5–13, 1958. Available at http://www
.fordham.edu/halsall/mod1958-aapc-res1.html.
Attwood, William. *The Reds and the Blacks: A Personal Adventure—Two
Tours on Duty in Revolutionary Africa as Kennedy's Ambassador
to Guinea and Johnson's to Kenya.* New York: Harper & Row,
1967.
Azikiwe, Nnamdi. *My Odyssey: An Autobiography.* London: C. Hurst,
1970.
Batsa, Kofi. *The Spark: Times Behind Me—From Kwame Nkrumah to
Hilla Limann.* London: Rex Collins, 1985.
Blouin, Andrée. *My Country, Africa: Autobiography of the Black Pasion-
aria.* New York: Praeger, 1983.

Brutents, Karen. *Tridtsat' let na Staroi Ploshadi* (Thirty years at the Staraya Ploshad'). Moscow: Mezhdunarodnye Otnosheniya, 1998.

Convention People's Party. *Program of the Convention People's Party: "For Work and Happiness."* Accra, n.d.

Davidson, A. B., and S. V. Mazov, eds. *Rossiya i Afrika: Dokumenty i materially, Tom. II, 1918–1960* (Russia and Africa: Documents and materials, Vol. 2, 1918–1960). Moscow: IVI RAN, 1999.

Davidson, Apollon, ed. *Komintern i Afrika: Dokumenty* (Comintern and Africa: Documents), compiled by Valentin Gorodnov. St. Petersburg: Aleteya, 2003.

Dayal, Rajeshwar. *Mission for Hammarskjold: The Congo Crisis.* Princeton, N.J.: Princeton University Press, 1976.

Dei-Anang, Michael. *The Administration of Ghana's Foreign Relations, 1957–1965: A Personal Memoir.* London: Athlone Press, 1975.

Devlin, Lawrence. *Chief of Station, Congo: A Memoir of 1960–67.* New York: PublicAffairs, 2007.

Dobrynin, Anatoly. *In Confidence: Moscow's Ambassador to America's Six Cold War Presidents, 1962–1986.* New York: Times Press, 1995.

Egorov, V. M. "Vozvrashenie v Afriku" (Return to Africa). In *Afrika v vospominaniyah veteranov diplomaticheskoi sluzhby* (Africa in the memoirs of veterans of the Foreign Service), vol. 5 (of 12 vols.). Moscow: Institut Afriki RAN, Sovet veteranov MID RF, 2004.

Eisenhower, Dwight D. *Waging Peace 1956–1961: The White House Years.* Garden City, N.Y.: Doubleday, 1965.

Epstein, H. M., ed. *Revolt in the Congo 1960–64.* New York: Facts on File, 1965.

Fursenko, A. A., ed. *Prezidium TsK KPSS 1954–1964, Tom. I: Tchernovye protokol'nye zapisi zasedaniei—Stenogrammy* (Presidium of the CC CPSU 1954–1964, Vol. 1: Draft protocol sentences of meetings—Verbatim reports). Moscow: Rosspan, 2003.

Gerard-Libois, Jules, and Benoit Verhaegen, eds. *Congo 1960.* Brussels: Centre de Recherche et d'Information Socio-Politiques, 1961.

Grinevskyi, Oleg. *Tysyacha i odin den' Nikity Serggevicha* (A thousand and one days in the life of Nikita Sergeevich). Moscow: Vagrius, 1998.

Kanza, Thomas. *The Rise and Fall of Patrice Lumumba: Conflict in the Congo.* London: Rex Collins, 1978.

Khrushchev, N. S. *Vremya, Lyudi, Vlast' (Vospominaniya: v 4 knigah).*

[Time, People, Power (Memoirs in four volumes)]. Moscow: IIK Moskovskie Novosti, 1999.

Khrushchev, Sergei. *Nikita Khrushchev and the Creation of a Superpower.* University Park: Pennsylvania State University Press, 2000.

Kirpichenko, Vadim A. *Iz arkhiva razvedchika* (From a secret service man's archive). Moscow: Mezhdunarodnye Otnosheniya, 1993.

Kornienko, Georgyi. *Kholodnaya voina: Svidetel'stvo ee uchastnika* (Cold war: Testimony of a participant). Moscow: Mezhdunarodnye Otnosheniya, 1994.

Laptukhin, V. V. "Nebyvalyi fenomen Hausa" (The unprecedented phenomenon of the Hausa). In *Pod nebom Afriki moei: Istoriya, yazyki, kul'tura narodov Afriki* (Under my Africa's sky: The history, languages, and culture of African peoples), vol. 2. Moscow: Muravei, 2003.

Mirskii, G. I. "Polveka v mire vostokovedeniya" (Half a century in Oriental studies). *Vostok*, no. 6 (1996).

Morrow, John H. *First American Ambassador to Guinea.* New Brunswick, N.J.: Rutgers University Press, 1968.

Mukhitdinov, N. A. *Reka vremeni (ot Stalina do Gorbatcheva): Vospominaniya* (The river of time [from Stalin to Gorbachev]: Memoirs). Moscow: Rusti-Rusti, 1995.

Namikas, Lise, and Sergey Mazov, eds. *CWIHP Conference Reader Compiled for the International Conference on the Congo Crisis, 1960–1961, Washington, D.C., September 23–24, 2004, Organized by the Woodrow Wilson Center's Cold War International History Project and the Africa Program.* Washington, D.C.: Cold War International History Project, Woodrow Wilson International Center for Scholars, 2004.

Nazhestkin, O. I. "Gogy kongolezkogo krizisa (1960–1963 gg.): Zapiski razvedchika" (The years of the Congolese crisis, 1960–1963: A secret service man's memoirs). *Novaya i noveishaya istortiya*, no. 6 (2003).

Nkrumah, Kwame. *Africa Must Unite.* New York: Frederick A. Praeger, 1963.

———. *The Autobiography of Kwame Nkrumah.* New York: Nelson, 1957.

———. *Challenge of the Congo: A Case Study of Foreign Pressures in an Independent State.* New York: International Publishers, 1967.

———. *I Speak of Freedom. A Statement of African Ideology.* London: Heinemann, 1961.

O'Brien, Conor Cruise. *To Katanga and Back: A UN Case History.* London: Hutchinson, 1962.

Patris Lumumba: Pravda o tshudovishnom prestuplenii kolonizatorov (Patrice Lumumba: The truth about the colonizers' monstrous crime). Moscow: Izdaniye Soyuza zhurnalistov SSSR, 1961.

Porter, A. N., and A. J. Stockwell. *British Imperial Policy and Decolonization, 1938–64, Volume 1, 1938–51.* New York: St. Martin's Press, 1987.

Rakhmatov, M. *Afrika idet k svobode* (Africa goes toward freedom). Moscow: Gospolitizdat, 1961.

Safonov, D. F. *A dughi gnut terpen'em . . . (Kak ya stal diplomatom-afrikanistom)* [And they sweep by patience . . . (How I became a diplomat-Africanist)]. Moscow: Institut Afriki RAN, Sovet veteranov MID RF, 2002.

Scott, Ian. *Tumbled House: The Congo at Independence.* London: Oxford University Press, 1969.

SSSR i strany Afriki 1946–1962 gg.: Dokumenty i·materially, Tom. I–II (USSR and African countries 1946–1962: Documents and materials, Vols. I–II). Moscow: Gosudarstvennoe izdatel'stvo politicheskoi literatury, 1963.

Subbotin, V. A. "Kongo: Leopool'dvil' v 1960" (Congo: Leopoldville in 1960). In *Afrika v vospominaniyah veteranov diplomaticheskoi sluzhby* (Africa in the memoirs of veterans of the Foreign Service), vol. 5 (of 12 vols.). Moscow: Institut Afriki RAN, Sovet veteranov MID RF, 2004.

Touré, Sékou. *Nezavisimaya Gvineya: Stat'i i rechi* (Independent Guinea: Articles and speeches). Moscow: Izdatel'stvo inostrannoi literatury, 1960.

United Nations, General Assembly. *Official Records.* New York: United Nations, 1960–64.

United Nations, Security Council. *Official Records.* New York: United Nations, 1960–64.

Urquhart, Brian. *A Life in Peace and War.* New York: Harper & Row, 1987.

U.S. Congress, Senate, Select Committee to Study Government Operations with Respect to Intelligence Activities. *Alleged Assassination Plots Involving Foreign Leaders.* Senate Report 94-465, 94th Congress, 1st Session. Washington, D.C.: U.S. Government Printing Office, 1975.

U.S. Department of State. *Foreign Relations of the United States, 1955–*

1957, Volume 18, Africa. Washington, D.C.: U.S. Government Printing Office, 1989.

———. *Foreign Relations of the United States, 1958–1960, Volume 14, Africa.* Washington, D.C.: U.S. Government Printing Office, 1992.

———. *Foreign Relations of the United States, 1961–1963, Volume 20, Congo Crisis.* Washington, D.C.: U.S. Government Printing Office, 1994.

———. *Foreign Relations of the United States, 1961–1963, Volume 21, Africa.* Washington, D.C.: U.S. Government Printing Office, 1995.

———. *Foreign Relations of the United States, 1964–1968, Volume 24, Africa.* Washington, D.C.: U.S. Government Printing Office, 1999.

Verhaegen, Benoit, ed. *Congo 1961.* Brussels: Centre de Recherche et d'Information Socio-Politiques, 1962.

Viktorov, Yu. P. Moi afrikanskie epizody (My African episodes), in *Afrika v vospominaniyah veteranov diplomaticheskoi sluzhby* (Africa in the memoirs of veterans of the Foreign Service), 5 (12). Moscow: Institut Afriki RAN, Sovet veteranov MID RF, 2004.

Von Horn, Carl. *Soldiering for Peace.* New York: David McKay, 1966.

Books and Articles

Albright, David, ed. *Africa and International Communism.* Bloomington: Indiana University Press, 1984.

———. *Communism in Africa.* New York: Macmillan, 1980.

Ambrose, Stephen. *Ike's Spies: Eisenhower and the Espionage Establishment.* New York: Doubleday, 1980.

Andrew, Christopher, and Vasili Mitrokhin. *The World Was Going Our Way: The KGB and the Battle for the Third World.* New York: Basic Books, 2005.

Ansprenger, Franz. "Communism in Tropical Africa." In *The Soviet Bloc, China and Africa*, ed. Sven Hamrell and Carl Gosta Widstrand. Uppsala: Pall Mall Press, 1964.

Azembskyi, Miroslav. "Reportaj s Berega Slonovoi Kosti" (Reporting from the Ivory Coast). *Novoye vremya*, no. 40 (1968).

Birmingham, David. *The Decolonization of Africa.* Athens: Ohio University Press, 1995.

———. *Kwame Nkrumah: The Father of African Nationalism.* Athens: Ohio University Press, 1998.

Borstelmann, Thomas. *The Cold War and the Color Line: American Race*

Relations in the Global Arena. Cambridge, Mass.: Harvard University Press, 2001.

Brands, H. W. *The Specter of Neutralism: The United States and the Emergence of the Third World.* New York: Columbia University Press, 1989.

Bretton, Henry L. *The Rise and Fall of Kwame Nkrumah. A Study of Personal Rule in Africa.* New York: Praeger, 1966.

Brzezinski, Zbigniew. "Conclusion: The African Challenge." In *Africa and the Communist World*, ed. Zbigniew Brzezinski. Stanford, Calif.: Stanford University Press, 1963.

Cartwright, John. *Political Leadership in Africa.* London: Croom Helm, 1983.

Colvin, Ian. *The Rise and Fall of Moise Tshombe.* London: Leslie Frewin, 1968.

Conn, Helen D. *Soviet Policy toward Black Africa: The Focus on National Integration.* New York: Praeger, 1972.

Cooley, John. *East Wind Over Africa: Red China's African Offensive.* New York: Walker, 1995.

Dallin, Alexander. *The Soviet Union and the United Nations.* New York: Praeger, 1962.

Davidson, A. B. "I. I. Potekhin i sovetskaya afrikanistika" (I. I. Potekhin and Soviet African Studies). *Sovetskaya etnografiya*, no. 3 (1974).

———. "Osnovatel Instituta Afriki (I. I. Potekhin)" [The founder of the Institute for African Studies (I. I. Potekhin)]. In *Stanoveniye otechestvennoi afrikanistiki: 1920-e–nachalo 1960-kh* (The formative years of African studies in Russia: The 1920s–early 1960s), ed. A. B. Davidson. Moscow: Nauka, 2003.

Davidson, Apollon, Sergey Mazov, and Georgiy Tsypkin, eds. *SSSR i Afrika 1918–1960: Dokumetntirovannaya istoriya vzaimootnosheniyi* (USSR and Africa 1918–1960: Documentary history of relations). Moscow: IVI RAN, 2002.

Davidson, Basil. *Black Star: A View of the Life and Times of Kwame Nkrumah.* New York: Praeger, 1974.

De Witte, Ludo. *The Assassination of Lumumba.* London: Verso, 2001.

Dowse, Robert. *Modernization in Ghana and the USSR: A Comparative Study.* London: Routledge & Kegan Paul, 1969.

Dunn, Kevin C. *Imagining the Congo: The International Relations of Identity.* New York: Palgrave Macmillan, 2003.

Fahnbulleh, Boima H., Jr. *The Diplomacy of Prejudice: Liberia in International Politics, 1945–1970.* New York: Vantage Press, 1985.

Foltz, William J. *From French West Africa to the Mali Federation*. New Haven, Conn.: Yale University Press, 1965.

Frank, Thomas M., and John Carey. "The Legal Aspects of the United Nations Action in the Congo." In *Background Papers and Proceedings of the Second Hammarskjöld Forum*, ed. Lyman M. Tondel Jr. New York: Oceana Publications for Bar of the City of New York, 1963.

Frenkel, M. Yu. *Istoriya Liberii v novoe i noveishee vremya* (Modern and contemporary history of Liberia). Moscow: Izdatel'skaya firma Vostochnaya literatura RAN, 1999.

Fursenko, Aleksandr, and Timothy Naftali. *Khrushchev's Cold War: The Inside Story of an American Adversary*. New York: W. W. Norton, 2006.

———. *"One Hell of a Gamble": The Secret History of the Cuban Missile Crisis*. New York: W. W. Norton, 1997.

Gleijeses, Piero. *Conflicting Missions: Havana, Washington and Africa, 1959–1976*. Chapel Hill: University of North Carolina Press, 2002.

Hamrell, S., and C. G. Widstrand, eds. *The Soviet Bloc, China and Africa*. Uppsala: Nordic Africa Institute, 1964.

Hann, Peter, and Mary Ann Heiss, eds. *Empire and Revolution: The United States and the Third World since 1945*. Columbus: Ohio State University Press, 2001.

Heldman, Dan C. *The USSR and Africa: Foreign Policy under Khrushchev*. New York: Praeger, 1981.

Hooker, James R. *Black Revolutionary: George Padmore's Path from Communism to Pan-Africanism*. London: Praeger, 1967.

Hoskyns, Catherine. *The Congo since Independence: January 1960–December 1961*. London: Oxford University Press, 1965.

Howell, Thomas A., and Jeffrey P. Rajasooria, eds. *Ghana & Nkrumah*. New York: Facts on File, 1972.

Kaba, Lanciné. "From Colonialism to Autocracy: Guinea under Sékou Touré, 1957–1984." In *Decolonization and African Independence: The Transfers of Power, 1960–1980*, ed. Prosser Gifford and William Roger Louis. New Haven, Conn.: Yale University Press, 1988.

Kalb, Madeleine G. *The Congo Cables: The Cold War in Africa from Eisenhower to Kennedy*. New York: Macmillan, 1982.

Kanet, Roger E., ed. *The Soviet Union and Developing Nations*. Baltimore: Johns Hopkins University Press, 1974.

Karabell, Zachary. *Architects of Intervention: The United States, the Third World and the Cold War.* Baton Rouge: Louisiana State University Press, 1999.

Khokhlov, N. P. *Patris Lumumba* (Patrice Lumumba). Moscow: Molodaya gvardiya, 1971.

Klinghoffer, A. J. *Soviet Perspective on African Socialism.* Rutherford, N.J.: Farleigh Dickinson University Press, 1969.

Kolko, Gabriel. *Confronting the Third World: United States Foreign Policy, 1945–1980.* New York: Pantheon Books, 1988.

Korbonski, Andrzej, and Francis Fukuyama, eds. *The Soviet Union and the Third World: The Last Three Decades.* Ithaca, N.Y.: Cornell University Press, 1987.

Kudryavtsev, V. "Afrika shagaet vpered" (Africa moves ahead). *Sovremennyi Vostok,* no. 4 (1960).

Kurtz, D. M. "Political Integration in Africa: The Mali Federation." *Journal of Modern African Studies* 8, no. 3 (1970).

Laidi, Zaki. *The Superpowers and Africa: The Constraints of a Rivalry, 1960–1990.* Chicago: University of Chicago Press, 1990.

Larkin, Bruce D. *China and Africa, 1948–1970.* Berkeley: University of California Press, 1971.

Laron, Guy. *Cutting the Gordian Knot: The Post–WW II Egyptian Quest for Arms and the 1955 Czechoslovak Arms Deal.* CWIHP Working Paper 55. Washington, D.C.: Cold War International History Project, Woodrow Wilson International Center for Scholars, 2007.

Lefever, Ernest. *Crisis in the Congo: A U.N. Force in Action.* Washington, D.C.: Brookings Institution Press, 1965.

Leffler, Melvyn P. *For the Soul of Mankind: The United States, the Soviet Union, and the Cold War.* New York: Hill and Wang, 2007.

Legum, Colin. "USSR Policy in Sub-Saharan Africa." In *The Soviet Union and the Third World. The Last Three Decades,* ed. Andrzei Karbonsky and Francis Fukuyama. Ithaca, N.Y.: Cornell University Press, 1987.

Legvold, Robert. *Soviet Policy in West Africa.* Cambridge, Mass.: Harvard University Press, 1970.

Lesiovskyi, V. M. *Taina ghibeli Hammarshel'da* (The secret of Hammarskjöld's death). Moscow: Mysl', 1985.

Lessing, Pieter. *Africa's Red Harvest. An Account of Communism in Africa.* London: Michael Joseph, 1962.

Lowenthal, Richard. "China." In *Africa and the Communist World,* ed.

Zbigniew Brzezinski. Stanford, Calif.: Stanford University Press, 1963.

Lukonin, Yu. V., and M. Yu. Frenkel, eds. *Istoriya Gany v novoe i noveishee vremya* (Modern and contemporary history of Ghana). Moscow: Nauka, 1985.

MacFarlane, N. S. *Superpower Rivalry & 3rd World Radicalism: The Idea of National Liberation.* London and Baltimore: Croom Helm and Johns Hopkins University Press, 1985.

Mahoney, Richard D. *JFK: Ordeal in Africa.* New York: Oxford University Press, 1983.

Marte, Fred. *Political Cycles in International Relations: The Cold War and Africa 1945–1990.* Amsterdam: VU Press, 1994.

Matusevich, Maxim. *No Easy Row for a Russian Hoe: Ideology and Pragmatism in Nigerian-Soviet Relations, 1960–1991.* Trenton, N.J.: Africa World Press, 2003.

Mazov, S. V. "Afrikanskie studenty v God Afriki v Moskve" (African Students in Moscow in the Year of Africa). *Vostok,* no. 3 (1998).

———. "Diplomatchicheskyi debut SSSR v Tropicheskoi Afrike: Iz istorii sovetsko-liberyiskikh otnoshenyi, 1945–1960 gg." (The diplomatic debut of the USSR in Tropical Africa: An episode from the history of Soviet-Liberian relations, 1945–1960). *Vostok,* no. 6 (2000).

———. "'Tsarstvo'" Kvame Nkrumi ("'The Kingdom'" of Kwame Nkrumah). *Vostok,* no. 1 (2010).

———. "Neizvestnaya istoriya sozdaniya Instituta Afriki AN SSSR" (The Institute for African Studies of the Academy of Sciences of the USSR: The unknown history of its creation"). *Vostok,* no. 1 (1999).

———. *Paradoksi "obraztsovoi" kolonii: Stanovlenie colonial'nogo obshestva Gany, 1900–1957 (*The paradoxes of a "model colony": The shaping of colonial society in Ghana, 1900–1957). Moscow: Nauka, 1993.

———. *Politika SSSR v Zapadnoi Afrike, 1956–1964: Neizvestnye stranitsy istorii kholodnoi voiny* (The policy of the USSR in West Africa, 1956–1964: Unknown pages of Cold War history). Moscow: Nauka, 2008.

———. "Soviet Aid to the Gizenga Government in the Former Belgian Congo (1960–1961) as Reflected in Russian Archives." *Cold War History* 7, no. 3 (2007).

———. "Soviet Scholar Comments on Nkrumah's 70th Birthday Anniversary." *Echo* (September 30, 1979).

———. "The USSR and the Former Italian Colonies, 1945–1950." *Cold War History 3*, no. 3 (2003).

Mazrui, Ali. "Nkrumah: The Leninist Czar." In *On Heroes and Uhuru-Worship: Essays of Independent Africa*, ed. Ali Mazrui. London: Longmans, 1967.

McKay, Vernon. *Africa in World Politics*. New York: Harper & Row, 1963.

Merriam, Alan P. *Congo: Background of Conflict*. Evanston, Ill.: Northwestern University Press, 1961.

Miller, Richard I. *Dag Hammarskjöld and Crisis Diplomacy*. New York: Oceana Publications, 1962.

Morgenthau, Ruth Shachter. *Political Parties in French-Speaking West Africa*. Oxford: Clarendon Press, 1964.

Mortimer, Edward. *France and the Africans 1944–1960: A Political History*. New York: Walker, 1969.

Namikas, Lise. "Battleground Africa: The Cold War and the Congo Crisis, 1960–1965." PhD dissertation, University of Southern California, 2002.

Nepomnyashyi, K. "Spasibo sovetskim lyetchikam" (Thanks to Soviet pilots). *Pravda* (July 31, 1960).

Nielsen, Waldemar. *The Great Powers and Africa*. New York: Praeger, 1969.

Noer, Thomas J. *Cold War and Black Liberation: The United States and White Rule in Africa, 1948–1968*. Columbia: University of Missouri Press, 1985.

———. "New Frontiers and Old Priorities in Africa." In *Kennedy's Quest for Victory: American Foreign Policy, 1961–1963*, ed. Thomas G. Paterson. Oxford: Oxford University Press, 1989.

Novikov, S. S., and D. P. Ursu. *Istoriya Mali v novoe i noveishee vremya* (Modern and contemporary history of Mali). Moscow: Nauka, 1994.

Omari, Peter P. *Kwame Nkrumah: The Anatomy of an African Dictatorship*. New York: Africana, 1972.

Padmore, George. *Pan-Africanism or Communism? The Coming Struggle for Africa*. London: Dennis Dobson, 1956.

Pechatnov, Vladimir O. *"The Allies Are Pressing on You to Break Your Will": Foreign Policy Correspondence between Stalin and Molotov and Other Politburo Members, September 1945–December 1946*. CWIHP Working Paper 26. Washington, D.C.: Cold War International History Project, Woodrow Wilson International Center for Scholars, 1999.

"Pod znamenem bor'by za svobodu" (Under the banner of national liberation). *Sovremennyi Vostok*, no. 1 (1960).

Ponomarev, B. "O gosudarstve natsional'noi demokratii" (On the national democratic state). *Kommunist*, no. 8 (1961).

Potekhin, Ivan. "Africa: Itogi i perspectivy antiimperialisticheskoi revolutsii" (Africa: The results and the perspectives of the anti-imperialist revolution). *Aziya i Afrika segodnya*, no. 9 (1960).

———. "Etnicheskyi i klassovyi sostav naseleniya Zolotogo Berega" (The ethnic and class structure of the population of the Gold Coast). *Sovetskaya Etnografiya*, no. 3 (1953).

———. "Politicheskoe polozhenie v stranakh Afriki" (The political situation in African countries). *Sovetskoe Vostokovedinie*, no. 1 (1956).

———. *Stanovleniye novoi Gany* (The formation of the new Ghana). Moscow: Nauka, 1965.

Ra'anan, Uri. *The USSR Arms the Third World: Case Studies in Soviet Foreign Policy.* Cambridge, Mass.: MIT Press, 1969.

Rahman, Ahmad A. *The Regime Change of Kwame Nkrumah: Epic Heroism in Africa and the Diaspora.* New York: Palgrave, 2007.

Remnek, Richard E. "The Significance of Soviet Strategic Military Interests in Sub-Saharan Africa." In *The Soviet Impact in Africa*, ed. Craig R. Nation and Mark V. Kauppi. Lexington, Mass.: D. C. Heath, 1984.

Ronin, Vladimir. *"Russkoye Kongo": Knigha-memorial* (The "Russian Congo": A book-memorial), 2 vols. Moscow: Dom Russkogo Zarubezhya imeni Aleksandra Solzhenitsina: Russkyi Put', 2009.

Rooney, David. *Kwame Nkrumah: The Political Kingdom in the Third World.* London: I. B. Tauris, 1988.

Sakhnin, Arkadiyi. "Raskayanyie zapozdalo" (Regret was too late). *Komsomol'skaya Pravda* (September 27, 1962).

Schatten, Fritz. *Communism in Africa.* London: George Allen & Unwin, 1966.

Schlesinger, Arthur M. *A Thousand Days: John F. Kennedy in the White House.* Boston: Houghton Mifflin, 1965.

Schmidt, Elizabeth. *Cold War and Decolonization in Guinea, 1946–1958.* Athens: Ohio University Press, 2007.

———. "Cold War in Guinea: The Rassemblement Démocratique Africain and the Struggle over Communism, 1950–1958." *Journal of African History* 48, no. 1 (2007).

Simon, Charlie. *Dag Hammarskjöld*. New York: Dutton, 1967.

Staniland, Martin. *American Intellectuals and African Nationalists, 1955–1970*. New Haven, Conn.: Yale University Press, 1991.

Statler, Kathryn C., and Andrew L. Jones, eds. *The Eisenhower Administration, the Third World, and the Globalization of the Cold War*. Lanham, Md.: Rowman & Littlefield, 2006.

Stevens, Christopher. *The Soviet Union and Black Africa*. London: Macmillan, 1976.

Stockwell, John. *In Search of Enemies: A CIA Story*. New York: W. W. Norton, 1978.

Suret-Canale, Jean. *Gvineyskaya Respublika* (Guinean Republic). Moscow: Progress, 1973.

Tareq, Ismael Y. "The People's Republic of China and Africa." *Journal of Modern African Studies* 9, no. 4 (1971).

Taubman, William. *Khrushchev: The Man and His Era*. New York: W. W. Norton, 2003.

Thompson, W. Scott. "The African-American Nexus in Soviet Strategy." In *Africa and International Communism*, ed. David L. Albright. New York: Macmillan, 1980.

———. *Ghana's Foreign Policy 1957–1966: Diplomacy, Ideology and the New State*. Princeton, N.J.: Princeton University Press, 1969.

Urquhart, Brian. *Hammarskjöld*. New York: W. W. Norton, 1994.

Valenta, Jiri. "Soviet Decision-Making on the Intervention in Angola." In *Communism in Africa*, ed. David E. Albright. New York: Macmillan, 1980.

Vinokurov, Yu. N., A. S. Orlova, and V. A. Subbotin. *Istoriya Zaira v novoe i noveishee vremya* (Modern and Contemporary History of Zaire). Moscow: Nauka, 1982.

Volk, S. "Perevorot v Mali" (The Mali Coup). *Novoe vremya*, no. 36 (1960).

Volodin, L. D., and O. L. Orestov. *Trudnye dni Kongo: Poiticheskyi Reportazh* (Troubled Days in the Congo. A Political Reportage). Moscow: Gospolitizdat, 1961.

Weissman, Stephen. *American Foreign Policy in the Congo, 1960–1964*. Ithaca, N.Y.: Cornell University Press, 1974.

Westad, Odd Arne. *The Global Cold War: Third World Interventions and the Making of Our Times*. New York: Cambridge University Press, 2006.

Wilson, Edward. *Russia and Black Africa before World War II*. New York: Holmes & Meier, 1974.

Young, Crawford. *Politics in the Congo: Decolonization and Independence.* Princeton, N.J.: Princeton University Press, 1965.

Yur'ev, N. *Expansiya SshA v Kongo* (U.S. expansion in the Congo). Moscow: Mezhdunarodnye Otnosheniya, 1966.

Zaher, Mark W. *Dag Hammarskjöld's United Nations.* New York: Columbia University Press, 1970.

Zotova, Yu. N., and I. V. Sledzevskyi, eds. *Istoriya Nigerii v novoe i noveishee vremya* (Modern and contemporary history of Nigeria). Moscow: Nauka, 1981.

Zubok, Vladislav. *A Failed Empire: The Soviet Union in the Cold War from Stalin to Gorbachev.* Chapel Hill: University of North Carolina Press, 2007.

Magazines and Periodicals

African Affairs, Oxford.

Aziya i Afrika segodnya, Moscow.

Echo, Accra.

Ghanaian Times, Accra.

Izvestiya, Moscow.

Journal of African History, Cambridge.

Journal of Modern African Studies, Cambridge.

Kommunist, Moscow.

Komsomol'skaya Pravda, Moscow.

Manchester Guardian, Manchester.

New York Times, New York.

Novaya i noveishaya istoriya, Moscow.

Novoye vremya, Moscow.

Pravda, Moscow.

Sovetskaya Etnografiya, Moscow.

Sovetskoe Vostokovedinie, Moscow.

Sunday Telegraph, London.

Vostok, Moscow.

West Africa, London.

Index